Systemic Silencing

Critical Human Rights

Scott Straus and Tyrell Haberkorn, Series Editors;
Steve J. Stern, Editor Emeritus

Books in the series Critical Human Rights emphasize research that opens new ways to think about and understand human rights. The series values in particular empirically grounded and intellectually open research that eschews simplified accounts of human rights events and processes.

Systemic Silencing

Activism, Memory, and
Sexual Violence in Indonesia

Katharine E. McGregor

The University of Wisconsin Press

The University of Wisconsin Press
728 State Street, Suite 443
Madison, Wisconsin 53706
uwpress.wisc.edu

Gray's Inn House, 127 Clerkenwell Road
London EC1R 5DB, United Kingdom
eurospanbookstore.com

Printed in the United States of America
This book may be available in a digital edition.

Library of Congress Cataloging-in-Publication Data

Names: McGregor, Katharine E., author.
Title: Systemic silencing : Activism, Memory, and Sexual Violence in Indonesia /
Katharine E. McGregor.
Other titles: Critical human rights.
Description: Madison, Wisconsin : The University of Wisconsin Press, [2023] |
Series: Critical human rights | Includes bibliographical references and index.
Identifiers: LCCN 2022048769 | ISBN 9780299344207 (hardcover)
Subjects: LCSH: Comfort women—Indonesia.
Classification: LCC D810.C698 M395 2023 | DDC 323.3/409598—dc23/eng/20230123
LC record available at https://lccn.loc.gov/2022048769

I dedicate this book to Tuminah and Mardiyem and all their fellow travelers for inspiring me to trace this story of incredible hardship and courage shown by Indonesian women.

Contents

Contents

Illustrations

Figures

Maps

Preface

t is difficult to discern when the precise seed for this research idea was planted. In the late 1990s, when I was completing my PhD research on the Indonesian military, I first heard about the topic of the so-called comfort women. I was meeting regularly with a group of women from the Gender Studies and History Programs at the University of Melbourne, including Antonia Finnane, Patricia Grimshaw, Maila Stivens, Kalissa Alexeyeff, Tracey Banivanua Marr, Amanda Whiting, Robyn Hamilton, and Jemma Purdey, to discuss gender in the Asia Pacific region. A leading historian of Japanese women's history, Vera Mackie, was an occasional visitor to this group. Around this time I heard her share her ongoing research about militarized sexual abuse and the new momentum of the movement for redress for the "comfort women," which was created by the 2000 Women's International War Crimes Tribunal on Japan's Military Sexual Slavery.

In 2008, when I was already on the teaching staff at the University of Melbourne, I had the extraordinary opportunity to hear the live testimony of Jan Ruff O'Herne (1923–2019) delivered in the law school to a somber audience together with a Korean survivor. Hearing their testimony was extremely powerful. I remained interested in this topic for years and began to teach about it in my popular honors and masters course called "History, Memory, and Violence in Asia" in the late 2000s. I frequently invited activist Anna Song to the class to talk about her work on this topic, which led to my deep fascination with how survivors drew global attention to their fate. I have also been inspired by student interest in this issue. A nagging question for me, however, was why there was relatively little activism or scholarship on Indonesian survivors and their experiences. In conversations with my sister Sarah McGregor, who is a psychologist and sexual assault counselor, I have been encouraged to reflect on the deep layers of trauma that survivors experience and think critically about the relationship between survivors and those with whom they interact, including the related duty of care.

In 2012 I put together a large grant application to the Australian Research Council centered on the process of transnational activism and confronting historical justice in Indonesia. The project focused on three historical episodes that connect Indonesia to different regions of memory. One of those case studies was that of activism around Indonesian "comfort women" that connected Indonesia to the region of East Asia. I devoted most of my time to this case study, and this book is the major outcome of my Future Fellowship (FT130100957). I am extremely grateful to the Australian Research Council for awarding me the extraordinary opportunity as a midcareer researcher to undertake a four-year research project that entailed research across four countries and multiple languages and enough time to reflect deeply on this topic.

There are many people I would like to thank for helping me bring this book to fruition. Vera Mackie inspired this project through her research and long-term interest in this issue. As a scholar, she has been an inspiration to me throughout my career and an important mentor for this project, my first foray into Japanese history. She hosted me as a visitor at the Centre for Critical Human Rights Research at the University of Wollongong throughout my research fellowship, listened to many of my papers as this project developed, provided ongoing advice and read and commented on the whole manuscript. I cannot thank her enough. Bambang Purwanto of the history program at Universitas Gadjah Mada (UGM) was another key supporter of this project and hosted me during the fellowship, providing opportunities for me to share my work with Indonesian history students and organizing a conference at Universitas Gadjah Mada with Yerry Wirawan and Ita Nadia on Indonesian women's history in 2019. Kate Darian-Smith has also been an important mentor and kept a dynamic focus on memory across the history program at the University of Melbourne during this project's gestation. I also thank the many audiences who listened to and gave feedback on papers related to this work in presentations to the History Programs at the University of Melbourne, Monash University, University of New South Wales, Universitas Gadjah Mada, Universitas Negeri Malang, and Universitas Negeri Yogyakarta and to the Gender Studies and Cold War Lives research groups at Australian National University, the Centre for Critical Human Rights Research at the University of Wollongong, and the KITLV (Royal Netherlands Institute of Southeast Asian and Caribbean Studies), as well the audiences of my conference papers and talks at the Berkshire Conference of Women, Genders and Sexualities, the Asian Studies Association of Australia (ASAA), the ASAA Women in Asia Conference, the Australian Historical Association Conference, the Indonesia Council

Open Conference, the Conflict and Women's Human Rights Conference and the women's rights nongovernmental organization Jejer Wadon (Female Subjects), based in Surakarta.

Along the road in writing this book, I have collaborated with and had conversations with many scholars working on gender and violence across and beyond Asia who have inspired my work in different ways. This includes Ruth Indiah Rahayu, Ana Dragojlovic, Susie Protschky, Eveline Buchheim, Francisca de Haan, Hani Yulindrasari, Mayuko Itoh, Nursyahbani Katjasungkana, Saskia Wieringa, Anna Mariana, Eka Hindra, Galuh Wandita, Jemma Purdey, Ruth Barraclough, Erik Ropers, Anna Song, Tessa Morris-Suzuki, Ken Setiawan, Hannah Loney, Sachiyo Tsukamoto, Rachel Hughes, Heather Goodall, Hilde Janssen, William Bradley Horton, Annie Pohlman, Louise Edwards, Mina Roces, Bronwyn Beech Jones, Annabelle Baldwin, Annisa Beta, Wulan Dirgantoro, and Dana Fahadi. At the University of Melbourne I also thank the steering committee of the Melbourne Research Alliance to End Violence against Women and Children (of which I am a member), which has sustained research and conversations across and outside our university on the topic of violence against women, which is an ongoing issue in every country of the world.

Across the life of this project, many people have helped me with finding sources, undertaking fieldwork and providing translation assistance and giving their time to me as interviewees. I thank Hani Yulindrasari, who worked as a research assistant for me in the early stages of research, and Eka Hindra and Nursyahbani Katjasungkana—two Indonesian activists who shared incredibly valuable insights with me. I am very grateful to Mayuko Itoh, who accompanied me during fieldwork to Japan and translated many Japanese sources, including our interviews, into English. I also thank the Japanese and Indonesian activists who gave me their time and shared their experiences of activism on behalf of Indonesian survivors. This includes the incredibly generous Kimura Kōichi, Kawada Fumiko, and Takagi Ken'ichi. I thank Paula Hendrikx, who assisted with archival research and translations from Dutch language; Faye Chan, who also assisted with Dutch translations; and the staff at the Women's Active Museum on War and Peace in Tokyo, including Yamashita Fumiko, for assisting with sources related to Japanese activism and the staff at LBH (Lembaga Bantuan Hukum, Indonesian Legal Aid) Yogyakarta for giving me their time and allowing me to view some collections of documentation related to activism. I would also like to thank William Bradley Horton for sharing tips on Dutch archive material and unpublished reports.

Earlier versions of small sections of this book across chapters 3, 6, and 7 have appeared in two publications that explore different dimensions of the history of the system and activism. Wherever I have used similar material and examples to those used in other publications, they have been cross-referenced with the two relevant publications: Katharine McGregor, "Living in a Conflict Zone: Gendered Violence during the Japanese Occupation of the Netherlands East Indies," in *Gendered Violence Across Time and Space in Indonesia and East Timor*, edited by Katharine McGregor, Ana Dragojlovic, and Hannah Loney (London: Routledge, 2020), pp. 39–58 and Katharine McGregor, "Emotions and Activism for Former So Called 'Comfort Women' of the Japanese Occupation of the Netherlands East Indies," *Women's Studies International Forum* 54 (January–February 2016): 67–78.

I am very grateful to the team at the University of Wisconsin Press and the editors of the Critical Human Rights Series for their strong interest in this book. Thanks in particular to the two reviewers, Saskia Wieringa and Ruth Barraclough, for their careful reading and important suggestions for improvement, to Amber Cederstrom, the acquisitions editor who shepherded me along the way, and Jessica Smith, who assisted with helpful editing.

I thank my colleague and friend Jemma Purdey, who has provided fantastic editing and proofreading support as an expert on the topics of gender, violence, and Indonesian history. She has helped me to improve this book. Any remaining errors are my own.

Last, I thank my family for tolerating many field trips away from home to conduct this research. Thanks especially to my daughters, Zahra Kelana and Khalila Kelana, and my partner, Kelana Jaya. Thank you also to my parents, sister, and friends for always supporting me and for listening to me talk about this book for quite a few years now.

Notes on Name Order, Spelling, and Translations

Throughout this manuscript I have used East Asian name order such that Japanese and Korean names in the text and references are given with family name followed by given name. I have made some exceptions, however, when scholars of East Asian background predominately publish in English language using Western name order. Despite some variances in Japanese names for publications in English and Japanese, I use consistent spelling of names so that it is easier to identify authors. For references originally in Kanji (Sino-Japanese characters), and the kana syllabary, I provide details only in Rōmaji (the Romanized version of Japanese language). Following recent trends, these Rōmaji spellings include macrons on long vowels in Japanese people's names and words although some individual authors do not use macrons for their names in English language publications. For Korean-language terms, I have followed the McCune-Reischauer system for romanization.

Over the course of Indonesian history, spelling patterns have changed. Generally I have elected to use modern spelling, except in cases of people's names where the old spelling is common practice (such as the use of the old *oe* instead of the modern *u*) or in the titles of older sources where old spelling was used. In many cases I refer to Indonesians, such as key survivor activist Mardiyem, only by one name as she, like many Indonesians, only had one name. In the bibliography where Indonesians have two names, I have listed sources under the second name for consistency.

Throughout this manuscript, I occasionally retain the original words used in a text in a particular language to draw attention to the nuanced meaning of these language choices. These terms are provided in the glossary. Translations of all titles from Indonesian, Japanese, Dutch, and French language appear only in the bibliography. All translations from Indonesian and French are my own unless otherwise indicated. All translations from Japanese and Dutch have been provided by my research assistants.

Abbreviations

Alg. Secretarie Ned.-Ind. Regering	Algemene Secretarie van de Nederlands-Indische Regering en de daarbij gedeponeerde Archieven
AWF	Asian Women's Fund
CEDAW	UN Convention on the Elimination of Discrimination against Women, 1979
CMI	Centrale Militaire Inlichtingendienst
GAKTPI	Gerakan Anti-Kekerasan Terhadap Perempuan Indonesia (Movement to Oppose Violence Against Women)
IMTFE	International Military Tribunal for the Far East Charter
JES	Japanese Debts of Honor Committee
JFBA	Japan Federation of Bar Associations (Nichibenden)
KCWU	Korean Church Women United
KNIL	Koninklijk Nederlands Indisch Leger (The Royal Netherlands Indies Army)
Komnas HAM	Komisi Nasional Hak Asasi Manusia (Indonesian National Human Rights Commission)
KSVRC	Korean Sexual Violence Relief Centre

LBH APIK	Lembaga Bantuan Hukum, Asosiasi Perempuan Indonesia untuk Keadilan Indonesia (Legal Aid Foundation, Indonesian Women's Association for Justice)
LBH	Lembaga Bantuan Hukum (Legal Aid)
NEFIS	Netherlands East Indies Forces Intelligence Service
NIOD	Nederlands Instituut voor Oorlogdocumentatie (Netherlands Institute for War, Holocaust and Genocide Studies)
Nl-HaNA	National Archives of the Netherlands, The Hague
OHCHR	United Nations Human Rights Office of the High Commissioner
PDI	Partai Demokrasi Indonesia (Indonesia Democratic Party)
PERADIN	Persatuan Advokat Indonesia (Indonesian Advocates Association)
PICN	Project Implementation Committee of the Netherlands
PKI	Partai Komunis Indonesia (Indonesian Communist Party)
PKPS	Perserikatan Kelompok Perempuan Sadar (Network of Aware Women)
POW	prisoner of war
PPPPA	Perkoempalan Pembasmian Perdagangan Perempoean dan Anak-Anak (Organization for the Eradication of the Trafficking of Women and Children)
SOMJII	Solidaritas Masyarakat Jepang untuk ex Ianfu Indonesia (Japanese Society for Solidarity with Former Indonesian Comfort Women)
VAWW-Net	Japanese based network Violence Against Women in War

VOC	Vereenigde Oostindische Compagnie (Dutch East India Company, 1602–1799)
YASANTI	Yayasan Anisa Swasti
YLBHI	Yayasan Lembaga Bantuan Hukum Indonesia (Indonesian Legal Aid Foundation)

Systemic Silencing

Introduction

Activism by and on Behalf of Indonesian Women

*Kami masyarakat Jepang menghormati kebesaraan dan ketabahaan hati Tuminah
sebagai pelaku sejarah "ianfu" Indonesia.*

[We the people of Japan respect the great spirit and the determination of
Tuminah as a historical actor, an Indonesian "ianfu"]

Engraving on the headstone at the gravesite of Tuminah (1927–2003)

In 2013 a small group of people gathered on the outskirts of
Solo, Central Java, to commemorate the newly renovated grave
of Tuminah (1927–2003). She was a survivor of the system of enforced prostitution used by the Japanese military and civilians during the Asia Pacific War
(1931–45), including its four-year occupation of the former Dutch colony of
the Netherlands East Indies from 1942 to 1945. In the 1990s, Tuminah spoke
publicly for the first time about her experiences. Ten years after her death, her
supporters added a headstone and plaque to her modest grave. The headstone
featured a photograph of her as a middle-aged woman and a dedication in
Indonesian.

The dedication inscribed on Tuminah's headstone (figure 1) tells us several
things about the history of the activism carried out by and on behalf of Indonesian survivors. A claim is made that Japanese citizens, represented here by a
small solidarity group, respect Tuminah, highlighting transnational sources of
support for Indonesian survivors. The dedication recognizes Tuminah as an
Indonesian *ianfu* (comfort woman). Indonesian survivors have long struggled
for recognition that they were also victimized alongside women from other
parts of the Japanese wartime empire, including China, Korea, the Philippines,

Tuminah

1927 – 2003

Kami masyarakat Jepang
menghormati kebesaran dan ketabahan
hati Tuminah sebagai pelaku sejarah
"ianfu" Indonesia.

Makam ini dibangun atas solidaritas
The Christian Society for Resolving the Issue of "ianfu"
di Kyusyu, Jepang

Figure 1. Dedication on the headstone of Tuminah's renovated grave, Solo. Photograph by author.

Malaya, Taiwan, and Singapore, as well as Japan. The reference to Tuminah's "spirit and dedication" recognizes her role in the early 1990s, at the beginning of a rising transnational movement for redress, for having the courage to speak out about her experiences. An English-language plaque also affixed to the front of the grave (see figure 2) puts it more directly, acknowledging Tuminah as the one who "broke the public wall of silence" in Indonesia about women's experiences during the occupation. The plaque recognizes the many other women victimized in the system of enforced military prostitution (hereafter "the system"), including Dutch women abused during the occupation of Indonesia. A few of these women also participated in the global movement for redress.

The decision to memorialize Tuminah follows a global trend of commemoration of women subjected to enforced military prostitution by the Japanese military. This trend dates back to 1998, when a memorial to survivors was erected in the city of Gyeongju, South Korea.[1] The most iconic and globally recognized monument, featuring a young Korean girl seated facing the Japanese embassy, was erected in 2011 in Seoul to commemorate related activism and the women (see figure 3). Memorials have since been erected in countries where

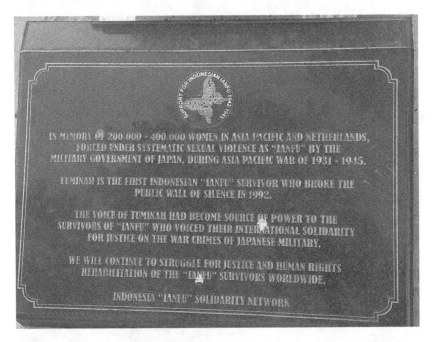

Figure 2. Plaque affixed to the front of Tuminah's renovated grave, Solo. Photograph by author.

local women were abused and in countries with significant Korean diaspora populations.[2] Each monument calls us to remember what happened to these women by making them visible and refusing to brush this history aside. Elizabeth Son describes the trend of memorialization as an act of care extended to survivors.[3] In Tuminah's case, the care extended to her is a product of her close personal connection with Kimura Kōichi, the Japanese activist who along with

Figure 3. *Pyeonghwabi*, Statue of Peace, Seoul. Photograph by author.

Indonesian activist Eka Hindra was behind the initiative to install the commemorative headstone. Tuminah had first shared her story with Kimura when he was working as a theologian in Indonesia in the 1990s, leading him to become a lifelong activist for Indonesian survivors of the system.[4] Through his ability to speak Indonesian and Japanese, he acted as an important bridge between activists in the two countries.

The decision to renovate one survivor's grave, as opposed to installing a monument to all Indonesian survivors in a more public space, provides clues about the context for activism and the status of human rights survivors in Indonesia. The renovation was a discreet gesture, reflecting a cautious approach. This can partly be explained by wariness about Japanese reactions to official memorials, as well as the Indonesian government's lack of support for survivors and related activism. An expression of disapproval from the local Japanese embassy, for example, led to the quick removal of a monument to survivors in a Catholic nun's shelter in the Philippines in late 2018.[5] As in the Philippines, the government and big business in Indonesia have had close economic ties to Japan since signing a peace treaty in 1958, which bound the countries economically and discouraged criticism of Japan's historical and contemporary role in the region.[6]

The survivors of the system who commenced activism in the early 1990s, were among the first groups in Indonesia to pursue collective redress for human rights abuses, yet there is still no national monument to survivors. This is not entirely surprising. Generally speaking, Indonesian victims of human rights abuses have had very little success in securing government or public acknowledgment of their suffering,[7] and there are very few such monuments.[8]

The Challenges of Human Rights Activism

In this book, I take up the question of why there was limited government and societal support for this issue by tracing the development of activism by and on behalf of Indonesian survivors of enforced military prostitution. I offer new insights into the ongoing challenges around achieving recognition of and redress for human rights victims in Indonesia and globally. I examine the obstacles that human rights activists face more broadly in promoting a cause, while extending care to survivors without exposing them to further harm in the process. To explain the enduring legacies of these women's historical experiences, the book begins with the longer story of unequal gender relations from the colonial period up through the Japanese occupation of the Indonesian archipelago, setting out the gendered context in which the violence took place and its aftermath. It unravels the reasons this history only began to be narrated (albeit partly and often from an unsympathetic viewpoint) in the early 1990s, thereby revealing the terrain from which Indonesian activism was born.

The book contributes to several fields of research, including histories of Indonesia, human rights, transnational activism, gender and history, and the so-called comfort women. It builds on an important body of research that documents and analyzes the empirical dimensions of the system.[9] This is the first systematic study of the development of Indonesian and related transnational activism by and on behalf of Indonesian women who survived being "comfort women." The driving questions I seek to answer are: what were Indonesian women's experiences of sexual violence during the occupation; how did these women negotiate living with such experiences; and how, when, why, and by whom was this issue opened up in Indonesia and with what response?

I interrogate the ways the survivors' experiences were framed in this process and the role they themselves played in activism. I ask why activism was slower to develop in Indonesia than it was in other countries, why these survivors were relatively marginalized in transnational activism, and why it took some time for critical framings of this issue to permeate Indonesian society. As I argue throughout the book, the answers are connected to ideas and practices that made disclosures about sexual violence difficult. They are entwined with the specifics of the system and to histories of Indonesian collaboration with the Japanese, the complex relationships not only between Japan and Indonesia but also between the Netherlands and Indonesia. Further contributing factors are the specific dynamics of Indonesia in the 1990s, when transnational activism began to escalate, as a militarized and increasingly religious society.

It is critically important to adopt a transnational and comparative frame for examining postwar activism. This is especially so when examining the case of the former colony of the Netherlands East Indies, where many Indonesian women, alongside a few Dutch women, were victimized and where decades later Japanese activists provided crucial support to Indonesian survivors. As Vera Mackie has noted, all activism for women survivors is necessarily transnational in its focus because it invokes calls for redress made on the part of non-Japanese citizens from the Japanese state.[10] Many studies have focused on activism in particular countries such as Japan, South Korea, China, the Philippines, the Netherlands, and the United States (especially across the Korean diaspora) and on advocacy directed at or conducted by international organizations.[11] Few studies, however, trace and compare the development of transnational activism beyond a single country and Japan. Furthermore, many studies on war memory and redress more generally focus almost exclusively on the zone of East Asia, meaning the countries of Japan, South Korea, and China, with far less attention to the historical legacies of Japan's occupation of Southeast Asia.[12]

First, I unpack the circumstances under which Indonesian activism began by comparing its evolution with the experiences in Japan and Korea. I examine how and why Japanese activists initially reached out to Indonesians to seek information about human rights abuses there. By reflecting on different perspectives and positionalities across activism on this issue in Korea, the Philippines, Taiwan and the Netherlands, I provide unique insights into the transnational dimensions of activism and its related complexity. What are the factors that enable activism to develop and thrive in some contexts and flounder in others? By tracing the development of Indonesian activism and the role of Japanese activists in supporting and driving it, I reflect on how operations of power, lack of access to resources, broad activist networks, and limited English language capacity acted as constraints. This provides an important non-Western case study of the dynamics of transnational activism across Asia.

Activism on the "comfort women" has played a critical role in addressing the marginalization that survivors have experienced, in extending hope to them as well as contributing to a broader project of challenging sexual violence. In this sense, this activism has made crucial contributions to advancing a human rights agenda in Indonesia. Despite these advances, it is important that both activists and scholars continue to reflect on lessons learned from this long-standing activism. For this reason, I provide a critical examination of how sexual violence has been portrayed within and outside the circles of activism in Indonesia. As a historian, I aim to examine the broader contexts within which the violence took place and within which activism developed. I seek to understand the reasons survivors have not received widespread recognition in Indonesia and the role transnational activism played in stimulating and sustaining activism on this issue.

My analysis of Indonesian and transnational activism focuses on the crucial decade of the 1990s, culminating with the Women's International War Crimes Tribunal on Japan's Military Sexual Slavery (hereafter Women's International War Crimes Tribunal) in 2000, which was a pivotal moment for many survivors. The year 2000 was the peak of Indonesian activism for survivors of enforced military prostitution by the Japanese army. This was also due largely to the enhanced attention by government and the media to the issue of sexual violence, following the fall of the Suharto regime in 1998.

Memory and Activism

This book tells the story of transnational activism conducted by and on behalf of the Indonesian survivors. I use the expression "by and on behalf of" to clearly position surviving women as activists and to recognize their contributions to activism. In doing so, I consider the roles they have played in activism; to what extent they have been able to control the direction of activism; and the effects that sharing their experiences have had on different audiences. Second, I use this expression to indicate the role of other nonsurvivor activists who have often acted as intermediaries between the survivors, journalists, and government representatives.

The study of activism by and on behalf of survivors and its effects requires analysis of memory. I use Joan Tumbelty's working definition of memory; "how a certain view of the past is incorporated, sustained or alternatively eclipsed in the mediums of the present—at individual and social levels."[13] Across this book I trace early narrations of women's experiences in popular mediums of memory, such as novels, museums, and media reporting; and attempts to reframe these memories in activist texts, such as testimony collections, media statements, campaigns, and activist publications. This work seeks to move the study of memory discourses beyond the frame of the nation by remaining alert to what Astrid Erll calls transcultural memory, which refers to memory's "continual 'travels' and ongoing transformations through time and space, across social, linguistic and political borders."[14] I provide an example of this in chapter 6, in analysis of the first Indonesian media reporting on the testimony and activism of a Korean survivor, Kim Hak-Sun, published in 1992 in the leading magazine *Tempo* and in chapter 8 when I reflect on the first Japanese language publication on the wartime experiences of Indonesian survivors.

To trace the processes or routes through which memory travels across cultures, I focus on analyzing the actions of particular "memory activists": those people engaged in mobilizing memory on this issue, including survivors, lawyers, writers, and historians. This is a term that has been increasingly used in the field of memory studies to more precisely signal a form of memory work that is directed toward changing understandings of the past for the purposes of historical justice and broader aims of reforming society. Carol Gluck uses the term "memory activists" in the context of activism for "comfort women" to refer to civil society groups of all political persuasions who "have tirelessly lobbied for recognition, compensation and commemoration."[15] In a study of Jewish and Palestinian Israeli activism directed toward disseminating formerly silenced Palestinian memories, Yifat Gutman defines memory activism as "the strategic commemoration of a contested past outside state channels to influence public debate and policy."[16] As Gutman observes, these memory activists "mobilize the past not for the aim of gaining power and status, but for advancing their moral and ideological visions."[17] As I will show in this book, in the case of activism related to the "comfort women," the moral and ideological visions motivating individuals and groups engaged in activism vary.

Motivation

Survivors themselves have played critical roles in sharing memories of their experiences. Together with other direct witnesses to the system, including other Indonesians and Japanese soldiers, they can be referred to as "carriers" of memory in the sense that they have direct experience of this history.[18] Though a painful process, survivors have been largely motivated to share their memories of experiences of sexual violence for achieving rehabilitation in society, as well as seeking forms of redress such as an apology and compensation from the Japanese government. Yet many women have also chosen not to publicly disclose their experiences.

In Indonesia, both local and Japanese organizations have provided support for this activism. These organizations made public the memories of the "comfort women" through a variety of public fora such as media reporting, court cases, solidarity meetings, and performance of testimony, as well as activist publications. One of the most active local organizations was the Indonesian Legal Aid Foundation (Yayasan Lembaga Bantuan Hukum Indonesia, YLBHI). As I will show, when YLBHI took up this issue in support of the women survivors in 1993, it fit in their organizational mandate to offer legal aid to marginalized people and to support broader social causes, including justice for forms of state-led oppression. By contrast, the Communication Forum for Ex-Heiho (Forum Komunikasi Ex Heiho), composed of Indonesian men who were formerly auxiliary soldiers for the Japanese military, took up this issue partly because it aided their own claims for redress. In Japan, a range of activists including lawyers and women's rights advocates and groups supported this activism in Indonesia for different reasons. At its broadest, this included the desire to see Japan address war-related injustices, as well as the more specific objective to achieve recognition and justice for the "comfort women" as survivors of military sexual violence.

Memory activists for former "comfort women" across the world have attempted to commemorate a new collective understanding of the experiences of survivors of enforced military prostitution. This perspective explicitly seeks to shift public understandings away from the tendency to attach shame to the women, toward one that views what happened to them as a crime.[19] Throughout this book, I analyze how effective this effort to commemorate and reframe the women's experiences has been. Acknowledgment of past injustices is a first step to achieving redress. Yet as this book will demonstrate, there is no simple relationship between narrating historical injustice and achieving redress for human rights abuses. In the interim comes a complex process of achieving what Dipesh Chakrabarty refers to as a social consensus on "historical wounds."[20]

Emotions

This brings us to a consideration of what forms of memory activism are effective in bringing about a social consensus. In his influential article on collective memory, Alon Confino argued that in order to have an effect, "it is not enough for a certain past to be selected. It must steer emotions, motivate people to act, be received, in short it must become a sociocultural mode of action."[21] As I will show, for activism related to the "comfort women," emotions are crucial. They help explain why particular people, including survivors, became long-running activists for this cause and perhaps shed light on why others have been hesitant to fully support the movement.

Debates about the history of the system are particularly charged because they center on sexual violence, which involves shame attached to the victims of the violence and those deemed responsible for it. In the postwar period shame was first attached to the former "comfort women" in many local societies on the basis that they had had sexual relations with enemy soldiers, and as such they were viewed as traitors or moral perverts, rather than victims. Following the logic that shame extends from the victims to the family and society in which the women live, some Indonesian government officials responded to the emergence of survivors with the view that the honor of Indonesia had to be protected. This rarely resulted in firm demands for redress and instead often equated to sweeping the issue under the rug.

Once the movement for redress began, a new process of shaming the Japanese military and state for their historical actions began, leading to some significant national apologies. This included the 1993 Kōno statement made by Chief Cabinet Secretary Kōno Yōhei, expressing remorse for the Japanese army's treatment of "comfort women" during the war (see chapter 7).

Beginning in the late 1990s, these developments were followed by a backlash against the movement that continues until now, and which more recently has been labeled "comfort women bashing."[22] Those attacking the survivors often react on the basis that they believe the survivors' claims shame Japan. In turn, they make the counterclaim that the women were not victims at all, but were volunteers in the wartime system.[23] The charged nature of these debates has influenced which women have shared their experiences of wartime abuse and which women are promoted by activists as spokespersons for the movement. I examine these dynamics in Indonesian activism in chapter 7. Ultimately, these underlying trends and the extraordinarily harrowing accounts that so many women have provided mean that activism on this issue necessarily engages the emotions of those to whom it is directed, including representatives of governments and broader populations who are called on to act.[24]

Naming

This brings us back to broader questions about the framing of sexual violence in Indonesia and who is considered a "worthy victim." Across Indonesian media reportage and activism on this issue, there has been very little reflection on the terminology used to refer to women subjected to enforced military prostitution. The term *ianfu*, the romanized Japanese language term for "comfort women," or *jūgun ianfu*, the equivalent term for "military comfort women," is commonly used to refer to Indonesian survivors. Shigeru Satō explains that the term *ian* means "comfort, solace, relaxation, consolation in English," but also has connotations of an expression of gratitude or a gift being given. In this case, it translates to mean that the military superiors presented girls and women as "gifts" to Japanese soldiers.[25] The use of the term *ianfu* by the Indonesian media and activists constitutes an uncritical but common practice of retaining the original Japanese term to describe the women. In Indonesia this term is almost never accompanied by quote marks, which are used elsewhere to indicate that the term is contested, particularly by survivors. Alternatively, the equally problematic Indonesian term *wanita penghibur*, meaning "woman entertainer," is sometimes used.

The term "comfort women" is contested because of its euphemistic connotation that the women willingly provided comfort to Japanese men. Survivors like Jan Ruff O'Herne, a woman of Dutch heritage (with a Dutch-Indonesian grandmother) who was forced into the system, strongly reject the use of the term "comfort women" to describe their experiences, instead claiming it is insulting because, as she put it, comfort "means something warm and soft, safe and friendly."[26] In other countries, perhaps due to more extensive reflection and the desire to honor survivors, more respectful terms have been used to refer to survivors. In South Korea, survivors are referred to as *halmŏni* or grandmothers; an honorific and kinship term that acknowledges the older status of survivors and conveys respect and affection.[27] In a piece titled "They Are Our Grandmas," Dai Sil Kim-Gibson draws attention to the urgent need in research and activism on this topic to humanize and not objectify survivors. She explains that she calls survivors "grandmas" partly as a term of affection, but also to acknowledge "they represent a human spirit that overcomes the most horrendous atrocities humans can inflict on one another."[28] In the Philippines the similarly affectionate term *lola*, meaning grandmother in Tagalog, is used by activists to affectionately refer to survivor activists. In my view the continued use of the word *ianfu* in Indonesia reflects the lack of a full critical reckoning with both the Japanese occupation as a colonial experience and the incomplete process of rehabilitating survivors and extending dignity to them. Throughout this book I alternatively use the term survivors or "comfort women" in quotes to signal the contested nature of this term, which unfortunately remains the most common way the women are identified across scholarship and activism.

Chapter Outline

The topic of this book brings together my interests in marginalized histories and processes of how survivors of violence live with traumatic histories: the measures they do or do not take to seek historical justice and with what effects. To set up the historical experiences on which this activism is based, the first chapters put into context the conditions in the colony of the Netherlands East Indies in relation to patterns of sexual exploitation of women by Dutch and local persons and introduce relevant discourses that help us understand women's experiences.

Chapter 1 begins with the premise that during the Japanese occupation there were social structures and norms, including patriarchal Dutch and Indonesian attitudes, which provided an enabling context for the system and other forms of sexual abuse of women. Part of this context included the practice of concubinage and *nyai*, live-in housekeepers, who were sexually exploited by local and Dutch men. There were links between these practices and colonial and feudal values. The chapter also points to the connections between imperialism and sex work in the colony, including the mobilization of Japanese women (known as *karayukisan*) from the late nineteenth century from the southern islands of Japan to labor-intense regions of the Netherlands East Indies for prostitution. The chapter surveys general attitudes to prostitution across local, Dutch, and Japanese societies, which included acceptance as well as condemnation. Beginning in the 1930s, this included efforts to prevent the trafficking of women and children and efforts to ban prostitution driven largely by the desire to maintain the "prestige" or "dignity" of each society or to secure greater control over women. These early debates signal a much longer history of the emotionally charged debates around sexual violence in Indonesia. In colonial Netherlands East Indies, these attitudes developed alongside an acceptance of prostitution in local society, where it supplied an income to a family.

Chapter 2 lays out Japan's prewar designs on the colony as a resource-rich territory and its wartime plans to extract labor and resources at almost any cost to locals. This chapter examines the occupation in terms of Japan's imperial ambitions, critically analyzing the ideology of pan Asianism that initially appealed to some members of the Indonesian elite, alongside the treatment of nonelite local people, especially forced laborers. The chapter explains how, amid conditions of economic desperation, forced labor was extracted from local people. It describes the position of forced and voluntary auxiliary soldiers or *heiho* who served as part of the Japanese military. I also examine the Japanese wartime regime's particular approach to women and the expectation of female devotion to the war effort, before opening up a discussion of the evolution of the system across the Japanese empire and its connections to Japan's system of licensed prostitution. In the final section of the chapter, I examine how this system was planned and implemented across the navy and army territories during the 1942–45 occupation of the colony.

Chapter 3 provides an overview of women's experiences of gendered and sexual violence during the occupation. The chapter outlines how the coerced "recruitment" of local sex workers unfolded and the assumptions underpinning it. It highlights patterns of deception in recruitment and local complicity, mostly through village heads as trusted community members whose actions should be understood in the context of the extreme coercion that characterized the occupation. I examine the false promises made to girls and women of jobs and education and why these promises would have been so appealing in the context of the occupation and patterns of colonial disadvantage. I survey other patterns across the system, of the forced transportation of women to outer islands and patterns of direct abductions of women. Extending the frame of analysis, I consider other forms of sexual abuse, such as rape outside of places of detention, attempts at resistance, and reprisals. The chapter also sets out patterns in the recruitment of a much smaller number of Dutch women, the connections between this and internment patterns, and examples of sexual abuse in internment camps. In the final section of the chapter, I reflect on the conditions in *ianjo* ("comfort stations"). I survey evidence from Japanese, Korean, and Taiwanese women in the colony and highlight Japanese efforts to assimilate all women in the system, which replicated the logic of colonialism. Finally, I examine the pattern of Japanese soldiers and civilians taking temporary wives or *nyai* by force or coerced negotiation.

In chapter 4 I focus on the immediate postwar lives of the women, early forms of war redress, and cultural memory of the occupation and the system in Indonesia and the Netherlands. I draw on testimonial evidence to consider what happened after the war ended to women who had been held in enforced military prostitution. I highlight patterns of abandonment of women on remote islands and the difficult choices they faced about whether to return home. This included public shaming of Indonesian women who returned home and Dutch women, who were put in specially demarcated camps for processing by the returning Dutch. I consider how, in this immediate post-war period, survivors lived with their experiences by making crucial choices about marriage. I analyze the Dutch temporary court-martials in the colony and the resulting prosecutions, which dealt mostly with crimes of abuse of Dutch women. Following these early justice measures, Japan's relationship with Indonesia was largely shaped by the 1958 treaty which set up Japan, in a Cold War context, as a US client state to oversee major investment in Indonesia. In Indonesia memory of the occupation has been characterized by ambiguity, whereas in the Netherlands the focus is on internment experiences. I reflect on how women and the system have been remembered in each country with close analysis of the influential 1982 novel *Kadarwati with Five Names*, which focuses on a former "comfort woman" and was written by a retired Indonesian soldier.[29]

In chapter 5, I widen the focus to examine the factors leading to the development of transnational activism for survivors in the 1980s and 1990s, paying careful attention to the evolving relationships between Japanese and Korean advocates and their support for survivors. I trace multiple roads to activism, beginning with the efforts of a group of lawyers from the Japan Federation of Bar Associations (JFBA) (Nichibenden). Their early work on cases of wartime redress for Koreans was motivated by a general concern among members about human rights issues. I focus on the role of Takagi Ken'ichi, who was a key advocate for redress for Indonesian survivors. Second, I examine feminist roads to activism in Japan. The confluence of a new emphasis on people's history and the history of women who were formerly *karayukisan* helped open up a space for writing the first life stories of Korean survivors still residing in Japan. Third, I examine the connections between Korean advocacy and the democratization movement and related critiques of militarism and military bases and the specific direction of women's activism. I analyze the links between Korean and Japanese women's rights activists, including their shared critiques of contemporary Japanese sex tourism to Korea. In the final section of this chapter, I examine the case of the most famous Korean survivor, Kim Hak-Sun, who shared her story openly with the media in a court case in Tokyo in 1991. Kim's testimony linked these patterns of activism together and turned the world's attention to the plight of survivors as victimized persons.

Chapter 6 shifts the focus back to Indonesia. As global attention was turning to this issue in the early 1990s, the situation in Indonesia was very different.

Indonesians continued to live under a military regime where, despite ongoing patterns of military abuse, there was complete impunity for human rights crimes. I compare the cases of Korea and Japan with the situation in Indonesia. I highlight the significant differences in terms of the very limited political space available to activists to advocate on human rights issues. I consider why women's activism was constrained until the mid-1990s and why this particular topic was not researched by either Indonesian historians or historians of Indonesia. The mass repression of the political left in the 1960s meant that unlike in Japan, "comfort women" and poor women more generally were rarely the focus of historical analysis. I examine how Indonesian journalists from the leading magazine *Tempo* reported on emerging global activism in the early 1990s and reflect on the journalists' decision to track down Indonesian survivors and ask them to share their experiences despite their reluctance to do so. I provide critical analysis of how survivors and their experiences were framed and narrated in this reportage before the emergence of Indonesian activism on this issue. The journalists conveyed an expectation that the women had an obligation to tell their stories for the historical record, yet at the same time they projected ambiguity regarding whether the women had been victimized. Meanwhile as *Tempo* was discovering this story, Tuminah came forward and told her story as a survivor.

Chapter 7 details how in 1993 a visit to Indonesia by JFBA lawyers to find out more about wartime experiences triggered more substantial activism in that country. The YLBHI took up the issue of war victims more broadly because of their commitment to marginalized people and the promotion of human rights values in society. The way YLBHI approached this case as a broader human rights issue was in contrast to the efforts of Japanese and Korean women's activists who focused more specifically on women survivors of military sexual violence and on recording women's life stories. YLBHI called on the survivors of wartime abuse to register with them and went on to document their experiences. Due to limited funding and an inability to mount a court case themselves, Indonesian survivors and activists were very dependent on Japanese lawyers for assistance. In this context of registering with YLBHI, survivors began to be profiled by the local media. I discuss why the story of one particular woman, Mardiyem, was repeatedly profiled and why Tuminah's story was relatively neglected. I show how Mardiyem subsequently became an icon for Indonesian survivors. With YLBHI's help and armed with data from multiple fact-finding missions, the Japanese lawyers lobbied their government for concessions on this issue. These efforts, combined with those of many other activists across the broader region of Asia, ultimately led to important forms of acknowledgment, including the 1993 Kōno statement.

In the early 1990s, activism drove increased attention to the issue of the "comfort women" in international organizations, including the United Nations. This led to further advances toward acknowledgment of the plight of surviving women. In this context, the Japanese government set up the Asian Women's Fund (AWF) in 1995, as a way to compensate individual women and avoid direct government payments. Chapter 8 discusses the creation of the fund and how it ultimately divided activists and led to new outreach efforts directed at Indonesians to convince survivors to reject or accept compensation payments from the AWF. The chapter traces how the citizens' group the International Committee of Asia-Pacific War Victims Organizations Claiming Compensation (Ajia-Taiheiyō Chiiki Sengohoshō Kokusai Fōramu Jikkō Iinkai) headed by Takagi Ken'ichi tried to extend support to survivors. I further analyze how the Communication Forum for Ex-Heiho for former Indonesian auxiliary soldiers or ex-*heiho*, became involved in "comfort women" activism, including documenting the women's experiences by means of questionnaires. The chapter also considers how and why women's activists and survivors with links to the Asian Women's Solidarity Conferences rejected the AWF. I compare Indonesian, Korean, Taiwanese, and Filipino responses to the AWF and detail how it split sections of the movement. In this period another Japanese civil society organization, the Citizens' Fund for Realizing Postwar Compensation (Sengo Hoshō Jitsugen Shimin Kikin), was also active in Indonesia. In 1995 and 1996 one of its members, feminist women's activist Kawada Fumiko, traveled to Indonesia to document the wartime experiences of Indonesian women to increase awareness about them in Japan. This led to the first book in Japanese on Indonesian women published in 1997. Mardiyem began to travel more frequently to Japan with YLBHI lawyer Budi Hartono to meet with different groups and publicize their cause. Around the same time, unexpectedly and without consultation with survivors or YLBHI, the Indonesian government signed an agreement with the AWF. The agreement was highly controversial for survivors because it included no individual payments to them, instead directing funds to building nursing homes based on the stated logic of protecting the honor of the women. This ushered in a new period of intensified activism in Indonesia and Japan, and the establishment of the Japanese Society for Solidarity with Former Indonesian Comfort Women (SOMJII).

Chapter 9 examines the climax of Indonesian activism on this issue, including the publication of the first Indonesian analysis of it, the effects of revelations of sexual violence in the May 1998 riots in Indonesia, and Indonesian participation in the Women's International War Crimes Tribunal for survivors of the system. I begin by examining how Indonesian activists regrouped after the disastrous AWF deal. I analyze the significance of the first Indonesian book on this topic, *Derita Paksa Perempuan: Kisah Jugun Ianfu pada Masa Pendudukan Jepang, 1942–1945* [The sufferings of forced women: Stories of "comfort women" during the Japanese occupation, 1942–1945].[30] The book was written by LBH lawyer Budi Hartono and sociologist Dadang Juliantoro in response to the government's failure to support Indonesian survivors. Part biography and part historical account, it includes an overview of the system and Mardiyem's life story. The book was the first detailed Indonesian language account of the life experiences of any victim of human rights abuses in Indonesia and therefore a pivotal publication in terms of introducing a human rights approach to the experiences of individual survivors.[31] Sexual violence against Indonesian women was propelled into the spotlight during the May 1998 riots in which ethnic Chinese Indonesian women were the targets of sexual violence, including rapes. As a result of intense activism, there was more public and political attention on cultures of militarism in Indonesia and a sanctioned investigation by the United Nations Commission on Sexual Violence. In the context of these major shifts, an Indonesian team joined the Women's International War Crimes Tribunal in Tokyo in 2000. This was a people's tribunal organized by activists in response to the failure of almost all legal avenues for redress. I provide an analysis of what the tribunal meant for Indonesian survivors and how they and other survivors were presented in the tribunal.

Archives, Testimony, and Hierarchies of Evidence

Covering more than a century of Indonesian history, this book necessarily draws on a broad range of primary sources. The diverse sources and the rationale for using them requires some discussion. Because this book constitutes a history of highly marginalized historical subjects, it is necessary to triangulate a broad range of sources to more fully understand their experiences and social contexts.[32] To write a history of sexual exploitation of Indonesian girls and women across the period of late colonialism in the Netherlands East Indies (1900–1942) through the Japanese occupation (1942–45), and of latter-day activism (1990–2000), I use materials from more traditional archival repositories and other repositories, which I consider alternative archives. Recognizing the limitations of state archives and their missions, which have generally been for the purpose of legitimating the state, many scholars have called for the definition of archives to be widened to include collections of sources that better represent groups frequently marginalized.[33] Across the book I reflect on the partiality or impartiality of the sources I use and critically consider how, why, in what context, and by whom various kinds of evidence was recorded. I take this approach to add complexity to the polarizing debates about hierarchies of evidence that are prominent in the field of research on "comfort women."

For the purpose of reflecting critically on all archives, it is useful to keep in mind the many assumptions and judgments that underpin the formation of archives. As Michel-Rolph Trouillot observed, "the making of archives involves a number of selective operations: selection of producers, selection of evidence, selection of themes, selection of procedures—which means at best the differential ranking and, at worst, the exclusion of some producers, some evidence, some themes, some procedures."[34] Underpinning this process are operations of power. Jacques Derrida goes so far as to refer to the archive's selectivity as "the violence of the archive itself," because the archive is both a place of preservation and a place for the forgetting and destruction of knowledge.[35]

For the colonial period, I use a range of sources including reports written by medical doctors concerned about venereal disease, reports from officials of the League of Nations who were concerned about the trafficking of women and girls, statements made by leading Indonesian nationalists and representatives of the women's movement, and colonial-era novels to understand related societal discourses around the sexual exploitation of Indonesian women and their stigmatization. For the marginalized history under study here, novels are an important source of contextual information. Laurie Sears has observed that Indonesian literature reveals another layer of Indonesian history, so much so that some novels may be considered what she calls "situated testimonies" of past experience, especially when an author has lived through this historical period.[36] Her observations are particularly true for the work of Indonesian novelist Pramoedya Ananta Toer, who has written about marginalized people in Indonesian history including *nyai* and "comfort women."[37] This framing can be applied to other novels as long as critical attention is paid to the positionality of each author. Further to this, novels can, as Pauline Stoltz suggests, offer an important form of resistance to state silence on issues of gendered violence and insights into the relationship between personal and collective memory.[38]

For the chapters covering the Japanese occupation, I draw on a combination of translated Japanese military documents, Dutch archival records from the Netherlands Forces Intelligence Service held at NIOD (Institute for War, Holocaust and Genocide Studies), and the National Archives of the Netherlands in the Hague, as well as the records of the General Office of the Dutch Indies government. I argue that Japanese military and Dutch intelligence sources detailing the experiences of Indonesian women need to be considered as "colonial" archives in the sense that Indonesian women are positioned in them as colonized or at least "occupied" subjects. Women's marginal position in these records means we need to critically evaluate what these sources reveal. Kirsty Reid and Fiona Paisley encourage scholars to consider "the extent to which the 'subaltern' (meaning variously colonized, oppressed or exploited) voices can be heard in the archive and what these traces might mean for our approaches and methods."[39] With this approach I work with these traces, combined with testimonial accounts, to identify patterns across the system. To contextualize archival sources requires consideration of how and why particular archives were formed, which documents were retained in these archives, and whose views were recorded in them and for what purpose. This involves paying attention to what Antoinette Burton refers to as archival "back stories" and thinking through how "specific political, cultural and socioeconomic pressures" shaped these sources.[40]

Surviving Japanese military archive sources confirm the military's role in coordinating the system. Yet the military records are frustratingly incomplete. There are several reasons for this. The Japanese military, like other militaries in wartime, documented its activities to record and memorialize wartime deeds. In that process, it could be expected that there was censorship, particularly of practices that might have contravened international and Japanese military laws. Rape was originally recorded as a crime punishable by death in the Lieber Code of 1863, which informed the formulation of the 1907 Hague Convention.[41] Japan became a signatory to this convention in 1912.[42] Yet Article 46 of the Hague Convention notably did not use the term "rape," and instead this article referred only to a soldier's duty to respect "family honor and rights."[43] This framing of rape as a crime against family honor, which generally meant against the head of a family, follows the patriarchal logic that husbands and fathers own their wives' and daughters' sexuality. This article and Japan's status as a signatory meant that the Japanese military had strong motives not to record evidence of the "comfort women" system.

The Japanese military concealed and destroyed evidence related to the system. A surviving telegram relating to the shipment of women across Japanese territories tellingly mentions that this telegram was a response to other "secret telegrams" in which requests were made by the Southern Army General Command for fifty "comfort women" to be sent from occupied Taiwan to Borneo.[44] Tessa Morris Suzuki has documented how a Japanese officer disguised the fact that a group of women captured with Japanese soldiers in the Netherlands East Indies were in fact "comfort women," claiming they were Red Cross hospital nurses.[45] Furthermore, the Japanese government systematically destroyed related records after the war.[46]

Despite the partiality of surviving Japanese military records, some scholars, in Japan especially, continue to view these military records as the only authoritative sources of information. One example is Japanese scholar Hata Ikuhiko, who played a key role in the 2014 government-backed Study Team on the Details Leading to the Drafting of the Kōno Statement. This study was prompted by claims from former Deputy Cabinet Chief Secretary Nobuo Ishihara at a Budget Committee hearing in 2014 that the testimonies survivors provided at a 1992 hearing, which informed the Kōno statement, had not been corroborated through investigations. Nobuo also claimed that the wording of the statement had been coordinated with the Republic of Korea. The 2014 study sought to investigate the process leading to the Kōno statement and potentially revise or retract it.[47] In his self-proclaimed effort to write a "neutral" history of this topic, published in English translation in 2018, Hata draws extensively on military archival records with almost no reflection on the partiality of these sources.[48] When he reflects on the value of women's testimony, however, he is utterly scathing.

Not unlike the Japanese records, which were compiled in the context of an occupying force, as the usurped colonial power the Dutch kept records for intelligence gathering during and after the occupation. To date these records have largely been used to survey or research the experiences of Dutch women. They were used extensively, for example, by Bart van Poelgeest in his 1993 report to the Dutch government on Dutch women, commissioned to try to discern the prevalence of forced prostitution of Dutch women during the occupation.[49] Historian Yuki Tanaka used some of these records to reflect on the postwar trials for crimes against Dutch women.[50] Select records were used in a report to the AWF written by Mayumi Yamamoto and William Horton in 1998, for the purposes of uncovering more information about the experiences of Indonesian women (see chapter 9).[51] Elsewhere I have drawn on these sources to consider broader patterns in gendered violence across the occupation.[52] In my analysis for this book, I place these records alongside women's testimonial accounts to create a more comprehensive picture of the system.

To write about women's experiences of the occupation, it is essential to use collections of testimonies from surviving women to understand how they survived the occupation and their lives after the war, including how they lived with the trauma and related societal stigmatization. There are a range of sources of testimonial evidence, including memoirs, biographies, published collections, and oral accounts given to activists and at activist events. Very few survivors have published their own memoirs due in part to limited literacy. Some exceptions are that of Jan Ruff O'Herne, who is of Dutch heritage, and that of Rosa Henson from the Philippines.[53] The life story of Indonesian survivor activist

Mardiyem was first published in a chapter in Hartono and Juliantoro's 1997 book and then in full book-length form.[54] She is not, however, the direct author of either of these accounts (see chapter 9). The Dutch publication *Geknakte Bloem: Acht Vrouwen Vertellen Hun Verhaal over Japanse Militaire Dwangprostitutie* (Broken flower: Eight women tell their stories about the Japanese military forced prostitution)[55] is a collection of testimonies of Dutch survivors published under pseudonyms. From the 1990s onward, Japanese and Indonesian researchers have sporadically collected testimonies of Indonesian survivors in many different forms, resulting most significantly in the first Japanese book on this topic, called *Indoneshia no "Ianfu"* (Indonesian Ianfu) published in 1997.[56] Indonesian women's experiences are also woven into the 2010 book by anthropologist and journalist Hilde Janssen, titled *Schaamte en Onschuld: Het Verdrongen Oorlogsverleden van Troostmeisjes in Indonesië* (Shame and innocence: The repressed history of comfort women in Indonesia).[57] Summaries and notes from interviews with survivors have also been published in reports from groups that have pursued advocacy, such as the 1996 report of the Communication Forum for Ex-Heiho and in the newsletter of Solidaritas Masyarakat Jepang untuk ex Ianfu Indonesia (Japanese Society for Solidarity with Former Indonesian Comfort Women), called *Suara* (meaning voice).[58]

Feminist historians working in this field who are concerned with capturing the experiences of people whose views do not usually make it into historical documents see testimonies as a valuable way to gain insights into the experiences of women in the system of enforced military prostitution. Like archive sources, testimonies are similarly partial accounts of the past. Yoshiko Nozaki acknowledges that testimony provided many years after events can contain "mistakes and inconsistencies" but also reinforces the fact the documentary evidence can contains mistakes and inconsistencies and sometimes, in the case of war documentation especially, "deliberate falsehoods and obfuscation."[59] I maintain that for victimized people, testimony is the most significant form of evidence regarding how an individual experienced and remembers traumatic events. As Nozaki argues, testimony is "among the most compelling and important kinds of evidence available for documenting the women's experience and the interplay between official policies and the peoples of colonized and occupied territories."[60] Testimony allows a victimized person to provide a version of events from their position. Furthermore, because it can be given verbally, testimony is a more democratic way of documenting the past experiences of Indonesian survivors of the system because they are a group of people with high rates of illiteracy.

In debates about the "comfort women," some scholars and opponents of activism reject testimonies on the basis that they are unreliable forms of evidence. At the more extreme end of this approach is the work of Hata Ikuhiko. In his history of the system, a chapter titled "personal stories of the comfort women" begins with the author noting that "there is an old saying about prostitutes telling their tales." He notes the "older and wiser people" often cite this saying when "admonishing the naive young for believing everything they hear."[61] In making this statement, he positions surviving women as prostitutes and excludes these women, most of whom are at least eighty-five years old, from the category of older and wiser people. He argues that any such "stories" must be verified "especially if the stories impinge on national honor and the enforcement of law."[62] In respect to the women's testimonies, Hata rightly points to the difficulties of remembering across decades. He does not, however, apply this same critique regarding the reliability of memory to soldiers' memoirs, also written decades after the war.[63] Combined together, archive sources and testimonies of women allow us to establish patterns in the collective experiences of women. This book highlights the strong correlation of patterns between testimonies and the archives.

Throughout the book, I draw on published testimonies of surviving women that have been recorded or collected, for the most part beginning in the 1990s. As will be discussed from chapter 5 onward, most testimonies were gathered in the context of a broader movement to document the life narratives of victims of human rights violations for the purposes of acknowledgment and redress.[64] This activist intention shapes the testimonies, but it does not discount their importance as another record of women's experiences. These sources should instead be seen as an alternative archive.[65] Published testimonies that are not written directly by survivors have unique properties as sources of historical evidence. They are undoubtedly influenced by the person collecting, writing up, and translating the oral testimonies. Published collections of testimonies and testimonies included in nongovernmental organization or advocacy reports are therefore further mediated sources of memory. Those who gather and record testimony select what is recorded on a page or discarded on the basis of whether it is considered relevant. More extensive published testimonies shed light on women's pre- and post-occupation lives as well as information on how they were "recruited" and the conditions of their detention. Where women have provided testimony in their own names, I have continued to identify the women by their names.

Another group of records that I draw on extensively throughout this book are those of nongovernmental organizations as related activist or intermediary groups, which could also be seen as forms of alternative archives. This includes documents produced by and on behalf of Indonesian survivors, such as the records of YLBHI, which included extensive press clippings on their activism, of the JFBA, of the International Committee of Asia-Pacific War Victims Organizations Claiming Compensation and of the Women's Active Museum on War and Peace in Tokyo, which includes documentation related to the 2000 Women's International War Crimes Tribunal and Japanese groups that support Indonesian activists. Similar to state archives, the material produced and retained by these groups reflects the priorities of each organization.

I also analyze sources of popular memory, including novels on this topic and related histories of sexuality and evolving Indonesian media coverage. Through this analysis I consider the changings ways women's experiences were framed and understood.

One further source that I have used extensively across chapters 5 to 9 are interviews with key activists from Indonesia, Japan, the Netherlands, and Korea. Following ethics approval from my university, I conducted around fifteen interviews on field trips taken between 2014 and 2018 with assistance from research assistants Mayuko Itoh and Hani Yulindrasari. I am extremely grateful to my interviewees from the YLBHI, the JFBA, the International Committee of Asia-Pacific War Victims Organizations Claiming Compensation, the Citizens Fund for Redress, the Korean Council, and the individuals who have been prominent in this activism, such as Kimura Kōichi, Kawada Fumiko, Nursyahbani Katjasungkana, Eka Hindra, and Kana Tomoko. The main focus of the interviews was to ascertain the activists' motivations, the strategies they used, the significance of transnational connections, the difficulties they encountered, and their reflections on the role of memory in activism and what forms of activism if any had been successful. These interviews were conducted mostly in Indonesian or English, apart from some interviews in Japan for which Mayuko Itoh assisted me as an interpreter.

As a white Australian woman, my position as a Western outsider from a prominent Australian university no doubt shaped the interview process and what was said to me. In Indonesia my former research on the history of human rights violations enabled me to connect with established networks of activists. Indonesia's democratization process, which began in 1998, has led to greater attention paid to gender-based rights in society and politics. At the same time, the country is dealing with new challenges in this space from conservative groups. In this context, my research was generally welcomed by those I interviewed. There was, however, a sense of disappointment among many activists that the movement had not achieved more, as well as a questioning of why this was so. I decided from the beginning of this research not to directly interview survivors of the violence because of the availability of many different accounts from women and because the most prominent survivor activists whom I wanted to write about, Mardiyem and Tuminah, had already passed away.

I have made it a principle in my research on historical violence to only interview survivor activists who have already made a choice to publicly share and engage in memory debates that entail remembrance of painful pasts. A significant deterrent to speaking with people who have chosen not to become survivor activists is consideration of the pain involved for survivors in sharing such difficult stories with an outsider again. Moreover, there is a history of disappointment with the lack of resolution for Indonesian survivors, despite years of advocacy and of women repeatedly sharing their stories. In Japan some respondents approached my questions with some caution due to the ongoing politicization of this topic in their country. In the Netherlands there was a sense that this history was relatively little known, given the focus on experiences of the war as it was experienced in the Netherlands itself; and in Korea there was a sense that Indonesian activists and survivors were quite peripheral to the larger movement for redress.

As I have outlined, a range of sources can be used to reconstruct a picture of the system, how it worked, who took part in it, and women's experiences of it, as well as public perceptions of, and activism related to, this history. In the next chapter I begin the story of this long history by considering the broader context of sexual exploitation in the colony of the Netherlands East Indies across the nineteenth to the mid-twentieth century.

1

Women, Sexual Exploitation, and Prostitution in the Netherlands East Indies

There were many precedents involving the sexual exploitation of women in Indonesia before the Japanese occupation of the Netherlands East Indies. This includes histories of girls and women being sold or given as concubines to men with high status, such as sultans and merchants, and in the Dutch era, bureaucrats or company officials. In this period, a combination of factors, including Dutch marriage laws and a shortage of European women in the colony, along with the preference of the VOC (Vereenigde Oostindische Compagnie, the East India Company, 1602–1799) and the colonial government, for Dutch men to abstain from visiting prostitutes, led to many men, including soldiers, taking local women as live-in partners or *nyai*. The experiences of *nyai* provide an important window into sexual relations in the colony, which varied across class and ethnicity. An understanding of the *nyai* and the broader feudal and colonial exploitation of Indonesian women also form an important historical context for interpreting the Japanese replication of the practice of forcibly taking local women as live-in partners during the occupation. This context also helps explain some of the continuities between the Dutch colonial period in terms of patterns of unequal relations between Dutch men and Indonesian women in an occupied colonial society and societal attitudes toward women who were subjected to enforced military prostitution in wartime.

During the colonial period, local and Dutch girls and women were engaged in prostitution. Patterns in sex work were closely connected with intensifying imperialism. Global capitalism and the demand for new goods and resources such as rubber, tobacco, and tin resulted in an influx of single or unaccompanied male laborers into the colony, driving up demand for prostitution. This demand and the desire to make money motivated Japanese men resident in the colony to recruit impoverished young Japanese women, known as *karayukisan*, to the colony. There were consequently Japanese civilian–controlled brothels, and several hundred Japanese women worked in the colony before the occupation.

Despite the increasing prevalence of prostitution, there was global, as well as local and Dutch, opposition to these practices. From the 1920s, for example, the League of Nations rallied its members to investigate the trafficking of women and children on the basis of an increasingly moral stance on this issue. This led to several reports in the 1930s on practices in the colony, which provide some insights into prostitution patterns at that time. Indonesian attitudes toward *nyai* and the prostitution of local women were hardening in the context of rising nationalism and a concern to protect the image of "the Indonesian woman." It is very difficult to access the views of women engaged in prostitution in the prewar era as very few recorded their stories. One exception to this is Tuminah, whose account will be examined later in this chapter. Her story provides unique insights into family pressure and prostitution and the sacrifice of daughters that was replicated in the coerced recruitment of the "comfort women."

Surveying these patterns in sexual exploitation helps us understand existing values, practices, and beliefs around prostitution at the time the Japanese military arrived in the colony, as well as the local networks, facilities, and the system of recruiters the Japanese army and civilians may have drawn on during the occupation. Women working in prostitution were among the first women to be forced by the Japanese army and navy to provide sex. There was some continuity in the venues used for prostitution before and after the war. Throughout this chapter I refer to persons working in prostitution as sex workers rather than using the passive term "prostituted women." This is because the latter term positions women as victims, assuming little agency on their part. However, I do wish to draw attention to processes or coercion behind sex work and broader forms of the sexual exploitation of women.

Understanding the *Nyai* as a Feudal and Colonial Practice

There is a long history of concubinage and temporary marriage in the territory today known as Indonesia. In court society, sultans and princes commonly had multiple wives and *selir* (concubines). In the late seventeenth century, for example, the Muslim Sultan Amangkurat I of Mataram was recorded as having four wives in accordance with some interpretations of Islam, and forty to sixty additional concubines.[1] Sultans had so many sexual partners because their virility was equated with the fertility of the land in the kingdom and the prosperity of the court. Concubines were often daughters "gifted" to sultans from other noble families, or presented as tributes from kings. In other cases, daughters were sold by impoverished families hoping for better social positions through new relationships with the courts. Javanese courts often recruited women from particular regions such as Indramayu, Karawang, and Kuningan in West Java; Pati, Jepara, Grobongan, and Wonogiri in Central Java; and Blitar, Malang, Banyuwangi, and Lamongan in East Java.[2] This practice of giving girls or selling young women to a sultan suggests that families saw daughters as something that could be exchanged by means of a sexual contract in return for an improved social and/or financial position.

Outside of Java, sultans in the Malay Peninsula and princes in Bali followed similar practices of having multiple wives and concubines.[3] Helen Creese observes that in nineteenth-century Bali, "access to women was a privilege of rank and royalty and a measure of a ruler's power or prowess."[4] According to the French observer Dubois, princes and princesses in the Balinese royal courts ran a lucrative system of organized prostitution, training young girls in performance and seduction from a young age. The girls were sent out from the court to find customers and offered as gifts to high-status visitors.[5]

As external trade with the archipelago, known then as the East Indies, increased beginning in the sixteenth century, Dutch and other foreign traders (including the Chinese) also took local women as concubines. Rich Chinese traders were sometimes gifted local women.[6] Usually referred to as *nyai* in Java and Sumatra, these women were live-in housekeepers with whom male heads of households had sexual relationships.[7]

There are several reasons it was more common for European men to live with *nyai* rather than have legalized wives. First, in the era of the VOC, the company tried but failed to attract Dutch women to the colony. One major reason women were reluctant to come was the great distance from home and particular concerns about the health of Dutch women in the colony since many Europeans suffered and died from tropical diseases.[8] Second, the company and local rulers together attempted to ban marriages between Muslims and Christians. As a result, many Dutch men took local *nyai* instead of wives.[9] Third, there were strict conditions set for marriage. According to Barbara Andaya Watson, marriages between Dutch men and local women were only allowed when the wives could speak some Dutch and when they had received

Christian religious instruction. Marriage was premised on the assimilation of local women to Dutch culture.[10]

There are divergent views about the extent to which the VOC and then the Dutch state accepted or opposed concubinage. For the reasons outlined already, until the early twentieth century there was a large discrepancy in the numbers of Dutch men compared with Dutch women in the colony.[11] Furthermore, some employers discouraged marriage between European men and European women. In the late nineteenth century, several different mostly plantation companies in East Sumatra, for example, only allowed Dutch assistants to marry after six years of service. Others specified the required salary or maximum debt an employee could hold before being granted permission to marry. The reasons behind these regulations included the idea that the plantations were unsuitable for European women; that young inexperienced employees could not balance taking care of their wives and children next to their work responsibilities, and moreover, that such employees would demand a higher income to support their families and thus be more expensive. In the eyes of company directors, European women could potentially reduce productivity and increase company costs.[12] As a consequence, in these communities, local concubines were more common than European wives.

The common practice of barracks concubinage is an important precedent in terms of patterns of unequal sexual relations between Dutch military men and Indonesian women. Barracks concubinage in the colonial army or the KNIL (Koninklijk Nederlandsch Indish Leger, Royal Netherlands Indies Army) was institutionalized from the 1870s during the conquest of Aceh.[13] Similarly to company employees, lower-ranked soldiers had particular financial difficulty supporting wives and were also required to achieve a certain level of seniority before they were permitted to marry.[14] As a consequence, these various conditions within the colony led to the relatively common practice of concubinage.

Under the Dutch colonial government, marriage between Christians and non-Christians remained illegal until 1848. Thus, as mentioned earlier, the practice of European men taking on live-in housekeepers, with whom they had sexual relations, was quietly accepted in Dutch and Chinese communities.[15] Liesbeth Hesselink argues that the Dutch colonial government also preferred Dutch men to have concubines rather than visiting prostitutes, due to concerns about venereal disease.[16] Hanneke Ming estimates that by the last quarter of the nineteenth century, half of all European men in the colony were living with concubines.[17] Chinese merchants and lower-level Chinese officials also lived with *nyai*.[18]

There are very few historical records relating to *nyai*, and much of the information we have about them, with few exceptions, comes from fictionalized accounts. In an effort to work around this lack of sources, some scholars have conducted interviews or attempted to triangulate sources to piece together aspects of the lives of these women. In interviews conducted in 1996 and 1997 about the colonial past, Ann Stoler and Karen Strassler found that women were reluctant to share stories of direct sexual exploitation by Dutch men, yet they mentioned instances of sexual exploitation of other distant women, including "Javanese servants made pregnant by the employees."[19] This reluctance suggests that there is shame attached to this historical experience. In her study of women living on Dutch tea plantations, Tineke Hellwig drew on the family archives, company records, court records, and a field visit to try to reconstruct some aspects of the stories of a *nyai* of a Dutch planter. Her subject was a Chinese woman named Goey La Nio whose father had business relations with the tea planter Kerkhoven, suggesting that through this patronage contact, the relationship came about.[20] Goey had three children but died giving birth to her third. During a visit to the plantation and a discussion with descendants, Hellwig learned that Kerkhoven had a further six Sundanese *nyai* and fathered a child with each woman.[21] However, he only officially recognized his children with Goey; when the other *nyai* had children, Kerkhoven found them local husbands to marry.

Why would these women have engaged in such sexual contracts with men? We know that through their relationships with Dutch and ethnic Chinese men, some women could potentially increase their social capital and acquire some wealth, although they had few legal rights.[22] In some circumstances they may have experienced improved living conditions, yet it was also the case that Dutch or Chinese men readily discarded these women. According to the Civil Code of 1848, *nyai* had no rights over any children born to a Dutch man.[23] As indicated in the example of Kerkhoven, it was entirely at the man's discretion as to whether he chose to recognize children he fathered. The situation of the concubines of lower-status Dutch men, such as soldiers, was considerably worse. The *nyai* of soldiers ranged in age from twelve to forty and lived in close proximity to the soldiers, often in partitioned rooms. They could be expelled from the barracks at any time, and once ousted, stigmatization meant that they and their children faced difficulties reintegrating into society.[24] These relationships across colonial society were therefore highly unequal and premised on colonial power. Despite the inferior rights of *nyai* compared with those of legal wives under Dutch law, in her study of precolonial mainland Southeast Asia, Trude Jacobsen has also argued that women in such relationships may in fact have been accepted by other members of society as legitimate wives, especially if they bore children with these men.[25]

Sexual Relations and Women's Varied Situations in the Colony

When thinking about the experiences of women in the colony, we need to consider how experiences differed depending on class and ethnicity. In the Netherlands East Indies, the attribution of ethnicity and nationality was complex. The government regulation of 1854 divided colonial subjects into "Europeans" and "Natives" for legal purposes. The category "Foreign Orientals" was later added. Identification generally followed the paternal line of descent. Because of years of interracial relationships, many people in the colony who were identified as European were of mixed heritage. There are differing views concerning the extent to which Eurasians were treated differently or demarcated as a separate community of people. Some scholars (such as Stoler) place a strong emphasis on interracial dynamics and the development of increasingly strict colonial hierarchies.[26] Ulbe Bosma and Remco Raben reject the suggestion that colonial society was "strictly racially stratified," arguing instead that class, gender, education, and culture also determined someone's position.[27]

Although an elite woman had higher status than a working-class man, this was the exception; the position of women in the colony was lower than that of men and they had fewer opportunities. A good indication of some of the issues that middle-class women found most pressing is provided in the reports at the first national congress of women, held in 1928. In her speech to this congress, R. A. Soedirman focused on inequality for Indonesian women in matters of marriage and divorce.[28] Another delegate, Tien Sastrowirjo, called for all schools to accept girls and for more schools just for girls and women to be able to serve alongside men as officials and representatives of government at all levels of society.[29] In general, women had less access to education than men did, and they were not permitted to serve as government representatives.

The composition of colonial society changed over time. With the opening up of migration and improvements in transport from the 1870s to 1930s, more and more Europeans came to the colony. Eventually the sex ratios began to shift and Dutch wives replaced *nyai*.[30] Scholars have suggested that changes in attitudes to mixed relationships accompanied this process.[31] In this period, while the practice of concubinage decreased, prostitution increased.[32]

Following the views of the Dutch government at home, the colonial government chose to regulate rather than ban prostitution. The 1852 Regulation to Counteract the Damaging Results of Prostitution required sex workers to register with the police and undergo weekly health checks.[33] Women found to be infected with venereal disease had to undergo treatment and be cured before returning to work. In reality, health checks were not enforced, and many women did not register with the police and instead engaged in "illegal" sex work.

The regulation of prostitution, however, was the subject of much criticism, with some arguing that it only served to subject women to added scrutiny and that it implied state endorsement of prostitution.[34] There were also associated moral concerns, as evidenced by the 1898 inquiry into the moral state of the Netherlands Indies army by the Dutch Society Against Prostitution and the Society for the Furtherance of Public Morality in Dutch Overseas Colonies. According to Hesselink, Dutch colonial thinking was characterized by the view that prostitution was a "necessary evil" and widespread acceptance of a biological determinist argument that both Dutch and local men in the military and working on plantations needed to "satisfy sexual urges."[35] As we shall see elsewhere in this book and across history, this kind of view occurs repeatedly in military sources and different historical contexts.

Prostitution in the colony intensified along with the expansion of global capitalism and increasing Dutch exploitation of Indonesians. As the demand for goods such as tin, tobacco, and rubber accelerated beginning in the early nineteenth century, and as shipping speeds increased and associated costs of passage decreased, colonial companies began to import indentured laborers to work in plantations and mines and to build infrastructure.[36] A majority of workers came from China, sometimes via British colonies, and a smaller number of Indians came from British India. Dutch companies also recruited indentured laborers from Java to work on other islands. The most common destinations for indentured laborers were first the plantations on Sumatra's East Coast, but also the tin mines of the islands of Bangka and Belitung off the Sumatran coast, the oil industry and coal mining in southeast Borneo, and the coal mines in West Sumatra.[37] On Sumatran plantations, colonial employees commonly paid the small number of local women "coolies" such low wages— half those of men—that women had to meet their financial needs by other means. Company officials did this in part to lure male workers rationalizing their actions on the basis of the women's presumed natural promiscuity.[38] As railways were built to facilitate greater commerce, migrant laborers also created a demand for sex work around the railways.[39]

In 1901 the government implemented the so-called Ethical Policy in recognition of the extreme exploitation of Indonesians. The result was an increasingly paternalistic approach to local people and efforts to lessen the colonial burden. It was in this context of a new concern about the excess of colonialism that a Dutch colonial commission of 1904 to 1905 on Declining Welfare found that increasing levels of prostitution were due to a number of factors. This includes the growing number of factory and plantation workers from outside the area, men and women working closely together, military garrisons, and difficult financial circumstances, which forced women and girls to look for money from multiple sources.[40]

Not just local and Dutch women engaged in prostitution in the colony. With the expansion of global capital, Japanese migrant women also arrived in Indonesia. In his study focused on the outer islands of the colony, Shimizu Hiroshi has documented how in the eastern islands such as Celebes, a strong gender imbalance among European officials, company employees, and imported Chinese workers led to an increased demand for prostitution in those places.[41] In this context, Japanese women, mostly from the impoverished villages of the Amakusa area in Kumamoto prefecture and Shimabara in Nagasaki prefecture, were trafficked to the colony. Their families were paid up front and the women were indentured to pay off this debt and the costs of their passage. Most of these women traveled to Indonesia through Singapore and Hong Kong in the British colonies, because these ports had direct shipping routes from Japanese ports before then traveling on to Medan, Surabaya, or Makassar. Medan was an important base because of the particularly high demand for prostitution generated by the Deli Tobacco Company in East Sumatra, which employed 62,000 male workers alongside only 5,000 women. A Japanese-run brothel in Medan, opened in 1888, also catered to Europeans. In 1896 there were fifteen Japanese brothel keepers, seventy-nine prostitutes, eighty-three female housekeepers, and nine domestic servants in the Sumatran east coast.[42] In this region, European men also bought Japanese women from brothels or imported them from Japan as *nyai*.[43]

In eastern Indonesia, Japanese women worked for the Celebes Trading Company in Celebes, Molucca, and Dutch New Guinea. By 1913 the Japanese consulate in Batavia reported there were twenty-three Japanese brothels, seventy sex workers, and forty-one concubines of different backgrounds in eastern Indonesia. Both the south west coast of New Guinea and Aru were prominent pearl and oyster fishing areas that recruited Japanese men as divers. By 1908, the industry employed 500 Japanese divers. These Japanese men created a demand for Japanese women in the area of Dobo harbor in the off-season.[44]

In 1913, due to mounting Dutch pressure, the regulation of sex work was abandoned, and new laws made "brothels, rendezvous houses and pimping illegal."[45] This led the government to abolish Japanese-staffed brothels in Batavia, but regulation of brothels outside Java proved more difficult. By 1916 the

Japanese consulate reported there were still 1,092 Japanese sex workers and 686 concubines in Sumatra.[46] Japanese consular reports note that many women stayed on and some women moved to the outer islands to escape regulation. While the scarcity of detail in archival records makes it difficult to establish precise links, we might assume that during the Japanese occupation this network of Japanese-run brothels in the outer islands was adapted to serve as *ianjo* for Japanese officers and troops. Hayashi Hirofumi has, for example, documented a case in neighboring Malaya during the Japanese occupation of the Japanese Quartermaster corps rounding up Japanese women in the territory, and engaging twelve former *karayukisan* to recruit local women for *ianjo*, and then to manage the *ianjo*.[47] As will be established in chapter 3, some Japanese women who were most likely former *karayukisan*, appeared to have played similar roles.

There were thus many women of different backgrounds engaged in prostitution. This included local women, women of ethnic Chinese background, Japanese women, and Eurasian and Dutch women, as well as local men engaged in prostitution. Data on these people are limited and must be pieced together from several sources, including colonial reports and inquiries, all of which were written for particular purposes.

One of the most insightful records of prostitution in the colony in the prewar period is a 1939 report by a Dutch expert on combating venereal diseases.[48] He recorded the patterns in prostitution that he observed in the port city of Surabaya. Simons noted that sex workers were all from the poorest classes and were usually "native" women.[49] In his view, Javanese women had the lowest status compared with women from, say, Manado, who were highly sought after for their predominantly European/Dutch clients. This may have been related to the fact that women from Manado were more likely to be Christian, because there were fewer taboos about relationships between people of the same religion, or because Christian women may have been perceived by their clients as having higher status.[50]

According to Simons, some women worked by parading through *kampung* (urban villages), waiting for single men to call them inside or waiting for drivers or houseboys to summon them. Other women worked from cafés after entertaining guests with drink and dance until closing around three o'clock in the morning. Some brothels were run by Chinese and Japanese. A major area for sex work in Surabaya was Banyu Oerip, where women would call out to men to try to attract some business.[51] In Surabaya, a restaurant functioned as a clandestine Japanese brothel. Simons suggests that several older Dutch women also worked discreetly in old-style houses. Restaurants, cafés, and old-style houses were similarly used by the Japanese as *ianjo* during the occupation.

Simons also reported male prostitution in the colony, including pederasty, prostitution of boys with older men.[52] Reflecting the tendency to see homosexuality as "unnatural," Simons attributed the demand for male prostitutes in part to the fears of contracting venereal diseases from women engaged in prostitution.

Simon's report focused mostly on "native" women, but he also made some observations about women of different ethnic backgrounds. He noted that Eurasian women, who were usually older at over twenty-five years, often worked in nightclubs, while Chinese women worked in brothels disguised as hotels and run by Chinese owners. Chinese sex workers were, he suspected, underage and generally only had Chinese men as clients unless men of other backgrounds were given invitations.[53] Perhaps largely due to colonial discourses that positioned Dutch women as exemplars of superior Dutch morality, in the colonial period prostitution by Eurasian women was always "denied by the authorities."[54]

Rising Global Concern for the Trafficking of Women and Children

As indicated by the 1913 crackdown, there was ongoing debate around prostitution and the sexual exploitation of Indonesian and other women in the colony. Opposition to this exploitation came from both international and local sources, including Dutch and Indonesian lobby groups. From the mid-1920s, global concern about trafficking women and children was rising largely as a result of the lobbying of an international women's movement. The Advisory Committee on Traffic of Women and Children in the League of Nations commissioned two international investigations into trafficking, one in the 1920s and another in the early 1930s. The first investigation, about which the most has been written, focused on Europe, South America, and Northern Africa and laid the blame for trafficking on state regulation of sex work, arguing also for greater protection of trafficked women and the equal application of standards of morality to be applied to men and women.[55]

The second investigation covering the so-called Orient focused on the traffic in women from the "Occident," especially Russian women (the so-called white slave trade), but also Chinese, Japanese, Filipino, Annamite, Siamese, Malay, Indian, Persian, Arab, and African women.[56] This included a study of the colony of the Netherlands East Indies. The 1932 report observed that in Batavia there were around 300 women working in prostitution, a quarter of whom were found in the port area of Tanjung Priok. Some women came from

Batavia, others from Sundanese villages in West Java, other parts of Java, and the archipelago. The report recorded the existence of small houses attached to restaurants, hotels, or boutiques where one, two, or three women would work. In the city of Medan, many small hotels owned by ethnic Chinese men were used for prostitution, and their owners were frequently charged by the police for such practices. The report noted a great number of young women, mostly of Javanese background on the plantations in Sumatra, who seemed to be the victims of trafficking.[57]

Reflecting on the social conditions that led to prostitution, the report's authors concluded that the majority of "native" women working in prostitution were divorcées temporarily making a living while looking for new husbands. There were a few Chinese women who almost exclusively served Chinese clients. Some touring singers and dancers who traveled to the countryside and plantations also engaged in prostitution. The report authors noted that European cabaret performers also engaged in prostitution after hours with clients they met at the Moulin Rouge–style venues where they performed.[58] Consistent with these passing observations about performers and prostitution, Helen Creese notes the term *ronggeng* was frequently used in the Indies to denote a sex worker, even though *ronggeng* traditionally referred to Javanese female dancers who performed enticing dances and invited men to sensually dance with them in public for a fee.[59]

In 1937, the League of Nations hosted a conference on the trafficking of women and girls in Bandung, West Java, to renew transnational cooperation on this issue. It remains unclear as to why Bandung was chosen as the location. A Dutch man, Jonkeer A. T. Baud, was chosen as president of the conference.[60] The specific purposes of the conference included exchanging information between police and other authorities and groups from diverse countries who were engaged in halting the trafficking of women and children; enhancing protection of migrants from trafficking; the potential abolition of houses of prostitution; greater collaboration between the authorities, police, and private organizations; employing more women to combat trafficking; and the targeting of Russian women.

Participants in the conference included government representatives from nine countries as well as international experts and members of benevolent organizations such as the Salvation Army. Representing the colony itself were members of the Indonesian organization Perkoempoelan Pembasmian Perdagangan Perempoean dan Anak-Anak (PPPPA, Organization for the Eradication of the Trafficking of Women and Children) and the Indo European Verbond Vrouwen Organisatie (Union of Women's Organizations).[61] There were calls for a future regional conference and a new bureau to oppose trafficking focusing on the Orient, with particular attention on the need for immigration reform to encourage more Chinese women migrants to the colony, to balance the number of Chinese men and thereby reduce their demand for prostitution.[62] The conference participants also raised medical reasons for the abolition of sex work, citing statistics on the rates of venereal disease in the Netherlands Indies army among both European and local troops, and the need to prevent syphilis in particular.[63] Health and disease prevention were major preoccupations of the League of Nations, taken up especially by the League of Nations Health Organization between 1921 and 1946.[64] Neither this report nor other sources offer specific information on patterns of trafficking of local women or the role of families and others in these practices.

What these sources reveal, however, is that at least six years before the Japanese occupation, there was evidence of heightened awareness in the colony of global practices of what was then referred to as the trafficking and enslavement of women. There were also efforts to stamp out such practices and to eradicate sex work. This raises questions about how Indonesians reacted to the forced prostitution of Indonesian women during the occupation. Did they view this through the same lens? The lack of documentation or sources on this sensitive topic means that it is very difficult to reconstruct a complete view of attitudes at the time.

Increased Nationalist Backlash against *Nyai* and Local Women Working in Prostitution

Despite the various legal and moral efforts of the Dutch colonial authorities to ban or regulate prostitution, it continued largely unchecked throughout the colony. Together with growing international condemnation, there were ongoing protests from Dutch and Indonesian groups. Dutch opposition to prostitution was based on religious perspectives and the view that sex outside marriage was unacceptable. Dutch Calvinists, for example, rejected all forms of regulation on the basis that it seemed to promote acceptance of prostitution.[65] Indonesian opposition to prostitution and concubinage similarly stemmed largely from Muslim religious condemnation of sex outside marriage. The organization Sarekat Islam, for example, strongly opposed the Dutch and Chinese use of local concubines, advocating that sex workers be isolated in a women's colony and shamed as an example to other women.[66] The proposed punishment and shaming of women engaged in sex work alerts us to an early example of intense stigmatization of women associated with sex outside marriage.

From the 1900s onward, the *nyai* became a popular subject of Dutch-language fictional short stories and novels, as well as in Malay-language newspapers and novels. One of the most famous Dutch novels is *Nyai Dasima*, written in 1896 by G. Francis, which narrates the story of an Indonesian woman who becomes the *nyai* of an Englishman.[67] In the novel the *nyai* is presented as highly sexualized, consistent with orientalist discourses about Indonesian women. Other Dutch colonial-era novels were more nuanced. The 1900 story *Tjerita Nyai Paina*, written by H. Kommer, is more sympathetic to the position of the central character who is forced by the owner of the sugar factory, where her mother works, to become his *nyai* to save her father from imprisonment.[68]

In Malay newspaper stories and novels, the figure of the *nyai* was frequently deployed to explore themes around the sexual exploitation of Indonesian women. Joost Coté observes that in these stories, the *nyai* is often taken on by a "wealthy and immoral colonial."[69] In some literary accounts, particularly those written by nationalist writers, including Tirto Adhi Soerjo's *Cerita Nyai Ratna*, family coercion and Dutch exploitation are highlighted in the process of recruiting *nyai*, but in these stories the *nyai* ultimately manages to improve her situation and become a "respectable" figure in society. The rehabilitation of the "fallen" woman is a key trope in these novels, most of which were written by men.

Despite the figurative use of *nyai* for multiple purposes in literary accounts, in local society both *nyai* and sex workers were increasingly stigmatized. This stemmed from the nationalist view that women were symbols of morality, representing the standard to which society at large should adhere. Indonesian women in prostitution lowered the status of all Indonesians.[70] Although there was a long history in feudal and colonial Indonesia of the practice of live-in unmarried housemaids, with the intensification of the nationalist movement in the 1920s, it began to be seen as an embarrassment. The women were considered to be living in sin, suspected of engaging in sexual relations outside of marriage with Dutch men.

The Indonesian nationalist movement increasingly asserted that Indonesian women should be modern women, but as "Eastern women," they should maintain their so-called *kodrat*—their biologically defined roles—and placed a high value on chastity.[71] Leaders such as Haji Agus Salim condemned Western culture for its loose morals, positioning Indonesian and Muslim culture in particular as morally superior.[72] In this context, Indonesian women who were cast as immoral were increasingly marginalized and resented.

Indonesian women took a different approach in campaigning to prevent the sexual exploitation of women. The movement, made up of a small layer of elite women in various groups and organizations, was mostly concerned with issues relating to women of their own class. In general, they did not pay attention to issues faced by *nyai* or sex workers. In 1929, however, the Indonesian Congress for Women petitioned the colonial government to prohibit concubinage.[73] In 1937, prominent female nationalist and writer Rasoena Said from West Sumatra questioned why Dutch men did not marry *nyai*, arguing, "If the government really is sorry about our girls and their lot, a regulation of this *nyai* system should be introduced or it should be abolished."[74] Arguments for abolition were made mostly on the basis of the lack of legal protection for Indonesian women in such relationships.

In this period, there was also growing local opposition to the trafficking of women. As noted already, Indonesian women in the PPPPA focused on the goal of "rescuing" women and children who were trafficked, based on strong moral objections to duping "innocent girls" into sex work.[75] This organization was chaired by Datu Tumenggung, who advocated that education, economic independence, and religious instruction were solutions to the practice of prostitution.

Following the release of a report from the colonial labor office on work conditions in the batik industry in 1931, attention turned to the broader issue of sexual exploitation of working women. The report exposed the practice of bonded work and the sexual exploitation of women employees.[76]

Middle-class Indonesian women, who made up the majority of the "movement" at this time, did not always organize on behalf of all women. In 1940, the PPPPA held a national conference on the trafficking of women, but rather than focusing on the victimized women instead highlighted the issue of public morality and called for middle-class women to be given an elevated role in society in policing morality.[77] They also called for greater controls on immigration and on imported films and reading materials to guard against immorality, again calling for Indonesian women to be involved.

The Lives of Sex Workers before the Occupation

A serious limitation inherent in the body of literature on prostitution in the colony of the Netherlands East Indies is the fact that very few works capture the experiences and motivations of women engaged in sex work. In an effort to fill this void, research into the historical phenomenon of the Japanese *karayukisan* offers some examples of different ways the experiences of these women may be conceptualized. In his study of *karayukisan*, for example, Bill Mihalopoulos advocates for increased attention to Japanese peasant women's historical and social formation as way of explaining their labor migration.[78] To recover women's agency he calls for closer analysis of local historical practices such that women's actions are understood in this context. To get beyond the singular perspective of exploitation by external parties only, he considers how child–parent relations worked in this period and obligations of reciprocity and child labor. He argues that in Japanese culture, a failure to secure the longevity of the household was much more shameful than prostitution. From this perspective, some women may have seen sex work as another form of labor, a way of maintaining the family and part of a commitment to parents and the family. He observed that "women could move out of sex work and in and out of marriage without carrying the heavily stigmatized social status usually associated with the category of 'prostitute.'"[79] They were not subjected to extensive moralizing, but instead were accepted as an important part of the community. Therefore, by making money, women had more social capital.[80] His work reminds us that is important to understand the social context in which women worked.

Through his research and writing, Mihalopoulus has tried to restore agency to *karayukisan*. Arguably, in doing so he may have gone too far in underplaying the effects of familial and community coercion and subsequent pressure on these women, especially in the context of patriarchal relationships with brothers, fathers, and other men in the community and traditions of deference to parents. In her study of prostitution in early modern Japan, Amy Stanley points out that most Japanese women had no volition, they were instead "indentured to brothels as children or young teenagers" by their parents in a process that was at the time labeled "body-selling" (*miuri*).[81] Like Mihalopoulus, Stanley stresses the economic basis of sex work, yet she suggests there is less agency on the part of the women involved. She observes that from the late eighteenth century, the economic capacity that sex work potentially gave women led to an increasingly negative value attached to such work. She argues that even though in reality they had little control over their earnings, sex workers' increasing visibility made them targets of anxiety because they potentially challenged the patriarchal family.[82]

In his study of *karayukisan*, Mark Driscoll adopts a far more circumspect attitude to understanding the position of *karayukisan*, suggesting that their agency was extremely limited. Focusing instead on recruiters and the historical records they left, he reaches very different conclusions. Driscoll focuses on the extreme exploitation by Japanese men who often kidnapped Japanese women from remote villages. He argues that these "pimps" were the first imperialists in Asia.[83] Recent studies of the *karayukisan* highlight the divergent approaches scholars have taken to writing the histories of sex work. They reflect debates across a much broader literature on sex work and indeed in contemporary activist circles about sex workers' levels of agency and whether they should be seen as victims or as agents.[84]

Complex perspectives have been applied to studies of contemporary sex work in Indonesia, but this is less so with regard to historical practices of sex work. In a study focusing on the Riau islands, Michele Ford and Lenore Lyons follow Rebecca Surtees's position that "sex workers do not conceive of their lives and experiences only in oppressive or empowered terms," to examine the diverse and shifting interpretations women make of their work.[85] Where it is possible to interview women, such perspectives may be gleaned. Due in part to limited sources and the fact that few sex workers left written records of their experiences and thinking, studies of sex work in the colonial era by contrast tend to focus on discourses around morality or interracial relations.[86] In her study of historical prostitution in Shanghai, Gail Hershatter suggests it is just not possible to piece together what most sex workers thought about their work through secondhand accounts.[87]

Scholars have had similar challenges in trying to access and understand the lives and stories of sex workers in the Netherlands East Indies from the women's own perspectives. In this case, however, we do have one brief account from a sex worker before the Asia Pacific War. As we learned in the introduction, Tuminah's story was documented primarily because she was later recruited to be a "comfort woman" and survived. Her insights, although shaped by the context of her recollections in the 1990s, help contextualize the broader historical and social formation of at least some sex workers in the late colonial era.

Tuminah recounts that she became a sex worker to help her family. In the last years of Dutch colonial rule, they were facing extreme financial hardship. At the age of fifteen she began work on the streets of Solo to, in her words, "feed my ten brothers and sisters."[88] She was the only person in her family with an income. She reported that she used to make ten *benggols* (equivalent to twenty-five cents) per customer, of which she had to use three for a hotel room. Tuminah stated that one of the most devastating aspects of her forced detention in an *ianjo* was that she could no longer provide for her family. It is striking that she narrates her story with apparent acceptance of the fact that she engaged in sex work to support the family. Similar to the case of the Japanese *karayukisan*, this suggests that a central motivation for such work was the pressure on children to provide for families.

Tuminah also told how her father sold her virginity to a Dutch man for five rupiah (*gulden*, equivalent to 500 cents).[89] Replicating historical patterns of viewing women as gifts, her testimony reveals that her family viewed her body as a commodity to be traded. Her account exposes the capitalist exploitation of young women under the Dutch. Tuminah noticeably does not mention coercion or volition in this process. One explanation for why she may not have questioned her parents' decision is that she viewed herself within the societal norms of a "dutiful daughter." In Indonesian society historically (and to some extent still), there are expectations that children will contribute to a family's income and, where possible, support their parents. Her story reveals how the family's economic needs were prioritized above her own. This raises questions, not yet answered, about how common the practice of selling daughters for sex was in Indonesian history.

In her study of the history of sex trafficking in mainland Southeast Asia, Jacobsen has called for far more critical attention to be paid to the roles of social and familial obligations in perpetuating trafficking. She suggests that all too often scholars and activists have assumed that a homogeneous individualism operates equally across societies at all times. In doing so, they fail to understand why some women have been and continue to be more susceptible to trafficking.[90] Building on this reflection, we can see that Tuminah seemingly accepted her fate due to ideas of familial obligation.

What this rare account also tells us is that in the late colonial period in Indonesia, alongside growing critiques of sex workers from nationalists, there were other societal values and expectations motivating women to engage in sex work. It also suggests the possibility that the immorality attached to sex workers in broader societal discourses at this time may have, to some extent, been negated in cases where women were supporting their families.

Conclusion

In this brief review of the history of sex work in the colony, I have begun to outline some aspects of sex work that shaped or ran in parallel with the "comfort women" system. The demand for local and Japanese sex workers was directly related to capitalist and imperialist economic expansion. Sex workers were some of the women who were forcibly recruited by the Japanese army on their arrival in the colony of the Netherlands East Indies. In chapter 2, I turn to examining the general approach the Japanese took toward local people as they began their occupation of the colony in 1942 before introducing the system of enforced military prostitution. In chapter 3, I examine the circumstances under which women working in prostitution and other women who were not formerly sex workers were "recruited" by the Japanese army and local collaborators.

2

The Japanese Occupation

Indonesians as Resources for War

By the time the Japanese arrived in the colony in 1942, Indonesian and Dutch opposition to the practice of trafficking women was growing. In the midst of rising nationalist sentiment among Indonesians at this time, this resistance was also a part of efforts to project a moral image of Indonesian women to counter colonial discourses about Indonesian backwardness. With the arrival of the Japanese, however, these debates quickly receded into the background as Indonesians began to adjust to a new regime. In this chapter, I examine how the Japanese approached Indonesians ideologically and practically. Ideologically, this included a promise from the Japanese to Indonesians of inclusivity and participation in a new era of pan Asianism. This pledge, however, was always qualified on the condition that the Japanese themselves would lead Indonesia toward a more autonomous future. In practical terms, the Japanese approached Indonesia and its people as a resource for its war effort and as a source of labor, in particular. Women were also perceived in these terms, not only to support the domestic side of the war effort but as a source available for sexual exploitation by the occupying forces.

Prior to the invasion, the Japanese undertook a close study of the colony and subsequently courted Indonesians as part of their plans for territorial expansion. I discuss pan Asianism, the colonialist view that underpinned this ideology, and its appeal to some (mostly elite) Indonesians. This attraction to Japan motivated some to collaborate, whereas for others the choice to collaborate was more pragmatic and based on the view that Japan would grant greater concessions toward self-rule. Understanding the sentiment of admiration for Japan and its achievements at that point in history, and the levels of collaboration in

Indonesia, helps explain why there is ongoing ambiguity about this period in Indonesia's national memory. Turning to the Japanese plans for the colony, I outline the process by which, in the midst increasingly difficult economic conditions, the Japanese procured labor from Indonesians for various projects and as auxiliary soldiers. I examine Indonesian collaboration at lower levels of society and the motives behind this, which further led to complicated views about the occupation at the time and until today. Last, I discuss the ideological approach the Japanese occupying forces took toward Indonesian women to secure their participation in the war effort on the domestic front especially by joining the organization Fujinkai (Women's Association). In stark contradiction with its professed mission of uplifting Indonesian women through participation in Fujinkai, the occupying forces perpetrated sexual violence against Indonesian women. The dualistic treatment of women in the colony mirrored views in Japan, where sex workers were subjected to extreme exploitation and by contrast, mothers were held in high regard.

Debate about the histories of and rationale for the system of enforced military prostitution across the Japanese colonies and occupied territories has led to various explanations for why it existed, how it operated, and the status of the women who worked within it. In the final section of this chapter, I discuss explanations that highlight the connections between this system and a longer history of licensed prostitution in Japan and its colonies, as well as those that focus on this as a military system originating in China in the 1930s. This discussion helps set up an understanding of the overall conditions of the occupation and Indonesian approaches to the Japanese, before turning to a more detailed examination of patterns in the system of enforced military prostitution in the colony in chapter 3.

Japanese Designs on the Colony

Japanese interest in the colony of the Netherlands East Indies began in the 1930s. Japanese businessmen and company directors who worked in the region were increasingly interested in southward expansion. A section of the Japanese navy supported this expansion, which would enable it to compete with the army's earlier northern expansion into Korea (made a colony in 1910) and China (from 1937).[1] During the 1930s, a focus on soft power initiatives saw Japanese officials courting Indonesian leaders in business and journalism as well as key nationalists, sending them to Japan for visits to encourage reverence of Japanese modernization. Through this process the Japanese molded a select group of Indonesians from the political and business elite who in turn became very pro-Japan.[2] Through his detailed study of these prewar alliances Ethan Mark demonstrates how "frustrated, ambitious members of Indonesia's middle-class civil society" became attracted to Japanese promises of an "Asian rebirth" as a way out of the colonial predicament.[3] This promise was particularly appealing after so many years of Dutch colonization and perhaps especially after the Dutch crackdown on nationalists in the 1930s. Some nationalists saw Japan as a potential model for modernizing without following Western patterns, while others, such as Mohammad Hatta, remained extremely wary of Japan.[4]

The German occupation of the Netherlands from May 1941 and Japan's bombing of Pearl Harbor in December 1941 saw intensified Japanese interest in the colony. The Japanese eyed the colony due to its geographic location, but also crucially, because it was resource rich and could support the growing demands of its war effort. In February 1942, the Japanese seized the colony from the Dutch and British forces with relative ease and also claimed the British colony of Singapore.[5] Prior to arriving in the Netherlands East Indies, the Japanese planned precisely which local resources and people they would target for exploitation and the lengths to which they were prepared to go to achieve their aims. The military's growing demand for raw materials such as oil, tin, timber, rubber, and minerals led to the prioritization of securing mines, plantations, oilfields, and factories.[6] This in turn dictated where troops were stationed and subsequently, the locations of "comfort stations" or *ianjo* to serve them.

During the occupation (1942–45), control of the regions was divided between different divisions of the Japanese military. The sixteenth division of the army ran Java and the twenty-fifth division ran Sumatra. The navy took administrative charge of the Eastern part of the colony, including Borneo, Celebes, Bali and the Maluku islands (see map 1).[7] In secret, the Japanese planned that eastern Indonesia would become its "permanent possession." For this reason, nationalism was not encouraged, and it is likely there was less concern for what the locals thought about the occupying forces.[8] This was in contrast to Java and Sumatra, where the Japanese actively engaged with and accommodated Indonesian nationalists, gave residents greater levels of autonomy, and continued to promote the promise of joint participation in a new age of pan Asian prosperity.[9]

Underpinning the occupation was Japan's fundamental motive to exploit Indonesia's labor and natural and agricultural resources. Local men and women were mobilized for a range of tasks to contribute to the war effort. The Japanese coerced local leaders such as village heads into recruiting "volunteers." This chapter first examines the exploitation of Indonesian labor broadly before

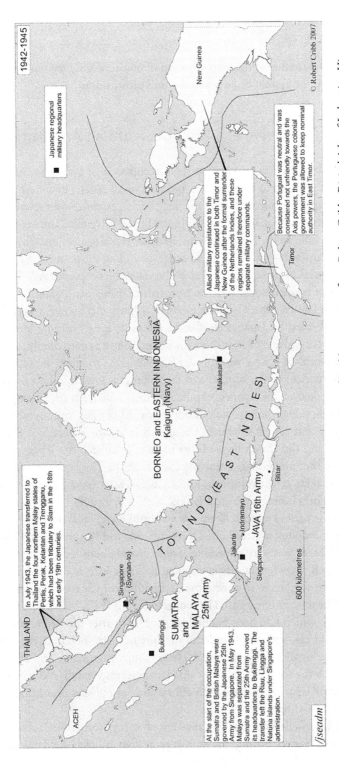

Map 1. Japanese administrative divisions in the Indonesian archipelago. Reproduced by permission from Robert Cribb, *Digital Atlas of Indonesian History* (Copenhagen: NIAS Press, 2010).

considering the particularities of the system of enforced military prostitution and its links to the system of Japanese licensed prostitution.

The Japanese Promotion of Pan Asianism

The Japanese justified their occupation of Southeast Asia on the basis of a promise to improve the position of all Asians in a new world order under Japanese guidance. This ideology, which extended on prewar ideas of an Asian rebirth in Japan was underpinned by the drive to secure new trade networks. In June 1940, Foreign Minister Arita Hachirō outlined the basic concepts underpinning this new world order, including the premise that close geographic, racial, and economic relations between the peoples of Asia should be the basis of peace, cooperation and prosperity.[10] His pan Asianist vision, which became known as the Greater East Asia Co-Prosperity Sphere, was enthusiastically embraced by Japanese leaders at the time, for whom the idea of a new global order replacing Anglo-American hegemony was particularly appealing. This concept of a new world order was designed to align the Japanese mission with anticolonial sentiments in the colonies it sought to take over.[11]

After the takeover, the Japanese emphasized their superiority over Europeans and asserted their intentions to help Indonesians.[12] They destroyed symbols of Dutch culture and rule and banned the Dutch language, pictures of Queen Wilhelmina, and the Dutch flag.[13] In its place they hoisted the Japanese flag alongside the Indonesian flag, attracting local support. The Japanese assigned a team of Japanese civilian draftees, known as *bunkajin* (persons of culture), with the task of winning over local people with propaganda.[14] The Japanese represented themselves as both liberators and brothers to local people.[15]

For many Indonesians, this anti-Dutch attitude and the promise of a new Asian world order was very appealing. Some directly admired the direction of Japanese politics, whereas others opposed it. There is little documentation of resistance to the Japanese during the occupation, which was composed of elements of the underground Partai Komunis Indonesia (PKI; Indonesian Communist Party), which had been banned by the Dutch after the PKI's 1926–27 uprisings,[16] but also groups of students and intellectuals, including those led by socialist nationalist Sutan Sjahrir.[17] These groups engaged in acts of resistance that took the form of spreading anti-Japanese propaganda and trying to sabotage major Japanese construction efforts such as railways and bridges to disrupt their war effort.

Despite Japan's declarations of a new era of Asian brotherhood, accounts from Japanese leaders during the war suggest that officials held far more patronizing views of Indonesians. In 1944, for example, Okada Fumihide, chief civil administrator for the South-Western Fleet, who was based in Celebes, wrote in an official report:

> The East Indies is now passing through a period that could justly be called "the Indonesian restoration." Japan has taken the place of Holland. The Indonesians who, as an ignorant, unhealthy and lethargic race became the victims of skillful Dutch tyranny, are now taking the opportunity of the Greater East Asia War to undertake a great political, economic and spiritual restoration. This restoration is based on our power. We Japanese must awaken the Indonesians in a manner which conforms with our unsurpassed nation and ideals, in order to muster their strength under the Rising Sun to resist and defeat the British and Americans . . . Under the Rising Sun and Japanese leadership, the Indonesians have been spiritually united with Japan, and as a result a glorious way of life has been opened up before them.[18]

This official report reflects a colonial viewpoint in which the Japanese were engaging in a civilizing mission to uplift Indonesians and bring them closer to the advanced Japanese, who are positioned as superior. The "Indonesian restoration" Okada imagined resembled Japan's own experience of modernization following the Meiji restoration of 1868, during which time Japan industrialized and adopted new traditions to compete with Western countries.

Like the European colonialists before them, in assuming a position of superiority, the Japanese categorized members of the societies they took over, ranking them in a hierarchical system. Indigenous Indonesians ranked second behind the Japanese. Ethnic Chinese and Indians, as minority populations, were included in the category of "Asian people," entitled to become Japanese nationals except in cases where their loyalty to Japan was questioned. Europeans were considered temporary residents and, with the exception of those who supported the Germans, placed in prisoner of war (POW) or civilian internment camps. Some of these internees became forced laborers on projects close to the camps or in distant locations such as Burma, where they worked on the Thai–Burma railway.

The Japanese policy toward the 200,000 Eurasians was more ambiguous and depended on whether they displayed loyalty to the Japanese.[19] In 1943, for example, the Japanese announced to Eurasians that they would be treated as locals unless they engaged in subversion.[20] As a consequence, with the rare exception of those openly loyal to the Dutch, many Eurasians, especially on Java, remained outside POW and internment camps.[21] Nonetheless, due to the economic crisis, many lost work and their financial positions deteriorated.[22]

Forced Labor and the War Effort

The Japanese recruited thousands of Indonesian men as laborers known as *rōmusha*. Densely populated Java was seen as a major pool of labor for the construction of wartime infrastructure and agricultural and textile production.[23] Shigeru Satō has estimated that one fifth of Java's 50 million people were mobilized during the war.[24] Recruitment was also intense across the eastern outer islands, which were controlled by the navy. In these regions there was a strong demand for labor to work in mines, shipyards, and airfields.[25] While most of the largely male *rōmusha* (laborers) workforce were employed inside the boundaries of the colony, some were shipped abroad to Japan's other colonies.

Initially, the Japanese had success attracting voluntary recruits. However, as news began to filter back home from *rōmusha* about their difficult working conditions and others failed to return to their villages, it became increasingly hard to find willing volunteers. In response, the Japanese commenced compulsory recruitment. Each regency (an administrative level under a province) was required to supply a quota of laborers for work inside and outside Java. In an effort to enhance the prestige associated with such work, the Japanese began to describe these workers as "economic warriors" on the basis that they were fulfilling this task for the war effort.[26] Signs bearing this term were erected on households that provided men as a form of recognition of their contribution. As the war progressed, it was also the case that the people's financial circumstances became more and more dire; "the occupation impoverished people to such a degree that in order to survive many had to accept any work that became available."[27]

The Japanese occupying forces in Indonesia, as elsewhere, had orders to use local resources to achieve self-sufficiency no matter the consequences for locals. A principle outlined for the occupation of southern areas (meaning Southeast Asia) dictated that "economic hardship imposed upon native livelihood as a result of the acquisition of resources vital to national defense and for the self-sufficiency of occupation troops must be endured."[28] During the occupation, peasants, facing coercion from local officials, were required to supply assigned quotas of rice for sale at below market value to the Japanese administration. This combined with inadequate facilities for transporting rice and smuggling led to severe rice shortages for local people.[29]

As a consequence of these conditions, people were willing to take on unusual levels of risk to survive and the risks for forced laborers were indeed significant. Most *rōmusha* did not receive sufficient rations, medical care, or shelter to sustain the arduous physical work they were required to perform.[30]

Socialist Tan Malaka, who was assigned to work in a mine in West Java during the occupation, reported seeing desperate and ill *rōmusha* abandoning work on the nearby railway line and trying to make it back to their hometowns only to die on the roadside.[31] Records show that death rates of Asian laborers on Japanese projects in the region, such as the Thai–Burma railway, were notoriously high, including an estimated 45,000 *rōmusha* from the Netherlands East Indies.[32] In his statement to the International Military Tribunal for the Far East in 1946, Dutch lawyer and POW Klaas de Weerd estimated from his extensive documentation of the occupation that 270,000 men were transported outside Java for work, of which only 70,000 returned after the war.[33] This represents a death rate of 74 percent. Further to this, every *rōmusha* who was forced to work on such projects away from their homes potentially deprived their household of a source of income, further accentuating the economic difficulties of families at this time.

As noted already, local officials, operating under varying degrees of coercion, were complicit in recruiting *rōmusha*. The most senior nationalist leader, Sukarno, was released from detention by the Japanese. He was wary of Japanese fascism but agreed in 1943 to encourage Indonesians to support the Japanese war effort in return for the promise of independence.[34] When circumstances became more difficult economically, Sukarno lobbied Indonesians to be creative and resilient in the face of shortages of things like soap and clothes. He rallied laborers to continue to sign up to work on projects such as railways, even though he knew of the terrible conditions and high death rates they would face.[35] This collaboration at the highest level, which was premised on sustaining the nationalist movement, continues to have bearing on how the occupation is remembered in Indonesian popular histories (see chapter 4).

Another category of laborer that was sometimes forced but sometimes voluntary, was the *heiho*, or auxiliary forces for the Japanese army. These men served as a secondary force of backup troops and laborers for the army and navy, alongside men from other Japanese colonies. The *heiho* membership included former Indonesian soldiers who had served in the Dutch military recruited from POW camps, unemployed men with no military service who were recruited on a voluntary basis, and forced recruits who were mostly recruited after March 1944.[36] Like *rōmusha*, there were varying degrees of coercion in the recruitment of *heiho*. In his statement to the Military Tribunal in 1946, de Weerd testified that Indonesian soldiers who had formerly served in the Royal Netherlands Indies army were "partly recruited and partly compelled to serve as a *heiho*."[37] Many men volunteered to become *heiho* rather than *rōmusha* because there was more prestige attached to this category of work. Wages were twice as high, and their families were guaranteed some protection.[38]

In her study of Indonesia's *heiho*, Kaori Maekawa estimates that 43,887 men served in this auxiliary role.[39] They were given military training at army or navy training schools, most of which were formerly military barracks or other installations of the Dutch colonial army.[40] The *heiho* were technically part of the Japanese military, and they received military ranks beginning with private second class and wore Japanese uniforms and insignia.[41] In reality, however, they were treated differently than Japanese soldiers, receiving lower wages and lower quality food, and they were made to bow to Japanese military of all ranks and civilians.

The Japanese mainly used *heiho* as a labor force in transportation, logistics, and construction and as guards for POW and internment camps. The conditions under which they lived varied depending on where they were located. Some were so poorly treated that Japanese soldiers overseeing them were later prosecuted for war crimes.[42] Others had better experiences. In the postwar era, former *heiho* subsequently retained a curious mix of pride at being part of the Japanese military and a sense of injustice at having been exploited (see chapter 8).

The experiences of *rōmusha* and *heiho* during the occupation are important to understand how they came to join with "comfort women" in claims for redress from the Japanese in the 1990s. As I discuss in chapter 4, the mixed and complex experiences of the occupation, within and among these groups, further complicate Indonesian attitudes to the occupation as a whole.

Indonesian Women and the War Effort

The Japanese viewed Indonesian women, similarly to Indonesian men, as a resource for advancing the war effort and more broadly as citizens in need of improvement under Japanese tutelage. Fujinkai branches were formed beginning in August 1943.[43] In Java, girls aged fourteen and over were called to join Fujinkai to support wartime "activities appropriate to women," such as child care, sanitation and nutrition, and overseeing first aid, savings, and home education.[44] Fujinkai branches were sometimes attached to work places that employed large numbers of women, such as factories. On Java, branches were formed in each regency, district, and subdistrict. They were later placed under the umbrella of the Jawa Hōkōkai (Java Service Association), which was formed on March 1, 1944. Fujinkai associations were most active in Java, but there were branches also in Madura, Kalimantan, Sulawesi, Sumatra, and other areas.[45]

Indonesian women had mixed attitudes toward Fujinkai, ranging from enthusiastic support to reluctant pragmatism, to a refusal to join.[46] Participation was technically voluntary, but some women joined out of fear of the Japanese military police or because this was the only women's organization the occupying regime allowed and thus one way to potentially further different goals. Other women, such as S. K. Trimuri, who opposed the occupation, rejected Fujinkai and instead joined an underground women's movement.

Fujinkai's particular focus reflected the wartime thinking of the Japanese military state and mirrored those of the Greater Japan Women's Association (Dai Nippon Fujinkai) based in Japan.[47] The example of Fujinkai helps illustrate how the Japanese sought to replicate Japanese organizations in the colony. A key difference between Japanese-based organizations and those in the colony, however, was that Japanese women were deemed to have "special qualities that were unparalleled in the world."[48] This was consistent with the idea that the Japanese people were more advanced than other "Asians." Furthermore, the Japanese military promoted the organicist idea that "the source of Japanese fighting spirit was the household (known as *ie,*); and that the person who protected the household materially and spiritually was the mother."[49] Japanese mothers were thus designated a special place in the war effort. On this basis, many Japanese feminists later critiqued earlier generations of Japanese women for being co-opted by the Japanese leaders into an imperialist and violent project (see chapter 5).

There were further and extreme contradictions between this state-professed ideology and the treatment of Japanese women in the system of enforced military prostitution. As it was in the prewar era, the demarcation between middle and upper-class women and the mostly lower-class women who worked in licensed prostitution reinforced women's roles in the higher classes as mothers at the center of the household to protect the image of the Japanese family state.[50]

Within the colony, there is evidence of a similar mismatch between the ideology of Fujinkai and the general treatment of Indonesian women by Japanese soldiers and civilians. The constitution of the Java Service Association, for example, recorded that local Fujinkai members were tasked with striving for "mutual moral improvement and for the exaltation of the womanhood of Java."[51] Despite this professed ideal, there are many examples of occupying forces abusing local women. In an account of the occupation given by S. M. Gandasubrata, a resident of Banjumas in Central Java, he hints at how the Japanese contradicted their own professed exaltation of womanhood, noting, "towards women the attitude of the Japanese was far from pleasing. Women had no value in their eyes. They considered as creatures of lower order than men; only useful as servants or to satisfy desire."[52]

In this rare account published in translation, Gandasubrata provides no explicit details of sexual violence against women. This is consistent with an overall lack of recognition of these acts as violence or as crimes. His reference to the use of women "to satisfy desire" references the power differential between these women and the men, resulting in sexual exploitation and slavery.

Indonesian women were viewed as a source of support for the domestic side of the war effort, but also as being available for sexual exploitation by members of the Japanese military and Japanese civilians residing in the colony. To understand why the members of occupying forces regarded women in this way, we need to consider not only the wartime system of enforced military prostitution but also that system's relationship to the prewar Japanese system of licensed prostitution and the extension of this system to Japan's first colonies of Korea and Taiwan.

Japanese Licensed Prostitution

In Japan and across its early colonies, the authorities endorsed licensed prostitution, that is, an officially organized and managed prostitution system. Licensed prostitution in Japan extends as far back as 1589, when "pleasure quarters" or licensed districts began to flourish in commercial and port cities.[53] The industry included women working as courtesans, as maidservants, and on the streets and those who provided sex for the military. Girls were often sold into this system by their families. As detailed in chapter 1, another part of the Japanese prostitution industry was the *karayukisan*, who were sent across the world on indentured labor contracts to pay off loans made to their poverty-afflicted families. The civilian sex industry provided "an infrastructural and logistical base from which the military was able to establish its comfort women station system, first within Japan and then abroad."[54] Japanese women were also part of the system.[55]

After Korea was forced to open its ports to Japan in 1876, the Japanese began to establish their own brothels, which operated through restaurants. Following the Russo-Japanese War of 1905, Japanese immigration to Korea expanded and the scale of Japanese-run prostitution increased. Five years later, in 1910, with the colonization of Korea, the Japanese introduced a licensed prostitution system and ultimately took control of prostitution in Korea. These controls included not permitting women to leave the premises except for compassionate reasons and a prohibition on married women engaging in prostitution. Song Youn-Uk suggests this regulation aligned with the Japanese ideology of *ie*, intended to clearly distinguish "wives and prostitutes."[56] As the economic situation worsened in the 1920s, jobs became scarce, and more Korean women were drawn into prostitution. Some of these women were deceived by Japanese and Korean procurers with promises of other kinds of work.[57] In this period, an extensive system involving private brokers saw Korean women traded and sent out to Japan and China. When the Pacific War expanded in 1942, these existing patterns in the state-managed system of prostitution in Korea enabled the rapid mobilization of Korean women into the system across Japan's occupied territories.[58]

Before the war, the Japanese state's attitude to prostitution was generally to allow it, while also seeking to regulate it. Opposition from a Christian abolitionist movement in Japan began in the 1880s, but with little effect.[59] Some small shifts in the state's position, including moves to curtail the *karayukisan* system from 1899 onward, were largely driven by a desire to protect Japan's national image.[60] In 1925, Japan endorsed the International Convention for the Suppression of the Traffic in Women and Children, which attempted to further regulate prostitution and forbid women under twenty-one years from working in the industry (see chapter 1). Although Japan adopted the protections for its own women, it actively excluded application of the convention to its colonies at the time: Korea, Taiwan, Kwantung, Sakhalin, and the South Pacific islands.[61]

The System of Enforced Military Prostitution

The beginning of the system of enforced military prostitution is commonly dated to 1931, when the Japanese navy first established an *ianjo* in Shanghai, following the Manchurian Incident in which the Japanese army secretly blew up the South Manchuria Railway as a pretext for military intervention.[62] To get around Chinese attempts to ban licensed prostitution, the Japanese government set up a "restaurant serving woman system" (*ryōriten shakufu*) in the city.[63] As more navy troops arrived in the area, more restaurants or stations were established. By 1936, there were ten restaurants employing 102 Japanese women and 29 Korean women, all of whom were examined twice a week for disease. A year later, the Japanese army followed the model of the navy and began to set up brothels in Shanghai, sending requests to Japan for women to be supplied from the area of Nagasaki, which had been the former center of the supply of *karayukisan*.[64] From 1937, when the war between Japan and China intensified, the system was expanded and Japanese women were sent to China to follow the troops. Chinese women were also rounded up by Japanese military police, placed in the stations, and forced to receive soldiers.

As the war progressed and the Japanese took more and more territories, the system was replicated in each new location. For the territories of Southeast

Asia, women were generally sourced locally because of the difficulties of sending women the long distances from Japan or its other colonies.

Estimates of the number of women across the system vary. It is often asserted that the vast majority of "comfort women"—up to 80 percent—were from Korea.[65] Research on the experiences on Chinese women, though, suggests that the number of "comfort women" from China was also large.[66] Kumagai Naoko explains that this variation is a product of how the number of women is estimated.[67] Because many women did not survive or chose not to come forward later, it is very difficult to accurately count the number of women affected. Some scholars have therefore estimated the number of women based, for example, on the number of stations recorded, the number of condoms used, and the turnover of women in stations, or they used ratios to estimate how many women to soldiers there would have been.[68] Yoshimi Yoshiaki estimated, for example, that if there was 1 comfort woman for every 100 soldiers and a turnover of 50 percent, this would lead to an estimate of 45,000 women for the 3 million soldiers in overseas service. Alternatively, if there was 1 woman for every 30 soldiers and a 100 percent turnover, this would lead to an estimate of 200,000 affected women.[69]

A key rationalization for the system was the view that providing women was necessary to satisfy the "sexual needs" of soldiers and to prevent the rape of local women.[70] Cynthia Enloe, although focusing on Euro-American contexts, argues that these beliefs were historically common in militaries and were underpinned by the myth that men, particularly soldiers as archetypal men, have "an uncontrollable sex drive" and that women in war are merely "camp followers," there to serve men's needs.[71] Reflecting on the cultural context of the "comfort women," Sarah Soh argues that the system reflected the values of "patriarchal fascism" according to which women were presented as "imperial gifts" to soldiers in return for their war service.[72] Highlighting the extreme objectification of women in this system, she refers to a 1938 report by Japanese military doctor, Aso Tetsuo, in which he suggested the stations should operate as "hygienic public toilets," within which the women were supposed to act merely as receptacles of male lust.[73]

One further rationale provided for the wartime system was that the soldiers needed to be protected from diseased women who might weaken their health. For this reason, women were subjected to regular health checks before being procured and throughout their time in the system to guard against sexually transmissible diseases.[74] The supply of "disease-free" women was thus seen by the military as another necessary part of the war effort.

Naoko Yamada provides evidence of some preplanning for the establishment of the system in the colony, which includes an emphasis on providing disease-free women. In 1941, a year before the occupation, during a Japan–Holland trade meeting in Batavia, a Japanese military doctor, Fukada, conducted a survey of venereal disease in Java. Following the rationale that soldiers had sexual needs, Fukada advised his government to set up *ianjo* to avoid rapes of local women.[75] He wrote, "most people are Muslims and have strong feelings about chastity. We need to pay stricter attention so as not to have rape incidents in order not to make natives distrust the Japanese military's discipline."[76]

To promote confidence in the occupation, the Japanese were very careful about how they approached issues related to Islam and religion and worked hard to keep a mostly male Muslim leadership on side, especially by emphasizing joint opposition to Western imperialism.[77] The references to "natives" in the quote is almost certainly targeted at male leaders. The sense that women were a "resource" to be exploited is anticipated. Fukada advocated that because venereal disease was quite widespread in the colony, the Japanese should seek assistance from village leaders to screen women before they were placed in an *ianjo*. His account makes clear that in advance of the arrival of its troops in the colony, the Japanese occupying forces planned for providing women, with concern expressed about the need to protect both the health and public image of its soldiers.

A range of Japanese and Dutch archival sources and military memoirs provide more information on military planning and implementation of the system in the colony. Yuki Tanaka has argued that there is clear evidence that "senior officers of each army issued orders to establish comfort stations, and that staff officers of subordinate units made a plan and put it into operation."[78] He cites an example of a noncommissioned officer, Nakamura Hachiro, being ordered by a commander to set up a station in Meulaboh (Aceh), into which Nakamura recruited four local women in March 1942.[79] Dutch archival sources reveal that in the first half of 1943, the Naval Garrison commander of Pontianak issued an order for establishing official brothels for use by navy and civilian personnel.[80] One of the most cited sources of proof of Japanese military complicity in establishing the system in the colony is a passage from the 1978 memoir of Nakasone Yasuhiro, who worked as chief of accounts of the second construction squad in Balikpapan during the war. Nakasone describes how, in response to attacks on local women by some of the men he commanded, he established an *ianjo*. He reports that in response "soldiers were just like potatoes packed in a barrel,"[81] presumably a reference to the soldiers being tightly packed into such stations. As we shall see in chapters 8 and 9, this particular admission was frequently highlighted by activists supporting survivors, because Nakasone Yasuhiro later served as prime minister of Japan (1982–87). His complicity exposed continuities between wartime leaders and postwar leaders.

Scholars have provided some details for how the system operated across army- and navy-controlled areas with some indications as to the precise role of the military in running these facilities. Drawing from a 1943 book of regulations of the twenty-fifth army, which initially oversaw the territory of Sumatra and the Malay Peninsula, William Horton demonstrates that there was a set of regulations for how stations were to be labeled, the terms of labor contracts, and requirements for regular reporting by those who ran the facilities.[82] The extent to which these regulations were followed is difficult to determine given the dearth of survivor testimony from Sumatra. Horton notes that the sixteenth army division, which controlled Java, appears not to have produced a similar manual. Nor is there mention across the literature of an equivalent navy manual, although it is of course possible that not all sources survived the war or have been made available to researchers.

In Java the Japanese resident and chief of staff of the sixteenth army needed to give permission for establishing army facilities.[83] Technically all women were supposed to be volunteers and older than seventeen years of age.[84] Testimony suggests that these rules, especially those related to women being volunteers, were not followed (see chapter 3). There are many and frequent examples of girls younger than seventeen. The army administration issued licenses for *ianjo* to be set up with the provision that regular health checks were to be performed and women had to be paid.[85] Some women in the system were paid, whereas others were not. The payment of the women does not lessen in any way the crimes of sexual violence perpetrated against them.

In the navy-controlled areas, military units and civilian administrations played key roles in running stations. The navy appointed its own officers to recruit women and make use of existing brothels. Navy units managed *ianjo* in locations such as Kendari, Amoit, Bau-Bau, and Rantepao. Japanese records indicate that the Civil Administration Department of the Navy issued twenty-two licenses for *ianjo* to be run by Japanese civilians and managed by the department.[86] The navy and the army often approved existing brothels to operate as *ianjo* and sometimes ordered local restaurants and hotels to convert their businesses into *ianjo*. They also constructed new facilities.

Based on a substantial number of testimonies from surviving women we know that there were "comfort" facilities across a broad range of locations in the colony (see map 2). Women were detained across the islands of Java, Sumatra, Borneo, Sulawesi (then Celebes), Buru Island, Bali, West Timor, Sumba, and West Papua. According to Tanaka, navy documents from 1942 include records (though rare) that detail the shipment of two batches of "special staff" to navy bases, including forty-five to Celebes, forty to Balikpapan, and thirty to Surabaya.[87] van Poelgeest and Yamamoto and Horton cite a wartime report prepared by the Office for Japanese Affairs in Batavia on seven stations

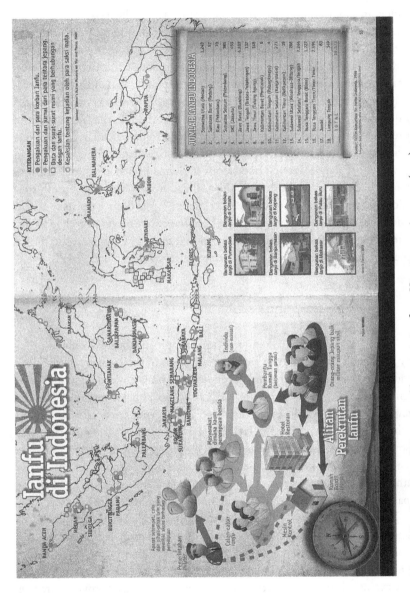

Map 2. "Comfort stations." Reproduced by permission from *Historia* magazine, no. 3 (2012): 52–53.

in Halmahera, the largest island in Maluku. The report lists the number of Indonesian, Korean, and Japanese women at each station, where known.[88]

The scholar activist Kimura Kōichi believes there were more "comfort women" in eastern Indonesia, which was controlled by the navy, than in Java.[89] When a group of former *heiho* in Indonesia, the Communication Forum for Ex-Heiho, attempted to create a register of survivors in the 1990s (see chapter 8), the largest number of women came from South and Central Sulawesi (7,244 women) and East and West Nusa Tenggara (2,994 and 1,727, respectively) women.[90] The concentration of stations in these areas may be related to the prewar networks of Japanese brothels and the fact that many areas in eastern Indonesia hosted large numbers of troops to protect strategic resources such as the oil and mineral deposits in Borneo or as part of the front line in the war effort. There were, 25,000 troops stationed in Ambon during the war. Ternate, Tidore, and Halmahera in the Maluku group of islands were all "strategic points in the Japanese defense perimeter."[91] We do not yet have a clear understanding of exactly how and by whom *ianjo* were set up in each location. Instead, we have fragmentary information that must be triangulated to form a general picture of the system and of wider patterns of sexual violence.

Conclusion

The system of enforced military prostitution can only be properly understood alongside the broader conditions of the Japanese occupation, Indonesian views of Japan, and Japanese intentions toward Indonesians as members of this occupied society. The use of forced labor reminds us of the prevalent Japanese wartime view that Indonesians, with the possible exception of the nationalist elite who the Japanese needed as allies, were seen largely as resources for the war effort. Wartime ideology included an alleged commitment to pan-Asian prosperity, which attracted some Indonesians and led to enthusiastic collaboration by others, but it became increasingly clear that the Japanese war effort was the primary driver of all activities in the colony.

The system of enforced military prostitution can be strongly linked to aspects of the established licensed prostitution system in Japan and its early colonies. The military system was first set up in China in the 1930s, before being implemented across all occupied territories. In the next chapter, drawing more extensively on archival records and women's testimony, I provide a broader survey of sexual violence during the occupation and methods of recruitment of Indonesian and Dutch women, local complicity, deception, and conditions of detention.

3

Patterns across the "Comfort Women" System in the Netherlands East Indies

My mother was crying. The soldier was yelling at her. I was forced to go.

Ema Kastinah, testimony in the film by Kana Tomoko
Mardiyem: Sex Slave of Japanese Army (Kana Tomoko, 2001).

Seventeen-year-old Ema Kastinah from Cimahi, a small military town just outside the city of Bandung in West Java, was out shopping with her mother when she was abducted by a Japanese soldier. Ema later recalled her experience at a so-called comfort station: "I had to [be ready to] work at any time. Even when I was asleep they woke me up to work. I wanted to run away and go home, but I could not."[1] Ema's experience reflects one of the methods used by the Japanese soldiers and others involved in procuring Indonesian girls and women into the system of enforced military prostitution. Her experience highlights the extreme conditions of the *ianjo*, including forced detention and no control over her work. In this chapter, I reflect on how Indonesian and Dutch women were sourced. This requires interrogating the dynamics in the occupied society, including the community situation from which women were recruited, and their relations with the occupying forces. It also involves reflecting on continuities with the colonial period and the introduction of new Japanese practices involving sexual enslavement of girls and women.

In Indonesia as elsewhere, the first "recruits" targeted by the Japanese to work in "the system" included sex workers, largely due to a common assumption that these women were expendable. There were also concerns about resistance to recruitment. The system of enforced military prostitution relied on strategies of coercing or duping girls and women, offering false promises of other types of work. I reflect on how such deception was possible and how and why during the occupation, local people and Dutch people collaborated to supply women. This involves considering the economic and social context of the occupation and how local structures of power worked against girls and women, the desperation of girls and women to take on work or seize new opportunities, and social pressures to obey orders.

A range of methods were used to procure girls and women for the system. As in Ema's case, some were abducted directly from the streets or from their homes. Dutch women were often taken from internment camps, and girls and women were shipped to other islands far from local sources of support.

Finally, I touch on aspects of life in the *ianjo*, including forms of abuse and control. I consider the presence of Japanese, Korean, and Taiwanese women in *ianjo* in the colony and efforts to assimilate the women to Japanese customs. I consider other forms of sexual violence perpetrated by the military and civilians during the occupation, including rape and forced marriages.

Sources

As I have already outlined, in scholarship and research on the topic of the "comfort women," the relative value of archival and testimonial evidence is one of the most hotly debated issues. Here I reflect more specifically on the sources available to reconstruct women's experiences and the limitations of these sources, including archives and testimony. I make the case for why archive and testimonial evidence should be considered together.

In relation to the "official" or "national" sources available to understand this history, Dutch intelligence sources that detail the experiences of Indonesian women must be considered as part of the colonial archive, whereby Indonesian women are positioned as colonized or at least "occupied" subjects. The marginal position of women in these records requires ongoing deliberation and examination. In using these records, I follow Michelle King's call for scholars to work beyond "the internal order" of archives.[2] This includes critically questioning the categories and framings in the archives.

The records of the Netherlands Forces Intelligence Service held in the NIOD (Nederlands Instituut voor Oorlogdocumentatie, the Institute for War, Holocaust and Genocide Studies) and at the National Archives of the Netherlands in The Hague include short testimonies and observations from former prisoners of the Japanese, farmers, former forced laborers, and men who worked in the Japanese police force or as *heiho*. Gathered as intelligence reports, these records include some useful details for understanding "the system," such as estimates of the numbers of girls or women "recruited," transported, or detained in different locations across the archipelago. Specific information related to sexual violence is commonly found under subheadings including "unethical practices" and "prostitution." This form of labeling and categorizing reveals the authors' moral judgments about these women, and therefore the exclusion of the women's voices from the archives.[3] These records rarely include detailed firsthand accounts from women about their experiences, and where they exist, they take the form of confessions by women accused of collaborating with the enemy.

Women suspected of collaborating with the Japanese, for example, could have their assets seized or they could be arrested.[4] These suspect women are described in the archive sources by a range of extremely derogatory terms. These included "Nippon whore," women of "bad reputation," and "loose morals" whose behavior was described as "perverted."[5] This language is consistent with that used to describe Dutch women in the metropole of the Netherlands who had relationships with German soldiers during the occupation.[6]

It must be kept in mind that the main objective of the Dutch intelligence agencies was to uncover espionage.[7] The positioning of women who had sexual relations with the Japanese as traitors replicates patterns across other wartime contexts. The so-called logic applied was that they had betrayed their country because they "gave" their bodies to the enemy.

The roles of Japanese, Dutch, and Indonesians involved in the system, in recruitment or control of facilities, are also documented in the records of the General Office of the Dutch Indies government (1944–50) (Algemene Secretarie van de Nederlands-Indische Regering en daarbij Gedeponeerde Archieven). These statements were gathered for temporary court-martials (see chapter 4) held after the war. In general, they only feature the views of Dutch or Eurasian women. Because the Dutch were particularly interested in exposing cases of collaboration, close attention is paid to whether women "volunteered" or were forced into the *ianjo*.[8]

In the available official Dutch archives, observations about Indonesian women are similarly brief. Indeed, individual testimony from Indonesian women is rarely recorded. One reason for this is that the Dutch were largely concerned with documenting crimes against Dutch people (Eurasians included). It also reflects the prejudices against Asian women of those gathering testimony.[9] For these reasons, when attempting to understand the system and write the history of this period, it is important to combine this archival record with testimonial evidence from its survivors.

The First Targets:
Women Working in Prostitution

The Japanese targeted a range of girls and women in the colony using different procurement strategies, with sex workers as their first targets. It is important to recognize that sex workers from Japan and from the other colonies of Korea and Taiwan were forcibly recruited into the wartime system alongside women who were not in sex work.[10] In the colony of the Netherlands East Indies, the Japanese initially sought women who had previously been sex workers for the Dutch army. In West Sumatra, for example, a Japanese veteran recalled they pursued such women and had them checked by a military doctor for venereal disease before installing four of them in a former Dutch tourist hotel as a makeshift *ianjo*.[11] In December 1943, in Pontianak, Borneo, sex workers were "assembled" to serve the navy, military administration and civilians across four stations in the city.[12]

To date, I can identify only one publicly available account from a former sex worker about her experiences of forced recruitment into the system: that of Tuminah, whose story was discussed in the introduction and chapter 1. In this account and various interviews, Tuminah explains how upon entering the city of Solo, Central Java, the Japanese army began their hunt for "street girls."[13] They scoured the three hotels where women frequently worked: the Julianna Hotel, the Rose Hotel, and the Selir Hotel (now Merdeka Hotel).[14] Tuminah was picked up at the Selir Hotel with some other women in late 1943 or early 1944 and immediately subjected to a medical examination. Once deemed to be clear of venereal disease, the women were installed in two inns used as *ianjo*: the Chiyoda Inn and the Fuji Inn, which serviced officers and soldiers, respectively. Tuminah was detained with fifty other women in the Fuji Inn for about one year. They were prohibited from leaving the premises.

What is particularly striking is that despite an escalation in concern about the trafficking and enslavement of women over the previous decade among elites in the colony, including Dutch and Indonesians, in the face of the Japanese occupation, nationalist and local leaders were quick to offer up sex workers as expendable. Indonesian nationalist and later first president of the republic, Sukarno, for example, assisted in supplying such women for the Japanese military, following his own release from a Dutch prison in Bukittinggi, West Sumatra. In his 1965 autobiography, he revealed that early in the occupation he acted as an intermediary between sex workers in Bukittinggi and the Japanese military. He claims he cautioned the local Military Commander Colonel Fujiyama that Minangkabau people were very religious and would be likely to revolt if the soldiers attempted to take local women.[15] He recalled that he informed locals that as "an emergency measure for the good of *our girls* and our country, I would like to utilize the services of prostitutes in this area. This way the foreigners will be satisfied and will not ravage our maidens."[16]

Sukarno reported that he negotiated with a spokesperson for the women who he claims responded enthusiastically, based on the assumption that the Japanese were wealthy and generous and because it would give the women a chance to be "great patriots."[17] This framing of the service of these women as part of a patriotic duty, which did not match with the treatment the women received after the war, is hauntingly similar to the framing that the famous Japanese survivor Kikumaru attached to her experiences.[18] Following his agreement, Sukarno gave instructions for 120 women to be placed in a segregated district with high walls. Soldiers would each be permitted to make a visit once a week.

The actions of both the Japanese military and Sukarno reveal their assumptions that the forcible detainment and "use" of sex workers was acceptable. Sukarno's own account of his conversation with a representative of these women suggests that the women anticipated being paid in return for their services. Due to the very limited sources on *ianjo* in Sumatra, it is not possible to verify whether this occurred, nor what conditions these women were subjected to. The agreement between Sukarno and the military commander makes clear that different standards seemed to apply to unmarried women and sex workers. Sukarno argued that by providing other women local "maidens" would be protected. Given the importance of keeping Indonesians on side due to the colony's value for the war effort and because of and religious sensitivities, Sukarno's intervention/guidance may have encouraged the Japanese military to target sex workers for recruitment first.

Deceptive and Coercive Recruitment

As the occupation progressed and the guise of Asian solidarity wore thin, the Japanese turned to "recruiting" girls and women not engaged in sex work through duplicity and force. Increasing rates of venereal disease among Japanese soldiers was one trigger for this shift, with military leaders seeking "young unmarried women free of sexual disease."[19] The Japanese attempted to entice women with promises of various types of employment.[20] Min Pyong Gap describes this tactic, also used in recruiting Korean women, as "employment fraud."[21]

Indonesian survivors have provided a range of accounts of being duped into the system with such promises. Sutarbini from Yogyakarta, Central Java was only eleven years old when she was encouraged by a local woman to take a job in Borneo with the promise of high wages, higher than those of her father, a civil servant.[22] The woman approached her after she had failed to get a job at a cigarette factory in Yogyakarta. Mardiyem, also from Yogyakarta, reported that she had heard about an entertainment job in Borneo and was encouraged to sign up by a local woman. She recalled, "The Japanese government was opening a restaurant and a performance venue. I was only just thirteen years old. I was interested in working."[23] Sutarbini's and Mardiyem's stories suggest that teenage girls were looking for whatever kind of work they could find to support their families.

As the occupation continued, the increasingly difficult economic conditions made job opportunities more alluring, especially to those from lower socioeconomic backgrounds.[24] Manual and service jobs were attractive because they were not perceived to require skills.[25] Lasiyem recalled that things were so difficult for her, she could no longer tolerate her circumstances. She took up the first offer of work, without telling her husband, because she wanted to buy food for her child. She ended up being forced into sex work.[26] At the age of sixteen, Mardiyah, who was from a village near Mt. Telomoyo in Central Java, accepted a job offer from a Japanese corporal as a laundry worker because her husband had been taken away to do forced labor on another island.[27] During the day she worked in the laundry at the military barracks in Banyubiru and then at Ambawara. With twenty other laundry women, she was not allowed to return home at night; instead, they were abused by different men in the barracks.[28]

To understand why girls were looking for employment in the colony at this time, it is important to recall that in the 1940s it was still relatively common for children to work. Strict rules concerning child labor were not introduced until the early twentieth century.[29] Established in 1919, the International Labour Organization advocated for abolishing child labor. The government of the Netherlands ratified the convention on child labor in 1922. With some reluctance, in 1925 the government of the Netherlands East Indies prohibited employment of children under the age of twelve in certain occupations deemed too heavy or dangerous. Children were also barred from work between 8 p.m. and 5 a.m.[30] These provisions still meant that children below and above twelve could legally work as laborers in agriculture and other industries with lighter and less dangerous work. At the 1928 Congress of Indonesian Women, Encik Siti Marjam observed that it was common practice for children aged seven to twelve to help their parents with work.[31] The fact that Mardiyem and Sutarbini were seeking work at the ages of thirteen and eleven is thus not remarkable, historically speaking. It was not until 1949 that the government of the

Republic of Indonesia raised the minimum age for the employment of a child to fourteen years.

The Indonesian girls procured into the system who appear in this chapter range in age from nine to seventeen years at the time of procurement. These ages indicate that very young girls were targeted, which accentuates the gravity of the crimes committed against them. The ages of targeted females are usually only provided in testimonies provided by the women themselves. By contrast, in archival records, the ages of Indonesian women are rarely provided and they are usually referred to by the broader terms of girls (*meisje*) or women (*vrouwen*).[32] Where ages are provided in these records, they range from twelve to thirty years.

A significant number of people in a variety of roles were involved in recruiting Indonesian girls and women for the system. To contextualize this complicity, it must be remembered that as an occupying force, the Japanese exerted considerable control over Indonesians. There were harsh penalties for disobeying orders, including the threat of violence and even execution. As individuals, families, and communities, Indonesians tried to navigate these difficult circumstances, sometimes sacrificing women and girls to save themselves. Ide Anak Agung Gde Agung, who served as a regional official in Gianyar Bali during the occupation, recalled that the kenpetai commander, Kawashima, gave unofficial orders to local officials to source women for the Japanese army.[33] In his account, the official described how they paid two sex workers to go to Denpasar to work for the Japanese so as to spare other women. The local army headquarters also used brothel owners or labor brokers to source women.[34] Presumably these intermediaries were given orders or offered enticements. Japanese reliance on the existing networks and infrastructure of the local prostitution industry is a pattern replicated across the wartime Japanese empire.[35]

Village heads also acted as procurers. Kasinem was summoned by the chief of her village in Central Java at age thirteen.[36] Japanese soldiers took her and other girls she did not know and forced them into prostitution at an *ianjo* in Solo. She was forced to stay there for three months. A Netherlands Forces Intelligence Service (NEFIS) interrogation report documents a case that took place in a village twenty kilometers from Kediri, East Java, in late 1942. The village head ordered a girl to accompany him to a Japanese doctor for examination, after which he handed her over to the Japanese and she was never seen again.[37] Other NEFIS reports document village heads near Cimahi filling orders from the Japanese military for girls and young women, who were subsequently taken to the nearby officers' quarters.[38] Outside Java, Rosa from Saumlaki, on the island of Babar in the South Moluccas, was fifteen when her village chief sold her and sent her to a Japanese naval brothel in the city.[39] In this case, there is explicit mention of payment changing hands. In Tanimbar, also in the Moluccas, village heads were also requested to produce lists of unmarried girls and women for recruitment.[40] This suggests that in some cases, married women were safe from trafficking, relative to unmarried girls and women.

Village heads collaborated in this process due to fear of reprisals from the Japanese if they disobeyed orders as well as from a desire to retain their positions in society. Others were paid for fulfilling orders. Some officials were pressured to recruit girls and women selected by Japanese officials.[41] Indonesia's most famous novelist, Pramoedya Ananta Toer, suggests that local officials, including regents, village heads, and government employees, even handed over their own children to save their jobs and status.[42] This pattern of coercing families was also seen in occupied China, where local officials faced threats to their lives if they disobeyed.[43] There are examples in Indonesia where officials also took action to protect women. Women's activist Umi Sardjono, for example, reports that if time permitted, some local officials made attempts to hide their teenage daughters in villages or small towns.[44]

To understand the position of girls and young women during the occupation and what enabled such deception and coercion, we need to reflect on the cultural values prevalent at that time, as well as the economic conditions of the occupation. In the first Indonesian-language book on the topic, written in the context of advocacy for surviving women in the mid-1990s (see chapter 9), Budi Hartono and Dadang Juliantoro suggest that the Japanese seemed to rely on networks of trust among local people who solicited help from the neighbors, friends and acquaintances of girls and young women.[45] They argue that feudal and patriarchal values, whereby daughters had no rights to challenge their parents or village officials, contributed to the Japanese decision to use local officials and parents to recruit women into the system.[46] Lucia Juningsih similarly points to the salience of social and familial conventions, which meant girls and women had to devote themselves to men, including societal elders. This sense of obligation is confirmed in Suharti's testimony, in which she describes how she accepted without question her father's orders to pack her things and leave the village along with other girls. She was not brave enough to ask any questions. Reflecting local values of patronage, in turn, her father seems to have not questioned the order passed on to him from a village official. Suharti believes that the local officials knew why the girls were being gathered and that they simply chose to sacrifice poorer people in the villages.[47]

This suggests that historical views of girls and women as objects to be traded persisted throughout the occupation. Girls and young women agreed to go because they feared the Japanese, had few alternative sources of information, and trusted the village officials who recruited them. Officials sometimes promised them attractive wages or schooling.[48]

As mentioned in relation to cases of local village heads involved in recruiting for the system, NEFIS archives also document examples of other locals recruiting from surrounding villages. For example, these records detail how a Javanese man and a Chinese man worked with senior members of the Japanese police to recruit girls and women in Magelang and Surakarta.[49] In Halmahera, eastern Indonesia, a Chinese woman acted as a madam, controlling a house in which women were held.[50] Indonesian men who served as *heiho* were also involved in the forced recruitment of women. Following the establishment of a brothel in Sintang, Borneo, fifteen *heiho* went out to find women on the orders of an official from the Minseibu, Department of Navy Civil Administration.[51] While records of these kinds of transactional relationships are numerous and significant, the archival records do not provide sufficient detail to ascertain how much coercion was involved in each of these cases, or the extent to which people were following orders or seeking personal gain.

Japanese people, both military and civilian, also played a part in sourcing women. NEFIS records include reports of a Japanese officer who, along with other soldiers, in 1943 went into villages around Cimahi to recruit women.[52] Several Japanese women also acted as recruiters.[53] One Japanese woman reportedly visited villages around Malang and selected young girls and married women whose husbands were absent.[54] Although no information is provided on the background of these Japanese women, it is possible that they were former *karayukisan* given that this was the background of most Japanese women in the colony before the occupation (see chapter 1).

Japanese civilian administrators were closely involved in establishing and managing *ianjo*.[55] In Pontianak, Borneo, for example, the garrison (*keibitai*) issued an order to the Minsiebu to set up brothels, which was then passed on to the Hōkōkai, an association of Japanese businessmen supporting the military effort.[56] The Hōkōkai operated around five *ianjo* in the city. A Japanese tailor declared unfit for war service was sent to Pontianak to manage a hotel previously run by the Hōkōkai.[57] The women were recruited by the Tokkeitai, Special Police Unit of the navy.[58]

There are also reports of Dutch women acting as recruiters and managers of *ianjo*.[59] Some Dutch women chose to recruit other women, perhaps in return for greater freedom.[60] Some Dutch civilian men were also complicit in recruiting Dutch and Indonesian women.[61] In one case, a former Dutch official in Padang ordered Minangkabau women to be handed over to the Japanese to spare "European" women.[62]

False Promises and Forced Transport

To entice girls and women to move far away from home to remote *ianjo*, the Japanese spread news of "opportunities" for study or work in Japan or Singapore. The news was passed along by word of mouth from the *kenpeitai* (military policy force) through all levels of community leadership down to village heads.[63] Sometimes women were promised training as midwives or nurses.[64] Usually women from the most populous island of Java who took up such "opportunities" were shipped to other islands or abroad. A village head in East Java promised Suharti, then aged fourteen, schooling outside Java, leading to an office, hospital, or restaurant job.[65] Instead, she was sent by truck to Surabaya and then by boat to Borneo, where she was forced to work in an *ianjo* in Balikpapan. Kevin Blackburn has also documented cases of Indonesian women being shipped to Singapore.[66]

Archive sources document many cases of girls and women being transported around the colony by ship. A former sergeant in the Dutch colonial army reported that many Javanese girls and women aged between twelve and eighteen were shipped to Ambon Island early in the occupation based on promises of a university education in Tokyo. They were instead held in "houses of ill fame," which were visited constantly by Japanese soldiers.[67] A ship hand testified to the NEFIS to having witnessed forty young Javanese women being shipped aboard the *Celebes Maru* from the port of Surabaya, East Java, to Halmahera, one of the Maluku islands, on January 24, 1944.[68] The women were promised jobs, but during the course of the voyage they gradually realized, much to their distress, that they would be forced to work in *ianjo*. Two of the women died during the journey. Another report records that 400 Javanese women were transported from Surabaya to Halmahera in November 1943.[69] An Ambonese nurse who was forced to care for women in brothels in Makassar reported that Javanese women from Magelang who were promised training and jobs as teachers were detained there.[70] Dutch archival records include accounts of women being sent from Manado in North Sulawesi to Makassar in South Sulawesi on the pretext of being provided with training as doctors and instead being forced into prostitution.[71]

Young women were enticed by Japanese promises of a new era for Indonesian girls and women. Given the limited opportunities they had had in the Dutch era when education was only provided for girls from the local elite, girls and women were attracted by the prospect of jobs or training under the Japanese. Though limited, the Japanese did provide training opportunities for male and female teachers to learn Japanese language and customs.[72] A program called the Special Overseas Students from Southern Regions saw a select number of young Indonesian men sent to Japan for training.[73] In this context, it would have been difficult to decipher which opportunities presented to young women by local or Japanese officials were genuine.

The prospect of taking up jobs far from home, such as on another island or as far away as Singapore or Japan, appealed to some young women, due to the confines of family control. Mardiyem recalled her strong desire to escape the strictures of her life in a family of Javanese court servants. From the age of ten, she notes that she was largely confined to her house inside the court compound.[74] At this time, Javanese girls and young women could not go out on their own, and they could not socialize without the permission of or accompaniment by their husbands, older brothers, or male relatives.[75] From his research, Pramoedya observed that girls and young women's "smothered familial circumstances" (*keadaan hidup yang mencekik*) made promises of a job or education far away from home appealing.[76] In a similar way, C. Sarah Soh has documented how Korean women, sensing a new age of colonial modernity with the arrival of the Japanese, were also attracted by false promises of jobs and education.[77]

There were several reasons girls and women were moved around within the Japanese wartime empire and frequently placed in *ianjo* far from their homes. First, in the system, women and girls needed to be located close to concentrations of soldiers. In Indonesia this meant large numbers were sent to the Eastern islands (see chapter 2). Second, the process of relocating to remote locations far away from home reduced the possibility of escape. The women would have been far less familiar with their surroundings; they would not be known by the locals in the area, and subsequently few would take the risk of helping them.[78] Third, it disguised from families exactly what had happened to the daughters, mothers, and sisters, thereby potentially limiting local resistance.

Abductions of Women

The abduction of women to work in *ianjo* across rural and urban areas was common in occupied China from as early as 1938 and continued throughout the war.[79] As described in Ema's case, in Indonesia, too, girls and women were abducted by Japanese soldiers. In Japanese researcher Kawada Fumiko's interviews with survivors carried out in Bandung, West Java, in the 1990s, several testify to this experience. Emi reported that when she was thirteen years old, a Japanese soldier abducted her from in front of her house where she was practicing *taisō*, a form of Japanese calisthenics, and took her to an *ianjo*.[80] Suhanah similarly reported that as a teenager she was abducted by six soldiers who threatened her with a bayonet.[81] Fourteen-year-old Omoh told how she was first summoned to report to the Japanese army headquarters before being forcibly placed in an *ianjo*.[82] These three women were held together with Ema, mentioned at the beginning of the chapter, in an *ianjo* on Simpang Street in Cimahi. The heavy presence of military in this area may explain the relatively large number of abductions of women to work in the system.[83]

Dutch researcher Hilde Janssen recorded similar cases of women and girls being abducted by Japanese soldiers, particularly in areas near military barracks, such as Ambarawa in Central Java. Three sisters from one family in Central Java were taken from their home after being noticed by Japanese soldiers. They were taken to Tawangmangu, a recreation spot in the mountains, and kept in a hotel for three months.[84] Each girl was visited by around five men every night.

Indonesian activist Eka Hindra documented the experiences of Sri Sukanti, who was abducted when she was only nine years old. Sukanti was the second youngest of twelve children in a family of limited means living in Gundi village, Central Java. In mid-1945, the commander of local troops came to her house in uniform armed with a samurai sword, accompanied by the village head. Sukanti was abducted in front of her parents with threats that the other children would be beaten if they resisted. She was detained for four days, during which she was repeatedly raped by the officer. She recalled that "at that time I felt like I wanted to die. Like I was no longer human."[85] Sukanti was returned to her family.

Resistance and Reprisals

In addition to the many cases where girls and women tried to resist abuse, some communities or small groups of people were able to help women escape capture. In Kabiarat in the Moluccas, eastern Indonesia, local pastors and nuns hid young girls when the Japanese invaded.[86] After village heads handed over two unmarried girls, parents in Kabiarat and nearby Tanimbar decided to marry off daughters in the hope this would shield them. To avoid these threats, in Java some women returned to the traditional practice of seclusion in the home (an elite traditional Javanese custom for girls between the onset of menstruation and marriage, called *pingitan*). Husbands also tried to prevent any contact between their wives and Japanese soldiers.[87]

In several cases, local resistance to taking women and girls took on more organized forms. Sumatran woman Rahmah El Yunussiyah formed the Organization of Local Women Members (Organisasi Anggota Daerah Ibu) to oppose the use of Indonesian women as entertainers for the Japanese army. These women leaders also demanded that the Japanese shut down *ianjo* because they contravened Indonesian cultural and religious norms. In response, the Japanese replaced the local women working at these venues with women from Singapore and Korea.[88] In Makassar, South Sulawesi, following refusals from local women to be prostituted into the system, fifty Japanese women were imported instead.[89] In September 1943, a successful opposition in Surabaya involved a protest by village heads against Japanese soldiers involved in a racket of repeatedly abducting married women from their homes and sending them back the next day. On this occasion, the Japanese army forbade Japanese troops from going into "native" areas after 10 p.m.[90] Locals closed the gates leading into housing complexes to protect their communities.

Other recorded cases where efforts were made to prevent women being taken by the Japanese ended in violent reprisals. Fathers or husbands who resisted were beaten or, worse, killed on the spot with a bayonet.[91] Early in the occupation, in Blora two Javanese men were killed when they drew weapons in an effort to protest the rapes of women by Japanese.[92] NEFIS reports include the rumor that villagers in Limboeng near Makassar in Sulawesi armed themselves against soldiers trying to take local women, killing a number of Japanese.[93] The killers were brought to Makassar and their fate remained unknown. In another case in Korido village in Papua, it was reported that a man who defended the Dutch was beheaded after being forced to dig his own grave.[94] His wife was subsequently forced to live with a pro-Japanese Papuan man. She was then moved to a converted hospital, with other widows, which functioned as an *ianjo*.[95]

Internment Camps and Dutch Women

As noted in chapter 2, Dutch people were treated as enemies by the Japanese, and most were interned as POWs or in internment camps. For this reason, the patterns of procurement of Dutch and some Eurasian women (who were treated as Dutch women), differed. In 1993, a Dutch government report into forced prostitution of Dutch women during the Japanese occupation estimated that between two and three hundred Dutch women were forced into *ianjo*.[96] Dutch and Eurasian women were sometimes recruited through advertisements for other jobs such as bar workers, which was seen as a chance to escape internment. A 1943 advertisement in the newspaper *Perwata Perniagaan* called for "polite" Dutch and "Indo" women aged seventeen to twenty-five to work in the navy house to welcome and talk with guests from 2 p.m. to 10: 30 p.m. each day.[97] In Bandung as the Japanese grouped women together in preparation for internment, they also approached some with an offer—a choice of prostitution with potentially better access to food or internment.[98]

The increasingly dire conditions in the internment camps influenced women's decisions. Living conditions grew progressively worse with less food, clothing, and medicine and declining sanitation.[99] Conditions were so dire that International Military Tribunal for the Far East records suggest that 13 percent of internees across all camps perished.[100] In a women's camp in Palembang, former internee Helen Colijn estimated a death rate of 37 percent, with women and children suffering from malaria, dysentery, and beriberi, a life-threatening disease caused by malnourishment.[101] Under such difficult conditions, the Japanese tried to lure women detained in internment camps into prostitution, sometimes with promises of other jobs.[102]

Dutch women were also forcibly taken into the *ianjo* when their husbands were interned.[103] They were usually coerced by Dutch collaborators or Japanese soldiers or civilians. In Jember, East Java, six to eight wives of planters were forced to work as "bar girls," which often entailed pressure to engage in sexual relations with Japanese clientele.[104]

Eurasian women for the most part were not interned, but as the occupation progressed they faced increasingly difficult economic circumstances and were forced to look for any kind of work. Some of these women took up jobs in bars or hotels. In these contexts, it was not always Japanese men recruiting women to do this work. A Eurasian woman in Salatiga encouraged her daughters to take up bar work to improve their collective circumstances. She tried to convince other woman to give up their daughters.[105] In the archival records, the ages of Eurasian women engaged in this type of work at this time ranged from fifteen to fifty years.

Due to the postwar trials focusing on cases involving Dutch women procured from internment camps into the system and the high-profile of Dutch survivor-activist Jan Ruff O'Herne, these experiences have been relatively well documented. For this reason, my discussion of these cases will be brief. There are documented cases of such procurement in Sumatra and Java. In Padang, Sumatra, between June 1942 and December 1943, Japanese officers running an internment camp repeatedly tried to persuade women aged eighteen to twenty-five years to work in the canteens and tea houses.[106] Strict conditions for recruitment were negotiated with a Dutch friar, including the condition that if a woman volunteered, her parents, brothers, and sisters would be freed from internment. In October 1942, two women consented and were taken to Bukittinggi (Fort de Kock) to work in the Unity Club (De Eendracht Club).[107]

This suggests intense familial pressure on Dutch women. Attempts were also made to abduct other women to work in this club, but the military police intervened to stop this process.[108] There is also evidence of some uncertainty among the Japanese about these processes, with cases reported of Japanese occasionally returning women to camps, as if in doubt as to their actions.[109]

In the latter part of the occupation, from late 1943 until mid-1944, internment camps were handed over from civilian to military control. During this time the "recruitment" of Dutch women into the system increased, although with an ongoing level of caution. Before establishing an *ianjo* involving Dutch women, teaching staff at an army cadet school in Semarang first sought permission from the army's Chief of Staff who instructed that to avoid legal problems they must obtain proof the women were volunteers. All women were forcibly required to sign contracts in the Japanese language stating they were volunteering.[110] William Horton has suggested such contracts were required across all army-controlled areas for all women,[111] but there are no preserved examples of such signed contracts and they have not been mentioned in Indonesian women's testimonies. The fact they were used for Dutch women could suggest greater caution was taken in these cases. Attempts were made to take women from internment camps in Bandung, Magelang, and Semarang.[112]

In March 1943, Ellen van der Ploeg was interned at Halmaheira camp in Semarang, together with her mother, younger sister, and brother.[113] In early 1944, all the girls and young women aged fifteen to twenty-five were summoned for an inspection during which the Japanese looked them over "from top to toe." Fifteen girls and young women, including Ellen, were taken away, ostensibly to "work" at a cigarette factory in Semarang. They were subsequently forced into *ianjo*. Highlighting the secrecy around the system, the women were explicitly told not to talk about their experiences.[114]

In February 1944, Jan Ruff-O'Herne was taken from Ambarawa camp. The Japanese military camp commanders compiled a list of women in the camp aged seventeen to twenty-eight and made their selection from a lineup.[115] Sixteen women were forced to quickly pack and transported to a Dutch colonial-style house in Semarang called "The House of Seven Seas." Some Dutch women were forced to live in the Semarang Club to receive men from the nearby South Army Cadet School.[116] O'Herne recalls that she refused to sign a document giving her consent. In April 1944, following an inspection by a senior officer in POW management, the facilities in Semarang were quickly closed down. The women were sent on to Bogor women's camp. This case became famous because it was the subject of a postwar trial (see chapter 4). The immediate closure of the facilities in Semarang reveals caution within the Japanese military about the forced detention of Dutch women.

Life Inside *Ianjo*

There was not one typical *ianjo*. These facilities were established using converted sites, including residential quarters, houses, hospitals, or boarding houses. The most common *ianjo* mentioned in archival sources are boarding houses, hotels, bars, restaurants, and clubs where women were forced to provide sex. In general, such venues allocated one room per woman or partitioned rooms. The variety of places used as *ianjo* closely replicates the range of prostitution sites used in Japan, including geisha boarding houses, geisha restaurants, hostess serving restaurants, and cafés.[117] Archival sources also refer to "military brothels" or "Japanese comfort houses" more specifically.

These sites, particularly hotels and boarding houses, were often surrounded by high walls or fences with barbed wire and guards or a guard post near a gate to prevent escape. References to the segregation of women from the rest of the community are found in sources related to camps in Java (including Malang, Magelang, Solo, Surabaya, and Semarang), Kalimantan (Bandjarmasin, Balikpapan, Pontianak), Sulawesi, Flores, and Maluku (Halmahera).[118] One example references a military hospital in Purworejo that was closed and used as a brothel. This hospital was "surrounded with barbed wire and the entrance gate was guarded by a Japanese policeman."[119] At the *ianjo* where Mardiyem was held in Borneo, a three-meter-high wooden fence surrounded the building.[120] Usually two or three policemen (*kenpeitai*) patrolled the fence to make sure no women tried to escape. Mardiyem said it was like "living in a jail." Women were occasionally permitted to go outside but were always accompanied by guards.[121] In the *ianjo*, women's movements and actions were carefully watched to ensure that they were not breaking any rules. Sometimes severe punishments were imposed. Other types of control and monitoring included regular invasive medical checks during which women were sometimes sexually abused.

Many *ianjo* used a ticket system that required the women to "sell" a certain number of tickets per week and would result in punishment if they did not meet requirements. The set number of tickets to be sold and the price of tickets ranged widely from *ianjo* to *ianjo* and from woman to woman. The women had little capacity to control the number and timing of "visits" they had to receive, and little to no control over their bodies and reproduction. The women stationed at Telawang Boarding House in Borneo where Mardiyem was held were forced to receive around ten to fifteen men a day. They could only refuse to receive soldiers when they were menstruating. In her *ianjo*, which was a long house on stilts in Balikpapan, Suharti recalls, "we had to be ready, every day, ten hours a day for the Japanese soldiers."[122] Some women were reserved exclusively for one Japanese soldier; presumably this involved more senior officers whose status enabled them to make such a demand. The majority of women were expected to receive a range of men in the hours determined by the manager of each facility.

The tickets distributed to the women in *ianjo* in exchange for their services were supposed to correspond to earnings or some form of payment. Mardiyem reports that the women never received money directly from clients. Instead they were given the tickets and told that when they had finished their work, they could cash them in for money to buy tickets home. Mardiyem stored the tickets in a basket under her bed, but she was never able to convert them. When the war ended, the boarding house was bombed and the women and the Japanese quickly dispersed.[123] Likewise, Tuminah reported that she was not paid regularly for her services and was forbidden from asking the Japanese soldiers directly for money.[124]

In addition to sexual violence and forced detention, Indonesian researchers have documented various other forms of physical and psychological violence toward girls and women held in *ianjo*. This includes experiences of being beaten, slapped, and kicked.[125] Dutch intelligence reports also recorded cases of physical abuse in *ianjo*. One Dutch woman taken from Halmaheira camp and held at Hinomaru brothel testified to Dutch authorities that those detained were beaten and threatened with rifles and guns.[126] There are repeated accounts from Dutch and Indonesian women of rough treatment also by doctors who were assigned to oversee the women's sexual health. Some women reported that the doctors also raped them. Pregnant women were sometimes subjected to forced curettes or iodine injections to induce miscarriages.[127]

One means by which women could navigate the abusive conditions of their detention was to source regular visitors who could then book them for longer hours. In general, such men treated them better, occasionally giving them money or treats and more rest time between acts of forced sexual intercourse. Even though the women were given rations, often the food was not sufficient.[128] Because she had regular visitors, Mardiyem reports that she was slightly better off. Other women had no money to buy more food. Mardiyem's accounts mirror a pattern uncovered by Ahn Yonson in her research on Korean survivors of select soldiers becoming "patrons" to women and providing them with minor forms of respite from abuse.[129]

In Dutch archival records, it is noticeable that despite condemnation of physical violence as abuse, the men who visited the *ianjo* are rarely attributed blame for sexual abuse. One report on the famous Semarang case states: "the officers who visited this club cannot be said to have committed crimes, but it was very regrettable from the viewpoint of morality."[130] The postwar court-martials (see chapter 4) attributed legal responsibility to those who set up such facilities and those who forcibly recruited women. By contrast, Dutch intelligence reports compiled at the end of the war continued to focus on documenting Dutch women's "immoral" behavior or potential collaboration with the Japanese. They distinguished between those who were deemed to be women of "ill repute" or "decent women."[131] This framing alerts us to the highly subjective and partial nature of archives and provides early evidence that sympathy for women was mediated by judgments about their moral standing.

Japanese, Korean, and Taiwanese Women in the Netherlands East Indies

Dutch archival records also mention the presence of women of other nationalities in the *ianjo*, especially Japanese, Korean, and Taiwanese women with Japanese women reserved for the highest rank of soldier.[132] A driver for Japanese officers, sergeant majors, and sergeants testified that the Grand Hotel in Bakmi Street in Surabaya functioned as a brothel for these senior-ranked military men and was staffed entirely by Japanese women. The same informant noted that another larger brothel enclosed by bamboo fences of at least three meters high was set up to service all ranks of the army and was, by contrast, staffed by women of "every Indonesian race."[133] A trader in Belawan similarly reported that Japanese women were imported to serve Japanese officers in Medan, East Sumatra, while other ranks of soldiers had access to Javanese women kept in other "brothels."[134] Fifty Japanese women were housed near a hospital in Tarakan, northeast Borneo, for serving Japanese officers. Again, a nearby facility housing around one hundred Javanese women served lower-ranking soldiers.[135] This practice reflects the status awarded to Japanese women in the ideology of the Fujinkai, as discussed in chapter 2.

Because Korean women were considered Japanese imperial subjects, it is also possible that some of those who were identified in the wartime reports as Japanese were actually Korean. The story of Chung Seo Woon, who was transported from Korea via Japan to Semarang, is well known because of her role as a prominent Korean survivor activist.[136] After being promised a job in a Japanese factory, she was taken to Japan and then put on a ship with other women. As they made their way across the region, women were dropped off at ports in Taiwan, Bangkok, Singapore, and finally, Jakarta. Chung then traveled on to Semarang with twenty-two other Korean women. By the end of the war, only nine survived. Chung reported that this was because the soldiers simply killed those who fell ill.[137] Unfortunately her testimony provides few specific details of the *ianjo* in Semarang where she was held, nor reflections on the local women who may have been detained with her.

There is also a documented case of a group of Taiwanese women being sent to the colony early in the war. In the first few months of the occupation in 1942, following a request from the Southern Region General Army Commander, fifty Taiwanese women and three brothel owners were sent to Kalimantan. A further twenty Taiwanese women were subsequently called for and supplied.[138] As discussed in chapter 2, evidence of the importation of both sex workers and brothel owners from Taiwan points to the links between this military system and civilian prostitution networks across Japan and its colonies.

The Dutch archival sources also include testimony from a Chinese Singaporean woman who detailed her experience of being shipped along with twenty-two other Chinese Singaporean women, to Halmahera Island in July 1942, after being promised restaurant work. Once the women realized they had been deceived, a Japanese officer helped release them, but the ship on which they traveled on return to Singapore was bombed, killing seven of the women.[139]

In the system, attempts were also made to present local women in a way that suited the tastes and fantasies of Japanese men. Consistent with the practice in colonized Korea and Taiwan of assimilating locals into Japanese culture, no matter their national background, women in the system were often given Japanese names. Indonesian and Dutch women mention being assigned Japanese names in the brothels, often names that related to flowers.

In Mardiyem's boarding house in Telawang, every woman was given a Japanese name, which was then displayed on an announcement board in the waiting room for men to choose from. Mardiyem was given the name Momoye, meaning peach tree branch.[140] She recalls that it was also the name of a famous Japanese actress before the war. A Javanese woman, Suharti, also held alongside Mardiyem, was given the name Masako.[141] A Javanese woman, Kasinem, who was held in Solo, was given the name Kanaku.[142] The Dutch woman, Jan Ruff O'Herne, was also given the name of a Japanese flower. She chose not to disclose it in her memoir or testimonies, perhaps because of its painful associations.[143]

This naming practice was presumably adopted so that soldiers could easily pronounce the women's names and be reminded of women at home. It also implied that these women in forced detention were now Japanese property. Anna Mariana characterizes this custom as fascist, in the sense that it replicated the idea that other races were lower than the Japanese race and therefore must be assimilated.[144] In some facilities, Indonesian women were also required to wear Japanese dress. The three sisters from Central Java mentioned above were required to dress in kimono in the hotels in Tawangmangu where they were held.[145] These practices all point to mimicry of practices across the Japanese civilian prostitution system.

Other Forms of Sexual Abuse

During the occupation, outside of the abuse of women and girls in *ianjo*, other forms of sexual violence were perpetrated against Indonesian and Dutch women. As noted in chapter 2, one of the rationales for the system was that it would prevent indiscriminate rape of women. Outside the *ianjo* rapes did take place, especially in the early stages of the invasion. A 1993 Dutch inquiry into sexual violence against Dutch women documented rapes by Japanese soldiers in Tjepoc, Tarakan, Manado, Bandung, Padang, and Flores.[146] The NEFIS records document cases of rape of European and elite Javanese (*priyayi*) women in Blora, Central Java, by soldiers from the forty-eighth division of the army between March 1 and April 4 in 1942.[147] It could be the case that these women were targeted because they were identified with the Dutch regime.

Apart from these seemingly targeted rapes, women were sexually abused in their workplaces or taken from their homes at night. Testimonies provided to the Netherlands Intelligence Service reveal that women were routinely abused and held for shorter periods of time, as opposed to the typically longer stays of women held in *ianjo*. The widespread cases of sexual violence reported in these archives indicate that one of the justifications for the system—that it would reduce sexual violence against other women—was false. As Qiu similarly observed in the case of occupied China, the system of comfort stations "did not prevent, but rather fostered sexual violence during the war."[148]

In Sorpong, western New Guinea, a farmer testified that local women were often caught and kept for a night, fueling resentment from the local population.[149] In Surabaya, East Java, witnesses reported that Japanese soldiers frequently attacked women on the streets at night.[150] In Kaloran Central Java and Kertosono in East Java, Japanese men took women against their will to their barracks and returned them to their homes the next day.[151] In her research on Indonesia's *ianfu*, Japanese researcher Kawada Fumiko documented the relatively common practice of soldiers spotting women on the street, following them home, and then abducting them. The women were abused once or held for a period of time for repeated abuse.[152] Sexual violence against women therefore extended well beyond the ongoing detention of women in *ianjo*.

Women were also vulnerable in their places of work. Nur worked at the Hotel Kopeng in Central Java. She recalls being extremely frightened when the Japanese took over the hotel. She was raped twice by the soldiers and was too afraid of being killed to resist.[153] Girls and women were constantly at risk of such violence and they felt little capacity to resist given that they could be killed if they did so. As Mardiyah put it, "where could we flee to at night? If I ran away I would have been shot, so whether I wanted to or not I had to serve him."[154]

Hilde Janssen has recorded similar accounts from women in Central Java. Paini from a village near Mt. Merbabu was thirteen years old when she was collected from her home by Japanese soldiers with her older sister to work in the barracks near her village. By day they had to cook for forced laborers, dig trenches, and source food from local villagers. Although they could return home at night, they were frequently picked up by soldiers and taken back to the barracks to be abused.[155] When she was sixteen years old, Siyem was taken from her village twenty-five kilometers from Solo and forced to work on the railroad.[156] At night, every evening for two months, soldiers repeatedly raped her in a train carriage that operated as an informal *ianjo*.

Dutch women in internment camps were also subjected to sexual violence. The number of Japanese staff running women's camps was generally small. Instead there was strong reliance initially on Indonesian police or *heiho* to guard and run the camps, and later on Korean and Taiwanese civilian auxiliaries (*gunzoku*).[157] Some women were subjected to sexual violence from camp guards. A former *heiho* member confessed to Japanese pastor Kimura Kōichi that during the war, Japanese men—himself included—forcibly took women from the camps and raped them.[158] The rapes of two women in an internment camp in Endeh (Flores) in May and June 1942 are reported in Dutch archives.[159]

There are documented cases of sexual violence against boys in camps as well. In Adek Camp in Batavia, young boys were forced to perform dances and kiss each other for a Japanese guard.[160] In Bangkong Camp in Semarang, a Japanese official forced boys into "lewd actions in the bathroom."[161] At an internment camp in West Sumatra, a Japanese *heiho* commander groomed boys and girls.[162] As will be explained in chapter 9, cases of sexual violence against boys were documented as part of the compensation scheme run by the Project Implementation Committee of the Netherlands (PICN) in the 1990s.

During the occupation, one practice that seemed to directly draw on local traditions involved Japanese civilian and military men forcibly taking local women to live with them and provide free manual labor and sexual services.[163] As detailed in chapter 1, this replicates the historical practice of Indonesian, Chinese, and Dutch men taking *nyai*.[164] In the Banda islands, Japanese soldiers took local women, ethnic Boetonese (Filipino), Javanese, and Dutch women, as "wives." Of the nine reported cases in the NEFIS archive, three women were the wives of laborers, and the Dutch woman was the wife of a POW.[165] There are also records of this practice occurring in Manado, North Sulawesi. Such women were referred to by the Japanese as *siang baboe, malam nyonya*, daytime maids, nighttime wives.[166] In the 1990s an Indonesian journalist uncovered more examples of these kinds of relationships during the occupation (see chapter 6).

The NEFIS archive includes details of Dutch or Eurasian women who were either forced or coerced into live-in relationships with Japanese military and civilian men. In 1942 the military police began to detain young Dutch and Eurasian girls from villages near Bondowoso and Banyuwangi. Some were placed in brothels, others were forced to become wives.[167] A Dutch woman working for the Japanese air force testified that from November 1944, she was forced to live with a Japanese police officer, resulting in her having a child.[168] In Makassar, a Eurasian woman was forced to live with a Japanese company man after her father was badly beaten when she first refused to do so.[169] She was repeatedly raped by this man and horribly treated. These accounts highlight the extreme coercion surrounding forced "marriages."

Archive records occasionally suggest that women "chose" to enter into these relationships or provide sexual services. Among the noninterned women who became the "wives" of Japanese soldiers were women whose Dutch husbands had already been detained.[170] Some Dutch women chose to live with a Japanese man to escape internment.[171] Others were given the choice of working in a hotel or brothel or living with one Japanese man.[172] Some women eventually moved out of club or bar work into such relationships, most likely in search of better conditions.[173] The fact that many of these accounts were collected for intelligence purposes means that firsthand accounts read like confessions by women who engaged in these relationships. Secondhand accounts consist of others informing on women with possible consequences for the suspected women in terms of constraints on their migration choices for resettlement in a new country given the ensuing independence war and exodus of Dutch people from the former colony.

Conclusion

Girls and women were coerced into the "comfort women" system by a range of measures characterized by force and deception and the broader context of coercion produced by the military occupation. The conditions of economic deprivation, Japanese propaganda, the threat of Japanese violence, and the local patriarchal order all contributed to the process of "recruiting" women. Once in the *ianjo*, girls and women were guarded, unable to leave freely, and forced to provide sex for most of the day and night. Some suffered physical abuse and violence. In addition to Dutch and Indonesian women there were Korean, Japanese, and Taiwanese women in some *ianjo*. The Japanese running the *ianjo* made efforts to culturally assimilate women by giving them Japanese names, usually the names of flowers, and sometimes requiring them to wear Japanese clothes. Beyond the *ianjo*, there was sustained sexual violence against girls and women more broadly. In the next chapter, I consider the immediate postwar period and what happened to women in the system.

4

Life after the War, Treaties, and the Occupation in Indonesian and Dutch Memory

Niyem was ten years old when she was taken from her home in Karangmojo, Yogyakarta, to a nearby military camp, where over the course of two months she was repeatedly raped. Years later, she recalled that after escaping and returning home, "I didn't dare tell anyone that I had been raped, I didn't want to hurt my parents. I was afraid that no one would want me, that I would be left out. But people still abused me calling me a 'Japanese hand-me-down.' Because I had been gone so long, they suspected what had happened to me. It hurt me tremendously."[1] Niyem's situation was similar to that faced by many girls and women at the end of the war. In the context of a volatile and evolving situation, they had to consider whether they could return home and whether upon return they would be accepted by their communities.

On August 15, 1945, after the US atomic and fire bombings of Hiroshima and Nagasaki, fire bombings of other major cities, and combat on Okinawa, Japan surrendered to the Allied forces. Two days later, Indonesian Republicans seized the opportunity to declare independence. As Allied forces arrived in the archipelago to oversee the surrender of the Japanese, the Dutch attempted to retake the colony, and Indonesians took up arms in resistance. This period of transition from the Japanese occupation to the Indonesian revolution (1945–49) was marked by violence, chaos, and uncertainty.

In this period, the experiences of survivors of the "comfort women" system differed depending on where they were held and how far they were from home. After the Japanese surrender, each woman was left to negotiate her own circumstances. Many Dutch survivors were held in temporary camps for processing. Indonesian and Dutch women had to deal with societal stigmatization and the sense of shame attached to their experiences.

As the Dutch forces fought to reclaim Republican-held territories, they launched a system of court-martials to punish Japanese leaders and their Indonesian collaborators for "conventional war crimes," which included "acts of brutality against and neglect of prisoners of war (POWs) and civilians in occupied areas."[2] Some cases of sexual violence against Dutch and Indonesian women were considered.

Less than a decade later, relations between the government of Japan and the new Republic of Indonesia were restored via a treaty signed in 1958. The treaty placed strong emphasis on financial reparations for Indonesia, ensuring ongoing Japanese economic influence in the country. The legacy of collaboration with the Japanese and the economic ties in its aftermath fostered ambiguity in Indonesian memory of the occupation. The period is remembered as a time of suffering, which Indonesians endured together, as well as sparking a necessary awakening that prepared Indonesians to seize independence. In contrast, for Dutch people who left Indonesia for the Netherlands after the war, the Japanese occupation is portrayed as a time of horror. In this chapter, I analyze examples of remembrance of this period, to examine how the "comfort women" figure in cultural memory of the occupation. This is set against the backdrop of Japanese–Indonesian and Japanese–Dutch relations from the 1950s to 1990s.

Indonesian Women's Experiences in the Immediate Postwar Period

After Japan's surrender, British and Australian Allied forces were appointed to take control of the colony in preparation for the Dutch to return. As they moved across the archipelago, the Allied forces frequently encountered women whom the Japanese had transported to remote and isolated locations, and they handed them over to the Netherlands Indies Civil Administration. On September 17, 1945, an Australian newspaper reported on the rescue of fifty-six Javanese women and girls abandoned on Timor island.[3] Traces of these women in archives are scarce primarily because they were not considered interesting or worthy historical subjects.[4] There are photographic and documentary traces in the Australian National War Memorial Archives of Javanese, Dutch, and Eurasian women abandoned in West Timor.[5] These women's experiences are, however, only briefly described in captions to the photos; for example, one reads, "Twenty-six Javanese girls who were liberated at Koepang [Kupang] from Japanese brothels."[6] Tracing the history of specific women is extremely difficult given the period of flux after the occupation, except for references made in the postwar testimonies of some women themselves.

Abandonment, Dislocation, and Stigmatization

The experiences of women in the period after the war can best be gleaned from testimonial sources and observations from people with whom they came into direct contact. Survivor testimonies reveal that Indonesian women held in *ianjo* situated close to their homes often struggled to fully reintegrate into local communities due to social prejudice. The three women whose cases were discussed in chapter 3—Emi, Suhanah, and Ema Kastimah—were taken from their homes in and around Cimahi to *ianjo* nearby. Each woman tried to return home after the war. Emi discovered her house had burned down and both her parents had died.[7] She subsequently lived with an uncle and never married. Locals taunted her for being the former "wife" of a Japanese man. She felt haunted by her experiences.[8] When Ema returned home, her parents were unwell because they had been so worried about her. Like Emi, her stigmatization as a former Japanese *nyai* meant she never married and lived alone.[9] Suhanah's father was killed by bayonet while trying to rescue her, and her mother died a year later. Suhanah was also stigmatized in her local community for being a former Japanese wife or *nyai* and did not marry.[10]

These brief descriptions of their postwar lives were provided by the women in the mid-1990s in interviews conducted by Japanese researcher Kawada Fumiko and assisted by Kimura Kōichi as translator (see chapter 5). The translator recorded the interview notes in Indonesian and referred to each woman in the third person. It is unclear whether these records contain direct quotes, but we know that locals used the term *nyai* to shame these women. As discussed in chapter 1, *nyai* implies that a woman is living with a man out of wedlock, and the term fails to capture the situation of women who were forced to have sexual relations with many men in the *ianjo*. Use of this term reflects an historical carryover from the late colonial era. It reinforces the perception that the acts of these women shamed all Indonesians.

In these three cases, where the women were held close to their homes, their experiences were widely known in the community. It was impossible for them to remain anonymous. This resulted in increased stigmatization. Iteng from the Sukabumi area, West Java, revealed in her interview with anthropologist Hilde Janssen that the Japanese took her and her sister on the pretext of work. As Iteng explained, when the war ended, they had little choice: "everybody in the village knew, we were too ashamed to go back."[11] These women experienced what Veena Das has referred to as a "social death," a societal refusal to accept women based on the view that those raped by enemy soldiers have been polluted.[12]

Very few testimonies exist from or about Indonesian women transported a great distance from their homes. These rare accounts illustrate the kinds of lives they led after the war. Mardiyem was held far from her home in Java, at Telawang Boarding house in Borneo. In her memoir she describes how the number of men attending the house began to dwindle until one day they disappeared altogether, and bombing commenced. The remaining women decided to flee and fend for themselves.[13] Rather than trying to return immediately to Java, with a fellow detainee, a Dayak woman whose nephew lived nearby in Belitung, Mardiyem initially sought shelter close to the *ianjo*, most likely due to a lack of funds.

After the war, Mardiyem stayed on in southern Borneo. Her friend's nephew, with whom she and her friend lived, joined the Indonesian Republican army fighting against the Dutch.[14] Mardiyem also joined the struggle, explaining that she was encouraged by those around her to marry Amat Mingun, an Indonesian man in the KNIL, so as to convert him to work as a spy.

For the duration of the independence war, she lived with her husband in the KNIL barracks, where she was mocked by the other wives. One soldier's wife warned others to beware in case Mardiyem tried to steal their husbands away.[15] In 1953 Amat Mingun took his pension, and they returned to Yogyakarta.[16] Initially Mardiyem lived with greater anonymity, as very few people knew about her experiences during the occupation. One day, during a visit to the central shopping district on Malioboro Street, someone recognized her and called out her Japanese name, Momoye. She was too embarrassed to return to the market for fear of shaming her family.[17]

In other cases, women were forced to make their own way home from their places of detention or find alternative shelter. In the late stages of the occupation, following an air raid on her *ianjo* in Balikpapan, Borneo, Suharti attempted to reach Banjarmasin with the intention of returning home to Java.[18] The women from her *ianjo* fled on foot. They walked for fifty-two days without changing clothes. Suharti explained that they did not stop to wait for those who fell behind. She recalled the names of four of the eight women who did not complete the journey: Kiku, Tumi, Tumini, and Tunn, all from Malang in East Java.[19] Along the way local Dayak people provided them with water and eventually transport. Upon reaching Banjamasin, rather than finding freedom, Suharti was forced to work as a "comfort woman" at Telawang Boarding House along with Mardiyem. When she was released three months later,

Suharti found a job in a nearby restaurant and was advised by her employer to marry and have a child. He matched her with a KNIL soldier, telling her this was so that upon her return to Java she could deflect any questions about her past. Living in the same army barracks as Mardiyem, she was subjected to similar taunting. She eventually returned to Java and had seven children.[20]

The fate of these women is largely undocumented, especially those who never made it home. In her memoir, Mardiyem recalled the story of fellow detainee Rosiyem. After the boarding house was bombed, Rosiyem told Mardiyem that she planned to leave Borneo with a Japanese soldier who loved her.[21] Mardiyem reported that her husband later discovered Rosiyem's mutilated corpse hanging from a tree in the jungle.[22]

While some of the women held at remote locations made their way home after the war, there were often significant barriers to doing so. Given that many women did not receive the payments promised by the managers of their *ianjo*, one impediment was simply lack of money for the return passage. A second was fear about social acceptance. In these circumstances, some women chose to stay on in the places where they were abandoned.

In his 2001 book, *Young Virgins in the Grasp of the Military*, Pramoedya Ananta Toer wrote about the experiences of some of these abandoned women.[23] He was imprisoned as part of the 1965 anticommunist genocide on the remote Buru Island. Pramoedya draws on recollections of discussions he and other detainees had with Javanese women left behind after the war on the island. Throughout the book he quotes a series of interviews conducted in 1978 in Java with families and witnesses to the system and interviews he conducted with survivors after his release from prison in 1979.[24]

Pramoedya weaves together the experiences of a handful of women from the point of their recruitment to their transportation and eventual abandonment in distant or remote locations, including Singapore, Thailand, and Indonesia's outer islands. One of his informants, Sukarno Martodihardjo, worked on a Japanese transport vessel during the war. He recalled encountering women of different backgrounds as they were shipped between Java, Bangkok, the Philippines, and Hong Kong.[25] In September 1947 on a trip to Bangkok, Martodihardjo met a woman, Sumiyati, who told him she had previously been taken by the Japanese from Java to Bangkok. She was wearing Thai-style clothes and had married a Thai man.[26] Sumiyati explained that after she was freed, she had nowhere to go. She and others all wanted to go home but were without money, protection, or local contacts. Martodihardjo observed that many women felt a heavy moral burden about their experiences and were ashamed to see their families again. As Sumiyati told Martodihardjo, she felt *ternoda* (stained).[27]

Pramoedya retells the story of Sri Sulastri, a resident on Buru in the 1960s, who shared her story with Sutikno W. S. Like Pramoedya, Sutikno was a political prisoner of the island. Sri recounted to Sutikno how in early 1945, the Japanese brought her and twenty-one other women who worked in a bar in Semarang to Buru. After the war she married a local Alfuru man.[28]

Why did many of the women held in the system quickly marry once they were released? Some may have been motivated to seek protection from further abuse. For others, marriage may have provided the financial means they were desperately lacking. In their testimonies, Mardiyem and Suharti convey a sense of gratitude that some men could accept their pasts. Suharti recalled her husband saying to her, "I dearly want to save you from your suffering. I promise that I will never hurt you because of your past. Please marry me." She initially rejected his proposal, but eventually gave in to his persistence and enjoyed a long, happy marriage.[29] Mardiyem also married a man who knew about and accepted her experiences. Given their view of themselves as tainted women, for both Mardiyem and Suharti marriage represented a form of refuge. In cases where women found loving spouses, they experienced care and understanding.[30] In other cases, experiences were less positive. One woman's husband blamed the fact that they could not have children on her past and eventually divorced her.[31]

The choice to remain in communities far from home did not always save these survivors from the public shaming they so feared. In Tebing Tinggi, North Sumatra, in late 1945, radical local youths stripped women who had been brought from Java during the occupation and paraded them through the streets.[32] This resembles scenes in postwar Europe, in which Dutch women who had consorted with German enemy soldiers had their heads shaven and were paraded in the streets as traitors. The women were frequently described using the derogatory term *moffenhoeren*, which connects "dislike of the enemy" (*mof* is a derogatory term for Germans) with prostitution (*hoer* means "whore").[33]

Indonesian survivors experienced ongoing physical and emotional effects as a result of their enforced prostitution. A survey of forty survivors in the Yogyakarta area carried out in the late 1990s found that seventeen experienced a physical disability, nine could not have children, and nineteen experienced physical disturbances, including high levels of fatigue and illness.[34] The researchers concluded that the women suffered deep psychological scars. All respondents felt that they were *rusak* (broken, damaged, or ruined) by the experience.[35] Thirty-five women identified as feeling *sakit hati*.[36] This culturally specific term combines the two words, *sakit* meaning ill or sick, and *hati*, which refers to the center of the body but also "the seat of emotions," similar to the idea of the heart in English.[37] The core features of the emotion *sakit hati* are described as "chronic resentment and anger closely related to being ill-treated or exposed to wrongdoing by others."[38] The women felt deeply injured by their experiences.

Some Indonesian survivors became pregnant by Japanese men and gave birth to their children. At the end of the war, those men who had not died in action returned to Japan, often cutting off all contact with the women and their children. This was an issue for which some Japanese later felt a degree of responsibility. At the end of the war, one Japanese officer, Shibata Yaichirō, called for the Japanese to seek out these women and pay them some form of support.[39]

Despite these shared challenges and the extraordinary resilience of survivors, there is no typical experience.[40] Some women never married, whereas others went on to have long and happy marriages. Some of those who married had no children due to injuries sustained through repeated rapes, but this was most likely an exceptional experience.[41]

Dutch Women's Experiences and the Onset of the Indonesian Revolution

Once released from the *ianjo* in the later stages of the war, due to protests about their treatment some Dutch women subjected to enforced prostitution were separated by the Japanese and placed in Paris camp in Batavia in May 1944, then in November 1944 moved to a special section of Kramat camp in Batavia.[42] This section of the camp was known to the Dutch by the term the "rabbit's hole," a derogatory reference to the frequent copulation of rabbits, or alternatively as "the department of women of ill repute."[43] After the occupation ended, the women were interrogated by the Netherlands Intelligence Forces to assess their potential knowledge of or collaboration with the Japanese. Jan Ruff O'Herne, who was held in Kramat from November 1944, believes the Japanese partitioned former "comfort women" into one section of the camp to conceal the women's experiences from others.[44]

Demonstrating a similar kind of stigmatization to that experienced by Indonesian women, inmates in the other section of the camp called them whores, traitors, or rabbits. After the Japanese surrender, O'Herne stayed on in the camp for another five months simply because there was nowhere else to go.[45]

As mentioned, the handover of control from the Japanese to the Allied forces was a time of extreme instability. The Indonesians were attempting to seize territory before the Dutch returned, which eventually led to the Indonesian Revolution. While formally denoted as beginning at the Battle of Surabaya on November 10, 1945, intense violence—known as *bersiap* (getting ready) in

Life after the War

Indonesian and *bersiaptijd* (a time of danger) in Dutch—had already broken out some months earlier. Frustrated by years of colonialism and emboldened by Japanese anti-Western sentiment, Indonesian youths attacked Eurasians, Dutch, Chinese Indonesians, and Moluccans.[46] O'Herne recalls attacks on the camps, which caused deaths and injuries among women and children.[47] The effects of *bersiap*, combined with the ensuing revolution and the forced departure of the Dutch, led to an enduring chasm between Indonesians and Dutch people who had formerly lived in the colony.[48] This divide may partly explain why Indonesian and Dutch survivors have rarely worked together to achieve redress from the Japanese.

During this period, many Dutch, including those who had been born in the Netherlands and those who had lived for generations in the colony, including Eurasians, known as the Indisch community, fled to the Netherlands.[49] O'Herne left for Holland in early 1946, in one of the first exoduses of Dutch from the former colony. She married a British solider she had met in Java, and they had two children. They lived in England for fourteen years before moving to Australia in 1960.[50]

Like O'Herne, Ellen van der Ploeg was forcibly recruited from a prison camp. She returned to Holland in 1947, and initially attempted to get fellow victims to speak out, but faced great resistance. Most women wanted to forget their horrific experiences, and those who had married were unwilling to jeopardize their newfound happiness.[51] van der Ploeg blamed both the Japanese and Dutch governments for their complicity in the silence.

The attitudes of Dutch families to the experiences of these women varied. O'Herne explains that she only ever talked with her mother about her experience once, but as she did not respond well, they never spoke about it again.[52] Marguerite Hamer de Froideville, who interviewed many Dutch survivors (see chapter 9), reports that some women who informed their loved ones were looked after very well by their families and (future) husbands.[53] Others were abandoned and rejected on the basis of the stigma attached to being "Japanese whores." Some mothers who knew what had happened to their daughters refused to listen or advised their daughters to "forget about it quickly" and "don't tell your father." In this context, many women chose to remain silent. Shame also played a significant role. The backlash in the Netherlands against *moffenmeiden*, a derogatory label meaning German maidens, also deterred survivors from speaking out about their experiences in the Indies.[54]

Like Indonesian women, some Dutch and Eurasian women became pregnant by Japanese men. Some had abortions, while others gave birth. Sometimes this led to further social prejudice and difficult childhoods for these children.[55] In some cases mothers concealed the identity of the children's fathers.[56]

The onset of the Indonesian Revolution meant that instability continued for another four years. Although research into the topic of sexual violence during the revolution is only just beginning, given the patterns in almost every armed conflict in history, it is likely that there was sustained sexual violence against women. Scholarship on the *bersiap* period generally makes only incidental mention of sexual violence committed by Indonesians, mostly against Eurasian and Dutch women.[57] Violence committed by the Dutch during the revolution has only recently begun to receive more critical attention.[58] This is largely due to a series of court cases starting in 2011, brought by the descendants of the victims of the Dutch massacres.[59] This has also led to revelations of cases of gang rapes of Indonesian women.[60]

There is even less documentation of women's experiences of sexual violence during the revolution than during the occupation. Susie Protschky has demonstrated that the Dutch military continued to take *nyai* in the revolutionary period and that this practice was also extended from the KNIL to the Dutch Royal Army especially in military barracks.[61] These findings raise new questions about the experiences of Indonesian survivors of the "comfort women" system, like Suharti and Mardiyem, who lived with husbands in KNIL barracks during the revolution.

It is still too early to draw conclusions about patterns of sexual violence in the 1945–49 period, but we can assume there were some continuities with patterns of violence against women during the occupation. A pressing question is whether there were similar continuums of violence in Indonesia to those observed by Yuki Tanaka in Japan. Tanaka described not only the Japanese military and civilian abuse of "comfort women" in the wartime system but also the abuse of Japanese women in postwar Japan by US and Australian occupying forces in the form of sexual assaults and providing sexual services.[62]

Postwar Prosecutions for Crimes of Sexual Violence

A key question that has animated activism until today is why there was so little justice for women abused in the system in the postwar prosecutions. At the end of the Pacific War, the terms of the surrender included an agreement for the United States, together with other Allied powers, to occupy Japan for a transition period. The allies established the International Military Tribunal for the Far East Charter (IMTFE), also known as the Tokyo Charter. Through this mechanism, Japanese leaders were tried individually for crimes against peace, as well as other war crimes committed in the context of an aggressive war.[63] The IMTFE Charter included rape and "the abduction of girls and women for enforced prostitution" as punishable crimes but did not list them as war crimes or crimes against humanity.[64] Nicola Henry notes that no rape victims were called as witnesses at the tribunal, and enforced prostitution was barely mentioned, despite considerable evidence on the practice being presented. This could be because the judges did not link rape and enforced prostitution to the process of waging an aggressive war, combined with the fact that the victor nations were primarily concerned with crimes committed against their people and not with crimes against Asian women.[65]

In addition to the IMTFE, Allied powers used their own national military tribunals to investigate lesser or "minor" war crimes.[66] The Dutch set up tribunals to prosecute crimes committed in the Netherlands East Indies. The investigating team gathered evidence of prewar espionage, maltreatment, torture, and unlawful killing of civilians, rōmusha, and POWs, as well as rape and forced prostitution of Dutch and Indonesian women. Across all national tribunals, the Dutch were the only country to prosecute the Japanese for the crime of forced prostitution. They were motivated by outrage at the abuse of Dutch women by Japanese men and the fact these women had been taken to ianjo from internment camps.[67]

Beginning in late 1947 and into 1948, the Netherlands established temporary court-martials in twelve locations in Indonesia: Ambon, Balikpapan, Banjarmasin, Batavia, Hollandia (Jayapura), Kupang, Makassar, Manado, Medan, Morotai, Pontianak and Tanjung Pinang. All were areas reoccupied by the Dutch.[68] In Java, prosecution was particularly difficult and often curtailed.[69] Overall 60 percent of the cases tried by the Dutch were for crimes against Indonesians. In those that dealt with cases of sexual violence, however, the victims were almost exclusively Dutch and Eurasian women. As Iris Heidebrink observes, for the Republicans, prosecuting the Japanese for war crimes was a low priority.[70]

The temporary court-martials in the Netherlands East Indies relied on internationally accepted definitions of war crimes, including the "rape and the abduction of girls and women for the purpose of enforced prostitution."[71] The Batavia court dealt with the now famous Semarang Affair, in which thirty-five interned Dutch and Eurasian women were taken from Ambarawa and other camps and subjected to enforced prostitution in the Semarang Club and other ianjo nearby.[72] In these trials Kramat camp became a focus for evidence gathering because of its location close to the court in Batavia and because Dutch women who had been held in Semarang brothels were relocated there.[73] This explains, in part, why this case made it to trial. Other cases brought before this court included those of Dutch women who had been taken from internment camps and placed in an *ianjo* in Batavia known as the Sakura Club, run by a Japanese civilian. Another involved a Dutch woman who was prosecuted for trafficking other Dutch women.[74]

Yuki Tanaka is critical of the almost exclusive focus in these court-martials on the prosecution of Japanese men for crimes against Dutch women, suggesting that crimes against Indonesian women were not taken seriously for racist reasons.[75] Race was undoubtedly one factor, however as explained already, it was also the case that the Dutch were more easily accessed and willing to testify as witnesses and victims. Naoko Yamada observed that the abuse of Indonesian women was sometimes addressed incidentally in trials focusing on other crimes, in some cases leading to prosecutions.[76] For example, a 1947 trial related to a large massacre in January 1944 in Pontianak uncovered cases of women who were forcibly recruited as "comfort women." Thirteen soldiers were subsequently prosecuted and found guilty. They were initially given death sentences, which were later commuted to ten years in prison.[77]

For reasons that remain unclear, a case involving the abuse of Indonesian women in Balikpapan was also investigated. A Japanese civilian brothel owner was tried for recruiting fifty-five women from Surabaya and forcing them into prostitution. He was found not guilty on the basis of there being no "forcible recruitment," despite two Indonesian women testifying to the contrary.[78] These examples indicate that while Indonesian women were not entirely ignored, neither were they accorded full procedural fairness in this legal process. As Yamada argues, in this case the court ranked a Japanese man's statement more highly than those of two Indonesian women. In these trials, not only race but also gender acted as a barrier to legal justice for Indonesian women. The failures of these court-martials to fully acknowledge the victims, and the relative neglect of Indonesian women in particular, is a point activists frequently return to.

Japan's Postwar Treaties and Relationships with Indonesia and the Netherlands

As they dealt with the fallout from the war through military tribunals, court-martials, and treaties, the Cold War began to increasingly influence relations between the Allied forces and Japan. While the initial postwar US impulse was to punish Japanese leaders for war crimes through the IMFTE process, in reality many sentences handed down to the war criminals by these courts were ultimately reduced and the perpetrators released.[79] Why was this the case? Why did the United States and Allied forces shift from a stance of wanting harsh prosecutions for Japan's war crimes to exonerating those found to have committed these crimes?

Within days of its formal surrender in early September 1945, US troops occupied Japan and set about remaking Japanese society, including suppressing remnants of the wartime militarist culture and sidelining former military leaders. During the Allied occupation, the Japanese government and bureaucracy continued to function. Within a few years, however, the dynamics in the region had shifted. The Chinese Communist Party's victory over the nationalists in 1949 and the outbreak of the Korean War in 1950 saw the United States and its allies increasingly looking to Japan as an important ally in the Cold War. In the context of these shifts and the rise of the left in Japan itself, the United States took a more lenient attitude to former war criminals, even rehabilitating some in exchange for strong support in Japan against communism.[80]

After the war, Japan was subordinate to the United States in its foreign policy. With US encouragement, Japan used war treaties with the governments of its formerly occupied territories to shape the direction of its economic and political relations in the region. The aim was to use reparations to forge ongoing economic cooperation.[81] The San Francisco Peace Treaty signed on September 8, 1951, was the principal instrument for this rebuilding. Article 14 dealt specifically with Southeast Asian countries, stipulating that Japan should pay "service reparations" to these countries with a focus on providing equipment for industrial production rather than monetary payments. In the context of the Cold War, this enabled the reconstruction of the Japanese economy and the reinstatement of Japan as a regional power with influence over Southeast Asian countries.

In Indonesia in the immediate postwar period, there was some wariness about relations with Japan. Sutan Sjahrir served as the first prime minister of the republic and also its foreign minister (1945–47). Unlike others in the republican movement, Sjahrir had refused to cooperate with the Japanese after being returned from exile in a Dutch prison camp at the beginning of the occupation. As prime minister he called for collaborators such as Sukarno, who was then president, to be punished and spoke about the need to purge Indonesian society of fascist influences.[82]

Meanwhile, the Japanese worked hard to secure the trust of the Indonesians. Aiko Kurasawa argues that the Japanese carefully positioned themselves in relation to Indonesia as another Asian country.[83] Japan secured an invitation to the Asia-Africa Conference, organized by leaders representing a coalition opposing colonialism, held in Bandung in April 1955. Three years later in 1958, the treaty signed between Japan and Indonesia included payment to Indonesia of US$223 million over twelve years, the cancellation of trade debt worth

US$177 million, and the payment of US$400 million in economic aid. It was to be paid in the form of products and services, mostly for improving industrial, communication, and transport infrastructure as well as agriculture, mining, and skills training for Indonesians.[84] The treaty resulted in Indonesian reliance on Japan for its development for the next decade and beyond.[85] The relationship was further strengthened by Sukarno's marriage in 1962 to a Japanese woman, Nemoto Naoko, who changed her name to Ratna Sari Dewi. During their marriage (1962–70), Dewi became a close adviser to the president and helped set up deals related to the treaty projects.[86]

During Guided Democracy (1959–65), a period during which elections and the party system were abandoned, President Sukarno grew increasingly critical of neocolonialism. He attacked the British for creating the new nation of Malaysia, which he viewed as a neocolonialist project, and began an armed confrontation with both the British and Malaysian forces. In 1963 this culminated in the president telling the United States to "go to hell with its aid."[87] Despite Japan being a US client state, Indonesia–Japan relations were not negatively affected. In this regard, it seems that ideas of Asian solidarity trumped Sukarno's critiques of new forms of imperialism. Japan's own imperial past was a blind spot, as was Sukarno's collaboration during the occupation.

On the evening of September 30, 1965, in the midst of an accelerating domestic political crisis, senior army generals were kidnapped and murdered in Jakarta. The army immediately blamed the popular PKI. The events of that night and the weeks and months that followed changed the country irrevocably. Led by General Suharto, the army used the opportunity to destroy the Indonesian left through campaigns of mass killings and imprisonments without trial. It is estimated that 500,000 people were killed and hundreds of thousands were detained.[88] Like many other Western-allied countries, the Japanese government took a "wait and see attitude," hesitating at first to support the army and then shifting its support from President Sukarno to Suharto.[89] At this time the Japanese supplied rice and textiles to Indonesia in cooperation with the army and assisted the United States in spreading anti-PKI propaganda.[90] During the transition from Sukarno to Suharto and the move to open up the Indonesian economy to foreign capital, the United States supported Japan as an intermediary to supply more development aid to Indonesia.[91]

By 1968, Suharto had taken over the presidency, installed a new army-dominated government, and adopted a pro-Western stance. Japan became one of the biggest contributors of aid and investment to Indonesia.[92] With the exception of the 1974 anti-Japanese Malari riots over Japanese investment (which were quickly suppressed by the army), twenty years on from the end of the war there was still no critical reckoning with the Japanese occupation nor with Japan's economic influence. One key reason for this muted criticism was the annihilation of the political left, the societal force most critical of Japan (see chapter 6).

Meanwhile Dutch relations with Japan were less complicated. In 1956, Japan signed an agreement with the Netherlands called the Protocol on the Resolution of Private Claims with the Netherlands. This was a rare exception to the terms of the San Francisco Peace Treaty, which specified that individual reparations would be excluded from treaties. The agreement allowed for US$10 million to be paid to 92,000 civilians as compensation.[93] The Dutch were far less economically dependent on Japan than Indonesia was, and perhaps partly for this reason, they received preferential treatment with regard to war compensation. The deal was a trade-off for the release of Japanese war criminals, prosecuted for crimes committed in the former colony.[94]

The Japanese Occupation and "Comfort Women" in Dutch National Memory

Because only a small section of the Dutch population lived in the Netherlands East Indies or had family who did, there is a strong perception amongst those in the Indisch community in the Netherlands that not many Dutch people know or care about their experiences. As Elizabeth van Kampen, a woman who was interned as a child during the occupation, puts it: "the Netherlands was occupied by Germany for five long years. The World War II enemy was Germany in Dutch eyes, not Japan."[95]

Across the Indisch community, the most dominant trope in memories of the occupation is of camp life. This is highlighted in the Indisch Monument in the Hague, inaugurated by Dutch Queen Beatrix in 1988, which features emaciated figures and children clinging to mothers.[96] The emphasis on camp experiences has led some to criticize the ongoing focus on Japanese abuses versus Dutch abuses in the colony. A former camp internee, Rudy Kousbroek, took up this delicate issue in his 1992 publication *The East Indies Camp Syndrome*.[97] The public reacted harshly to the work, forcing Kousbroek to leave the Netherlands temporarily.[98]

In comparison to this emphasis on the camp experience, the stories of former Dutch "comfort women" are largely silenced in public memory.[99] The Dutch Resistance Museum in Amsterdam, for example, focused largely on representations of the German occupation and war in Europe. A small section in the museum is devoted to experiences in the former colony. Reinforcing the emphasis on camp experiences, the exhibition features enlarged photos of women and children in internment camps.[100] Alongside these photographic exhibits are a number of pullout wooden compartments. The slots, which snap back into the wall if not held open, contain the museum's only representation of the experiences of Dutch "comfort women." This alerts us to the fact that the case of the "comfort women" remains shameful not only in Asian societies, as is often alluded to in general scholarship on this topic, but also in European societies, such as the Netherlands. Dutch historians only began to write about the topic of the "comfort women" in the 1990s when activism commenced.[101]

Advocacy for wartime redress from members of the Indisch community commenced in 1990 with the establishment of the Japanese Debts of Honor Committee (Stichting Japanse Ereschulden).[102] Every week its members demonstrated outside the Japanese embassy in The Hague. Their key demands were for an admission of guilt, an expression of regret, and compensation for war victims.[103] The foundation brought a number of cases before the Japanese courts in the early 1990s,[104] and eventually extended its support to former "comfort women" (see chapter 9).

The Japanese Occupation and "Comfort Women" in Indonesian National Memory

As a nation, Indonesia does not commemorate or mark the Japanese period of occupation and related suffering. Ethan Mark attributes the lingering ambivalence toward the occupation to the fact that there was extensive local collaboration.[105] Nevertheless, there is a tendency to emphasize one experience of suffering over others—that of forced labor. Japanese cruelty and the harshness of the forced labor system is generally emphasized, which also glosses over the fact that it disproportionately affected poorer Indonesian men.[106] Ken'ichi Gotō has argued that the *rōmusha* became a trope standing in as a symbol for the "three and half years of occupation darkness."[107] The emphasis on the *rōmusha* experience is closely tied to a story of national endurance, a pathway to Indonesian independence, rather than any claim for historical justice. This adheres with the Indonesian New Order's emphasis on so-called Pancasila values, according to which the group is emphasized over the individual and associated individual human rights.[108]

During the early New Order period, Indonesia's growing economic dependence on Japan was further reason for not advocating for more war-related compensation. The government went so far as to censor representations of the occupation. In 1973, the Ministry of Information refused to approve Soviet-trained Indonesian filmmaker Sjumandjaya's film *Romusha*, which depicted the Japanese occupation. The decision followed interventions from the Japanese embassy and the Japan Club, which was dominated by the leaders of large Japanese corporations and companies that invested heavily in Indonesia.[109] This prompted some public backlash over perceived Japanese paternalistic attitudes to Indonesia, which mirrored those during the occupation.

Although *rōmusha* remained the dominant trope referencing the darkness of the occupation, from at least the 1980s the experiences of former "comfort women" were explored in popular culture, including films and novels. The most famous novel from that time dealing with this topic is *Kadarwati Wanita dengan Lima Nama* (Kadarwati the Woman with Five Names) written under the pen name Pandir Kelana.[110]

The man behind the pen name, retired Major General Slamet Danusudirdjo, explained that the novel was based on facts, which he had fictionalized.[111] Danusudirdjo was seventeen years old when the Japanese arrived in Indonesia. After participating in the student army during the Indonesian Revolution he became a customs director, then head of the Economic Planning Board and then head of the Jakarta Arts Institute in the 1980s.[112] He wrote several novels about the revolution under the same pen name.[113]

Kadarwati: A Woman with Five Names

First published in 1982 by mainstream publisher Sinar Harapan, the novel begins with the fictional writer of the story asking permission of a woman, Mirah, to write her life story and thereby fulfill the wish of the woman's lover and the author's friend, that her remarkable story be told. The one condition Mirah gives is that her real name is not disclosed. From the opening, therefore, it is established that the story is recorded by a man because another man deemed it important. The male authorship of the novel and the fact that Mirah's story is narrated in the third person means that her story is repeatedly filtered through men's eyes.

It is important to understand the framing of this novel and the context within which it was written, as it remains one of the most well-known forms of cultural remembrance of the "comfort women" in Indonesia until now. The book influenced early perceptions of survivors. A film by the same name, based on the novel, was made one year later by director Sophan Sophiaan.[114] The novel begins in 1942, with Kadarwati taking a train journey home to her parents. From the opening, there is sustained attention paid to her physical appearance and sexuality, including detailed references to her body and facial features. She admires her appearance and is aware of the frequent attention her looks attract. During the train ride, she observes that the train conductor, "full of passion, observed my body, especially the part just below my neck."[115] Her parents also warn her that her body might "drive men crazy."[116] The early message of the novel, which goes on to describe the sexual abuse and exploitation of the "comfort women" system, is that women are responsible for arousing men's lust.

Kadarwati receives a false offer from the Japanese occupying forces to study abroad. She gains her parents' permission to study in Singapore, but is surprised when she is instead appointed as a nurse assistant and moved to Malaya, where she receives domestic training. It finally becomes clear she will be a housekeeper, an occupation with historical connotations of sexual exploitation. Her complaints are met with threats against her family.[117] She is taken to a British rubber plantation and trained by a Japanese housekeeper to manage a house headed by Harada, the local superintendent. Her job is to serve him and his guests, and she is told that one of her jobs is to bathe him. This results in consensual sex, which is described over two pages. Kadarwati lives with Harada for several months until he is called back to Tokyo.

Harada is replaced as head of the plantation by Nakamura, a lecherous man who rips off Kadarwati's clothes and rapes her. She successfully plots to take revenge on Nakamura by making him jealous of other guests, such that he hits a senior guest, General Tanaka. Tanaka then becomes her protector. Kadarwati is still forced to sleep with other soldiers. In a dream, she strips naked in front of a mirror and reflects on who she is now. She is no longer Kadarwati because "her soul has been lost in someone else's country." Readers are told that her spirit was lost, but her body remains. Reflecting her despair, she calls herself Astuti, after a woman who hung herself from a tree at home.[118] This sets up a continuum of shame attached to these experiences. At this point in the novel, she blames herself for her fate, explaining, "I felt I was not Kadarwati. I was the sugar (*gula-gula*) of so many people. The sugar of Nippon [the Japanese], a paid prostitute. It's true I was the housekeeper of the Japanese officer's mess, but who would want me. I always asked for something like money or jewellery—whatever was of value to me. I am a prostitute, prostitute, prostitute (*pelacur, pelacur, pelacuuuuuur!*)."[119] Astuti directs her resentment only toward Nakamura and not at the Japanese army. She sees herself as a lowly person of little worth, repeating the label "prostitute" to emphasize the loss of dignity she feels.

Despite his character's journey to despair and self-loathing, throughout the novel Kadarwati/Astuti is portrayed as a woman who exercises some agency in the context of terrible circumstances. She repeatedly refers to her desire for revenge. She describes the Japanese men as "bestial" (*manusia-manusia binatang*).[120] To plot her revenge, she tries to stay in Japanese circles of influence. Astuti saves up sleeping medicine and one night spikes the Japanese soldiers' drinks and then sets the building on fire, watching the men burn alive. She escapes with her friends, only to discover that Sukarno has declared independence.[121] Reflecting the arrival of a new era, the narrator tells us the woman decides to use the name Tasmirah or Mirah.

Later in the novel, Mirah sets up a shelter in Balokan, Central Java, to help lessen the burden of "lost women" (*wanita-wanita tersesat*), meaning women who have lost their way, which could mean both sex workers and "comfort women."[122] The term "lost women" has religious connotations (both Muslim and Christian) of having veered from the path of a righteous life. Mirah's experiences have led her to empathize with these women.

As the story continues, the narrative extends to the Indonesian revolution. Mirah convinces the women in Balokan to provide sex for Dutch soldiers so they can learn the men's secrets and share them with the Indonesian National Army and earn money to live. The framing in this section of the novel is highly nationalistic. Similar to the framing in Sukarno's memoir (mentioned in chapter 3), women's bodies are positioned as a resource. One volunteer suggests this work would be a form of *perjuangan*, part of the struggle for independence.[123] Mirah is torn about engaging in prostitution again and asks for Allah's forgiveness.[124] She mentions several times that she would not be worthy as a wife for Bargowo.[125] This lack of self-worth reflects the assumption that she has been "ruined" by her experiences. The women are ultimately successful in providing information on Dutch strategies to the Indonesian National Army.[126]

It was not until the book was republished in 1992, when the "comfort women" issue was escalating internationally and public interest along with it, that it became a bestseller.[127] As will be discussed in chapter 7, this novel is important because in the 1980s and 1990s, it was a seminal representation of the "comfort women" story in Indonesia. While in Japan and Korea, people began to research and write the history of sex workers as early as the 1970s, there was almost no interest in these women among Indonesian historians. It was only in the realm of fiction that this history was being represented. The tropes in this novel, written by a retired general sixteen years into a military-dominated regime, mirror the New Order's gender values in the sense that the protagonist is depicted as an immoral woman unworthy of marriage and distant from the regime's ideal of a housewife. Because she commits herself to the nationalist cause, though, she is ultimately redeemed (see chapter 6).

Conclusion

The experiences of former "comfort women" across the Indonesian archipelago differed depending on where they were detained. For women in both Indonesia and the Netherlands, sharing their personal histories was difficult because of ongoing stigmatization and shame. In the decades after the war, the Indisch community in the Netherlands remembered the Japanese occupation largely through the experiences of Dutch POWs and those detained in internment camps. Like the Indonesians, the experiences of Dutch survivors were viewed as a shameful issue and rarely discussed. In Indonesia, the Japanese occupation was remembered in ambiguous terms, as Japan emerged as a key postwar trading partner, investor, and ally. Through the 1960s, 1970s and 1980s, while sexual violence against Indonesian women was not entirely forgotten, representations of these stories in popular culture reinforced the trope of a fallen woman who redeems herself through sexual self-sacrifice, but these failed to consider the experience from a woman's point of view.

5

Pathways to Activism
in Japan and Korea,
1980s–1990s

peaking to fellow protesters at a rally in South Korea in
1997, Kim Hak-Sun explained why six years earlier she
had decided to testify about her experiences as a "comfort woman": "Before
I die, I had to say what I wanted to say . . . So I started. On the evening of
August 14, I opened my mouth in front of all the reporters from the news
media. I was so furious. I wanted all the Korean women to open their eyes and
face the truth."[1] Kim's 1991 testimony is often lauded as a turning point for
attracting international attention to the "comfort women" issue. Why did she
and others who came after her choose to publicly share their experiences of
wartime rape? Kim explains she was motivated by her advancing age and a
desire for people to know what had happened to her, and by anger directed
mostly at the Japanese government for not admitting this history. To fully answer
this question, it is necessary to understand the role of national and transnational activist support networks advocating for redress. Kim was supported by
Japanese and Korean activists who took different, but somewhat connected
pathways toward recognizing and then supporting survivors. Japanese support
was premised on recognizing Japan's historical colonization and exploitation
of Korea, as well as recognizing ongoing inequities across the two countries.

Although Indonesian experiences of the "comfort women" system were
mentioned in cultural memory from as early as the 1980s, it took significant
shifts in public discourse for their experiences to be reframed as human rights
abuses. The origins of these shifts, however, are not located in Indonesia, but
in East Asia, particularly South Korea and Japan. A number of parallel developments in these countries facilitated a slow reframing of the experiences of all

survivors, and from the early 1990s onward eventually had effects for Indonesia. In the broader context of a movement for wartime redress in Japan and Korea, far greater attention was given to the plight of survivors of militarized sexual abuse.

Japanese and Korean activism evolved in the context of particular developments in these countries, which can be traced back at least as far as the 1970s, including continuing and critical reflections on the legacies of the war and imperialism. As will be discussed, this criticism arose in part due to shifts in the geopolitical landscape, including the escalation in US intervention in Vietnam in the mid-1960s, the associated use of military bases in Korea and Japan, and increased US presence on these bases. Demands for war compensation from female survivors arose because of increased awareness of the plight of these women, resulting in feminist research on women's histories and increased attention to the sexual exploitation of women, violence against women, and ethnic discrimination.

This chapter traces the evolution of activism in Japan and Korea beginning in the 1970s, on the issue of the "comfort women." It outlines the motives and strategies of the Japanese activists—who later assisted their Indonesian counterparts—and the development of transnational activism. The approaches of Japanese and Korean activists to this issue provide important context for understanding how Indonesian activism later developed and the forms it took. Comparing these cases helps explain why human rights activism may flourish in some countries and fail in others and highlights particular contexts in which transnational activism may be most resilient and effective.

Japanese Lawyers and Early Cases of Wartime Redress

Japanese legal advocacy for redress for wartime crimes and hardships constituted one part of the drive toward transnational activism for the former "comfort women."[2] Since the 1970s, a small number of Japanese lawyers acting independently have supported those seeking legal redress for a range of wartime experiences of hardship and suffering, along with advocacy from the Japan Federation of Bar Associations (JFBA).

In its role of supervising attorneys, the JFBA is an influential body and an important mechanism for human rights protection in Japan. It is beholden to the guidelines of the 1949 Attorneys' Act, which reflects the principles of the 1946 Japanese constitution. Article 1 prescribes that attorneys are responsible for "protecting human rights and achieving social justice."[3] In 1950, the JFBA set up a Human Rights Protection Committee, which researches human rights issues and investigates complaints of human rights abuses, which can lead to policy and legislative recommendations. The JFBA holds regular conventions on protecting human rights and submits reports to the UN High Commissioner for Human Rights.[4]

In 1965, Japan signed a treaty with South Korea that included providing US$300 million in goods and services from Japan to South Korea, as well as US$200 million in long-term low-interest development loans.[5] The treaty strengthened economic and political ties between South Korea and Japan, while increasing South Korea's dependence on its neighbor.[6] As noted in chapter 4, the majority of Japan's postwar treaties ignored the individual rights of those who were subjected to violence and exploitation. In the decades since, the Japanese government has (with very few exceptions) taken the view that all cases for war reparations were settled with these treaties and the associated payments to the governments of affected countries.[7] Representatives of the Japanese government argue that individuals are not entitled to demand compensation for violations under international humanitarian law according to The Hague Convention of 1907 or customary international law. They invoke the Japanese legal principle of nonresponsibility of the state (*kokka mutōseki*)—a prewar doctrine that holds that "the government is not responsible to its citizens for the damages caused by the acts that it performs in the exercise of official authority."[8]

From the late 1980s and 1990s, as demands for individual redress emerged, the JFBA undertook research to advise the Japanese government on the best ways to address such claims. In this period, there was increasing attention globally to war redress because of what Elazar Barkan observed as "a new international emphasis on morality . . . characterized not only by accusing other countries of human rights abuses, but also by self-examination."[9] Japanese lawyers have written extensively on postwar compensation, reflecting precisely this trend.[10] They have also engaged in comparative research into how Japan and Germany dealt with war responsibility.[11] In postwar Japan, lawyers have established a deep commitment to and sense of obligation for protecting human rights and dealing with past human rights abuses.

The strong institutional support for human rights advocacy encouraged some lawyers to work in this area, while others had more personal motives.[12] Takagi Ken'ichi, for example, founded the advocacy organization International Committee of Asia-Pacific War Victims Organization Claiming Compensation (Ajia-Taiheiyō Chiiki Sengo Hoshō Kokusai Fōramu Jikkō Iinkai). He explains that he was strongly motivated by a sense of injustice relating to his family's wartime treatment and his years as a student activist in the 1960s and

1970s to critically question the actions of the Japanese government. Takagai was born in 1944 in Japanese-occupied Manchuria, where his Japanese father worked in a factory. At the end of the war, his civilian family was abandoned without assistance while the army was repatriated.[13] In the late 1960s, the New Left student movement, of which he was a part, was focused on opposing the renewal of the 1952 US–Japan Joint Security Treaty, which allowed US bases in Japan, including full control of Okinawa.[14] The use of these bases to support the war in Vietnam triggered more critical discussions about Japan's collaboration with the United States and its historical and contemporary relationship with the rest of Asia.[15]

Takagi Ken'ichi was one of the earliest Japanese activists to work on behalf of those claiming damages from the Japanese government for their wartime suffering. In 1975, his first legal case was a pro bono compensation claim by Korean laborers who had been abandoned after the war in the Russian-controlled territory of Sakhalin.[16] Approximately 60,000 Korean men were taken to work in mines in Sakhalin, a mineral-rich island to the north of Hokkaido.[17] The four plaintiffs in the 1975 case came from the South Korea–based Association of Separated Families in the Soviet Union.[18] Takagi Ken'ichi filed a suit in a Tokyo district court. In 1989, the case was finally dismissed after three of the four plaintiffs had died. In 1990, the government declared it had a moral responsibility to repatriate Koreans remaining in Shakhalin.[19]

This shift reflected changes in local and international sentiment about war responsibility. In 1988, for example, the US government passed the Civil Liberties Act, according to which the US government offered an apology and payment of US$20,000 to every surviving Japanese and Japanese American who was forcibly detained during the war.[20] Takagi's reputation from the Sakhalin case led to approaches from other claimants seeking wartime damages. He established the International Committee of Asia-Pacific War Victims Organizations Claiming Compensation in 1991.[21]

Beginning in the 1970s, through their roles in these types of legal cases, Japanese lawyers began addressing the legacy of the Pacific War and how it was understood. In addition to the Sahkalin case, Korean claimants demanded equal treatment in the postwar reparation claims process (sengo hoshō saiban).[22] One of these early cases was brought by Korean citizen, Sun Jin-to, a former forced laborer who became a victim of the atomic bombings in Japan in 1945 (a *hibakusha*). Unlike Japanese citizens, he was not initially considered eligible for medical assistance or recognition from the Japanese government. He won the case first at a district court (1974), then the high court (1975) and appeals court (1978), paving the way for other Korean *hibakusha* to receive treatment and compensation.[23] The growing number of court cases and Korean demands for redress triggered Japanese legal activists to pay greater attention to the issue of war compensation, with a particular focus on victims of forced labor.

Alongside these developments, progressive historians fought to ensure that Japan's role in the Pacific War was not censored in history textbooks. In the 1980s, historian Ienaga Saburō used the courts to challenge government certification and the effective censorship of history textbooks to exclude mentions of Japanese war crimes.[24] This high-profile case enhanced public debate in Japan about the legacies of the war. Such debates escalated around the fortieth anniversary of the end of the war in 1985 and with the death of the wartime Emperor Hirohito in January 1989. In 1988, the JFBA escalated its investigations into "the realities of war victims" and sought "measures which would provide compensation for victims."[25] The end of the Cold War in 1989, which reduced US reliance on Japan as a regional ally, was another important stimulus for action on this issue.

The foundational work of Japanese lawyers on wartime compensation and war memory paved the way for "comfort women" legal activism. In taking on such cases, many lawyers approached this issue as part of broader concerns for human rights and war compensation for a range of victims. Others adopted a specific focus on advocating on the issue of violence against women in the context of imperialism and militarism. Despite very limited legal success, lawyers, activists, and survivor activists have consistently and persistently used legal process and the courts in Japan to raise the profile of the issue.[26]

The Feminist Road to "Comfort Women" Advocacy in Japan

Several trends in Japanese society from the 1970s onward led Japanese feminists to turn their attention to "comfort women." The first of these began in the 1950s and involved intensifying debates around sex work and histories of debt bondage in Japan. As discussed in chapter 2, in the early twentieth century prostitution was state-regulated, but by 1955, due to public pressure, the Japanese state nullified all indentured sex worker contracts and a year later passed a law banning prostitution. At this time, the women's movement began to critique the "commodification of sexuality," including sex work and pornography.[27] These critiques extended beyond the circles of feminist academics. At the same time the women's liberation movement of the 1970s was stimulating debates worldwide about many of these issues.

Japanese feminist debates in the 1980s were facilitated in part by a flourishing print culture, an economic boom, greater participation of women in higher education, and the emergence of "female and feminist voices in academia."[28] Activism was propelled by the fact that women's studies began to be taught in universities and women's studies organizations, founded in the 1970s, began to publish books and journals.

Representations of the Karayukisan and "Comfort Women"

Published in 1972, one of the most important works to open up the issue of the history of sex work and debt bondage in Japan was *Sandakan Hachiban Shōkan-Teihen Joseishi Joshō* (Sandakan brothel no 8: A prologue of the history of Japanese lower class women), written by an amateur historian, Yamazaki Tomoko.[29] This work stands out first because the author was not a university-trained historian, second because she used oral history, and third because of the nontraditional subject of the book. The book reflected a new trend in Japan called "people's history" (*minshūshi*), which rejected the view that only professional historians could write history and focused on writing local histories and histories of everyday life and nonelites. Moreover, *minshūshi* included critically reexamining people's past complicity in imperialism and the war.[30]

These historians typically used oral history to write "histories from below." Carol Gluck describes this field of research as a form of protest.[31] Despite some criticism of the people's histories approach, this book and others brought public attention to new categories of historical experience.[32] *Sandakan Brothel No 8* tells the story of a young Japanese woman from Amakusa-Shimo island who was a *karayukisan* in Singapore and then at Sandakan, a port city in British Borneo.[33] The book is based on oral testimony from Osaki, a former *karayukisan*, collected by Yamazaki between 1968 and 1970. Yamazaki was motivated to tell Osaki's story because she believed that the history of these women had been silenced.[34] One chapter lays out Osaki's life story, describing how she is shipped abroad in 1916 at the age of ten, with the promise of work as a cleaner. When she turns thirteen, she is forced to work in a brothel in Sandakan.[35] Like former "comfort women," Osaki tried to conceal her past (see chapter 4) and was rejected by family members.[36]

Yamazaki's book was one of the first published works to narrate the experiences of a lower-class Japanese woman from her perspective, contextualizing her experiences alongside the economic and social conditions of her community. Following several chapters introducing how the author found Osaki comes a chapter detailing Osaki's experience, written in the first person. We are told that she agreed to go abroad because she wanted to make enough money for her brother to buy land and then marry.[37] Her brother, with whom she lived, received ¥300, but the procurer set ¥2,000 as their debt.[38] After working in the brothel, for six years Osaki lived and worked as a concubine for an Englishman. Other chapters detail Osaki's recollections of other *karayukisan*.

Weaving research into other chapters in the book, Yamazaki tells readers that Japanese people ran the majority of the brothels in Sandakan.[39] She criticizes the state for its treatment of former *karayukisan*, pointing out that after overseas prostitution was prohibited by Japan in 1920, some women were simply abandoned. She details how some, like Osaki, followed the imperial army into China in the 1930s, thereby linking the *karayukisan* with wartime practices of sexual exploitation. In the epilogue the author also links the *karayukisan* to prostitution around US military bases in Japan in the 1970s.[40]

Although there was some criticism about how evidence was presented, including allegations of distortion, Yamazaki's book met with broad acclaim in Japan.[41] The book received the Ōya Sōichi Prize for nonfiction literature and became a national bestseller. In 1974, the book was made into a film of the same name, produced by Kumai Kei. The film was nominated for an Academy Award in the Best Foreign Language Film category that year.[42]

James Warren, a historian of *karayukisan* in colonial Singapore, commended *Sandakan Brothel No 8* for reflecting on how age and class shaped Osaki's experiences.[43] Yamazaki's work inspired an increase in the use of oral history to capture the experiences of other elderly, lower class, and by definition marginalized women in Japan, including former "comfort women."

New Spaces for Marginalized Voices

While histories of the *karayukisan* were opening up, the first publications on the "comfort women" emerged, although not all works adopted a survivor-centric approach. Often overlooked, Erik Ropers has argued that the 1970s was a pivotal decade for scholarship and research related to enforced military prostitution.[44] One of the better-known works from this time, *Jūgun Ianfu*, was written by journalist Senda Kakō and published in 1973, a year after *Sandakan Brothel No 8*.[45] A bestseller, the nonfiction book sold half a million copies, with twenty-five printings in the first two months of sale.[46] Senda's main sources were witness testimonies from Japanese military veterans and information collected by Korean journalists. Although the work has many shortcomings related to the methods for gathering sources, Ropers argues that the work is "illustrative of the beginning of thinking-through Japanese war responsibility in regards to women in its former colonies and territories."[47] C. Sarah Soh describes it as one of the first sympathetic Japanese accounts of "comfort women."[48]

In the 1970s, Japanese and Korean historians began to use oral history to document the life stories of marginalized Korean residents in Japan, known as *zainichi kankojin/chōsenjin.*[49] Following Japan's colonization of Korea in 1910, *zainichi kankojin/chōsenjin* were brought to Japan as forced laborers, with around 600,000 Koreans still in the country at the end of the Pacific War.[50] After the 1952 San Francisco Peace Treaty, the position of Koreans in Japan became precarious, as the agreement revoked the Japanese nationality of former colonial subjects living there. Due to ongoing advocacy from this community, the Japan–South Korea Treaty of 1965 included a special provision for South Koreans to gain permanent residence in Japan, entitling them to welfare, education, and health care.[51]

Inspired by growing awareness of discrimination against resident Koreans and other minority groups, in 1970 women from the New Left in Japan founded the Conference of Asian Women Fighting Against Discrimination=Invasion (Shinryaku=Sabetsu to Tatakau Ajia Fujin Kaigi), known as the Asian Women's Conference. The conference focused on linking multiple forms of discrimination and tied their critiques to both the United States and former Japanese empire.[52] At this time, the status of Okinawa was a key issue. According to the terms of the surrender agreement, Okinawa, a Japanese territory since 1879, was retained as a US territory beyond the initial US occupation of the mainland (1945–52).[53] The prefecture did not revert to Japanese control until 1972. In making this agreement with the United States, the Okinawans felt that the Japanese government had sacrificed them. In the following decades, their protests escalated as the military bases became increasingly pivotal in US campaigns in the region, including the Korean War (1950–53) and during the most interventionist phase of the Vietnam War (1965–75).

During this time, Japanese researchers increasingly documented the life histories of Okinawans, including Korean migrants who were subjected to conscripted labor and forced military prostitution during the war.[54] In the last phase of the war, as Japanese troops retreated to the homeland, they set up more *ianjo* in the Okinawan islands, bringing Korean women with them.[55] After the war, some of these women stayed on in Japan.[56]

In 1971, in the lead-up to the transfer of Okinawa from the United States to Japan, Okinawan resident Bae Bong-gi, who was of Korean background, publicly identified herself as a former "comfort woman."[57] She came forward not from a desire to speak about her past nor to replace or to seek compensation but because of a procedural necessity as part of her application for Japanese residency, to prove that she came to Okinawa during the war. Eventually successful, in 1975 her case was reported in the newspaper *Kōchi Shimbun*.[58] In 1977 she shared a fuller account of her life story, including her experiences as a "comfort woman," with a newspaper affiliated with Korean residents in Japan and associated with North Korea, which had extended support to her.[59] Her story attracted significant national attention. In 1979, filmmaker Yamatani Tetsuo produced a documentary based on interviews with her, and published a book featuring her testimony alongside those of Japanese soldiers and one Korean soldier.[60]

Journalist and feminist writer Kawada Fumiko also took an interest in Bae Bong-gi's life story because it accentuated the multiple axes of discrimination faced by women.[61] The local newspaper *Kōchi Shimbun* covered Bae's employer's campaign to obtain social welfare from the Japanese government after she fell ill. Upon reading it, Kawada was alerted to the marginality of Korean residents in Japan.[62] The fact that Bae Bong-gi had come to Japan as a "comfort woman" also piqued Kawada's interest. At that time, Kawada was working for a magazine called *Sekai Gahō* that covered social and political issues, such as the Vietnam War, opposition to US military bases, new treaties between Japan and the United States and between Japan and Korea, the peace movement, and related Japanese activism.[63] Kawada was researching the ongoing trend of poor families selling their daughters into prostitution on indentured contracts.[64]

After first meeting her in 1977, Kawada interviewed Bae over a period of five years. As a consequence of her trauma, Bae was socially withdrawn, so it took her a long time to reveal her story.[65] The resulting book, *Akagawara no Ie: Chōsen kara Kita Jūgun Ianfu* (A house with a red tile roof: A military comfort woman from Korea), published in 1987, documents Bae's life history and provides historical context surrounding her experience as a *zainichi* and a former "comfort woman."[66] When it was first published, this was one of the most detailed life histories of a "comfort woman" and provided rare information on the system as a whole. The initial public response to her book in Japan and Korea was relatively muted, with around four thousand copies sold. In the 1990s, as activism on this issue began to escalate, demand grew, with the book reaching its seventh edition, including a Korean translation published in 1992.

Kawada Fumiko was increasingly called on to provide media commentary and join fact-finding missions, including to Indonesia (chapter 8). She continued to publish accounts of women's experiences of the system. She joined with several activist groups including the Centre for Research and Documentation of Japan's War Responsibility founded in 1993 by Yoshmi Yoshiaki (see later discussion).

Advocating for Change

Other Japanese women came to the issue of the "comfort women" through critical reflection on the historical and contemporary relationships between Japanese women and other Asian women. Beginning in the

1970s, Japanese and Korean women linked to Christian networks formed an alliance to oppose Japanese prostitution tourism to South Korea, known as *kisaeng* tourism. Historically *kisaeng* were a hereditary status group during the Chosŏn dynasty trained from childhood as courtesans to serve higher status men. In 1894 the caste system was abandoned, but these practices continued in part because of Japanese colonial demands. In the 1970s, the term *kisaeng* referred to young women who entertained small groups of men at drinking parties, where sex was often expected.[67] Sex tourism, like tourism more generally, was booming due to the success of the 1970s income-doubling plan and increased societal wealth. In 1973 students led protests against Japanese sex tourism at airports in Seoul and Haneda, shaming men who engaged in the practice. Journalist Matsui Yayori expressed this outrage at the time: "previously Japan colonized and pillaged Korea, raping many of her daughters as army prostitutes. Now they go back to the same land and disgrace her women again, this time with money."[68] In 1977, Matsui established the Asian Women's Association (Aija no Onnatachi no Kai) with Gotō Masako to protest against Japanese sex tours to other Asian countries.[69]

Like lawyer Takagi Ken'ichi, Matsui Yayori was influenced by her family's wartime experiences. Born in 1934, she lived through the war as a child. In 1945, her father was drafted into the army and sent to China. A dissenter, on his return to Japan, he strongly condemned the Japanese army's conduct.[70] Matsui frequently published articles in the press about women's rights. She canvassed issues such as the feminization of migration, the effects of development projects on women, as well as the trafficking of women, sexual violence against women, and women's efforts to resist the sources of their oppression.[71]

The Asian Women's Association reached out to Korean women in particular. The choice of the organization's founding date—March 1, 1977—marks the anniversary of the Korean uprisings against Japanese colonialism in 1919. As Vera Mackie observed, this was both an acknowledgment of Korean women's struggle against Japanese imperialism and an expression of admiration for Korean women's more radical political practices.[72] Many Japanese activists became increasingly critical of their government's relationship with South Korea based on the criticisms of Korean democracy activists that the Japanese government supported authoritarian regimes in South Korea.[73] Enhanced awareness of the plight of *zainichi kankojin/chōsenjin* and immigrant workers in Japan strengthened ties between women activists from the two countries.[74]

Japanese members of the Asian Women's Association recognized that ongoing relationships of inequity across the Asian region sustained Japanese companies' exploitation of Asian women's labor.[75] Its members began to examine the historical relationships between Japan and these countries, including the system of enforced military prostitution. Matsui Yayori drove this process.[76] In 1984, when working as a foreign correspondent for *Asahi Shimbun*, Matsui interviewed a Korean survivor who had been forcibly shipped to Thailand as a "comfort woman" during the war and had stayed on after it ended.[77] Matsui also supported the work of early Korean feminist scholars researching this issue, such as Yun Chung-Ok, whose work is discussed later.[78] From 1990 onward, members of the Asian Women's Association began to participate in a network supporting survivors.[79]

By the 1980s, Filipino, South Korean, and Thai women were working in brothels and bars in Japan, leading to more thorough critiques from women's rights activists of unequal relationships across the region.[80] Organized abolitionist groups who opposed sex work existed in these countries as early as the 1980s. In South Korea, this included church groups. In Thailand such groups included the Friends of Women in Thailand, and in the Philippines the Third World Movement against the Exploitation of Women, which also protested sex tourism to the Philippines.[81] These four countries shared a history of military bases and sex work surrounding the bases. Through these organizations, women formed international networks to oppose sex work and sexual violence.[82] These networks were important when attention later turned to the "comfort women."

The Korean Road to Advocacy

Korean advocacy by and on behalf of survivors developed out of advocacy supporting demands for war redress more broadly, women's activism, and the democratization movement. Following the devastating Korean War and the division of the country, South Korea was ruled by a succession of authoritarian governments until 1987. From 1948 to 1960, the country was governed by anticommunist dictator Syngman Rhee, then by the military regimes of Park Chung-hee (1961–79) and his successor, Chun Doo-hwan (1980–87), both of whom focused on economic development. During these regimes, all forms of protest faced constraints, and relations with Japan were prioritized as part of a Cold War alliance with the United States.

Changes in Korean society, including increased awareness of the exploitation of women, contributed to greater openness to the issue of the "comfort women." The regimes of Park and Chun used conservative Confucian values to co-opt women workers into pursuing development goals. Throughout the 1960s and 1970s—the so-called second phase of Korean industrialization—women's labor drove the manufacturing boom, yet women workers generally were paid half the wages of men.[83] Women workers organized and led some of the earliest labor disputes, demanding higher wages and improved labor rights. They protested against widespread sexual violence committed by managers, but also by police and thugs involved in repressing their protests.[84] Ruth Barraclough goes so far as to say that "sexual violence regulated the lives of women who went out to work in the factories" and underpinned the entire process.[85] Although this abuse was endemic, women faced difficulties in securing recognition of it due to social discourses about working-class women's sexual availability and because sexual assault was not considered a crime.[86]

Korea's Women's Movement

Working-class women played a key role in drawing attention to sexual violence in Korean society. Initially the women's movement, which was dominated by the middle class, was wary of the working-class movement due to entrenched anticommunism resulting from the Korean War.[87] The Minjung movement, a mass movement for democracy and against the exploitation of the working classes, created new alliances.[88] The movement combined the goals of ending the authoritarian regimes of Chun and Park, eliminating dependence on foreign powers (the United States), uniting North and South Korea, and ending class struggle.[89] Amid growing opposition to the Chun government, and inspired by radical women's labor activists, middle-class women also became increasingly politically active.[90] In an expression of solidarity, some middle-class women took up factory work, part of a broader student-led movement called *hakch'ul*.[91]

An important development in the formation of critical understandings of the issue of the "comfort women" was the increased theorization of women's oppression in Korean society more generally. In 1977, Ewha Woman's University in Seoul established the first women's studies department in Korea, pioneering feminist teaching and research in other universities across the country.[92] The program proved to be extremely popular. At the same time, a reinvigoration of the women's movement was under way. In collaboration with activists, women's studies departments organized study groups focusing on the history of the Korean women's movement, the division of Korea, human rights abuses, military rule, and the relationship between military rule and male domination in society more broadly.[93]

Throughout the 1980s, brutal police attacks on women protesters in the Minjung movement triggered criticism of the use of sexual violence by the military and police.[94] Women's groups demanded responses to police violence by initially framing it as a human rights issue, rather than an issue of sexual violence, with no success. In 1986, after a policeman at Bucheon police station sexually assaulted imprisoned student activist Kwon Insook, women's organizations joined with prodemocracy and religious groups to demand the police officer be brought to trial. Their outrage led to the founding of two organizations, the Women's Council against Sexual Violence and the Joint Committee against Sexual Violence at Bucheon Station. Their actions attracted broad support, including that of the Korean Bar Association, which acted for Kwon and secured a five-year sentence for the police officer. In the midst of a growing protest movement, known as the June democracy movement, this incident helped mobilize broad support against the military regime, which was eventually toppled in December 1987.[95] Kwon went on to become a feminist scholar.

Public condemnation of sexual violence against women was strengthened through two pivotal cases in 1991 and 1992 involving women who took revenge by killing men who had sexually abused them as children. Kyungja Jung argues that these cases helped shift public discourse from a culture of always blaming the women and was a catalyst for the formation of a new organization, the Korean Sexual Violence Relief Centre (KSVRC) in 1991.[96] Feminist scholars began to make connections between high rates of sexual violence in Korea by the military and police and the dominance of the Korean military in society, including compulsory military service and experiences of militarism during the Japanese and US occupations.[97] Women's activists linked this history of militarism and US bases in Korea with the growth of sex work and sexual violence against women.[98]

Activism on Behalf of War Victims

As noted above, from the 1970s, Korean survivors in Japan and at home stepped up their demands for war compensation. A key organization driving this activism was the Association of Pacific War Victims and Bereaved Families, founded in 1973.[99] The association initially focused its efforts on seeking the repatriation of the remains of Korean war dead and uncovering the fate of the missing. It also lobbied the Japanese to fund scholarships for the children of Koreans killed or wounded in the war.

Scholars at Ewha University played a crucial role in generating critical debates about sexual violence and the "comfort women" issue. The university supported the founding of the KSVRC and stimulated Korean feminist research into the system. Driving this process was Yun Chung-Ok, a professor of English.[100] As early as 1980, she traveled across parts of Asia and the Pacific to gather information on the system.[101] In February 1988, along with members of the Korean Church Women United (KCWU), she conducted fact-finding trips to Okinawa and in Korea and ran a survey on the system. In April 1988, the findings of this research were presented at a KCWU seminar run focusing on *kisaeng* tourism to Korea.[102] This seminar led to the formation of the Committee on Military Sexual Slavery by Japan and sparked new efforts to work with Japanese women's groups to pressure the governments of Korea and Japan to disclose the truth about this history.[103]

Korean women activists followed debates over wartime redress in Japanese politics. Beginning in 1990, a member from the Japanese Socialist Party, Motooka Shōji, began to ask questions about the "comfort women" in Japan's national legislature, the Diet. He demanded that the government investigate the forced recruitment of these women and apologize. The government responded with claims that the women were all prostitutes who worked voluntarily for private entrepreneurs and that it would not accept responsibility. In reply, the Korean Women's Association sent an open letter to the Japanese government requesting an apology, a memorial to the women, and a thorough inquiry.[104]

In a watershed moment in his 1990 visit to Japan, South Korean President Roh Tae Woo raised the issue of the "comfort women" for the first time and requested a list of women drafted into the system. The list provided to the Koreans included only the names of women, with no other details. Motooka pushed the Diet to reveal whether the women were forced draftees, claiming he had evidence they were. In April 1991, the Japanese government responded to this demand and the letter from the Korean Women's Association by reiterating its position that the system was privately run and stating that there would be no apology, memorial, or compensation.[105] As will be discussed, because of these denials, a Korean survivor, Kim Hak-Sun, testified publicly about her experiences a few months later.[106]

Korean women continued to organize and form new activist organizations. The most significant of these was the merging in November 1990 of thirty-seven women's groups to form an umbrella organization called the Korean Council for Women Drafted for Military Sexual Slavery by Japan, commonly known as the Korean Council. Yun Chung-Ok was a founding co-representative of the council.[107] The council continued to research the history of the system, opening up a hotline in September 1991 for Korean survivors or witnesses to call in and provide information.[108] By 1994, around two hundred women had shared their stories via the hotline.[109] The Korean Council remained the driving force behind South Korean activism, bringing together church groups closely associated with democratization and women's movements. The Christian Academy, founded in 1965, played a key role in the movement.[110] From January 1992 until today, the Korean Council have organized demonstrations in front of the Japanese embassy in Seoul every Wednesday at noon. At the very first protest, the women shouted slogans such as "apologize," "punish," and "compensate."[111]

Alongside the Korean Council, the Association of Pacific War Victims and Bereaved Families continued to gain support, and by the early 1990s it had 300 local offices and 20,000 members across South Korea. Its goals evolved to focus on protecting the rights of surviving war victims, uncovering "the truth about the past," and fighting for restitution from the Japanese government and the corporations involved in using Korean conscripted labor. The association also lobbied the United Nations to block Japan's admission to the Human Rights Committee until it apologized and made reparations.[112] Its members used public protests to draw attention to wartime issues, including a month-long march in summer 1991 from Busan to Seoul to publicize the plight of those victimized during the war. In this period, the association attempted to gather testimony from survivors about their wartime experiences with varying success.[113] Although some victims remained hesitant to come forward, in 1991 a group of survivors connected to this project filed a class-action suit against the Japanese government for a range of cases of wartime abuse.[114] Survivor Kim Hak-Sun was one of the claimants. She gave her first public testimony on August 14, 1991, the day before the anniversary of Japan's surrender. Her testimony and participation in the court case marked a turning point for activism in Korea, Japan, and around the world.[115]

Kim Hak-Sun and the Escalation of Demands for War Redress

Kim Hak-Sun was one of more than thirty-five South Korean claimants in the case, including two other survivors of the "comfort women" system.[116] Unlike Kim, they did not reveal their names beyond the court.[117] Other complainants in the class action included former forced laborers and family members of people killed in the war. The claimants demanded a compensation payment of ¥20 million each.[118] Lawyer Takagi Ken'ichi took on this case pro bono.[119]

As the first class action involving former "comfort women" in Japan, not unexpectedly it drew a great deal of public attention. Outside the courthouse in Tokyo, the Association of Pacific War Victims and Bereaved Families held street demonstrations. Korean women protesters wore white *hanbok* (Korean dress) with photos of war victims hung around their necks.[120] The color white symbolizes mourning in many Asian cultures.

Further to Kim's media testimony on August 14, 1991, the media conference held on December 6 provided another pivotal moment for getting the public's attention. Takagi's team called the conference to speak about the range of cases being brought in the claim. Kim Hak-Sun stood beside other claimants, including an injured Korean former forced laborer.[121] As Takagi remembered it, the press was only interested in Kim's story.[122] Kim cried as she recounted her experiences of abuse. In Takagi's view, there was something particularly striking about her story of suffering and the visual image of an elderly woman crying, which touched people in ways that other activism had not.

Kim told the assembled media how, at the age of seventeen in 1941, her foster father had taken her to China to find her a job.[123] She had completed training in singing and dancing to work as a *kisaeng*. In China her foster father was arrested and accused of being a spy, and she was taken by truck to a house where she was later raped by a Japanese officer. She was kept in an *ianjo* next to a military unit. She was one of five Korean women held in the house. All were given Japanese names and kept under guard, unable to leave without permission. Over four months Kim was repeatedly subjected to rape, beatings, and invasive medical examinations. She looked for ways to escape, eventually convincing a Korean businessman who came to the station and abused her to take her with him.

Kim's story attracted media interest around the world, with many follow-up effects. Over the next three years, a succession of court cases were brought by Korean, Filipino, and Dutch survivors.[124] Her testimony prompted more survivors to come forward, including Jan Ruff O'Herne, then residing in Australia, and Maria Rosa Henson from the Philippines (see chapter 7). Women from the Philippines were noticeably quick to take up this issue, most likely because of their long-established connections with Japanese activists who opposed sex tourism to the Philippines.

Another significant outcome of Kim's public testimony was that it motivated other Japanese citizens to act. In December 1991, as the Kim Hak-Sun trial was under way, Chief Cabinet Secretary Katō Kōichi claimed that the government was unable to locate records indicating government involvement in "the system."[125] In direct response to hearing Kim's testimony and Katō's denials, researcher Yoshimi Yoshiaki found and published documentary evidence linking the Japanese government to the system held in the Library of the National Institute of Defence Studies in Tokyo.[126] These documents had been scheduled for destruction in the closing days of the war, but were seized by the Allied forces, preserved, and later returned to Japan.[127] Yoshimi was already engaged in debates about wartime responsibility and had challenged the idea of the innocence of Japanese civilians in his 1987 book *Grassroots Fascism*.[128]

On January 11, 1992, the influential Japanese newspaper *Asahi Shimbun* published summaries of the six documents Yoshimi had uncovered, which implicated the Japanese government in the wartime system of enforced prostitution.[129] This documentary evidence prompted the Japanese government to finally acknowledge the state's role in the system. The next day, Katō Kōichi publicly acknowledged the military's participation in its organization. On January 17, during an official state visit to South Korea, Prime Minister Miyazawa Kiichi apologized to the Korean people for the "comfort women" issue.[130]

In Korea over the course of 1992–93, public support for the surviving women grew. In response to claims from some Japanese that the women participating in the trial were only seeking money, some Koreans decided that rather than the women having to accept Japanese funds, they would instead raise money from Koreans to support survivors, and they gathered US$250,000 in a relatively short time.[131] The Buddhist Committee for Human Rights in Korea funded a House of Sharing, providing a home for six survivors.[132] In April 1993, the Korean government also agreed to make a onetime payment of US$6,250 and a monthly subsidy of US$1,890 to survivors, in addition to providing food and medical support.[133]

International Advocacy and Support for Survivors

Since it was established in 1990, in addition to playing a major role in keeping the issue of the "comfort women" in the public eye in Korea and Japan, the Korean Council has advocated on this issue in international fora. In March 1992, Hyo Lee-Chae, cofounder of the Korean Council, petitioned the United Nations Human Rights Office of the High Commissioner (OHCHR) to investigate atrocities against Korean women during the war and pressure the Japanese government to pay compensation in a suit that was being prepared (see later discussion). At a meeting in Geneva in August 1992, members of the Korean Council together with a survivor testified to the OHCHR. This resulted in a statement from its Sub-Commission on Prevention of Discrimination and Protection of Minorities, that "the system" was a "crime against humanity that violated the rights of Asian women and the international agreement prohibiting forced labor that Japan signed in 1932."[134]

In the same month, feminists from Japan, Korea, the Philippines, Thailand, and Taiwan formed the Asian Women's Solidarity Forum, and the Korean Council hosted their first conference in Seoul. The conference focused on connecting militarism, patriarchy, war, and abuses of women's human rights.[135] A second conference was hosted a year later in Japan.

In May 1992, the Korean government opened a fact-finding investigation titled Committee on the Damage of the Japanese Imperialists during Their Occupation of Korea.[136] The Korean vice premier and minister for Foreign

Affairs at the time, Kim Yong Nam, presented the committee's findings to the United Nations in August 1993. They requested UN assistance to clarify the truth about the "comfort women" and to find a solution to the issue of compensation and damages.[137] This contributed to the formulation of the UN Declaration on the Elimination of Violence against Women (see chapter 6).

Meanwhile, Kim Hak-Sun's class action and the Japanese government's ensuing apology sparked further activism in Korea and Japan. Japanese feminists continued to work closely with Korean feminists on research and advocacy, especially through the Asian Women's Association.[138] Historians, activists, and lawyers joined together to host the International Public Hearing on Japan's Postwar Compensation in December 1992, inviting numerous delegations to attend. This hearing included testimony from six former "comfort women" and four former forced laborers.[139] At the public hearing, Murayama Akira from the JFBA's Human Rights Committee explained that there was an urgent need to make clear the damage Japan had inflicted throughout the war and seriously address compensation because "along with the increasing awareness of human rights, international public opinion has come to expect postwar compensation of the individual."[140] Immediately after the hearing, the JFBA held an international human rights seminar on the theme of "War and Human Rights—Legal Analysis of Postwar Reparations," initiating a broad investigation into wartime victims.[141]

The JFBA subsequently conducted investigations in most countries affected by the war, including those formerly occupied and from which POWs were taken. This included China, North Korea, South Korea, Taiwan, the Philippines, Hong Kong, Malaysia, Singapore, Australia, and Indonesia.[142] An investigation team, consisting of one to five members, was sent to each country. The JFBA aimed to document the number of victims in these countries but, most crucially, to hear directly from the victims and their supporters to learn what had been done so far.[143] Through this pathway, Japanese activists first came into contact with Indonesian survivors (see chapter 7).

In April 1993, some Japanese supporters of the 1992 hearings established the Center for Research and Documentation of Japan's War Responsibility, focusing on the wartime victimization of Asian people. The supporters included researchers, lawyers, and citizen activists committed to addressing Japan's war responsibility.[144] The center published its research findings in August 1993, and the following month its members founded a journal called *Sensō Sekinin Kenkyū* (Research on Japan's War Responsibility).[145] Members claim that their initial report was instrumental in prompting the 1993 Kōno Statement.[146] The center collaborated with the Korean Council to share research findings.[147] Yoshimi

Yoshiaki was a key figure in the center, and he was joined by other concerned researchers, such as Kawada Fumiko, who continued to research this issue independently.

In the early 1990s, the "comfort women" issue seemed to strike a particular chord with the Japanese and Koreans in a way it had not in the 1970s, when the first survivor accounts were made public. Multiple developments in these societies over the decades led to the creation of an increasingly supportive environment for a movement of redress for survivors. Vera Mackie has characterized the 1990s as a time when the broader discursive context was shifting globally in relation to sexual violence.[148] Carol Gluck highlights how particular developments such as the end of the Cold War and the death of Emperor Hirohito, which she calls the "chronopolitics" of memory, aligned in this period.[149] This created a break from the past in Japan and an opportunity for reevaluations of the war.

More broadly, the end of the Cold War stimulated the opening up of human rights abuses, which had been swept under the rug in the interests of Cold War alliances. The sense of a new historical era is reflected in the comments made by Arai Shinichi, chair of the International Public Hearing on Japan's Postwar Compensation in 1992: "Today all countries of the world are trying to build a new, peaceful world order. In this effort of ours, we must pay greater attention to the importance of human rights. The creation of a new world order will depend on our awareness of the importance of human rights."[150] Arai stressed that the Japanese response to this issue would be an indicator of the extent to which Japan embraced democratic principles.

Conclusion

In the 1980s and 1990s, evolving relationships between Japanese and Korean advocates and the support they offered for survivors were critical to the development of activism. There were multiple roads to activism, first through the work of lawyers from the JFBA on cases of wartime redress for Koreans. The feminist road to activism was connected with a new emphasis on people's history and the history of women who were formerly *karayukisan*, which opened up a space for the life stories of Korean survivors still residing in Japan to be heard from the first time. Japanese feminists' new anti-imperial critiques of women's position in the war connected the work of Korean and Japanese women's activists. They shared critiques of contemporary Japanese sex tourism to Korea and the sexual violence around military bases in both countries, usually committed by US soldiers.

Korea's road to advocacy was informed not only by the Minjung movement and related critiques of militarism and military bases but also by the direction of women's activism, which included opposition to sexual violence. In Korea the first research was propelled by a new emphasis on women's studies at Ewha University. In 1991 Kim Hak-Sun's personal bravery to share her story publicly shone a global spotlight on survivors. Her testimony was the catalyst for other women to speak out, including one Indonesian woman, but with markedly different results. In the next chapter, I analyze media responses to this Indonesian woman's testimony and the attempts of Korean activists and journalists to push Indonesian survivors to come forward.

The Early 1990s

Indonesian Media Reporting on Korean Activism and Indonesian Survivors

In 1992, some of the first Indonesian media reports on the "comfort women" carried statements from two Indonesian men who worked in an *ianjo* in Manado, Sulawesi. They recounted how after promising to send women to sewing school the Japanese "rounded up about one hundred women, all under twenty years old," placed them in ten houses and "then erected fences around the housing complex." The men commented that the women were paid and their health was protected. They also revealed that any woman who tried to escape would be returned and that the "boarding house" was known as Mahakeret—in local language meaning "to scream"—because locals frequently heard women's screams coming from the complex.[1] The inconsistencies in this article are typical of early Indonesian reporting on this issue and reflect a lack of critical questioning around this case of historical injustice.

As explained in chapter 5, new awareness about histories of debt bondage and historical and contemporary Japanese exploitation of Korean people gave rise to new framings of the issue and different channels of activism in other countries, which intersected with broader considerations of wartime redress. This chapter returns to the context of Indonesia in the early 1990s, as Kim Hak-Sun's story triggered global attention to the issue of "comfort women." I compare the Indonesian situation with that in Korea and Japan and examine how Indonesians responded to Korean activism and the factors that constrained activism on this issue domestically.

By the early 1990s, unlike South Korea, which was experiencing democratization, Indonesians still lived under a military regime. Despite ongoing patterns of military abuse in Indonesia, there was almost complete impunity for human rights crimes and limited tolerance for human rights activism. Other key differences between Korea and Indonesia were the lack of a comparable critique of Japan's place in the global order among democracy activists, limited public critique of the culture of militarism, and limited activism against gendered violence. Each limiting factor was the result of particular developments reaching back to the 1965 violence in particular and the subsequent rise of the New Order regime. In turn, this impacted on the development of women's activism and class consciousness, including the topics chosen by Indonesian historians for investigation. Of particular note here are the New Order regime's violent repression of militant women and its promotion of a conservative gender ideology, which slowed the development of women's studies programs in its universities. I consider each factor to assess how they obscured the larger context of the "comfort women" issue in Indonesia.

I examine the how in the early 1990s, the Indonesian media reported on the emerging activism by and on behalf of "comfort women." Through their reporting on global developments, Indonesian journalists played a key role in drawing attention to this issue at home. Through interviews with former soldiers, witnesses, and women survivors, journalists began to open up Indonesian experiences of this system, which they considered hitherto hidden. I analyze how Indonesian journalists framed the story; how they positioned Indonesian survivors; and how they reported on sexual violence.

Indonesia in the Early 1990s: Constraints on Activism

When comparing activism in Indonesia to that of South Korea and Japan in the early 1990s, it is important to first consider how the social and political contexts differed. President Suharto was in his third decade of rule, with little sign of the New Order regime (1966–98) weakening. As discussed in chapter 4, Suharto was a former military general who had risen to power in the mid-1960s through his role in directing the mass killings and imprisonment of Indonesians on the political left and sidelining Sukarno. The destruction of the Indonesian left muted what had once been strident criticism of global fascism, the Japanese wartime regime, and rising militarization during the Cold War. The core ideological rallying points of the New Order regime were anticommunism, development, and stability.[2] In this way the regime's ideology paralleled that of the South Korean regimes of Park Chung-hee (1963–79) and Chun Doo-hwan (1980–88), noted in chapter 5. The Indonesian army, however, marked a dual social and political role for itself, whereby many men of military background also served in the government. Combined with censorship, this meant that open critique of the military was difficult. Suharto repeatedly used the army to crush dissent. This process began with the 1965–66 genocide against the Indonesian left and extended to the repression of regional separatist movements. Beginning with the Indonesian invasion of East Timor in 1975, the military violently repressed opposition here and in other provinces.[3] In its attacks on all forms of dissent, the military repeatedly used sexual violence against women as a means of terror and intimidation.[4]

Indonesian women activists and historians have pointed to the long-lasting effects of military-led attacks from 1965 onward on politicized women in the leftist organization Gerwani (Gerakan Wanita Indonesia, Indonesian Women's Movement) and on the development of women's political activism more broadly. Feminist activist and writer Ruth Indiah Rahayu argues that the nature of this violence produced fear in circles of women's activists for decades.[5]

Gerwani (1954–65) brought together women with a range of activist commitments, including nationalism, feminism, and socialism. The organization became increasingly popular due to its efforts to support poorer working women by establishing kindergartens, running cooperatives, conducting literacy campaigns, training women as leaders, and campaigning for women's labor rights.[6] They also challenged child marriage and polygamy. Gerwani members wrote about the history of the women's movement and the various forms of suffering Indonesian women faced, including domestic and military violence. In the 1950s, Gerwani Vice Secretary-General Sulami published a three-part article on the history of the women's movement in an international publication of the Women's International Democratic Federation. The article included specific mentions of sexual violence against women as a feature of the Japanese occupation.[7]

It is important to acknowledge this historical referencing of sexual violence during the occupation to counter any suggestion that Indonesian women's activism lagged behind Korean or Japanese activism. Instead, as I will show, this activism was forcibly derailed due to the destruction of the Indonesian left after 1965. Like Japanese women in the 1970s, in the 1950s Gerwani members were critically evaluating the history of the women's movement. They were similarly alert to and actively monitoring militarism around the world.[8]

Through their activism, they connected with women across the world, including those in the Netherlands, China, Korea, and Japan who linked women's oppression to its broader structural causes, such as colonialism, militarism, and economic exploitation.[9] From the late 1950s through the early 1960s, due to their work at home with women across all classes, and along with its international reach, Gerwani experienced rapid growth in its membership. It went from having 100,000 members in 1957 to 700,000 in 1960 and 1.5 million in 1963, with branches in every province of Indonesia and subbranches in 40 percent of villages.[10]

In the 1965–68 genocide, the military targeted Gerwani members for persecution. In an elaborate propaganda campaign directed at them, the women were demonized as immoral and accused of sexually torturing six military generals killed in the September 30 movement. This campaign resulted in a lasting stigma attached to politicized women, even to now.[11] The regime singled out Gerwani members for brutal treatment, including widespread sexual violence and torture in addition to murder, imprisonment, and forced labor.[12] The consequent destruction of Gerwani spelled an end to progressive women's activism based on the critique of structural inequities and global processes such as militarization and capitalism. This persecution deterred some women from taking a more political approach.[13]

After coming to power in 1966, Suharto's New Order government tightened its control of the women's movement and promoted an extremely conservative gender ideology. Similar to the anticommunist military governments of South Korea that mobilized the values of Confucian capitalism, the military dominated Indonesian government focused on rapid economic development. Women's voluntary or low-paid labor was seen as integral to achieving this goal. The New Order was represented as a family state, which built its legitimacy on patriarchal ideology according to which the *bapak* (father), meaning President Suharto, was in charge.[14] The regime's approach to women was to view them as part of the masses to be co-opted and controlled.

Women were controlled through a variety of state development programs, such as the family planning and family education schemes, Family Planning (*Keluarga Berencana*) and Family Welfare Education (Pendidikan Kesejahteraan Keluarga). The 1992 National Guidelines of State Policy (Garis Besar Haluan Negara) set out the primary role of Indonesian women as that of mother.[15] Feminist writer Julia Suryakusuma used the term *ibu*, meaning older women and mother, to describe the New Order's gender ideology as "state *ibuism*," arguing that in this system women were prescribed the primary roles of being housewives and mothers.[16] The state ideology promoted the middle-class wife as ideal, ignoring the reality that most Indonesian women worked both inside and outside the home.[17]

The New Order government paid lip service to women's issues largely because of international pressure and global developments. In 1978, a Ministry for Women's Affairs was established, and in 1980 the government ratified the 1979 UN Convention on the Elimination of Discrimination against Women

(CEDAW), while rejecting any international oversight into its implementation. In 1993, Nori Andriyani observed that these ratifications appeared to be part of an effort to project an impression of making progress on women's rights to align to the emphasis in international aid agencies on women's position as a measure of the "quality and success of development" at that time.[18] She pointed out that there was in fact very little effort made to implement the principles of CEDAW. Nonetheless, CEDAW did provide an international mechanism for Indonesian women to engage with for lobbying the government.

History Writing and the Invisibility of Marginalized Women

In Japan, the histories of *karayukisan*, the product of new attention to minorities and social difference, contributed to opening up the issue of militarized sexual abuse. There were no such comparable trends in Indonesian history writing in the postwar period. After formally achieving independence in 1949, most Indonesian historians committed to writing Indonesia-centric history or history for nation-building.[19] This led to a strong focus on histories of revolutionary heroes who had struggled against the Dutch, for example. During the period of Guided Democracy (1959–65) which saw the promotion of socialist values, historians paid greater attention to the everyday or ordinary person. These works tended to document the histories of categories of people, such as working-class involvement in particular events, rather than the life stories of specific workers.[20] The first histories to pay attention to women emerged in the late 1970s and 1980s. One trend in these new histories was to document the roles of women in the national revolution.[21]

Up to the 1990s, the subjects of and ways Indonesian history was being written served to further obscure the histories of largely lower-class women who were victimized during the Japanese occupation. Rahayu points out that Indonesian historiography is not only male-centered but also has a colonial *pribumi* focus, by which she means that writing that does consider women focuses on elite Dutch educated women or those who organized the first women's congress in 1928. The exemplar of this cohort of women is Raden Adjeng Kartini (1879–1904) the daughter of a Javanese aristocrat and colonial official, who became famous largely because of the letters she wrote to progressive Dutch women, which were later translated into Indonesian. Rahayu explains that when at last the drive to write new feminist histories began in the 1990s, it focused on documenting the women's movement, which again meant a focus on elite histories.[22] This raises questions about how lower-class Indonesian women were viewed in historical accounts and whether historians even considered them worthy historical subjects.

In the 1970s and 1980s, a historian from the University of Gadjah Mada, Sartono Kartodirdjo, pioneered new research into working-class Indonesians. Based on his thesis on a peasant revolt in the colonial era,[23] Kartodirdjo's work inspired other research on peasants and the histories of villages, but a strong focus on the Dutch colonial period remained and therefore a reliance on Dutch colonial records.[24]

Oral history was first used in Indonesia in the 1970s by the state, largely for recording the historical experiences of Indonesian elites of key periods, including a study conducted in the 1980s on experiences of the Japanese occupation.[25] No "comfort women" were interviewed for this project. It was not until the late 1990s that independent researchers began to use oral history to unearth the stories of more marginalized historical subjects, particularly victims of the 1965 genocide.[26] One reason for this relatively slow start were the dangers associated with conducting research on topics like this. While the end of the Suharto regime in 1998 made research into the genocide and other cases of human rights abuses more possible, a movement in Indonesia akin to that in Japan, researching the histories of lower-class women including former "comfort women," did not emerge.

There were multiple reasons for the lack of Indonesian research on "comfort women" until the 1990s. As discussed in chapter 5, the development of women's and gender studies programs at Japanese and Korean universities in the 1970s and 1980s, underpinned by women's activism, was crucial for generating critical research into histories of gendered violence, contemporary gender relations, sexual violence, and sexual exploitation in these societies. In Indonesia, the first women's studies program was established at the University of Gadjah Mada in 1991 and then at the University of Indonesia in 1992. This is nearly two decades behind such programs in Japan and Korea. It took another three years for the program at the University of Indonesia to develop a curriculum.[27] This means that at the time the "comfort women" issue was escalating internationally in the early 1990s, these programs could not yet have had significant societal effect.

The founder of the women's studies program at the University of Indonesia, Saparinah Sadli, admits that because the conservative military regime was still in power when it was established, they were very cautious. This included eschewing the term "feminist" so as "to avoid unnecessary irritation within the academic community at the university."[28] Their work was concentrated on policy objectives and improving the rights of working women versus a more direct focus on violence against women, including state and military violence or the structural causes of gender discrimination.

Indonesian Women's Advocacy around Women's Rights

Beginning in the late 1980s and early 1990s, more women's organizations began to focus on defending women's rights and promoting feminist critiques of existing gender relations. In 1985 a group of women in Jakarta established Kalyanamitra (Women's Communication and Information Center). The secular organization focused its advocacy on exposing gender discrimination in government development programs.[29] Kalyanamitra attempted to counter New Order gender ideology, working on issues such as military coercion, lack of consent in the government's family planning program, and sexual harassment. In the early 1990s they began to provide training on issues such as gender equality and gender relations.[30] According to a former member, the organization faced resistance from some sections of society in relation to its discussions of domestic violence and objections from the state to discussions of state violence against women.[31] An example of organizations advocating on women's issues at the micro- or local level, is the group Gerakan Kesadaran Wanita (Movement of Conscious Women). The organization was formed in 1987 by women in Salatiga, Central Java, to protest in solidarity with a victim of domestic violence who was prosecuted after killing her abusive husband.[32] In 1990, another national secular organization, Solidaritas Perempuan (Women's Solidarity) was founded with a focus on Indonesian overseas domestic workers, including violence against these women.[33] Following its founding in 1995, the Indonesian Women's Association for Justice and Legal Aid legal Aid (Lembaga Bantuan Hukum, Asosiasi Perempuan Indonesia untuk Keadilan, LBH APIK), also set up women's crisis centers across Indonesia.[34]

At this time, women's groups with a religious basis began to focus on the issue of violence against women. The Islamic feminist group Rifka Annisa, founded in Yogyakarta in 1993, focused its work on domestic violence, refuting religious justifications for such violence. It established its own women's crisis center in the same city.[35] The Christian umbrella organization Network of Aware Women (Perserikatan Kelompok Perempuan Sadar, PKPS) used a theological approach to draw attention to the plight of female victims of violence.[36] PKPS worked with international networks, such as the Women's Commission of the Ecumenical Association of Third World Theologians and the

Asian Women and Culture Movement. These organizations began to commemorate November 25 as the international day of opposition to violence against women.[37]

As discussed in chapter 5, in South Korea women workers were crucial to the democratization movement and to raising awareness of violence against women. Throughout the 1980s, in Indonesia female factory workers were increasingly used as a cheap source of labor, yet only a very small number of women joined unions to protect their rights.[38] In 1982, in response to violence against women workers, women formed the advocacy organization Yayasan Anisa Swasti (YASANTI), named after a female worker who was sexually assaulted.[39] YASANTI members advocated for the rights of women factory workers and the economic rights of rural women.

The organizations mentioned here all worked in a difficult political and social environment. However, women activists who confronted the military or police faced even greater risks. In a climate of impunity, the military remained undeterred from using violence against politically active women. In May 1993, a female labor activist was murdered. Marsinah had joined a protest over low wages at the watch factory where she worked in Sidoarjdo, East Java.[40] The owners of the factory, PT Catur Pura Surya, called in the local military to handle the dispute. It was strongly suspected they played a role in Marsinah's killing. She had gone to the military headquarters to find out what happened to her fellow protesters. Marsinah died from internal injuries sustained through rape by a metal object that was repeatedly forced into her vagina.[41] To deflect from military culpability, nine people were arrested in connection with her murder, and it was presented as a criminal case. The suspects were tortured and forced to confess to killing and raping her. Marsinah's case raised the profile of the issue of violence against factory workers and union organizers and led to national and international condemnation.

Compared with national women's movements elsewhere in Asia, including in the neighboring Philippines, Indonesian women activists were not well connected to international networks. In part this was due to the depoliticization of the women's movement since 1965. It was also likely attributable to language issues and Filipinos' relative fluency in English.[42] Moreover, unlike the Korean, Japanese, and Filipino women's movements, the Indonesian women activists did not yet have a significant voice in emerging global debates. One such debate, in which Korean and Japanese women were deeply involved, concerned whether prostitution constituted violence against women or work. Women activists from Japan, Korea, and the Philippines tended to side with the view that prostitution constituted violence against women.[43] This view was informed by a number of factors but most significantly, the strong condemnation of Japanese sex tourism to Korea and the Philippines and the long-term presence of foreign military bases within their borders, as discussed in chapter 5.

By contrast, Indonesia did not host foreign military bases, and there was not the same trend of Indonesian women traveling to Japan to participate in sex work or entertainment. Nor was there an influx of Japanese sex tourists to Indonesia on the scale seen in Korea and the Philippines. In the early 1990s, Indonesia's sex industry was not as heavily reliant on either foreign tourists or foreign soldiers.[44] The government's overall attitude to sex work was one of toleration and attempts to control the industry.[45]

In the early 1990s, some local women's organizations began to take up cases of military violence against women in the disputed provinces. In the context of the separatist movement in the province of Aceh, for example, Flower Aceh, established in 1989, focused on issues of discrimination, including violence against women.[46] In general, however, in the early 1990s women's organizations were reluctant to discuss "military rape and the gendered effects of war and communal violence on women."[47] The lack of more widespread critique of the military at the time is directly related to the antisubversion law then in place, according to which Indonesians could be charged with the death penalty for criticizing the government or its institutions. Although the tide was beginning to change in the early to mid-1990s, compared with women's activism in Korea and Japan, activists in Indonesia were not yet united in their approaches to tackling sexual violence against women and the broader structural connections between domestic and military violence.

The years between 1989 and 1994 represented a turning point in the rule of the decades-old New Order regime. A series of changes shifted the degree of control the government exerted over the media and public debate in what was termed a period of *keterbukaan* or openness.[48] In practice, it meant an emboldened media more willing and able to openly and critically discuss government policy and issues like human rights and democratization.[49] Key triggers for increased attention to human rights were a series of incidents of military violence, including the killing of civilians in Lampung in 1989 and the December 1991 Dili massacre in East Timor. The latter killings, in which the army shot and killed two hundred people during a peaceful protest in Dili, were captured on video by British journalist Max Stahl and broadcast to the world's media, placing the Suharto regime under increased international pressure, especially from aid donors including the United States and Japan. In a very rare exception to the usual impunity the military enjoyed, some soldiers involved in the killings were punished (albeit not severely), and the Suharto government went so far as to admit that Indonesia faced human rights challenges.[50] In June 1993, the government established the Indonesian Human Rights Commission (Komnas HAM).[51] The commission provided legitimation of the discourse of human rights in Indonesia and to the surprise of many, appeared steadfastly independent and willing to take on controversial cases.[52] While the commission was given a broad mandate to address human rights, it did not yet have a particular focus on gender-related issues. Though it ended abruptly in June 1994, this period of openness may have contributed to *Tempo*'s bold coverage on "comfort women" in 1992 and 1993.

Indonesian Media Responses to Developments in Korea and Japan

Carol Gluck contends that in global terms, the role of the media was crucial for "generating the activism" on the issue of the "comfort women."[53] The first steps involved sharing the views and accounts of survivors, followed by coverage of the subsequent Japanese government response. This process began in late 1991 when, as explained in chapter 5, Kim Hak-Sun testified in a court case brought against the Japanese government, which introduced a new framing around the issue. Japanese sociologist Ueno Chizuko suggests that "when former comfort women testified as victims, a forgotten past was recovered for the first time as a distinct, different reality. History was made anew by this act. And, after fifty years, a 'retrial' of that history has now become possible."[54] This process of making history "anew" and of survivors reconceptualizing themselves as "victims" via testimony was not, however, an immediate or universal one. Many women chose to remain silent, and not all media reporting on this testimony was immediately sympathetic. Moreover, survivors were not alone in presenting their views on this history. Some in Japanese society and the societies where survivors lived continued to blame the women for their experiences and view them as shameful. Instead, evolving narratives reveal evidence of a gradual but not universal or complete shift toward reconceptualizing the women's experiences.

The Case of *Tempo*'s Special Coverage

Throughout 1992 and 1993, the Indonesian magazine *Tempo* followed the story of the "comfort women" in Japan and Korea closely.[55] An analysis of this reporting offers one way of gauging Indonesian views about the topic. Although this is not a comprehensive survey of Indonesian media, nor of public opinion, it provides some insights into how the issue was presented to the public by what was then Indonesia's preeminent news magazine.

Tempo was founded in 1971 by former student activists who had aligned themselves with the army in late 1965 and supported the banning and subsequent attacks on the Indonesian left that helped bring an end to President Sukarno's rule.[56] Its editors were connected with New Order leaders, which provided them with a certain level of protection from media censorship and surveillance of reporting that criticized the government.[57] Nonetheless *Tempo*, like other publications at the time, was very aware of the need to carefully navigate the regime's censorship regulations.

Tempo was known for its in-depth investigative reporting, and its editorial content regularly highlighted issues of justice and the plight of victims of injustice.[58] The magazine's focus on the "comfort women" in the early 1990s was in many ways groundbreaking in Indonesia. *Tempo*'s reports, translated and published elsewhere, constituted a singular reference for most commentary and writing on this issue for some time.[59] As I will show, however, its framings of this issue suggest that understandings of gender-based injustice among its journalist and editorial team were limited. Below I consider how Indonesian journalists reported on and positioned survivors in their reportage.

Tempo's readership was mostly middle class, and it is estimated that around 86 percent of the readership in 1992 and 1993 was male.[60] Most of the journalists reporting on the "comfort women"—generally poor Indonesian women who had rarely been the subject of historical inquiries—were, like their readers, middle-class men. They also employed foreign correspondents. Ōkawa Seiichi, a graduate of Waseda University, worked as the Japanese correspondent for *Tempo* starting in 1982.[61] Ōkawa cowrote many of *Tempo*'s articles on the "comfort women" together with Indonesian journalists.

Tempo's early reports focused on the issue of Japanese responsibility and the emergence of Kim Hak-Sun as spokesperson for surviving women. In January 1992, *Tempo* ran a short piece with the headline "Miyazawa Says Sorry."[62] This article, jointly written by Ōkawa and a second journalist only attributed with initials ADN, outlined the court case in which Kim participated, mentioning the three women who were forced to become "comfort women." The romanized Japanese term *jugun ianfu*, which is translated in the article as "special prostitutes of the Japanese army," is used throughout. The story reported on a press conference in which Kim gave an account of her experience of being taken from Pyongyang to North China at age seventeen. There she was forced to "serve" three hundred soldiers and threatened with death if she tried to escape.[63]

The story features a photo of Kim. She is shown standing on a street wearing a white *hanbok* with other women protesting the visit of Japanese Prime Minister Miyazawa Kiichi to South Korea. Her fist is raised in the air. This photograph may have been supplied by her support group or taken by other reporters, and it positions Kim as an activist survivor. Use of this image, together with detail from Kim's shocking testimony, is in tension with the overall emphasis of the article, which positions the issue as one to be negotiated between governments, rather than highlighting its importance for survivors.

The article leads with the public apology of Prime Minister Miyazawa to the "comfort women" during his visit to South Korea and quotes Kim's response that an apology on its own was insufficient and that some form of compensation for victims was necessary. The authors wonder at the feasibility of such claims, as the larger problem, they opined, was that "many other *countries* (*negara*) in Asia had suffered the same fate" (emphasis added). They posed the question: "would Indonesia [not surviving women] also put forward a case?"[64] Their choice of language signaled an emphasis on "nations" as the harmed parties, reflecting "a patriarchal logic" that the state owns the individual and women's sexuality.[65]

Reports on Indonesian Survivors

By July 1992, international media coverage, and *Tempo*'s reporting on the "comfort women" issue at home was intensifying due to the Japanese government's acknowledgment that the Japanese military was officially involved in recruiting women from across Asia into the system. Media outlets approached government officials from the region for comments. The governments of North and South Korea, the Philippines, and Taiwan, in particular, made clear their expectations that the Japanese government should address the issue and pay compensation. When one Indonesian lawmaker called for Indonesia to join this protest to the Japanese government, the Defense Minister, General Benny Murdani, made a cautious statement about the need for more information regarding Indonesian women being forced into the system.[66] At the same time, Foreign Affairs Minister Ali Alatas stated that "the moral violation against the honor of those who have been recruited as comfort women by the Japanese army cannot simply be forgotten."[67]

Days after these conflicting comments from Indonesian government officials, in July 1992, the first Indonesian woman, Tuminah of Solo, came forward to publicly testify. Tuminah shared her story with Japanese theologian Kimura Kōichi, who worked in the Baptist Theological Seminary in Central Java. Her story was published with her permission on July 17 by her nephew, a journalist working at the Semarang-based newspaper *Suara Merdeka*. It also appeared the next day in the national daily *Kompas*.[68] At the time she gave her initial testimony, Tuminah was interested in claiming compensation and potentially pursuing a case through Japanese courts.[69] This was the first time an Indonesian survivor had broken her silence on this topic; however, her testimony triggered no responses from nongovernmental organizations or the Indonesian government, nor was she interviewed by *Tempo* for their series of articles on "comfort women."

In late July 1992, barely a week after Tuminah went public with her story, *Tempo* published a special report on the "comfort women," featuring six articles following further developments in Japan and Korea. The anachronistic image accompanying the lead article in the series featured a reproduction of an 1862 wood-block print by Utagawa Hiroshige II, set in a licensed district of Edo (the former name for Tokyo). The scene depicts Japanese geisha, wearing heavy makeup and dressed in kimono, walking in a garden beneath cherry blossom trees.[70] This image conveys what are widely regarded as exoticized views of Japanese women and culture. The geisha has long been an object of fascination for foreign men, as exemplified in Giacomo Puccini's opera *Madama Butterfly* and in Arthur Golden's popular novel *Memoirs of a Geisha*.[71]

The lead article uses as its title the aforementioned controversial Japanese term for the women, *jugun ianfu*. Author Bambang Bujono, then also a senior editor, reflects on the differences and similarities between wartime and peacetime prostitutes (using here the derogatory word *pelacur*) and the issue of the forcible recruitment of women, noting the common occurrence of coercion and deceit of young women in both contexts.[72] Given the accompanying image, Bujono may have been referring to historical practices of the forced recruitment of Japanese women into sex work (see chapter 2).

Japan's Chief Cabinet Secretary, Katō Kōichi, had recently admitted that the military was involved in the system and in recruiting women, while also denying that the women were forced to do so.[73] Bujono responded to this statement noting that it was difficult to accept the Japanese government's view that all women freely volunteered, given that "the Japanese military had it all[,] including power, weapons and sexual needs due to the pressures of war."[74] On one hand, the journalist recognized the power differences between armed soldiers and civilian women in an occupied territory; on the other hand, he replicated stereotypical ideas about the sexual needs of soldiers in wartime.

Another article in this edition, "Japan Can No Longer Avoid It," cowritten by Ōkawa Seiichi and Didi Prambada, emphasized Japanese responsibility. The article updated readers on the ongoing struggle of Korean women to *meluruskan sejarah* (straighten out history) as the authors described it. It included discussion of the second court case in 1992 in Tokyo brought by nine Korean women against the government of Japan under the guidance of Takagi Ken'ichi.[75] The authors noted that one of the seventy-year-old claimants, who went by the pseudonym Kaneda Kimiko, wore a wig and sunglasses to the trial so she would not be easily recognized. They directly quoted Kaneda's explanation that "if she was recognized by workmates she might be forced to step down from her job due to shame."[76] The journalists acknowledged and conveyed to the reader the fear these women felt of being judged by others and discrimination if they were identified.

The article referenced a statement from Indonesia's Minister for the State Secretariat, Moerdiono, who proclaimed, "we want to forget the past."[77] Given the government's position, the authors concluded, "it seems that if Indonesian women or others want to pursue compensation they will have to take the path followed by Korean women."[78] This was a curious conclusion to make, considering that by July 1992, only Tuminah had identified herself to the media (a report *Tempo* had not yet covered), raising little public response. Early signs indicated that the success of such a process, barely started in Indonesia, seemed highly unlikely.

Although Tuminah's account was not included, the July 1992 edition was the first in which *Tempo* featured some form of testimony from surviving women. Rather than being the main focus of the articles, however, the women's testimony was interspersed with other commentary. One article in the special edition featured comments from Major General Slamet Danusudirdjo, author of *Kadarwati*, the fictional novel discussed in chapter 4.[79] Its writers, Sri Indrayati and Ōkawa Seiichi, referred to the Japanese documents Yoshimi Yoshiaki had uncovered detailing the operation of *ianjo* in the Netherlands East Indies. In passing, they recorded the stories of a former Indonesian sex worker Ngairah, who was forced to work for the Japanese in a hotel, and Malaysian Chinese woman Since Kew, who with nine other women was sent to Halmahera Island in eastern Indonesia. After the war ended, they wrote, Since Kew was too ashamed to return home. Indrayati and Ōkawa acknowledge that it was not easy for women to come forward because they, like Korean women, "tended to hide these stories and pass them off as jokes so as not to shame their families" (*mereka ini memendam cerita sampai mereka hanya sebatang kara, agar tak membuat malu keluarga*).[80] When writing about what the women were required to do once they were detained by the Japanese military, the authors adopted the term the women used in their testimony, *melayani*, literally meaning "to serve men," which is commonly used to refer to having sex. The term implies volition, however, and the authors notably avoided using the more direct term "rape" (*perkosaan*).[81] Another article in this edition, by Prambadi and Krishna, reporting largely on the experiences of Dutch women as detailed in Dutch archives, again used the term *melayani* to describe the role these women carried out.[82] This is a deliberate softening of the experiences of sexual violence, which implies discomfort about calling out or naming sexual violence.

In August 1992, *Tempo* published two long articles on the "comfort women" issue. This time, they featured testimony from several Indonesian women. Once again, the accounts were mediated by including commentary from other witnesses to the system, including Indonesian and Japanese men who had worked in or gone to *ianjo*.[83] The editor explained that a team of fourteen journalists from Ujung Pandang, Toraja, and Manado in Sulawesi; Medan in North Sumatra; and Bali and East Kalimantan had "tried to track down" former "comfort women."[84] The journalists recounted how, in response to their investigations and requests for interviews, many women were reticent to talk to them or give their names, let alone make public claims for redress.

The first of these articles, researched by a team of writers but with a byline for Ōkawa and Indonesian journalist Bunga Surawijaya, was sensationally titled "Screams from the Bamboo Hut."[85] The authors explained that their informant, a seventy-year-old survivor in Pangkalpinang, Bangka Island, unlike Korean women, "did not want to loudly protest against the government of Japan and ask for compensation." Observing that it was not easy to ask her to recount her experiences of Japanese brutality, they said, "it was not that she had forgotten, but she did not know why she should talk about her experiences, when it could all make her grandchildren ashamed. When finally, she told of her experiences, she requested that we not use her real name."[86] What is remarkable is that despite noting the woman's protests and obvious discomfort, the journalists proceeded to relate her story. Moreover, despite asking not to be identified by her real name, they identified her by the Japanese name—Fumiko—she was given during the occupation. Surawijaya and Ōkawa were not alone in taking this approach in their reporting.

Their initial description of "Fumiko's" appearance focused on a photo of her at twenty years old. The description was overtly sexualized, as having "a small body, but a pronounced bottom and breasts," so as to assist the readers' imaginations and provide titillation.

They went on to narrate her story. One day, when she was twenty—the age depicted in the photo—and already a widow, Japanese soldiers picked her up from her house, near to a soldier's barracks. She was promised marriage, a trip to Tokyo, and adequate provisions for her struggling parents.[87] Instead, she was taken to a large house. She had almost given up hope when one day a soldier, who the authors describe as having "used her before," took her to live with him. She remained there until he returned home after Japan's defeat.[88]

Despite hearing from "Fumiko" directly about the circumstances she faced and her cruel choice to either continue to work in the bar or live with a man who had already abused her, the authors described the man as *kekasihnya*, "her loved one."[89] This problematic use of language conveys the confusion the journalists undoubtedly felt about how to talk with women about their experiences and how to write about them.

Because "Fumiko" ended up in such a relationship, Surawijaya and Ōkawa concede that her story "may perhaps not be that convincing in terms of her being forced to be a comfort woman."[90] Given that relatively few women had spoken out about their experiences as "comfort women" up to this point, it is interesting that there was already an impression of what was typical and thus a sense of an ideal story. The influence of Kim Hak-Sun's account is possibly one explanation. The journalists did, however, place Fumiko's wartime experiences in the context of her whole life, noting that she married after the war, had children and grandchildren, and she was very thankful for this. In doing so, they conveyed a sense of her life experiences beyond being a "comfort woman."[91]

The article juxtaposed stories from "Fumiko" and other women of their experiences of sexual violence, with other accounts about the system, including the views of people who deny that sexual violence took place. This included quotes about setting up *ianjo* taken from the 1975 memoir of Nogi Harumichi, a Japanese officer who had served in Ambon, eastern Indonesia.[92] In an attempt to deflect blame from the Japanese army, Nogi claims that the Japanese targeted women who were already working as sex workers or wanted to perform this work. However, there are inconsistencies in his account. As Surawijaya and Ōkawa note, Nogi also wrote that when the Japanese tried to move women to another location, they were met with protests from the locals. The article draws on accounts from two Indonesian men, Urbanus Tulus and Alex Lelengboto. They presented ambiguous accounts about the women and the extent to which they were victimized or well treated. Their testimony also revealed that "former members of the Korean and Taiwanese armies, even *heiho*" (who were serving as part of the Japanese army), also used *ianjo*.[93]

One of the most striking aspects of this article is that it also features comments from a former Japanese soldier. Taira Teizo became an Indonesian citizen after the war and Indonesianized his name. In his testimony to *Tempo*, he strongly rejected the claim that women were forced into the system. He admitted that there had been "comfort women," offering as proof the sordid expression *saya merasakan sendiri*, which literally means "I tasted the women myself." He explained that the Japanese army set up brothels everywhere on the basis that "they recognized men's biological needs."[94] Such comments parallel the relative openness in Japanese soldiers' memoirs about their wartime experiences. Former soldiers often narrate their experiences in a matter-of-fact way, with little sense of shame.[95] Taira insisted that women were not forced, but that "the women were recruited through announcements made by local officials."[96] Expressing no sympathy for the position of women who were held in these fenced compounds, he sought to normalize the experience. "Functions in these places with high gated fences usually began with drinks, as is our habit in Japan. Then after midnight those who wanted to continue the party took the comfort women to rooms . . . I really didn't see any force there. Everyone was laughing and singing because they were all drinking. I never knew of any women who were so stressed they committed suicide."[97] In using the phrase "as is our habit in Japan," Taira equates what happened in an *ianjo* with geisha parties in Japan, which typically begin with women serving men alcoholic drinks. He tried to normalize the experience, describing a partylike atmosphere. Taira focuses only on the public faces the women presented, assuming that if things were really so bad they had a choice to commit suicide. Including Taira's commentary without any rebuttal can only suggest that the journalists did not find his views problematic.

A former *heiho* soldier, Sulchan, was also interviewed for this article as a witness to the system. His comments were similar to Taira's. He maintained that if the women working in the Hotel City in Rembang, which functioned as a brothel during the occupation, were not all professional prostitutes, they were all there voluntarily. In his view the women just wanted to live well: "so they could eat bread and wear nice clothes." Adding, "as far as I know, there was no force. The lives of the *geisha* [his term] were more secure than those of most of the population."[98] As outlined in chapter 3, economic conditions had increasingly deteriorated throughout the occupation. Along with coercion and the threat of violence, this no doubt shaped the choices women made.

Another witness included in the article, Badar, was a seventy-five-year-old former guard who worked at a hotel in Denpasar during the occupation. He told *Tempo* that women were given half the payment the hotel received for each "guest," adding, "they could not refuse clients for fear of being killed."[99]

By including the views of multiple witnesses in this report, *Tempo* was following the journalistic practice of covering all sides of a story. What is noticeably absent from the reporting, however, is open condemnation of these forms of sexual abuse or any signaling of who might be to blame.

Following this article, a second story focused on women who lived with Japanese men during the occupation. This article, titled "They Had No Choice," put more emphasis on the issue of coercion.[100] The all-male team of Indonesian writers tells the reader that not all women "who fell at the feet of the Japanese army" in the system ended up in brothels. Some Japanese officers and leaders, they explain, "took women for themselves and protected them" (*ada saja pemimpin atau perwira Jepang yang lalu melindungi wanita itu untuk diri sendirinya*).[101] The choice of the words is revealing. The expression "fell at the feet" indicates that they became victimized, yet the use of "protected" implies patriarchal ideas of male protection. This is problematic given that the women were often forced or coerced into these relationships. Perhaps the journalists meant to convey that the women were protected from greater abuse, but this is not clear. Whatever the intention, it disguises the fact women were still subjected to sexual violence in those "relationships."

"They Had No Choice" profiles the experiences of two women from Central Java, two women from Toraja in Central Sulawesi, and one woman from Minahasa, North Sulawesi, all of whom lived with Japanese men during the occupation. Two of the women were picked out by Japanese men from their workplaces (a restaurant and factory) and forced to live with them. The two Torajan women were forced to legally marry Japanese men. As the article explained, all were too afraid to refuse the men. Lai Rapung explained that she was given an ultimatum: "if I refused, my father and I would have been beheaded."[102]

The language used in *Tempo*'s framing across its reporting on the "comfort women" noticeably lacked reference to human rights discourse. The issue was instead framed more cautiously as a possible case for redress with coverage of a wide range of views about the system. Human rights scholar Cheah Wui Ling reminds us that "patriarchal cultures and familial pressures" not only silenced women but also "failed to generate debate or feelings of injustice among the wider public for surviving women."[103] The sense of injustice is ambiguous because no blame is attributed to the soldiers or the Japanese army more broadly and the terms *kekerasan* (violence), *perkosaan* (rape), and *kekerasan seksual* are almost never used. Furthermore, there were no references to the spectrum of sexual violence women can experience, nor the cultures of militarism in which it is able to thrive.

Although some of *Tempo*'s reports depict the women as people who could demand restitution, the journalists did not condemn the behavior of soldiers or emphasize the specific rights of women violated in these cases. This may reflect the women's framing of their experiences and their reluctance to label the violence against themselves or to only refer to it indirectly because of shame. Hilde Janssen noted such patterns in the cases of survivors giving testimony to her.[104] Annie Pohlman has made similar observations about women victimized in the 1965 violence.[105] It may suggest that at this point, the women had not reframed or recognized their experiences within the language of human rights.[106] The journalists were aware that many women were reluctant to share their stories and understood the ongoing social stigma they faced. Nevertheless, they believed these stories should be investigated and exposed. Ultimately, therefore, the women were not portrayed as victims or survivors of the system; instead, they were treated as historical witnesses (*saski sejarah*) who could and should share their experiences for all. This returns us to the issue of how women of a particular class are viewed in Indonesia and the extent to which they were considered historical subjects or simply sources of information.

Conclusion

In Indonesia in the early 1990s, the political and social context was far less conducive to the development of activism than it was in South Korea. *Tempo* reported on emerging activism, and its journalists went in search of survivors. The accounts replicate the patterns of abuse of women detailed in archival sources, including stories of being taken from their homes with false promises, being forced into the system when engaged in other forms of work, and being forced to become wives or live-in partners for Japanese men. Reporting on this issue in Indonesia, however, reflected the lack of a broader critique of militarism and sexual violence.

Although domestically there was hesitation to present these as cases of human rights violations, internationally the "comfort women" issue was having ripple effects. The media reporting in Indonesia helped raised awareness of this issue, but efforts to more fully advocate for the women only began after a delegation of Japanese lawyers visited in 1993. The fact that activism did not develop organically in Indonesia reinforces the many constraints around this issue. In the next chapter, I turn to examining how Indonesian activism finally began in earnest.

7

The Japan Federation of Bar Associations and Escalating Indonesian Activism

> My motivation arose after I read the news in the paper, especially about the efforts of the advocates in Jakarta who were bravely defending our fates.
>
> Mardiyem, quoted in "Pengakuan Bekas Ianfu dari Yogya,"
> *Jawa Pos*, April 29, 1993

A key stimulus for Indonesian activism was a visit by a group of Japanese lawyers in 1993. The most iconic Indonesian survivor, Mardiyem, was moved to come forward after the lawyers began to ask about women's experiences in reconsidering Japanese responsibilities for war redress. As noted in the previous chapter, this was an important shift because until then Indonesian press reports had taken a cautious approach and generally fell short of describing the women as victims of human rights abuses. Condemnation of those responsible for the violence was also muted. Moreover, once they were published, the women's stories had attracted little public outcry or support from government officials.

In 1993 a group of Japanese lawyers from the Japan Federation of Bar Associations (JFBA) visited Indonesia on a fact-finding mission to document forms of wartime abuse, prompting unprecedented interest in the "comfort women" issue there. The visit led Indonesia's minister of Social Affairs to issue a call for victimized people to step forward. This opened the door for the YLBHI, which acts as a central coordinating organization for all legal aid (LBH) offices, to begin activism on behalf of the victims of wartime abuse, including former "comfort women" and former forced laborers or *rōmusha*. The JFBA delegation's interest in wartime abuse led to an increased emphasis on identifying victims of such abuse, and for this reason the term "victim" became increasingly prominent in Indonesia media reporting and activism. When using the term "victim" throughout this chapter, I am reflecting the dominant terminology of this period even though I personally prefer to view former "comfort women" as survivors.

Beginning in May 1993, LBH branches proceeded to collect and process the details of men and women who had experienced wartime abuse. YLBHI hoped that by gathering this data and passing it on to lawyers from the JFBA, various forms of redress might be achieved. Consistent with their mission to increase awareness about human rights in general and generate public sympathy for these cases, LBH lawyers adopted a strategy common across human rights movements of turning to the media to publicize the plight of former "comfort women" and *rōmusha*.[1] In relation to women, in particular, LBH lawyers encouraged the survivors and the public with whom it was engaging to reconceptualize these experiences as violations of human rights. This approach was crucial because of the stigma associated with the women's experiences.

In this chapter I investigate how the Yogyakarta branch of LBH—the most active on this case—approached this issue and the limitations of their activism. The lawyers believed it was essential that the women's testimonies were put on the record. This was despite acknowledging the many difficulties women had to overcome to testify and despite the fact LBH could not promise definite outcomes.

Through LBH's activism and networks, Indonesian survivors began to be represented both nationally and internationally. Through this process one survivor, Mardiyem, became the focus of media attention. The reasons LBH's lawyers initially put her forward as a spokesperson are partly related to her strength and resilience and her strong memory, but also to the nature of her particular experiences of "the system." I argue that her case closely conformed to the "ideal" story of a survivor across the movement, especially when compared with that of Tuminah.

Upon their return to Japan, the JFBA reported to their members and passed their recommendations to the Japanese government. While there were no direct outcomes from this process, I argue that this visit marked a turning point in activism on this issue in Indonesia, and to some extent it changed how the stories of the women survivors were framed in media reporting from this point on.

A JFBA Delegation Goes to Jakarta

As discussed in chapter 5, by the early 1990s in Korea and elsewhere across the Asian region there was increasing interest in Japan's actions in the Pacific War, including demands for redress from people victimized during the war. As the peak body representing lawyers in Japan, the JFBA was keen to better understand the scale of this historic victimization and had already begun research into cases across the region. In April 1993, a delegation of five lawyers arrived in Jakarta, led by Murayama Akira, a member of the JFBA Committee for Human Rights Protection.[2] Murayama explained that the purpose of the short visit was to find out more about the experiences of Indonesian victims and their demands. The delegation did not have very high expectations about the mission, and neither did they expect to make much progress.[3] This was primarily because unlike in the countries to which they had already sent delegations, such as the Philippines, in Indonesia they did not yet have connections with organizations that had commenced collecting testimony from survivors, nor with survivor groups.[4]

In carrying out their investigations and as an entry point for each country they visited, the Japanese lawyers engaged with bar associations to identify local contacts and find out how to reach victims. In Jakarta the JFBA delegation first met with lawyers from the Indonesian Advocates Association (Persatuan Advokat Indonesia, PERADIN),[5] which in turn referred them to YLBHI.

YLBHI was founded in the 1970s by Adnan Buyung Nasution and other members of PERADIN to provide free legal aid for the poor. It was one of only a few human rights organizations permitted to operate during the Suharto era.[6] YLBHI used its connections with the media to announce the delegation's visit, their interest in meeting affected persons, and the possibility of offering them some concrete support. This led to people who had experienced wartime abuse coming forward to meet the delegation. Given their low expectations for the trip, it was a surprise to the Japanese lawyers that they were able to meet a small number of war victims including forced laborers, survivors of massacres, and former "comfort women" during their short stay.[7]

According to Murayama, at the time, YLBHI's briefings to the media about the possibility of redress for victims was a point of tension, as the JFBA had not made such a promise. Instead, Murayama explains that they had made it clear that the purpose of their visit was to conduct "an investigation, no more than that" and listen to the demands of lawyers and potentially victimized people.[8] Nevertheless, as will be discussed, media reports covering the visit contained conflicting information about the potential for compensation.

A Question of Timing: Indonesia's Human Rights Problem

The media interest in the JFBA delegation's visit prompted the minister of Social Affairs, Endang Kusuma Inten Soeweno, to issue an unexpected statement. Newly installed into her office only a month before, the minister called on victims to report to local LBH branches.[9] Given that it marked a significant shift from the government's position on this issue as laid out a year earlier by the Minister for the State Secretariat Moerdiono, this support came as a surprise. Soeweno's altered position reflected increasing public attention to human rights issues more broadly and the government's plans to establish the National Commission of Human Rights (Komnas HAM). The JFBA visit came precisely when the Indonesian government was attempting to shift the narrative on its human rights record. Moreover, they would have been aware that two months before the JFBA visit, due to persistent Filipino activism, Japanese Foreign Minister Watanabe Michio had apologized to the Philippines for the wartime abuse of women forced into prostitution.[10]

Relatively speaking, the issue of Japanese war redress was less sensitive than cases of human rights abuses for which the Indonesian government or military itself stood accused, especially because the abuses were of Indonesians, and not those inflicted by Indonesians. It is also significant that this case was brought to the government's attention by a delegation of Japanese rather than Western lawyers.

Although the Indonesian government remained firmly nationalist when it was criticized for human rights abuses, it appeared to react more strongly when such critiques came from Western organizations or countries. In the 1970s, for example, such a strong response was made in reply to activism carried out by Amnesty International calling for the release of political prisoners.[11] In the 1990s, this can also be understood in the context of the use of culturalist ideas to defend "unique" Asian values at that time.[12] In the wake of the Dili massacre, such varied responses to international condemnation were obvious. Both the Netherlands and Japan threatened to withdraw their aid to Indonesia. Suharto called out the Dutch government as a former colonial power for trying to intervene in Indonesian affairs, but there were no such condemnations for Japan even though Japan had also occupied and exploited Indonesian people.[13] The Indonesian government could not so readily dismiss the JFBA delegation's investigations into human rights abuses committed by the Japanese as another arrogant "Western" intervention in Indonesia. Arguably, ideals associated with Asian solidarity and putative Asian concepts of human rights promoted by political leaders may have also prompted greater openness to the Japanese law-yers and their message.[14]

Another possible explanation for the minister's shift in position on Japa-nese war redress and support for victims to register with the LBH was that the government was trying to distance itself from the claims and thereby avoid potential conflict with the Japanese government.[15] This was potentially a strat-egy to avoid direct government criticism of Japan.

Growing Momentum: LBH Takes on Advocacy

As already mentioned, despite its low expectations, during the JFBA's visit a significant number of people claiming to have been victimized during the occupation responded to YLBHI's call. The unexpectedly positive response, along with time constraints, meant that delegate members could not hear the testimonies of all who came forward.[16] The delegation interviewed a total of thirty-three people, which included forced laborers and their families. Of these, eight were former "comfort women."[17] The women recounted their different experiences. One told the delegation of how she was taken by Japa-nese soldiers from a rice field, raped, and then detained for seven months; another of how she was kidnapped by Japanese soldiers and then confined and raped repeatedly for four months. Another woman told how she was taken by a *heiho* to a Japanese army tent, where she was detained for the next two years.[18] One witness reported the story of a former "comfort woman" who died of starvation while hiding in a forest at the end of the war.[19] It became clear to the JFBA delegation that many were affected by the war, and none had yet received compensation. As Murayama Akira explained, it was only fair that they would expect assistance in return.[20]

The JFBA visit attracted national media attention, which included reports and interviews with some of the women who had come forward. One of these women was sixty-three-year-old Raijah from Tangerang, West Java. She told *Tempo* journalists that her parents were pressured by the Japanese and she was finally forced to work in a brothel. In the same report, sixty-four-year-old Fatimah from Kendal, West Java, told of being gang-raped by Japanese sol-diers and forced to work in a brothel. When a journalist asked the women if they would follow the examples of Korean and Filipino women and demand compensation, Raijah answered that if they were to receive compensation that would be a blessing, "but if not, maybe that's my fate."[21] Her comments sug-gest she was neither prepared nor willing to mount a fight for compensation but would accept it if offered. Despite the hesitation of some women to speak to journalists, a volunteer accompanying them, Armien Kelana, adamantly told the media that these "human rights abuses must be exposed."[22] In making such a statement, Kelana appeared to impose a responsibility on the women to share their stories for the greater good, even if it was to their own detriment.

Todung Mulya Lubis, the head of the Jakarta Lawyers Club that cohosted the Japanese delegation with YLBHI, threw his support behind the collection of data, telling the media he hoped war victims including forced laborers and "comfort women" would register at LBH offices. He acknowledged that there were significant challenges in this process, including the fact that many survivors were old and that many women were not prepared to identify themselves as former "comfort women" due to the shame (*aib*) associated with this experience.[23]

There are several reasons working on behalf of persons victimized during the Japanese occupation fit well with YLBHI's general program at that time. According to its constitution, its mission was to "provide legal assistance, in the broadest sense, to those whose civil, political, socioeconomic, and cultural rights are violated, including the right to development, in particular for those groups lacking wealth and political power."[24]

YLBHI recognized that former "comfort women" and former forced laborers were victims of civil rights violations. Many were not well off, and they were certainly not well connected politically. The YLBHI lawyers may not have initially understood the extent of the ongoing disadvantages the women faced due to their wartime experiences, as discussed in chapter 4, but their awareness of the vulnerability and marginality of these women grew over time. Writing about the case a few years later, lawyer Budi Hartono characterized the backgrounds of most survivors as women of poor health who had suffered trauma and were socially marginalized. Hartono's impression was that due to the stigma attached to their pasts, the women faced psychological pressures and, because it made finding employment hard, poverty.[25]

The case for wartime redress from the Japanese fit with YLBHI's interest in taking on cases that addressed broader issues of inequality and provided opportunities to educate victimized persons and the public about human rights. Recognizing the limitations of the New Order's flawed legal system, where many judges were not impartial, YLBHI followed a structural approach. As its founder, Nasution, explained, this meant choosing cases with "a major structural element" and the potential to increase awareness and educate different groups of people about their rights. Generally this meant that cases had to fit into one of YLBHI's four key areas of concern: land use and ownership, environmental protection, labor relations, and political crimes (related usually to subversion charges).[26] By the early 1990s, YLBHI was working on cases such as protecting villagers evicted from lands by wealthy real estate prospectors, striking workers, children forced into prostitution or sweatshops, and women subjected to domestic violence or sexual abuse.[27]

It is important to note that even as YLBHI was taking up the case of the "comfort women," the organization's position in relation to gender-based violence and discrimination was uneven and unclear. Nursyahbani Katjasungkana, a feminist lawyer and former head of YLBHI in 1987–93, has described this as a disconnect within the organization. Around this time, she recalls often being told by other lawyers that cases of domestic violence were private matters and therefore not appropriate for YLBHI lawyers and was sometimes challenged when she took on such cases.[28] For this reason, in 1995, a group of women lawyers including Katjasungkana from YLBHI broke away and formed LBH APIK. The new organization provided counselling and legal aid for female victims of violence, including domestic violence and even some cases of state violence.[29] LBH APIK formulated a concept of structural gender legal aid aimed at challenging gender inequalities in the law and legal system.[30] These lawyers viewed the law as a key site of struggle because it discouraged classifying sexual violence as a crime against women. Indonesia's criminal code (Kitab Undang-Undang Hukum Pidana), formulated by the Dutch in 1918 and carried over into Indonesian law, classified rape as a crime against morality.[31] According to Katjasungkana, this was predicated on the view that the most serious crime is not against the woman but is the violation of family or community-based morality.[32] On this basis, even within YLBHI, there was a high degree of uncertainty about addressing cases of marital rape in terms of whether this met the definition of a crime.

This ambiguity is significant in the context of YLBHI's decision to take on the case of redress for wartime human rights violations, which included sexual abuse and rapes. Although the case did not precisely match the organization's key areas of focus, it contained a strong structural element. The case raised the issue of state responsibility (here, Japan) for individual victims of human rights abuses. It also fit with YLBHI's more general aim to promote democratization by defending human rights and the rule of law.[33] Internationally, this period saw an increased emphasis on human rights and a willingness by the international community to act to address historical injustices.[34]

LBH's Approach to the "Comfort Women" Issue

By the early 1990s, YLBHI had offices in Indonesia's major cities, including Jakarta, Bandung, Semarang, Yogyakarta, Surabaya, Medan, Ujung

Pandang, Manado, Palembang, and Jayapura. The Yogyakarta branch was the most active on the issue of the "comfort women." The decision to commit significant resources to this case locally is partly explained by the specific leadership in the Yogyakarta branch. Edward Aspinall observed that the level of commitment to the structural approach to legal aid varied across different LBH offices at this time.[35] In 1993, LBH Yogyakarta was led by then forty-five-year-old Budi Hartono. Hartono was a strong supporter of the structural approach to legal aid and a regular commentator on law and human rights issues in the media.[36] He was willing to advocate for difficult cases and was soon identified as a leading activist on behalf of the surviving women.

Immediately after the JFBA's visit, LBH Yogyakarta announced that it would open a complaints post (*pos pengaduan*) for wartime victims. The formal process of documenting experiences of human rights abuse took place from April 26, 1993, to September 14, 1993.[37] LBH used a very broad definition for registering women, deciding to document any and all forms of sexual abuse by the Japanese army during the occupation, as opposed to restricting registration to women who had been forced to be "comfort women."[38] The Yogyakarta branch employed a team of paralegals who worked across towns in Central Java, including Purworejo, Kebumen, Cilacap, and Wonogiri. This network of branches meant they were able to quickly disseminate information about the registration process into regional and rural areas.[39] As a consequence, the response was strong, leading to 249 registrations.[40] Most of the women who came forward were from areas where there had been a concentration of Japanese military during the occupation, including Gunung Kidul and Magelang.[41]

LBH aimed to document the women's experiences in a way that would meet legal standards. Assistants prepared declarations for each registration based on a survivor's statement or that made by a member of a survivor's family. Each declaration was then witnessed. Winarta Hadiwiyono, who worked as a student volunteer for LBH around this time, recalled that "the form included information on the survivor such as a chronology on how they became a comfort woman."[42]

The subsequent verification process included collecting statements from other family members, members of the local community, and sometimes heads of villages or hamlets. The women were also interviewed by LBH staff. As Hadiwiyono explained, "We recorded how they became comfort women, what year, who first approached them, what was promised, where, what happened when they became a comfort woman, how they were freed."[43] There were therefore multiple checks on the women's recollections. As the LBH members described it, they were always mindful to approach their collection of testimony with sensitivity. This meant that they would meet the women several times and frame the questions carefully so as to verify testimony but not offend the women.

Other than the collection of the witness statements and brief testimony, LBH did not attempt to record longer oral histories of these women's lives and experiences before and after the occupation. This contrasts with the approach taken by the Korean Council and the networks of Korean and Japanese feminist activists supporting women survivors in those countries. As discussed in chapter 5, the Korean Council and associated feminist groups carefully collected the life histories of survivors and published these in the collection *True Stories of the Comfort Women: Testimonies*, first in Korean in 1993 and later in English.[44] In Indonesia, the importance of life testimony and testimonies in women's own words for advocacy and for generating empathy for the cause, was not yet recognized. As explained in chapter 6, using oral history to record the stories of survivors of human rights abuses and of marginalized women was still not common practice in the Indonesian academy and activist circles.

When they registered with LBH, some of the women openly expressed concerns about their privacy but also admitted they had come forward to record their experiences because they were convinced to do so by others, or for their own reasons, including expectations of compensation. Some women did not want their names released, nor for LBH staff to visit their houses for fear that their neighbors would find out.[45] This suggests that even fifty years later, some of the women were still concealing their pasts from their families and communities.

In accordance with LBH's mission to promote democratic values and generate greater awareness of human rights, Budi Hartono contacted the media early on to ensure coverage of their efforts and in the hope of gaining government support. Hartono's approach was typical in the organization, which was to "move beyond a traditional lawyer-client relationship and instead treat each case, as LBH leaders put it, as the focus for development of a 'social movement.'"[46] Hartono and LBH hoped that this case would gain broader social and political traction.

Hartono's outreach to the media had an impact. The day after LBH opened registrations, local and national media reported on the registration process. Early coverage featured short profiles of *rōmusha* and former "comfort women" who had registered at LBH on the first day. A noticeable difference in the coverage of the two cases was that most former *rōmusha* provided their full names and places of residence and were frequently photographed; while agreeing to be interviewed some women did not want their photographs taken, nor did they disclose their names or places of residence.

An article in *Kedaulatan Rakyat* on April 27 included a profile of Tohir bin Harto, aged eighty-three, who wanted to demand compensation from the Japanese government for being a forced laborer (*rōmusha*), in Tanjungpinang, Riau, during the war.[47] He was identified by his place of residence as Karang-gondang, near Jepara in Central Java. It is common in Indonesian news reporting to include witnesses' places of residence. This is due to the Indonesian convention of always noting the place from which someone comes, as an identifier of their communities. By contrast, in the case of the woman most frequently profiled in these early reports, neither her address nor real name was used. Instead she was referred to either by the Japanese name she was given during the occupation, Momoye, or as Ny My, meaning Mrs. My. It was reported that she asked not to be identified because she had not yet consulted with her son on this matter. One journalist reported her asking, "Please don't identify me so my son is not shocked."[48] In another article in which the same woman expressed her concerns about her identity becoming public, she was quoted as saying, "I am afraid that this registration will lead to taunting from my neighbors."[49] Some time later, "Mrs. My" publicly identified herself as Mardiyem of Yogyakarta.

Mardiyem Becomes an Icon of the Movement

In her 2007 memoir, told to Indonesian and Japanese activists Eka Hindra and Kimura Kōichi, Mardiyem describes how she became the focus of intense media attention at that time. She recounts how, upon registering at the Yogyakarta LBH, Budi Hartono asked the journalists to help publicize her case as part of the broader campaign to raise awareness. She tells how the journalists immediately started photographing her, without asking her permission first, making her feel uncomfortable. She asked that her name and the name of her *kampung* be changed. It was clear that she was not prepared for the public exposure, nor for the reactions of those in her community once the news reached them.[50] Her hesitation to give her name and place of residence and to be photographed suggests how difficult it was for Mardiyem to publicly reveal this aspect of her past. As she explains in her memoir, she was acutely aware that members of society still stigmatized former "comfort women," labeling them "as prostitutes and immoral girls, even though this happened decades ago."[51] Despite her initial hesitation and undoubtedly due to her personal courage, Mardiyem emerged as the most prominent of the Indonesian survivors and a spokesperson for the movement. Mardiyem herself partly explains this evolution, but it is also important to ask why was it that from the 174 women who presented themselves to the LBH offices in those few months in 1993, she stood out and became the icon of the movement.[52]

For the thousands of women who passed through the Japanese system of the "comfort women," only a few have spoken out. Elazar Barkan suggests that because at first only a handful of women came forward, "the group of victims existed primarily as a *category*, and only implicitly as individuals."[53] Arguably, in this process particular women became icons of the movement standing in for the larger group of yet-to-be-identified women. As the first woman to use her name and publicly advocate for compensation, Korean Kim Hak-Sun quickly gained international notoriety and became the foremost global icon of the movement. Her photo frequently appeared in newspapers and in activist publications and commemorations, and a statue of Kim now adorns the San Francisco monument to the "comfort women."[54]

In other countries, comparable icons emerged. Maria Rosa Henson became the face of the movement in the Philippines. Henson came forward in 1992 in response to a call from the Task Force on Filipino Comfort Women.[55] In 1993, she participated in a lawsuit against the Japanese government and published her memoir.[56] She was a member of the Hukbalahup resistance in the early years of the Japanese occupation and at the age of fifteen was taken by the Japanese army and held in a military garrison. Detained for nine months, she was forced to have sex with soldiers every afternoon and evening under military guard.[57]

Jan Ruff O'Herne emerged as another icon for the movement representing the experiences of Dutch women. O'Herne came forward in 1992 after seeing Kim Hak-Sun on television.[58] As detailed in chapter 3, O'Herne was taken from Ambarawa internment camp to a Dutch house in Semarang and forced to have sex with Japanese soldiers for a period of three months.[59] Her first public act as a survivor was to lay a wreath at the Adelaide War Memorial to commemorate the fiftieth anniversary of Java's surrender to Japanese troops on March 8, 1992. O'Herne was frequently invited to international advocacy meetings, and when it was first published in English in 1994, her memoir became one of the most well-known survivor accounts.[60]

There are several possible reasons Budi Hartono initially chose Mardiyem's story to profile in the media at the time of the LBH registrations, why her story was regularly repeated, and why she subsequently became the icon for the movement in Indonesia. Although many women registered at the LBH offices and others had come forward earlier, Hartono's decision to promote Mardiyem's story to the media relates to the particularly shocking experiences she recounted having endured.[61] This included not only repeated rape but also a forced abortion when she was five months pregnant at age fifteen. The accounts of the abortion, in particular, appeared regularly in early reports of her case.[62] Several aspects of her story were very similar to those of the now exemplary case of Kim Hak-Sun. As a thirteen-year-old girl, Mardiyem was duped into the system and transported far from her home in Yogyakarta to Borneo island. She testified that although she was given tickets for each visit by a soldier and promised these would later be converted to money, by the end of the war they were worthless. The reference in her testimony to a lack of payment positioned her, in the eyes of the movement, as an "ideal" victim.

The emphasis on ideal victims became increasingly important as the movement evolved and was forced to confront denialists. Soon after the women began to speak out, those associated with a neo-nationalist backlash in Japan claimed that because payments were made to the women, this was proof they were "prostitutes," regardless of coercion. Despite various statements of remorse and regret from successive Japanese Prime Ministers Miyazawa Kiichi, Hosokawa Morihiro, and Hata Tsutomo, in May 1994 Japan's Justice Minister Nagano Shigeto told the media that in his view the women demanding apology and compensation were in fact "licensed prostitutes."[63]

Tuminah's Dilemma

Mardiyem's experience of the system and her background contrasts with that of Tuminah, the first Indonesian survivor to publicly testify. Tuminah did not attract anything like the media attention Mardiyem did. As noted in chapter 6, her story was published by her journalist nephew in the Semarang-based newspaper *Suara Merdeka* on July 16, 1992, and then in the national daily *Kompas* on July 17, 1992.[64]

In her testimony, Tuminah was open about the fact that she was working as a "street girl" prior to being forcibly recruited into the "comfort" system. She referred to her past as sex worker and former "comfort woman" as sinful,[65] and to herself as *cah nakal*, meaning immoral person.[66] Commenting on broader societal perceptions of sex workers who are the subject of violence, Hilary Gorman argues that the intense stigmatization of sex workers as "bad women" eventually leads to their moral exclusion, whereby "the harm that is inflicted on people who are perceived to be outside the scope of justice is rationalised."[67] By representing herself as immoral in her interviews with the media, Tuminah may have reinforced a societal perception that she was not a worthy victim.

Tuminah was not an appealing figure to represent the movement because of several complicating factors. As well as her background as a sex worker with its associated negative connotations, Tuminah testified that her basic needs were provided for at the inn. This included food provisions, which were not rationed, and she also testified to receiving occassional payments for her services.[68] Although this does not negate the fact she was forced into the system and held against her will, her experience is not represented in media reports as being entirely exploitative. Tuminah testified that she had decided to speak out to encourage other women to come forward and demand compensation, but the media attention her story initially attracted faded quickly. Once the LBH registrations opened, any attention she may have garnered as the first to speak out soon shifted to Mardiyem.

In contrast to Tuminah's story, Mardiyem's narrative more closely approximates a "model victim" who is young, duped, tries to resist, suffers physical harm, and is unpaid. Sarah Soh refers to this as a "paradigmatic story."[69] This term draws attention to the fact that activists choose to emphasize women whose testimonies fit this narrative on the basis that they are more likely to receive empathy and support in societies where there are strict ideas around women's morality and less likely to be dismissed by denialists. In her criticisms of the "model" story, Ueno Chizuko has observed that such an ideal places pressure on women who do not conform. It creates a boundary between the "pure" and "impure" victim.[70] In this context, Ueno has problematized what she calls the "prostitution paradigm." This presumes that because the women were sometimes paid, participation was voluntary. Ueno argues that even if payment occurs after rape "it does not mean the crime of rape is erased."[71]

The dismissal of claims to victimhood for women who were former sex workers has also been challenged in the movement. Scholar and activist Yamashita Yeong-ae observed that in Korean activism, Japanese women who were prostituted prior to being recruited into the "comfort women" system have sometimes been excluded from the category of "worthy victims." This is based on the fear that any suggestion of volition or choice expressed by the women, would render the state unaccountable. Yamashita argues that Japanese "comfort women" who were former sex workers should be included as victims.[72] Under Japan's state regulated prostitution system girls and women were in fact commonly bound by debts incurred by their impoverished families, and male household leaders often made decisions on behalf of their daughters.[73] Tuminah's story, as recounted in chapter 1, similarly implies that she was bound by family debts or the burden of providing for them. In the early days of Indonesian activism, it seems that choices were also made to promote the experiences of particular women over those of others.

The stark reality that activists need to make the most persuasive case when it comes to compensation claims, has sometimes led to a simplification of the wide range of experiences of former "comfort women." Activists' tendency to promote the stories of women with a particular set of experiences can explain why

Mardiyem emerged as the most well known of the local "comfort women" in Indonesia, and why she was most frequently invited to speak at international events related to the movement. Like O'Herne in Australia and Henson in the Philippines, Tuminah first came forward in 1992. Unlike them, she was not invited to testify at the International Public Hearing Concerning Japan's Postwar Compensation in Tokyo in December that year.[74] The hearing was organized by concerned lawyers, activists, and historians and attended by over eight hundred people. Four other women from the Republic of Korea, the Democratic Republic of Korea, China, and Taiwan provided testimony, along with four former forced laborers, including one from the Netherlands.[75] Sarah Soh described the 1992 hearing and its emphasis on testimonies and analysis of life stories as an important part of the emergence of "the era of the survivor."[76] The opening to the report on the hearing emphasized that it was intended to provide a platform for nongovernmental organization workers and UN representatives in attendance, including former director of the UN Centre for Human Rights Theo van Boven, to "hear directly from the victims."[77]

The noninclusion of Indonesian survivors at this hearing may reflect the fact that, apart from Tuminah, very few survivors had come forward at this stage. It was also most likely because Indonesian women had not yet formed an identifiable organization representing survivors. In each case, with the exception of O'Herne and one woman from China, survivors were supported by organizations from their home countries. Indonesian activism on this issue was late to develop and thus relatively less visible globally.

Mardiyem's Choice

The reasons so few survivors came forward are similar across all the societies from which affected women come. Mardiyem explains that she only decided to register as a survivor because her husband had already passed away. She explained if he had still been alive she probably would not have registered so as "not to cause him shame." Here she expresses the view that her experience of rape is not only personally shameful but also brings shame to her husband, implying that her chastity and sexuality belong not just to herself but also to her husband.[78] In her memoir she connects her feelings of shame to her deceased father, suggesting that her rape was also an insult to his dignity.[79]

As noted throughout this book, survivors and activists variously used the terms *ternoda* or *aib*—both meaning stained—to describe the shame placed on and felt by women and their families. The concept of being stained is crucial for understanding why some survivors have not shared their experiences.[80] The concept is consistent with the Islamic emphasis on purification of the body before prayer, after sexual relations, and during the fasting month, and it implies a sense of being unclean or impure (see also chapter 9). It implies not only that these women's bodies are defiled but that disclosure of their experiences may "stain" the reputations of those around them. It reflects strong taboos about disclosing cases of sexual violence. The label applies not only to a woman who is perceived to have broken standards of acceptable sexual morality but also to her family because of the associated patriarchal belief that men must guard women's sexuality. As a consequence, the concept of stain is still used by survivors to refer to the sense of shame they attach to their experiences.

In the end, several factors motivated Mardiyem to tell her story publicly. One was a sense of duty to her fellow survivors. She explains how they motivated her to continue her struggle. After registering with LBH, she looked for other women who were detained in the same boarding house in Telawang during the war and encouraged twelve of them to register. In her narrated memoir of the stories of her friends, she gives brief accounts, detailing how most died in circumstances of poverty and how that further motivated her to do more.[81]

Mardiyem was also greatly encouraged by the eagerness of the Japanese lawyers to collect evidence from women survivors about their experiences because it entailed recognition of suffering and the violation of their rights. As she explained: "Decades after the war, I still felt followed by sin because I had against my will carried out a dirty job. I felt I wanted to rebel and look for justice, but I did not know from whom I should seek it."[82]

Though it haunted her still, Mardiyem was able to reframe her experiences in a new way—as a harm inflicted on her as an individual who was worthy of compensation from the Japanese government.

Mardiyem's memoir also reveals that after making the decision to register and putting her trust in LBH her experiences were not immediately positive. She recalls how a former *rōmusha* who was also registering suggested that she had had it easy during the war because all she had to do was "work in bed."[83] She recalls how she almost threw an ashtray at him: "He did not know that the suffering of a woman who is forced to provide sexual services is so deep. I not only suffered being physically beaten, but also suffered spiritually for decades, together with a feeling that would not go away that I had done wrong."[84] Foremost, her comment suggests that even as a fellow "victim" of the war, there was little understanding about the effect of this crime on women. Such a view, that former "comfort women" were undeserving of justice, may also have played into public perceptions.

Mardiyem's memoir includes many observations about her journey to becoming a public figure, activist, and icon of the movement, which included more personal challenges.[85] As she put it, "At that time, I appeared frequently in the newspaper, in magazines and television so that many people began to know about my past as a Japanese hostage. I was insulted and heckled because I had been a Japanese hostage."[86] Even though she represented the "ideal" victim in activist terms, in broader Indonesian society Mardiyem continued to be branded as an immoral person. After her public revelation, she was excluded from social activities in the *kampung* where she had once headed the local Family Welfare Program. Over time the situation in her community improved, but she clearly suffered in the short term. On this basis, some of her fears about going public appeared to have been justified.

The Registration Process and its Outcomes

Early media reporting on the registration of *rōmusha* and "comfort women" acted as a stimulus for other victims to come forward.[87] By the close of registrations in September 1993, 17,245 former forced laborers (all men) and 249 women had registered.[88] Of those 249 women, 25 were deceased and 46 had never returned to their place of residence, meaning that these women's experiences were registered by relatives.[89] The low number of women registering partly reflects the fact there were far fewer "comfort women" during the occupation than there were forced laborers. Undoubtedly, barriers related to the stigma associated with their experiences also prevented others from coming forward.

Though formal registrations for reporting to the JFBA closed in September 1993, LBH continued to document the experiences of survivors for the next decade. By 2007, 1,156 women had registered.[90] Many of these later registrants came forward in 1996 and 1997 when the issue again became a focus of significant public attention (see chapter 8).

The archives of documents collected through LBH were held in hard copy at its Yogyakarta office. The use of computers in organizations such as LBH, even in the mid- to late 1990s, was not yet widespread.[91] By 1999, most of the hard copy files in the Japanese redress case held at LBH Yogyakarta's offices had been destroyed by termites.[92] An attempt was made to digitize some of the remaining files, but not all.[93] In 2006, an earthquake in Yogyakarta destroyed many of the remaining hard-copy documents and digitized records. Today LBH Yogyakarta retains documentation for only ten or so of the women who reported to them in the 1990s.

Through the process of registering with LBH and sharing their stories, survivors developed expectations about the outcomes of the process. As Hadiwiyono observed, "Many women had hidden their stories for years, so when this began to open up the response was large; the women's expectations were strong. They hoped that if they testified then perhaps there would be help for the problems they had faced."[94] Given that the decision to tell their stories incurred great risk of social and familial isolation and stigmatization, it is reasonable and logical that they would have had some expectation of compensation.

At the time, the media reported somewhat contradictory statements from various YLBHI officials about the potential outcomes of the registration process. The day after registration opened in late April 1993, for example, Budi Hartono told journalists that the Yogyakarta LBH office would assist their clients with "whatever requests they had."[95] Two days later, *Kompas* reported that Hartono would demand an apology and compensation for his clients from the Japanese government.[96]

Around the same time, an official from the head office of YLBHI in Jakarta, Luhut M. P. Pangeribuan, was quoted as making a very contrasting statement: "LBH does not promise anything. Those registering should not make the mistake in thinking that simply by registering they will receive compensation. We are at the very beginning of the process."[97] Luhut sought to clarify the Japanese lawyers' position: that they would raise this case for discussion at their October symposium and that YLBHI would wait to receive their informed advice.

The fact that legal action could only be pursued in Japanese courts presented several challenges for YLBHI.[98] The reality was that it was very dependent on Japanese assistance due to its funding constraints and because it had not yet secured their support to bring a case on behalf of Indonesian claimants. While YLBHI could have initiated a class action to be heard in a Tokyo court—as Korean complainants did in 1991 and Filipino complainants in 1993—it chose not to take this route. Former "comfort women" in Indonesia did not have an independent organization to support them or fundraise for them, and given that survivors were mostly poor, YLBHI would have needed sufficient funding to cover transport, accommodation, and living expenses for them, as well as the significant costs involved in pursuing a case in Japan.[99]

Moreover, although always difficult, YLBHI's funding position was particularly dire at this time. Beginning in April 1992, in response to international protests over the Dili massacre, the Indonesian government had curtailed aid transfers from Dutch nongovernmental organizations to their Indonesian counterparts. At that time, 88 percent of LBH's US$650,000 annual budget came from the Dutch group Novib. In mid-1993, when YLBHI took on this advocacy for persons victimized during the occupation, it was facing an extreme financial crisis. There were also serious doubts about the preparedness and capacity of survivors to endure a long and drawn-out legal process.[100] These challenges meant that in handling this case, YLBHI had always been and continued to be greatly reliant on the JFBA for direction. This was coupled with the belief in YLBHI that the data they gathered could be passed on to the JFBA for consideration in their upcoming symposium on wartime victims.[101] However, the JFBA saw it somewhat differently. After they returned to Japan in mid-1993, the JFBA's contact with YLBHI was limited and the delegation maintained that they had always seen their visit to Indonesia as a preliminary fact-finding mission only.[102]

In August 1993, a month before the deadline for registrations at LBH and two months before the JFBA symposium, Japan's Chief Cabinet Secretary Kōno Yōhei responded to the findings of a Japanese study on the "comfort women" issue.[103] In a now famous statement, Kōno admitted that in many cases "women were recruited against their own will, through coaxing, coercion etc." and that "the Japanese military was, directly and or indirectly, involved in the establishment and management of the comfort stations and the transfer of comfort women." He also offered "sincere apologies and remorse" to surviving women.[104]

The head of YLBHI, Adnan Buyung Nasution, responded to the secretary's apology, saying that he expected further steps would follow. He suggested that the issue should be included in the Japanese history curriculum (a detail also mentioned in the Kōno statement), that a monument should be built for the women in Japan, and that the women could demand compensation for their "inhumane treatment by the Japanese army."[105] Seeing an opportunity to apply further pressure, Nasution suggested that the "Indonesian government should take clear steps so that the Indonesian women continue to be respected by every country."[106] The Indonesian government, in his view, should have followed the examples of the governments of North and South Korea in showing support for the women by firmly demanding compensation. Indeed, throughout 1992 and 1993, governments and activist groups from North and South Korea and from the Philippines led sustained lobbying for Japanese redress.[107] In contrast, since giving its support to the YLBHI registration process in April 1993, the Indonesian government had remained remarkably silent on the "comfort women" and wartime redress issue more broadly.

After the Apology

The main outcome of the JFBA's investigations across the region, including in Indonesia, was its *Report of the Overseas Investigation on War-Time Victims*.[108] In the lead-up to the report's release in October 1993, JFBA representatives commented to the media that victims' claims for compensation were strong and that the government should make "an appropriate post war settlement."[109] The published report includes accounts from investigations in China, South

Korea, Taiwan, the Philippines, Hong Kong, Indonesia, Malaysia, Singapore, and Australia. Its Indonesia report is thirteen pages long and includes a summary of wartime victimization, cases of sexual violence including the "comfort women," forced laborers, *heiho* (for unpaid wages), mass killings of civilians, and other damages. It features extracts from testimonies of those abused and requests for appropriate compensation. The relatively brief coverage of Indonesia suggests that very little of the data gathered by LBH was used. The summary report was distributed and discussed at the JFBA symposium in Kyoto in October 1993,[110] where its members passed a resolution stating that there were many wartime victims who had never been compensated and called for further investigations.[111]

The JFBA report did not elicit a direct response from the Japanese government on the basis of the enduring view that compensation claims had already been resolved in accordance with the relevant treaties. With regard to Indonesia specifically, the Japanese government's position was that that the issue of wartime compensation was already settled. It had signed an agreement with the Indonesian government and was providing financial aid. As JFBA delegate Murayama Akira explained, however, this was not the position of their organization. He stated: "Our standpoint was focusing on the victim's redress. Japanese society was required to properly redress the victims. Japan should take a position to apologize and redress the victims. We understood this as a principle of human rights protection, so we passed the resolution."[112] In addition to making recommendations to the government, the JFBA shared their findings with Japanese society more broadly. They made efforts to increase awareness about human rights issues connected to the war, campaigning for textbooks to include this history.[113] Indeed, the issue of the "comfort women" was included in Japanese history textbooks passed by the Ministry of Education starting around 1992.[114]

As mentioned, after handing over their report to the JFBA, YLBHI's activism on this issue did not stop, but its financial limitations forced it to take a nonlitigation approach. Rather than building a court case, the documentation YLBHI collected was used as a form of evidence for their lobbying efforts, including letters written to the Japanese prime minister and in correspondence with the United Nations.[115] Hadiwiyono explains, "We tried to push especially the government of Japan to acknowledge that they had a problem [and] they had to take responsibility for this issue."[116] Tim Lindsey and Melissa Crouch describe this type of approach as "cause lawyering."[117] Cause lawyers combine activism with legal work and often seek to achieve social justice for less privileged groups. For YLBHI, cause lawyering forms part of its program of structural legal aid.[118]

Through collaboration with the JFBA, YLBHI lawyers sought advice on how to handle this historical case of sexual violence. Budi Hartono credits the Japanese lawyers with motivating the women to speak because in his view they "encouraged Indonesian survivors to reconceptualize their experiences in terms of the violation of their rights" and convinced them that this problem could be negotiated with Japanese representatives.[119] Cheah argues that for survivors, this process of "rights naming sought to overcome culturally ingrained mind blocks that had silenced these women for so long."[120] At the same time, others, including activist Eka Hindra, who later worked intensively with the survivors over a period of twenty years, were less certain of the degree to which Indonesian survivors had undergone such a transformation to seeing themselves as survivors of human rights abuses.[121] In her view, this failure to reach such self-realization was largely because survivors needed not only the opportunity to tell their stories, but also psychological support to heal from their traumas and further human rights education and training. While LBH provided the first of these to the women who came forward, neither it nor any other organization stepped up to offer ongoing support or education.

The Yogyakarta-based LBH activists who recorded the women's stories seem to have been aware of the difficulties women faced in sharing their experiences, while also emphasizing its positive effects. Hadiwiyono commented, "Giving testimony was a positive experience for some because they could release that which they had held on to, but there was also a sense of awakening their suffering that they experienced and some would cry."[122] Hadiwiyono reflects a commonly held view that talking about experiences of violence constitutes a form of healing of a person's trauma. It is not necessarily true that speaking is therapeutic for all people, and in fact some people choose silence as a deliberate strategy in response to their trauma.[123] On its own, speaking is not sufficient, and other organizations recognize that therapy is also needed.

YLBHI's work helped the women see their experiences in a new way: in terms of their victimization. When compared with the South Korean and Filipino cases, though, which had strong support from feminist groups, Indonesian women clearly missed out. Such guidance could have enabled them to form their own organization to fight for their own cause and provide ongoing support.

Conclusion

As this chapter has described, activism for Indonesia's "comfort women" began in a very different context to that seen in South Korea and the

Philippines. With the encouragement of Japanese counterparts, Indonesian lawyers began by documenting women's stories. YLBHI took on this issue as part of its broader commitment to democratization, and in this context the cases of all wartime victims, not just women survivors. In YLBHI's efforts to promote awareness of this issue, Mardiyem was repeatedly profiled and eventually became a spokesperson and icon for the movement in Indonesia.

Although women's organizations in Indonesia had begun to take up contemporary issues of sexual violence by the mid-1990s, very little attention was given to military sexual violence. There was no specific organization devoted to opposing military violence against women, nor to the historic cases of the "comfort women." In 1993, as a consequence of the YLBHI registration process—precipitated by the JFBA delegation's visit to Indonesia and press coverage—the cases of surviving Indonesian women finally came to light. In the next chapter, I outline how this public attention, coupled with connections forming between survivors and their advocates across the region, began to escalate, ultimately leading to the establishment of the Asian Women's Fund.

The Asian Women's Fund and Increasing International Outreach, 1995–1997

ollowing the 1993 Kōno statement, activist demands for redress for "comfort women" intensified. Debates at the United Nations and emanating from the 1993 Vienna Declaration and Program of Action quickened this process internationally. In 1994, the International Commission of Jurists, issued a report arguing that every survivor who came forward should be paid compensation.[1] These calls from leading human rights defenders and institutions increased survivors' expectations that compensation was imminent.

In August 1994, due to domestic and international pressure, the Japanese government approved the establishment of the Asian Women's Fund, "a hybrid national public organization" to address Japan's "moral responsibility" to survivors.[2] The fund, originally named the Asian Peace and Friendship Fund for Women, was established to issue atonement payments to former "comfort women" funded by donations from private individuals and to initiate welfare projects funded by the Ministry of Foreign Affairs.[3] This clear demarcation between the private and government funds sought to protect the government's unwavering position against paying compensation to individuals. The Asian Women's Fund (AWF) was established on July 18, 1995, with the dispersal of funds to begin in August 1996.

The AWF was formed during the term of Prime Minister Murayama Tomiichi, leader of the Japan Socialist Party, who presided over a coalition government. To mark the fiftieth anniversary of the war, Murayama set up a Ruling Parties Project to Consider War Responsibility.[4] On this anniversary, the prime minister issued what is known as the "Murayama statement," an apology for the war. Three days later he announced the AWF.[5] A cross section of Japanese public figures supported the AWF,[6] but from the outset it was considered controversial. On one hand, activists supporting survivors objected on the grounds that the compensation payments were not being paid from government funds, while on the other hand, it was opposed by Japanese who did not believe the women should be paid compensation at all.

Likewise, many activists from outside Japan opposed the AWF, largely because they saw it as a way of sidestepping state responsibility and avoiding accountability. At the same time, some felt that the AWF was the best chance at any form of compensation. These differences led to intense splits across the activist movement. These divisions and their effects on Korean and Taiwanese survivors are well documented.[7] What is less understood is the AWF's effect on Indonesian survivors who remained marginal in the transnational movement and felt neglected by the AWF.

Competing Responses

In Indonesia, the formation of the fund precipitated efforts from the AWF and other Japanese organizations to reach out to survivors. Throughout this period, Mardiyem began to receive invitations to attend international conferences and other events. These invitations and approaches included sincere efforts to understand her views on the AWF, whereas others sought to influence her position. The absence of a dedicated organization representing Indonesian survivors meant that certain organizations and people in Japan and Indonesia became crucial conduits for activists and survivors, acting both for and against the AWF proposal.

For example, the International Committee of Asia-Pacific War Victims Organizations Claiming Compensation (see chapter 5) turned to the Indonesian veteran's group, the Communication Forum for Ex-Heiho, to identify women survivors and sign them on to AWF's compensation program. At the same time, the Japanese organization Citizens' Fund for Realizing Postwar Compensation (Sengo Hoshō Jitsugen Shimin Kikin) attempted to raise alternative funds to support the women and dissuaded them from taking AWF funds. At the Fourth Asian Solidarity Conference held in Manila in March 1996, women activists lobbied various country-based organizations to encourage a consensus on rejecting compensation through the AWF.

Individuals including Indonesian lawyers at LBH, such as Budi Hartono, and Japanese advocates like Takagi Ken'ichi, Kawada Fumiko, and Indonesia-based Japanese theologian Kimura Kōichi, held varying positions regarding the AWF, and each assumed prominent roles in connecting with and speaking for survivors. The LBH tried to negotiate these various and multiple positions while also lobbying the Indonesian and Japanese governments for meaningful outcomes.

Transnational debates also intensified in this period due to a report filed by the UN Special Rapporteur on Sexual Violence. The Special Rapporteur was first appointed in 1994, following the 1993 Declaration on the Elimination on Violence against Women. The rapporteur's role was to work with nongovernmental organizations and governments to monitor and document violence against women, issue reports, and pressure states to address violations.[8] Based on her visits to South Korea and Japan in July 1995, Special Rapporteur Radhika Coomaraswamy's 1996 report recommended issuing individual compensation payments to surviving women, making individual apologies to women who are substantiated as victims, punishing perpetrators, and including this topic in school textbooks.[9] These recommendations strongly mirrored those of activist organizations in Japan and Korea and were taken up by Indonesian activists.

Meanwhile, in June 1994 the period of political openness in Indonesia that had begun in the early 1990s ended abruptly with bans imposed on several news publications, including *Tempo* magazine, making human rights activism more difficult. In July 1996 the government led an attack on the headquarters of the opposition party, the Indonesia Democratic Party (Partai Demokrasi Indonesia, PDI). This episode marked the beginning of a general crackdown on dissent.[10] At the same time, international pressure on Indonesia over its human rights record continued to build. In December 1996, the Nobel Peace Prize was jointly awarded to East Timorese activists José Ramos-Horta and Bishop Carlos Filipe Ximenes Belo, who had spoken out against military violence in the province. Elections held in May 1997 saw growing public unrest and targeted outrage at candidates running for election, including Suharto's children and cronies. In this domestic and international climate, ongoing debates about how to resolve the case of the "comfort women," and whether to accept money from the AWF, played out in Indonesia.

Japanese Outreach to Indonesia

One of the major players in the transnational debates over the AWF was the International Committee of Asia-Pacific War Victims Organizations Claiming Compensation, founded in 1991. The committee was funded by donations from the Japanese general public and from admission fees collected for their regular conferences.[11] Its members sought to secure individual compensation for a range of war victims, versus state-to-state reparations. As Takagi Ken'ichi argued in his keynote address to the 1996 conference, international law was increasingly addressing compensation especially for vulnerable people. He proposed that "states that disregard damage of the weak cannot be trusted. Germany placed importance in individual compensation for the Jews and other war victims. U.S.A. and Canada implemented individual compensation in 1988 for its repression against Japanese-Americans during the war."[12] In his view, payment of compensation represented a question of "justice and morality for Japanese society."[13] Takagi frequently tried to leverage international developments to make a case for Japanese compensation payments and draw attention to recognition of human rights violations. At the 1996 conference, he invited an expert to report on the consequences for women of rape during war, drawing on evidence from the 1992 mass rapes committed by Serbian men against Muslim women during the Balkan conflict in Bosnia.[14]

Before the "comfort women" issue emerged, due to his interest in broad compensation for victims of war abuses, Takagi already had links to an Indonesian advocacy organization. This was the Communication Forum for Ex-Heiho, which was established in May 1990 with two key missions: to retrieve the remains of former *heiho* from across Indonesia and to build a monument to remember *heiho* who died in Morotai in Halmahera island.[15] Takagi was introduced to this organization through Japanese researchers on Indonesia.[16] Takagi recalls that his first impressions of members of the forum were of men who were proud to be former *heiho*.[17] When the forum's representative, Tasrip Rahardjo, attended the first International Committee gathering in Japan in 1991, he asked for help to gain recognition of the *heiho*'s status in the Japanese army and for retrospective military promotions to be honored. Takagi recalls being surprised because such requests did not entirely convey a sense that the former soldiers were "victims" of the occupation.[18] Usually, wartime survivors chose to "testify as victims" at these conferences. Instead, Rahardjo's presentation reflected a semi-nostalgic remembrance of being part of the Japanese army. Their viewpoints further elucidate sources of ambiguity around how the occupation is remembered.

As a result of the outreach of the International Committee and other global developments, members of the forum slowly shifted their positions concerning wartime redress. In July 1992, when news of Korean advocacy for surviving women reached Indonesia, Rahardjo told the press he estimated there were 60,000 Indonesian 'comfort women.' At that stage, only one woman had come forward. Rahardjo did not provide a source for this estimate, but he told *Tempo* magazine he was going to Tokyo the following month to claim US $700 million for the women.[19]

Why did Rahardjo believe that his organization, made up of former soldiers, could best represent the women survivors of the occupation? In part this seemed to reflect a patriarchal assumption, as Ute Frevert observes, that men are "expected to restore honour whereas women are often deemed incapable of doing so."[20] There was no suggestion that surviving women might represent themselves. Potentially, the forum also acted based on an assessment of their power and visibility relative to that of the women. After the war, many former *heiho* went on to have careers in the Indonesian military and other professions. They had vastly more political and social capital than former "comfort women," who had extremely limited educational and employment opportunities after the war. The forum's status as an organization also meant the former *heiho* were more visible in Indonesian society than the women were.

From 1992 onward, as the "comfort women" issue gathered momentum, the forum noticeably altered its strategy and approach, particularly on the question of redress. Rather than asking for recognition of their status, and relatively quietly calling for their entitlements and payment of lost wages, the forum demanded that Japan pay former *heiho* compensation of US$20,000–US$30,000 per person to replace the forced savings and wages of soldiers.[21] If Japan did not concede, they insisted they would bring the case to the International Criminal Court in The Hague.[22]

Once again, the fact that Indonesian survivors of the "comfort women" system did not have their own organization had multiple ramifications. By this time Filipino women had formed the Task Force of Filipino Comfort Women (later called Lila Pilipina), which had begun to document survivors. Japanese lawyers, including Takagi, contacted Filipino survivors via the task force and worked with it to achieve some goals. In 1993, this connection led to eighteen Filipino women filing a lawsuit against the Japanese government in Tokyo district court. The suit eventually included forty-six claimants, all of whom demanded ¥20 million per person as compensation.[23] This direct relationship with survivors meant that Takagi continued to involve women from the task force in the annual conferences of the International Committee. By contrast, in Indonesia the key advocacy organization was a legal aid body not exclusively focused on seeking justice for surviving women. Ultimately, this lack of dedicated organizational representation made Indonesian women less visible to the AWF.

The 1995 Conference of the International Committee

Takagi Ken'ichi openly supported the AWF as a mechanism for compensation. This was in keeping with his long-standing commitment to seeking this form of redress for wartime victims, and perhaps his experience advocating for many survivors in Japan's courts, most of which were unsuccessful. Takagi was involved in the discussions around establishing the AWF and explained that the formula for compensation was carefully considered. He pushed for including the obligation for the Japanese government to pay ¥3 million for medical and social welfare support for each victim, in addition to the proposed ¥2million for each victim, paid for by donations from the Japanese public.[24] He felt that securing larger payments from the government for medical and welfare expenses helped address the perception that the AWF was mostly funded by private money.[25] Speaking twenty years after the AWF was created, Takagi was still of the view that not taking money from the AWF was a missed opportunity.[26]

In recognition of her growing profile in Indonesia and beyond, Mardiyem was invited to the International Committee's 1995 conference, accompanied by LBH representative Rita Serena Kolibonso. Takagi explained that he invited her to speak at the conference because "Mardiyem was symbolic like Kim Hak-Sun."[27] He used this opportunity to encourage her and other survivors to consider taking the AWF money.[28]

For Mardiyem, attending the conference was important in various ways. In her short speech, she gave an account of her experiences during the occupation.[29] Her testimony was reported in the Japanese media; Eka Hindra, an Indonesian activist who worked closely with Mardiyem from 1998, claims that this conference and Mardiyem's testimony opened up the issue of Indonesian "comfort women" to the international community.[30] This was not an easy experience for Mardiyem, who was approaching seventy years of age. She reported that she felt very emotional remembering and talking about her past in an open forum.[31]

The Ex-Heiho's Report on the Comfort Women

In addition to establishing a connection between the International Committee, Mardiyem, and the LBH representative, Takagi turned to the Communication Forum for Ex-Heiho to help document Indonesian victims. He decided to involve the forum in this process based on the part they played in the system as guards at the *ianjo* and other sites where women were held.[32] He assumed they could have information that could be useful in the search for survivors. Takagi traveled to Indonesia in late 1995 and met with members of both the forum and LBH. The forum arranged for him to meet and interview five former "comfort women" in Bogor.[33] He visited Mardiyem and conducted follow-up discussions with LBH representatives regarding the AWF, once again attempting to convince them to accept the compensation offered.[34]

It is likely that Takagi took this two-pronged approach because he believed the forum would be more amenable than LBH to using the AWF as a strategy for pursuing broader compensation. A week before the 1995 International Committee meeting, the Yogyakarta branch of LBH (led by Budi Hartono) decided to oppose aspects of the AWF. In a letter to Prime Minister Murayama Tomiichi on August 2, 1995, LBH praised his apology for the treatment of women during the war but demanded that the government of Japan "pay compensation to the former Indonesian comfort women on an individual basis (not in the form of a project)."[35] Echoing broader criticism of the AWF offering, they expressed their dissatisfaction that the Japanese government was only funding welfare projects.

Meanwhile, following encouragement from Takagi, the forum had already begun to document surviving women.[36] They advertised the AWF's offer in newspapers and through the forum's network of offices throughout Indonesia, relying on the assistance of local LBH offices to register those who came forward. An astounding 22,454 women did so in the space of nine months from August 1995 until April 1996.[37] A crucial reason for women coming forward appears to have been the advertising concerning the amount of money women could potentially receive from the AWF: US$28,500.[38] The forum recorded biographical data for the women and their responses to a simple questionnaire comprising twenty-five multiple choice questions.[39] To establish that harm had been caused, the questions focused on coercion and maltreatment.

A translated version of the questionnaire in imperfect English was included in an Indonesian-language report presented to the International Committee in April 1996 titled "Compensation for the Jugun Ianfu."[40] From the more than 20,000 questionaries completed, the report summarized the women's "answers" for each question. On the key question of how the women became "comfort women," they could choose from the following responses: (a) being deceived to become nurse, further education, be given work; (b) being forced if not willing, family threatened to be killed (by the Japanese); (c) based on own intention after being seduced or flattered; and (d) kidnapped on the way home from school (years old). Overall 45 percent of respondents chose (a), 45 percent choose (b), one percent selected (c) and 9 percent chose (d). Another question asked the women: what was the attitude of the soldiers? Eighty-four percent described it as rough and fierce, 7 percent as normal, 6 percent as natural, and 3 percent as good.[41] There is no further elaboration on these findings.

Other questions focused on the women's experiences of having "sexual intercourse" or sexually "serving" the men. One question asked, "how did you feel during or at the time of serving the soldiers (*heitai*)?" This is a highly personal and private question. Asking it demonstrates absolutely no sensitivity to the women's experiences of sexual violence and completely disregards the fact that the women had been raped (indeed, 84 percent had already testified that the attitude of the soldiers was rough and fierce). The vast majority selected the answer (a) that they did not enjoy, only feeling tired and fed up (66 percent) or (b) no longer remember or feeling as if in hell (32 percent).[42]

The forum's 1996 report also included background on "the system" in Indonesia and an estimate of the number of "comfort women" across the colony based on the number of troops in Indonesia during the war. The authors of the report estimated there were 150,000 troops in Java and Sumatera and assuming that every seven soldiers needed one woman for "sexual services," they concluded there must have been 21,428 "comfort women" in the colony.[43] This is a similar method of estimation to that used by Yoshimi Yoshiaki to estimate the total number of women in the system (see chapter 2). The figure has been repeatedly used by activists to refer to the total number of Indonesian "comfort women." It is remarkably close to the number of women documented by the forum, but it should be noted that like LBH, the forum documented all women who had experienced sexual assault and not exclusively former "comfort women."[44] The results of the questionnaire indicated that 57 percent of documented women were held in *ianjo*, which might be the closest estimation available of how many of these women were "comfort women."[45]

The report featured extracts of interviews with surviving women across multiple branches of the forum. Some of these interviews were conducted by Japanese activists, including Takagi Ken'ichi and Kawada Fumiko (see below). The authors of this report note that many women had "endured suffering and hidden their feelings" and had only become brave enough to reveal their experiences after hearing about the possibility of compensation, which they argued would be a form of healing for the women "after fifty years of suffering."[46]

Members of the forum were determined to advocate on behalf of the women. They argued that they were documenting this case "to provide assistance to victims of brutal sexual assault."[47] In this, the report explicitly referenced the types of violence women experienced, which represented a definitive shift from early news reporting on the topic described in chapter 6. This suggests a new awareness of the specific nature of the crimes against the women.

The forum had other motives. In the opening pages of the report, its authors reminded the International Committee of its earlier recommendation that the government and people of Japan quickly compensate all victims of the Asia Pacific War.[48] Referring to the 1993 Kōno statement, which gave many wartime victims hope for compensation, the forum argued that "without payment of compensation to all victims, an apology has no meaning, instead it becomes a lie to the international public."[49] The intention of the report on the women survivors was clearly in support of a collective claim for compensation. However, at least one aspect of this claim is problematic. Evidence provided to *Tempo* and in scholarly work, primarily by guards of "comfort stations," indicates that *heiho* soldiers were also responsible for abusing women.[50]

Nonetheless, such an emphasis on joint victimhood and using the "comfort women" case to open up redress for all wartime victims was consistent with the way Takagi Ken'ichi and the International Committee framed this issue.[51] He reassured the *heiho* that the committee wanted to help secure compensation for all victims. He conveyed his frustration with critiques of the AWF, noting that many victims were dying while these debates were playing out, arguing that "concrete actions to implement immediate and substantive redress are more precious than hundreds of criticisms."[52] His criticism was most likely directed at the Korean Council, one of the most vehement opponents of the AWF, but also at some Japanese activists who opposed the fund.

The Asian Women's Solidarity Conference and Outreach to Indonesia

From its inception, in apparent recognition of their prominence in the redress movement, the AWF initially focused its attention on South Korean and Filipino women seeking compensation and always tried to work toward a solution through their respective governments. In 1993, the Japanese and Korean governments initially discussed the idea of a foundation financed by Japan and run by the South Korean government.[53] When the Japanese eventually decided to establish the AWF, they did so without any prior consultation with survivors or activists, nor did they recognize Indonesian women.

As detailed in chapter 5, the Korean Council played a leading role in activism globally, such that their views on the AWF significantly influenced the movement as a whole. The Korean Council opposed the AWF, arguing that it was an inadequate solution. They looked to rally international opinion on this issue by using existing networks with the UN, International Commission of Jurists, and the Asian Women's Solidarity Conference.[54]

In March 1996, Filipino survivor organization Lila Pilipina (formerly the Task Force for Filipino Comfort Women) hosted an Asian Women's Solidarity Conference in Manila, with the support of the Korean Council, the Asian Women Human Rights Council, and another local organization, the Gabriela

Women's Alliance. Attendees included forty-nine Japanese activists, twenty-seven Korean activists (including survivors), forty-three Filipino activists, six Taiwanese activists, and two Indonesians—LBH lawyer Dewi Novirianti and Mardiyem.[55] The theme of the conference was "Why the Japanese-sponsored Asian Women's Fund is not the solution to the 'comfort women' issue." The organizers hoped to formulate a plan of action based on the recently released Coomaraswamy report. The delegates called on the Japanese government to make formal individual apologies to the survivors, disband the AWF, pay direct reparations to survivors and the bereaved families of victims, create a special administrative tribunal for reparations, include the issue in textbooks, and punish the perpetrators.[56]

In August 1996, as the AWF began to issue its first payments, Koreans formed a new organization called the Citizens' Coalition for the Resolution of the Forced Recruitment of the Comfort Women by the Japanese Military.[57] This group raised funds to support survivors who rejected the AWF payments and lobbied the South Korean government to increase the stipends already given to some survivors.[58]

In January 1997, as a result of AWF outreach, seven Korean women agreed to accept compensation. All were members of the Association of Pacific War Victims and Bereaved Families.[59] By late 1997, under pressure from the Korean Council and its followers and exhortations that the women needed "to maintain the honor of the survivors and the pride of the nation," all seven women recanted their deals with the AWF.[60] Chunghee Sarah Soh is highly critical of the position of Korean activists and the Korean government who, in her view, denied the rights of victimized women to decide whether to take the AWF payments.[61] She argues that survivors' rights to personal autonomy were curtailed due to relationships of dependence between survivors and organizations like the Korean Council.

These forms of dependence and the ties between activists and survivors are important to consider across all cases of human rights activism. There is a tension between viewing survivors as controlled or manipulated and seeing them as able to make independent choices. Writing in 2008, Hideko Mitsui, offered a different perspective on this issue. She was critical of what she perceived to be a backlash against activists based on the assumption that "the subaltern *should* not be able to speak for herself, and thus, when she demands something as obscure as justice at the expense of monetary gain she must be ventriloquizing those with the power to prescript her speech."[62] Mitsui objected to the view that survivors were being manipulated, arguing that every position on this issue was inevitably political.[63]

Another critique raised by Yamashita Yeong-ae, who worked for the Korean Council, was that responses to the AWF were sometimes framed as a nationalist issue. In this way they disregarded the individual women affected and what compensation might mean for them.[64] An example of this approach is seen in the language used by the Citizens' Coalition for the Resolution of the Forced Recruitment of the Comfort Women by the Japanese Military. The coalition called on its members to "protect our *halmŏni* [grandmothers] so that they are not hurt again by imperialistic Japan's dirty money, so that our national pride is not insulted."[65] Yamashita strongly rejected the women being framed as national symbols alongside a very one-sided view of Japan.

In Taiwan, the government and leaders of the movement represented by the Taipei Women's Rescue Foundation took a similar position to the Koreans and decided to raise alternative funds for the women. Likewise, they rejected AWF payments "to protect the dignity of victims and the pride of the country."[66] These responses from Korean and Taiwanese advocates were premised on the availability of alternative funds from sympathetic governments who understood compensation as an issue of national pride. Taiwan's and South Korea's responses are connected to strong anticolonialist sentiments in these countries.

In the Philippines, the situation was different. At the Asian Women's Solidarity Conference in March 1996, there was strong Filipino support for a rejection of the AWF, yet the first recipients of AWF money in late 1996 were Filipino women. This largely reflected the different economic realities of Filipino women, compared with their South Korean and Taiwanese counterparts, who were offered alternative funds by their governments and citizenry. Maria Rosa Henson was among the recipients. Henson had brought a legal case against the Japanese government beginning in 1993 and was a high-profile participant in the 1996 conference. At the time she was offered the compensation payment in late 1996, her legal case remained unresolved. Henson explained that she decided to take the money after listening to advice from Takagi Ken'ichi and representatives of the AWF.[67] She faced backlash from some activists and survivors, but she argued that she was old and sickly and needed the money to meet her daily needs, while she continued to pursue legal redress through the courts.[68] She died in 1997, a year before the decision in her case, which was to dismiss all of her claims, was eventually handed down.[69]

To receive the AWF funds, Filipino survivors had to provide birth certificates and marriage certificates (where available and relevant) and produce an affidavit filled out by a local nongovernmental organization or government representative detailing their experiences and the conditions they faced as "comfort women."[70] The documentation process was not dissimilar to that followed by

Indonesia's LBH (chapter 7). The Philippine government formed a special committee to verify documents, and then the Department of Justice interviewed survivors and checked applications to decide who would be given compensation. Representatives of the AWF held up Filipino recipients as success stories, but there were multiple struggles in the Philippines and between external players over whether survivors should accept AWF money. Organizations like Lila Pilipina helped some survivors with their applications to the AWF while continuing to advocate for state redress.[71]

The Citizens' Fund for Realizing Postwar Compensation

Maria Henson's decision to accept the AWF's compensation payment had an immediate effect on the movement. The Citizens' Fund for Realizing Postwar Compensation mobilized to raise money from independent sources and connect Japanese supporters directly with survivors.[72] Supporters sent around ¥5,000 a month to around eighty women, mainly in the Philippines, on the condition that if they accepted AWF funding, the money from the Citizens' Fund would stop.[73] The Citizens' Fund kept up payments to women for about three to four years, later extending assistance to Indonesian women—perhaps recognizing that they faced a similar context and could not hope for support from their own government. Some Indonesian women received 400,000 rupiah for their medical needs, and some received further compensation for medicines. A total of 3 million rupiah was received by LBH for distribution to the women.[74]

The Japanese activists behind these programs of alternative compensation strongly objected to what they saw as attempts by the Japanese government to sidestep state responsibility. As Mitsui observed, from the very beginning the AWF obscured who had committed crimes against the women. The appeal made to citizens to contribute funds, for example, was prefaced by the following description of the harms against women: "The war caused enormous horror and ravaged the people of Japan and of many other nations, especially those in Asia. Particularly brutal was the act of forcing women, including teenagers, to serve the Japanese armed forces as 'comfort women,' a practice that violated the fundamental dignity of women."[75] Here, Mitsui emphasized, the harms were blamed indirectly on "the war" rather than soldiers, and Japanese victimhood is foregrounded.

The Citizens' Fund took various steps to counter the AWF. They posted advertisements in newspapers in Japan, South Korea, and the United States dissuading people from donating to the AWF.[76] The Citizens' Fund also escalated its outreach programs to connect with women who had not yet made deals with the AWF. In 1995 and 1996, just after the AWF was set up, representatives of the group made three visits to Indonesia, requesting help from LBH and the forum to locate women.[77] Arimitsu Ken and Kawada Fumiko were members of the delegations to Indonesia. Kawada explained that the purpose of her trip was to gather information to increase awareness about the Indonesian "comfort women" in Japan.[78] Supporters of the Citizens' Fund felt that the results of Indonesian investigations into the "comfort women," including those conducted by LBH and the Communication Forum for Ex-Heiho, had not yet been sufficiently socialized in Japan.

During their visits, Arimitsu set up bank accounts for several Indonesian survivors so they could receive payments for their medical and health expenses. Kawada focused on collecting testimonies from the Indonesian survivors she met. These were longer and far more detailed than the typically short bio data collected by LBH and the forum. With the help of Kimura Kōichi as an interpreter, she interviewed six women in Yogyakarta. In her interview, Mardiyem spoke about her experiences during and after the occupation, explaining that she visited LBH as a way to control what she called the "devil's circle" of recurring feelings of guilt and ongoing stigma related to her experiences.[79] Kawada also recorded the life story of Sukarlin, a friend of Mardiyem who was held in the same boarding house in Telawang, Borneo. Sukarlin told Kawada about the strict surveillance and violent sanctions the women faced during the occupation and her chronic health problems.[80]

Kawada interviewed six more women in Sukabumi, West Java, and six in Cimahi, West Java. Kawada also interviewed four women who were the forced wives of Japanese men. They spoke of the struggles they and their children experienced during and after the occupation.[81] Kawada believes she was welcomed by the women because she was Japanese and perhaps because of the expectation of compensation.[82]

The testimonies of these women were published in Japan in 1997 in a book titled *Indoneshia No "Ianfu"* (*Indonesia's Comfort Women*). Consistent with the style of similar popular publications in Japan at the time, the book uses very few to no quotation marks, meaning it is unclear precisely when the women are being quoted directly.[83] This may also reflect the difficulties of translation from the Javanese or Indonesian language to Japanese. The book drew on several Japanese sources, including documents discovered by Yoshimi Yoshiaki, such as a telegram detailing an order for women to be sent from Taiwan to Borneo.[84] It included the accounts of several retired military men, including former Prime Minister Nasakone; [85] Shogenji Kango, who had served as a mayor in Banjarmasin during the war; [86] and the testimony of Miyamoto Shizuo.[87] This evidence was later used in the Tokyo Women's Tribunal (see chapter 9).

On her second visit to Indonesia in December 1995, Kawada traveled with a Japanese film crew to document the stories of Indonesian survivors in Sukabumi. The documentary about the Indonesian "comfort women" was broadcast by Chukyo TV in Nagoya city the following year.[88]

In July 1996, just before the funds from the AWF were to be paid out to the women who had registered, Mardiyem and Budi Hartono traveled to Tokyo. They submitted a petition to the JFBA asking for help to fight for the rights of Indonesian survivors, using the JFBA system of appeals,[89] and met with representatives of the Japanese government.[90] They held meetings with women survivors from four countries (Korea, China, the Philippines, and Taiwan), all of whom had rejected the AWF. The women participated in a street protest demanding acknowledgment of the Indonesian survivors, an apology, and direct compensation from the Japanese government.[91]

A few months later, in September, Mardiyem and Budi returned to Japan, this time at the invitation of a local organization to visit Hokkaido and several other cities to present information about Indonesian "comfort women" on several campuses.[92] Mardiyem spoke of being moved when meeting the students because some were the grandchildren of Japanese forces who had fought in Indonesia. She had not expected such a positive response from the younger generation, while questioning why there was not the same response from the older generation.[93] On this visit, Mardiyem also met with AWF representatives in Tokyo to demand direct compensation and make clear that Indonesian survivors had been greatly offended at not being initially acknowledged.

In addition to Japanese outreach to Indonesians, Koreans were also trying to build and maintain connections across the movement. Yoong Mee-Hyang from the Korean Council explained that it was not easy to contact Indonesian survivors directly.[94] One way was via the regular regional Asian Women's Solidarity conferences. Recognizing the financial barriers women from poorer countries faced, the Korean Council often funded women from these countries to attend. In the March 1996 conference in the Philippines, for example, the Korean Council supported Mardiyem and an LBH lawyer to attend.[95]

During this period, as Mardiyem's transnational activism was escalating in intensity, at home in Indonesia the government launched a crackdown on potential sources of political opposition. In July 1996 the headquarters of the PDI were attacked by hired thugs with military and police backing. This resulted in rioting and the quashing of all sources of opposition to the regime.[96]

By late 1996, Mardiyem's travels to Japan had elevated her profile, and she was recognized as the icon of the Indonesian movement.[97] The Communication

Forum for Ex-Heiho completed their report and sent it on to the International Committee, following the report from the LBH to the JFBA sent two years earlier. Kawada Fumiko's book on Indonesian survivors was also under way. Nonetheless, despite the growing international activism on the "comfort women" issue, Budi Hartono remained deeply disappointed that this issue had not triggered public support in Indonesia as it had in Korea and the Philippines. In those countries, widespread interest saw mass actions, general meetings, conferences, open seminars, and broad use of pamphlets to "make the comfort women issue a lively discourse which would at the same time bombard the government of Japan."[98] Hartono had hoped that a stronger public response would pressure the Indonesian and Japanese governments to resolve the issue in a way that took into account the wishes of the survivors.

The Indonesian Government's Deal with the AWF

The combined effect of these reports and Mardiyem's increasing global profile may have contributed to the Indonesian government's decision to negotiate directly with the AWF.[99] On November 14, 1996, the government made the announcement that it "empathizes with the endless psychological and physical trauma and pain of the women who were victims of violence. However, the Government, representing a people who are imbued with the Pancasila philosophy, does not intend to introduce measures of policies strongly colored by emotion, and will work hard to protect the honor of the women who were victimized and their families."[100] This emphasis on Pancasila values, which in New Order rhetoric meant an approach that emphasizes social harmony and the oneness of the state and society, made clear that the state would not act on behalf of individuals.[101] In many ways this mirrored the so-called Asian human rights discourse advocated by some leaders in the early 1990s, especially via the 1993 Bangkok Declaration, which suggested that Asian societies prioritized communal over individual rights and economic social and cultural rights over civil and political rights.[102] The comment in relation to the protection of honor suggests that it would be shameful for women to speak up, when of course several women had already gone public and given media commentary. This statement replicated the idea of sexual violence as extending an *aib* or stain on families.

This moralistic framing is consistent with the position at the time in the Ministry for Social Affairs, which handled this issue, and coincided with a concerted campaign of moral rehabilitation of sex workers. Reflecting a culture where only women are blamed for "lapses in morality," the ministry regularly published guides on how to rehabilitate sex workers and overcome the problem of loose morals or *tuna susila*.[103] In late 1994 and 1995, the ministry authorized raids on sex work locations in Boker and Kalijodo in Jakarta, evicting workers and forcing them to undergo rehabilitation.[104]

Throughout 1996, Indonesian government representatives reiterated their position that the right to claim from the Japanese government was settled with the 1958 treaty. Their preference was for the AWF to promote projects and assistance programs through the Ministry of Social Affairs, not through any other organization.[105] After three years of LBH advocating on this issue, this was a direct snub from the government and likely related to LBH's increased involvement in oppositional politics. In the lead-up to the May 1997 general election, LBH formed a coalition with student groups and others to create an organization to monitor the election. LBH workers were intimidated and their Medan office was burned down.[106] In July 1996, the Jakarta LBH office allowed activists to use their premises to launch a new political party, the Indonesian Democratic Party (Partai Rakyat Demokrasi), defying laws on political parties.[107] It is likely that the government was deliberately rebuking the LBH on this issue.

As a prelude to its formal agreement with the AWF, the Indonesian government representatives argued that due to the apparent difficulties of verifying who the women were, it would be better that funds were used to establish facilities for the elderly more broadly. They claimed such an arrangement would inevitably benefit former "comfort women." This framing ignored the fact that at the ministry's request, LBH had already taken statements of women's experiences and verified them through a process that appeared to differ little from that used for Filipino claimants. The real source of objection to direct compensation payments seemed to be the Indonesian government. Indeed, the AWF's own website, set up to provide an open and transparent record of their activities, claimed that some members of the AWF had a strong preference for individual payments to Indonesian survivors. Eventually the AWF agreed to the Indonesians' deal on the condition that the nursing homes should be established in places where surviving women were concentrated and that these women would be given priority.

On the March 25, 1997, the Ministry of Social Affairs signed an agreement with the AWF for the payment of ¥380 billion yen. The agreement was discreetly labeled a "Memorandum of Understanding between the Department of Social Affairs and the AWF Concerning Promotion of Social Welfare Services for Elderly People in Indonesia."[108] The surviving women were not named in the report's title, but the agreement affirmed that this was connected to "comfort women." The second line stated that it was premised on "recognizing that victims, who underwent immeasurable painful and suffering experiences and suffered incurable physical and psychological wounds as 'wartime comfort women,' exist in Indonesia."[109]

This was formal recognition that Indonesian women had also been victimized. The agreement focused on the Ministry of Social Affairs overseeing the establishment and running of nursing homes for a period of ten years in regions "where war time comfort women seem to exist."[110] Because it was not an agreement between the AWF and individuals, no letters of apology signed by the Japanese prime minister were issued to individual survivors. One Japanese organization reported, however, that the prime minister expressed regret in a letter addressed to President Suharto.[111] Yet in Indonesia, there was no announcement to this effect, and the letter was never made public. This lack of individual recognition of survivors created a further source of grievance for activists and survivors.

Given that she had only relatively recently met with representatives of the AWF, Mardiyem's response to the deal was outrage. The media immediately looked to her and LBH for comment. Mardiyem made her objections clear: "there are no 'comfort women' who want to be asked to move into a nursing home."[112] She explained the cultural preference for the elderly to live and be cared for by their families and further stated that she was angered by implied government statements that "if Indonesian women received money this would mean they sold themselves." She saw no direct benefit for survivors in the agreement. She argued that the Filipino women who had received money from the AWF had been tricked and that Indonesian women needed to be careful not to be tricked as well. She noted that Indonesian survivors had agreed that if one woman receives money, they all should receive money.

Budi Hartono called on the minister to change her views so that individual victims could be directly compensated.[113] On April 19, he announced that although survivors were still trying to resolve the dispute, they were also prepared to sue the minister.[114] Hartono explained that many Japanese people disagreed with the AWF, viewing it as a form of "extortion by their government to shift the burden of responsibility to the public and treat the comfort women's situation at arm's length."[115]

In the context of this heightened public interest, together with anger among the survivors and activists at the government's deal with AWF, a new organization called the Movement to Oppose Violence against Indonesian Women (Gerakan Anti-Kekerasan Terhadap Perempuan Indonesia, GAKTPI) made a public statement in support of the women.[116] GAKTPI's mission was to increase gender equality in Indonesia through a particular focus on addressing cases of violence against women. In May 1997, the group issued a press release containing a copy of a letter sent to the minister of Social Affairs requesting that the government cancel the agreement for the nursing homes, which in their view amounted to theft, and instead pay the money directly to the women.[117] They challenged the minister, who had just been campaigning for the legislative elections, to see to it that like women in other countries, Indonesian women received the compensation directly.

The Significance of People-to-People Links

The agreement between the Indonesian government and the AWF also prompted responses in Japan. Writer Kawada Fumiko and theologian Kimura Kōichi were the key Japanese advocates to speak out and denounce the deal.[118] In her book, Kawada exposed widespread views among the Japanese military that Indonesian survivors were not victims, but instead registered prostitutes. Using examples from her interviews with Indonesian survivors, she highlighted the forced recruitment of women, including those who were not previously sex workers. She concludes the book with firm criticism of the AWF's project in Indonesia and alerts readers to a growing countermovement demanding individual compensation.[119]

Kimura Kōichi's multilingualism and close connections with the women meant he often acted as an intermediary between Japanese and Indonesian activists. When LBH needed help, Kimura would assist with translations of Japanese documents and connect Japanese activists with Indonesian survivors and to LBH.[120] Kimura became particularly close with Mardiyem and Suhanah, sometimes traveling with them as their interpreters. He assisted Kawada Fumiko with translating thirty-three interviews.[121] In 1996 he was also a key translator for a Japanese documentary film that helped increase awareness of the case of Indonesian survivors in Japan.[122] The film crew returned to Indonesia to make a second documentary in July 1997.[123]

In Japan from June to September 1997, a small group of Japanese activists including Kawada and Kimura launched an advocacy group called Japanese Society for Solidarity with Former Indonesian Comfort Women (Solidaritas Masyarakat Jepang untuk ex Ianfu Indonesia, SOMJII). SOMJII's mission, as announced in their first newsletter *Suara*, was to address the lack of information in Japan on the situation of Indonesian survivors and to "inform as many Japanese citizens as possible about their plight."[124] SOMJII also acted as a lobbying group for Indonesian survivors, calling on representatives of the AWF to be more transparent in their dealings with the Ministry of Social Affairs about how Japanese funding would be used.[125] It sent its own representatives to inspect the nursing homes built under the agreement and to check if they were in fact accommodating survivors. SOMJII also shared information with LBH and Indonesian survivors to assist in their advocacy.

In July 1997, Budi Hartono accused the AWF of discriminating against Indonesian women on the basis that women in other countries had received funds directly.[126] He expressed his disappointment at the Indonesian government's view that this issue was an *aib* noting, "their suffering is part of history. They did not do something that should be considered a stain. They were forced and pressured. If they are considered a stain by the government, why is the government willing to accept the money?"[127] Hartono's direct challenge to the concept of a stain stands in marked contrast to statements made by journalists in 1992, when this issue first began to be discussed. Dadang Julian-toro, the head of LAPERA, a Yogyakarta organization, agreed that if the government's excuse "was that this was a stain that should not be opened then it was appropriate to ask. If these were the actions of the Japanese army, and history was indeed like this. Why must it be hushed up?"[128] In response to the media attention and motivated by the possibility of compensation, by July 1997 a large number of Indonesian women had registered at LBH's Yogyakarta office and were calling on them to challenge the government. Some made posters and put them up outside of Yogyakarta LBH office, carrying slogans such as "restore our rights," "don't steal from us what is ours by right," "where are our rights, we want justice," "why are we being silenced, we have suffered so much," "Mr President, pay attention to our fate. Only the veterans get your attention."[129]

The language of human rights used in these posters is striking and in firm contrast to the way the survivor women had very tentatively framed their experiences in the earliest reports given by *Tempo* journalists in 1992. There are also pointed references to the perceived favoritism of war veterans over the women.

By August 12, three hundred women from the Yogyakarta area and Central Java and five hundred women from Kupang, eastern Indonesia, had asked the LBH to fight for compensation on their behalves.[130] Budi Hartono explained to the press that every woman's experience was being verified. A group of former *heiho* wearing batik shirts and caps decorated with small Japanese flags gathered in front of the Japanese embassy in Jakarta to demand compensation.[131]

Meanwhile, the activism of these survivors of the Japanese occupation was gaining attention from society more broadly. In August 1997, Mardiyem was invited by activists to open a campaign opposing violence against women.[132] She was very moved by this invitation because in her view, "the concern shown towards victims of violence, including rape was very limited. Even though this occurred at all levels of society, those who suffer are the ones at the bottom."[133]

In October 1997, the AWF finally offered a formal response to the Indonesian protests about the deal. They argued that they could not pay the women directly because there was already a consensus-based agreement between the AWF and the Indonesian government to use the money for social welfare projects, namely nursing homes.[134] They pointed out that this money came directly from the Japanese government, not the Japanese people.[135]

Nonetheless, SOMJII continued to pressure the AWF in Japan. In December they requested clarification of several points of the Indonesian agreement; first, as to whether the AWF recognized that there were former "comfort women" in Indonesia, and if so, how many women they believed there were. Further, they asked "what kind of investigation has the Fund conducted on the issues of 'comfort women' in Indonesia so far? Is there any plan of further investigation? If so, provide us with the detail of the plan."[136] They asked whether any money had been paid to Indonesia yet, and if so, to whom and how much, and about the progress of the construction of nursing homes. They requested clarification about the relationships between survivors and the nursing homes, exactly what costs for the women would be met. SOMJII also pushed the AWF to acknowledge the public response in Indonesia to the agreement with the government.[137]

Following a similar line to LBH, SOMJII also pressed the AWF to ask why there were no plans for "a letter from the prime minister" and "support for medical treatment, care, and residence," which the AWF had described as "the inseparable set of tasks for the implementation of our plan."[138] Finally SOMJII questioned whether cases of individual women wanting to receive compensation from the AWF would be considered.[139]

The AWF replied by explaining they required "authorization from the government or an equivalent authority" of any country before proceeding to pay individual compensation.[140] The AWF noted that they were given assurances by the Indonesian government that the nursing homes would support survivors and be set up in the areas where these women were concentrated.

In 1998, in a visit by SOMJII representatives to a nursing home in Binjai near Medan in North Sumatra, they found not a single "comfort women" survivor residing there.[141] The Japanese Ministry of Foreign Affairs reported to SOMJII that by the end of 1998, eleven homes had been completed with ten residents in each, yet only one survivor resided in one of these facilities.[142] There was thus a significant gap between the expectations of the AWF about how the funds would be used and the reality of implementation by Indonesia's Ministry of Social Affairs.

Conclusion

The establishment of the AWF led to an escalation in domestic and transnational activism for survivor women. Groups on both sides of the AWF debate attempted to contact Indonesian survivors and bring them on board with their views. Mardiyem was invited to international events and became the representative of Indonesian women. Apart from LBH, another victims' group, the Communication Forum for Ex-Heiho also advocated on behalf of the women. The newly formed Japanese support group SOMJII lobbied the Japanese government and the AWF on behalf of Indonesian women.

In this period, survivors became more vocal and began to articulate their demands more clearly in the language of human rights. LBH and Mardiyem were increasingly in the media spotlight following the Indonesian government's controversial agreement with the AWF not to pay individual compensation to Indonesian women. They became more forceful in the demands they made of the Japanese and Indonesian governments and increasingly critical of negative discourses around survivors.

9

The End of Suharto

Sexual Violence under the Spotlight

n Indonesia, between 1997 and 2000, there was increased focus on human rights, and more specifically sexual violence, due to a number of developments related to reform and democratization. While this produced an environment that was more conducive to activism, at the same time there were many cases of human rights abuses competing for activists' attention. Beginning in 1997, the Asian financial crisis was the first blow to the military-dominated Suharto regime, which had relied on its development credentials for legitimacy. At this time, Indonesian activists and student protesters became increasingly brazen in their demands for reform at all levels of society, including an end to elite corruption and greater attention to human rights. In this context and in the wake of the government's deal with the AWF, LBH published the first major work in Indonesian on Indonesian "comfort women." This was a landmark publication on human rights in Indonesia because it encompassed both the life story of a survivor and because it took an intersectional approach to the issue. The book aimed to fundamentally change societal views about survivors of wartime sexual violence.

The events of May 1998, including organized riots in the major Indonesian cities, led to a new spotlight on sexual violence. The reason for this was the shocking revelation of mass rapes of mostly ethnic Chinese women during the violence. The riots prompted President Suharto's resignation and a new era under the leadership of the former vice president and interim president Habibie. Facing international pressure, Habibie sought to quickly democratize Indonesia. This included the abolition of the Ministry of Information, which had previously censored the press, especially reporting related to human rights abuses. Women's rights activists became increasingly prominent in this period and began to raise cases of military sexual violence against women.

Meanwhile, internationally, Dutch advocacy organizations signed a deal with the AWF that resulted in better outcomes for women of Dutch background. Women's activists from Korea, Japan, and the Philippines began to plan a people's tribunal as an alternative way of seeking redress for survivors from all affected countries. The tribunal, which took place in Tokyo in 2000, became a new focus for Indonesian survivors and brought Japanese and Indonesian activists together again.

The First Indonesian Book on the Comfort Women

In early November 1997, LBH began to publicize a forthcoming book about the Indonesian "comfort women" coauthored by lead LBH lawyer Budi Hartono and sociologist Dadang Juliantoro.[1] The book was promoted as a form of protest against the Indonesian government's position on this issue, especially the deal with the AWF, and to raise awareness about Indonesian survivors.[2] In a comment to the media, Budi Hartono explained that "besides caring about the usefulness of expressing the truth about the history of the comfort women, which until now has been covered up, the book forms one kind of protest about why the Korean, Filipino, Taiwanese and Chinese governments and Japanese NGOs have done a lot to help the struggle of the comfort women, whereas the government of Indonesia has taken a passive attitude."[3] Hartono and Mardiyem continued to criticize the Indonesian government for its handling of the case, often comparing Indonesian actions to those of other governments. The book challenged the government's view that this was a shameful issue. Budi Hartono explained, "with this book it will be understood that the *jugun ianfu* were not dishonorable women, but victims who deserve to be respected."[4] Although his comments indicate that he was attempting to morally rehabilitate these particular women by distinguishing them from "dishonorable" women (presumably meaning sex workers), whom it is implied are less worthy of respect, he unwittingly discounted the experiences of women such as Tuminah and reinforced negative attitudes toward sex workers.

The book, *Derita Paksa Perempuan: Kisah Jugun Ianfu pada Masa Pendudukan Jepang, 1942–1945* (The sufferings of forced women: Stories of "comfort women" during the Japanese occupation, 1942–1945), provides an overview of women's experiences of sexual violence. The words LBH used to refer to survivors in both the book title and the text, *jugun ianfu* or *wanita penghibur*, both mean "comfort women." The most distinctive feature of this book was the focus on the story of Mardiyem. Such is her predominance in the book that one media report referred to her as one of its coauthors. Given her limited literacy, however, the truth is that Mardiyem provided extended testimony and observations only.[5] This was the first book in Indonesia to focus in depth on the story of a victim of human rights abuses told from her perspective. One chapter was devoted solely to her story, commencing with her life as a young girl up to the end of her ordeals during the Japanese occupation.[6] The book's cover, which can easily be found in an online search, featured a photograph of Mardiyem engaging in a street march in Tokyo demanding recognition of Indonesian survivors, holding a banner in Japanese with another image of her holding a poster in English reading "redress now."

It was the first book to consider the history of a nonelite, relatively poor Indonesian woman. In the year before this there had been some publications, also supported by LBH, about murdered labor activist Marsinah, but these books did not focus on her life story, nor on the specific forms of violence directed at her, which included sexual violence.[7] Rather, their focus was on her representation as a symbol of the oppression of labor activists and legal corruption.[8] As noted in chapter 6, until then, histories of Indonesian women had focused largely on elite women who had participated in the women's movement or fought against the Dutch.

In this sense, *Derita Paksa Perempuan* was a major breakthrough. Furthermore, like the first histories of the *karayukisan* in Japan (discussed in chapter 5), Hartono and Juliantoro took an intersectional approach, paying attention not just to the actions of the Japanese army but the surrounding culture of patriarchy that had enabled this system. They explained why daughters or young women would often unquestioningly follow the requests of their fathers or village heads to sign up for work opportunities (see also chapter 3).[9]

The authors of the book were highly conscious of Japanese–Indonesian economic ties and pointed to this as a factor hindering government support for survivors. In their introduction, Juliantoro and Hartono reflect on the extensive Japanese investment in Indonesia, which may have prevented attention to this issue. In media reports Hartono also frequently stated that he hoped monetary reasons were not behind the AWF deal.[10] The book's launch in November 1997 coincided with the onset of the Asian financial crisis, and its effects were beginning to be felt in Indonesia. That month, sixteen banks were closed down and the rupiah had lost over 40 percent of its value.[11] Indonesia was turning to all possible international donors, including Japan, for help.

To attract broader sympathy and generate outrage, the authors represented the issue as a problem for the nation of Indonesia, not one for the women alone. They stated, "the lowering of Indonesian women to become just the sexual servicers of the Japanese army, is nothing other than a reflection of how low the Indonesian people were in the eyes of Japan."[12]

In representing survivors this way, they replicated what Ueno has referred to as "the patriarchal paradigm of the nation's shame,"[13] which dominated Korean public discussions about "comfort women." Ueno critiques this paradigm on the basis that it "denies women's agency, and reduces the infringement of women's sexual human rights to a dispute over property rights between fellow men within the patriarchal system."[14] This example suggests some of the difficulties that activists face in trying to rally support. In the end, they sacrifice the women's personal experiences and agency by making them into symbols of a larger claim of the infliction of national shame.

Different promoters of the book presented contrasting messages about its meaning and purpose. The book launch was celebrated at Hotel Sartika in Yogyakarta on November 14, 1997.[15] In her launch speech, Mardiyem repeated the story of how she was recruited, stressing her young age, "at that time I was still 13 years old, I had not even begun menstruation."[16] She affirmed the sense of indignity she felt at the government's actions, stating, "the feelings of hurt are there until today. It's so bad that we are treated worse than rubbish. At least in the case of rubbish there are scavengers. What about me? I am harassed! There are even some people who spit on me whilst saying you were just a Japanese ration."[17] She reminded the audience that she had already engaged in a struggle for the violation of her rights to be recognized, mentioning that this had also cost her personally. She related that after she began to speak publicly about her experiences, orders for her catering business declined and eventually stopped altogether because people considered her dirty due to her history.[18] She expressed her hope that with this book the history of the "comfort women" would also be acknowledged alongside that of the rōmusha. She compared herself to other victims of the occupation, observing that they had at least received recognition in history texts. Mardiyem posited that this history was part of the struggle of all Indonesian women.

The book was promoted as part of a campaign to include this history in Indonesian history textbooks, to counter the view that this was shameful, and to challenge stereotypes about the women. At the launch, Budi Hartono commented, "the tragic fate that our women experienced has never been included in our history books."[19] The demand from Budi Hartono and Mardiyem for this history to be included in textbooks is consistent with the resolutions of the 1996 Asian Solidarity Conference and the recommendations of the Coomaraswamy report and demonstrates how activist demands were converging internationally.

The book attracted broader sources of support. Rosalia Scortino was the program officer for Gender, Human Development and Reproductive Health at the Indonesian and Philippine offices of the Ford Foundation from 1993 to 2000. The Ford Foundation was one of the joint publishers of the book. Scortino placed the book in a broader context, commenting to a journalist that this issue was connected to the effects of war on women who always become victims of physical violence and sexual violence. Reflecting her interest in the book and its potential effects, Scortino commented, "one aim is to socialize the case of the jugun ianfu in Indonesia, but also to build gender awareness in broader society."[20] Apong Herlina from YLBHI stated that the effort to record this history and carry out advocacy was "a new step in the defense of women's rights."[21] These comments reinforced the significance of the book for promoting awareness of sexual violence and women's rights.

Elsewhere in November 1997, political activist and performance artist Ratna Sarumpaet held performances across Indonesia of a provocative monologue called "Marsinah Accuses."[22] The play's title mirrors that of Sukarno's famous 1931 address to the Dutch colonial court when he faced charges of subversion leading to his exile to Boven Digul. In the play, Sarumpaet retraces the final hours of Marsinah's life. Mardiyem attended a performance along with Budi Hartono and Kimura Kōichi. At the end of the play, Sarumpaet invited Mardiyem to the stage, where she presented her with a book by the same title as the play, and Mardiyem reciprocated, gifting Sarumpaet a copy of *Derita Paksa Perempuan*.[23] Sarumpaet linked these human rights abuses on the basis that each involved impunity for crimes committed against women. This pattern of linking different cases of human rights abuses against Indonesian women intensified after the May 1998 riots and led to more dynamism in efforts to publicly discuss and oppose military sexual violence against women.

The May 1998 Riots: Military Sexual Violence in the Spotlight

Beginning in late 1997 and early 1998, as the economic crisis began to deepen, the demands of the prodemocracy movement grew louder. This movement for change came to a head with the events of mid-May 1998. From May 12 to 14, a series of police shootings of student protesters, riots in the major Indonesian cities that destroyed shops and resulted in mass deaths, and the rapes of mostly Chinese Indonesian women changed Indonesia in fundamental ways. These events led to President Suharto's resignation and Habibie's appointment as interim president. The nature of the violence led to severe scrutiny of the police and military for at the very least simply standing by during the rioting, and at worst, playing a key role in the violence itself. The revelations of sexual violence against Chinese Indonesian women galvanized women's rights activists to raise loud protests against sexual violence more generally and demand answers for who was responsible for the May 1998 rapes in particular. The nature of this violence combined with an increasing climate of democratization, during which press restrictions were lifted and activism became less constrained, enabled nationwide discussion of other cases of sexual violence against Indonesian women, especially cases committed by the Indonesian military. This prompted more sustained critiques of patterns of military sexual violence.

The sexual violence committed against mostly Chinese Indonesian women in Jakarta, Medan, and Solo included sexual assault, gang rape, rape by objects, and women being forced to have sex in front of other family members, as well as the murders of some raped women.[24] Revelations about this violence, combined with a general push for reform, prompted diverse responses to the issue of violence against women. An initial response to support survivors and their families, included groups emerging out of existing organizations and activists' coalitions. This included two established women's rights groups, Kalyanamitra and Mitra Perempuan, which became new centers of solidarity between ethnic Chinese and other Indonesians who had suffered in the riots.[25] Mitra Perempuan issued one of the earliest public calls through advertisements in newspapers to support survivors of these sexual assaults.[26] One of the main organizations supporting victims was the Volunteer Team for Humanity (Tim Relawan Kemanusiaan) led by Catholic priest Sandyawan Sumardi. In June 1998, a subteam within this organization was formed, called the Tim Relawan Divisi Kekerasan terhadap Perempuan (Volunteer Team Division for Violence against Women), led by Ita F. Nadia of Kalyanamitra. This group worked with survivors providing medical assistance, legal support, and counseling, and sought to document the women's experiences. By July 13, 1998, they had completed a report in which they estimated that 168 women had been assaulted in Jakarta, Solo, Medan, Palembang, and Surabaya.[27]

The assaults against Chinese Indonesian women prompted new media discussion around sexual violence, but very few survivors were prepared to give direct testimony to the press. One woman's account appeared in a tabloid, where she reflected a reluctance to disclose her experiences similar to that expressed by former "comfort women." She noted, "Really I don't want to tell anyone about this shame . . . What for, what good does it do me? It's just one more burden for me. I am ashamed in front of people, especially my friends."[28]

Like former "comfort women" in the early 1990s, this woman was reluctant to talk to the press because of shame. She refers to her male partner's feelings of disgust at her, thereby implying an unquestioning and problematic sense of male ownership of women's sexuality. Some women also feared reprisals for speaking out and further persecution on the basis of their position as Chinese Indonesians.

Reporting on the 1998 rapes and social constructions around the victims reveals more about public attitudes to sexual violence and who could be considered a worthy victim. Ariel Heryanto observed that commentary on female victims of the rapes tended to stigmatize the women in stark contrast to the heroic representation of male student kidnapping victims. He attributed this to the emphasis on virginity and chastity for women and the view that women should "have only one sexual relationship with the man to whom they are married legally."[29] Jemma Purdey notes that both ethnic Chinese victims and the urban poor victims of the May 1998 riots were considered unworthy victims due to their ethnicity or class.[30] These observations remind us that just as in the case of the "comfort women," social class and gender determines who is perceived a worthy or legitimate victim.

In June 1998, soon after it was installed, Habibie's interim government responded to pressure from women's groups and other human rights groups to form a Joint Fact-Finding Team (Tim Gabungan Pencari Fakta) to investigate the riots, including the sexual assaults and rapes. The team included members of human rights and women's nongovernmental organizations as well as government officials, police, and military officials. Not surprisingly, in this process, representatives from the government and security forces pressured other members of the team not to implicate the military in the rapes. In November 1998, the Joint Team concluded that although there was evidence that the riots themselves were highly coordinated, data on the rapes did not allow them to conclude whether the rapes were part of the same riot system.[31] The Joint Team and human rights groups were repeatedly challenged on the basis of the proof they could produce, including criticisms that indirect testimony was insufficient.[32] These challenges all overlooked the difficulty survivors of sexual violence have in speaking about their experiences. Activists repeatedly tried to explain why victims would not come forward, connecting this to the lasting stigmas attached to rape and feelings of shame felt by victims.

Although there was a tendency both in Indonesia and abroad to represent the violence as ethnic violence, several scholars rejected this analysis and drew broader comparisons. Heryanto viewed the rapes as more akin to militarist state terrorism, pointing to the military use of sexual violence in the disputed territories of Aceh and East Timor as a form of intimidation.[33] Indonesian feminist and lead editor of *Jurnal Perempuan*, Gadis Arivia, similarly connected the occurrence of rape in the May riots with the repressive Indonesian state and earlier cases exposed in 1996 of military rape in East Timor, suggesting the prevalence of "a culture that supports male sexual aggression and violence against women."[34] The May 1998 rapes, therefore, generated a new focus on patterns of military sexual assault in Indonesia. This led to organizations "mapping of the New Order's repressive structure" such that people in "conflict-ridden areas" could "see that their plights were not unrelated."[35]

At this time, activists and academics also began to hold public seminars and workshops comparing patterns of military sexual violence from Aceh and East Timor, but also internationally with cases like Bosnia and Croatia.[36] Some sections of the media offered more systematic analyses of military sexual violence. In October 1998, *Gatra* magazine ran a special story on military violence against women in East Timor, focusing on the so-called village of widows in Villa Verde and exposing patterns of "rape, local wives and comfort women like the *jugun ianfu*."[37] In this report, a direct link is made to the case of the Japanese occupation through the use of this term. Other papers drew parallels between gang rape used in multiple contexts by armies, including in Bosnia in the 1990s, Bangladesh in the 1970s, and the Japanese in their wartime system.[38] SOMJII members monitored Indonesian reporting on this kind of violence and the fact that connections were starting to be made with wider cases of sexual violence against women in periods of conflict within and outside of Indonesia.[39]

Some Indonesian government officials responded defensively to perceived international shaming of Indonesia related to cases of sexual violence in the May riots.[40] General Wiranto, as commander of the Armed Forces and minister of Defense, repeatedly denied the rapes had occurred.

A significant result of these collective efforts to pressure President Habibie to acknowledge and take responsibility for the May 1998 rapes was the formation of the National Commission on Violence Against Women (Komisi Nasional Anti Kekerasan terhadap Perempuan, Komnas Perempuan), an independent body established on October 15, 1998, to handle cases of violence against women.[41] The commission included academics, medical professionals, nongovernmental organization activists, and members of state institutions. Further to this, the Habibie administration established the National Human Rights Action Program (Kegiatan Rencana Aksi Nasional Hak-Hak Asasi Manusia Indonesia) for 1998–2003, acknowledging women as a marginalized group, in addition to children and the elderly. The program included a plan to implement conventions that had already been ratified, such as CEDAW, and a national program to eliminate violence against women.[42]

The high profile of the May rapes internationally, combined with increasing information coming to light related to other cases of military sexual violence against women, culminated in a visit in late 1998 by UN Special Rapporteur Radhika Coomaraswamy with the support of the Indonesian government. During her trip from November 20 to December 4, Coomaraswamy investigated the May rapes and cases of military violence against women in Aceh, Irian Jaya (the New Order name for West Papua), and East Timor.[43] She was not permitted to travel to Aceh and West Papua ostensibly because of limited time, but she still investigated these cases through other evidence.

Her visit galvanized women's activists, leading to a nationwide observance of the International Day of the Elimination of Violence against Women on November 25. The Women's Coalition for Justice and Democracy (Koalisi Perempuan Indonesia untuk Keadilan dan Demokrasi), headed by feminist lawyer Nursyahbani Katjasungkana, organized a National Congress on December 18, 1998, in Yogyakarta, mirroring the historic Indonesian Women's Congress of 1928. Five hundred women from twenty-six provinces attended the congress.[44] At the opening of the gathering, delegates played musical instruments to symbolize breaking the silence on the issue of violence against women.[45] Members also agreed to work toward increasing the quota of women in the legislature.

Overall, responses to the May 1998 riots saw a broadening of debate about violence against women. There was an increasing number of publications on the subject of sexual assault and rape.[46] One result was "more public education about the nature of rape as a crime" and more open discussion about the public obstacles to testifying.[47] When it was published on January 21, 1999, the Special Rapporteur's report, which included anonymized testimony of victims of sexual violence, drew significant local attention to the issue of sexual violence more broadly. Coomaraswamy concluded that "rape was used as an instrument of torture and intimidation by certain elements of the Indonesian army in Aceh, West Papua and East Timor" and that women in these regions were also often subjected to forms of sexual torture.[48] She also reported on cases of sexual slavery by Indonesian soldiers and the children who were born as a consequence of this abuse. In relation to the May rapes, she confirmed that despite evidence that they had taken place, among criminal justice officials, the attorney general, and other sectors of society, there was a worrying culture of denial. She attributed this to a lack of gender awareness and recommended gender training for the police, military, and criminal justice officials.

Coomaraswamy strongly condemned the Indonesian military, calling for its role in society to be severely reduced, noting that "a human rights culture cannot emerge within a militarized state."[49] She highlighted the worrying trends of intimidation and threats toward human rights activists that remained un-investigated, and the general impunity for many cases of sexual violence. The high-profile announcement of Coomaraswamy's findings was met with an angry response from representatives of the Indonesian government.[50] From this point on, there was ongoing UN monitoring of violence against women in Indonesia, intensifying again after the 1999 military and militia-led violence in East Timor, which eclipsed the focus on the May violence.[51]

As mentioned in earlier chapters, as Special Rapporteur, Coomaraswamy was also responsible for continually monitoring developments on the "comfort women," emanating from her 1996 special report on this issue. However, in her 1999 report, the "comfort women" were not mentioned, nor were Indonesian women a specific focus of her ongoing monitoring on the issue of the "comfort women."[52] It seems that contemporary cases of violence against women in the Indonesian context simply overshadowed the historic cases. Meanwhile, the focus of UN attention on the "comfort women" issue remained firmly fixed on East Asia and the positions of Japan and South and North Korea on this topic.[53] This was most likely a result of sustained South Korean lobbying on this issue.

New Deals with the AWF and Continuing Advocacy for Indonesian Survivors

Alongside dramatic political changes in Indonesia, internationally negotiations and advocacy related to the "comfort women" issue continued to unfold. The AWF carried on its negotiations with different women and organizations. In the Netherlands, the key organization advocating for the rights of surviving women, the Japanese Debts of Honor Committee (JES), was more broadly concerned with war redress for Dutch victims of the Japanese occupation of the Netherlands East Indies. Members of the JES in principle rejected the AWF because it did not constitute legal compensation, while also agreeing to assist some JES members to pursue compensation. Retired General Huyser and Marguerite Hamer de Froideville subsequently left the JES board to set up a committee known as the Project Implementation Committee of the Netherlands (PICN), which was willing to work with the AWF.[54]

A deal between the PICN and the AWF was reached in in July 1998. As PICN's vice chairperson, Hamer de Froideville oversaw the process. She explained that with the assistance of the AWF they were able to set up a compensation scheme and allowed survivors to choose whether they wanted to be part of it. She notes that this differed to other countries, where particular organizations or governments made the choice for women or where women might have received the money directly from the AWF.[55]

The PICN received ¥255 million from the AWF over three years and was responsible for determining who was eligible to receive the money.[56] In general terms, the criteria included that the women had to have spent World War II in Southeast Asia and were forced against their will by means of deception or threats to work in army brothels or similar places. Women captured from outside the camps or women taken from the camps and subjected to rape were also eligible. The PICN provided compensation to women who were in coerced sexual relationships with Japanese military men over an extended period of time. Advertisements were placed in the JES's monthly magazine calling on women to register via a confidante. Dutch women, like other women from countries across Asia, were also reluctant to come forward, and many only did so because they were not required to publicly identify themselves.

In addition to the funds, the PICN received a copy of a signed letter of apology from Japanese Prime Minister Hashimoto Ryūtarō to the Dutch Prime Minister Wim Kok, apologizing for what had been done to the Dutch victims.[57] There were no individualized letters for recipients, but Hamer de Froideville sent a copy of the letter to all recipients. She noted that this meant a great deal to them.

After processing, seventy-eight Dutch applicants were determined to be eligible for the fund. This included four men who had been eight- to twelve-year-old boys at the time of the occupation and who had endured "systematic sexual abuse against their will." Two boys were abused outside the camps and two within the camps. Hamer de Froideville refers to these boys as "comfort boys" and reflects on the fact that they had experienced great shame related to their experiences.[58] The fact that male victims have only been recorded in the Netherlands raises the issue of how widespread the abuse of boys and men was across other occupied territories. The recipients of fund money came from the Netherlands, Indonesia, the United Kingdom, Canada, the United States, Australia, and India.

According to Hamer de Froideville, to respect the privacy of the women and men involved, the PICN tried to keep the issue fairly low profile, which included not involving the media. The women's and men's identities were at all times protected, and each signed consent agreements to determine whether the documentation they supplied to the PICN on their experiences should be destroyed or kept under embargo for twenty years.[59] This is in stark contrast with the strategy employed in Indonesia by LBH, which sought to gain public sympathy for the women through media exposure. There were some Dutch objectors to the PICN process. Jan Ruff O'Herne strongly rejected the PICN and did not want to have anything to do with it or the AWF.[60] Ellen van der Ploeg took a similar position.

When the Dutch deal was announced in mid-1998, Indonesian media outlets reported on it. One journalist claimed that Dutch women would receive compensation of 3.5 million guilders in total from Japan while also noting Indonesian women had suffered the same fate: hundreds of women were forced by Japan to become sex workers in military barracks spread across the archipelago.[61] Given the comparative wealth of Dutch to Indonesian women, rejecting the AWF was potentially a difficult position to sustain. According to Hartono, however, at stake was not just an issue of compensation but "the pride of the Indonesian nation and especially of the women who have been offended by the government of Japan."[62]

By the time the Dutch deal with the AWF was announced, ¥38 million of the ¥380 million yen agreed between the two governments had already been paid to the Indonesian Ministry of Social Services, and nursing homes had been built in Semarang, Magetan, Pare Pare, Medan, DKI Jakarta, Yogyakarta, Kalimantan Timur, Sumba, West Java, and South Sumatera. Budi Hartono continued to demand that the Indonesian government "return the money to the AWF" and then "urge the Japanese government to quickly apologize in a formal capacity and individually to each former ianfu. Only then will we think about compensation."[63] He remained insistent that the money be returned even though this now seemed highly unlikely. In following this line, he mirrored the thinking of the SOMJII group who at a meeting in Indonesia in June 1998 led by Kimura Kōichi committed to a plan of action to try to stop the AWF deal.[64]

In the midst of these persistent Indonesian protests, lobbying in Japan by both the SOMJII group and the JFBA, and the perceived success of the Dutch resolution on this issue, the AWF commissioned a report into the Indonesian "comfort women" to focus in particular on what evidence was in Dutch archives about the experiences of Indonesian "comfort women." This appeared to be a direct response to SOMJII's questions (see chapter 8) regarding the existing research (if any) concerning Indonesia. This archival report, released in September 1998, titled *Comfort Women in Indonesia: A Report on Dutch Archival Materials for Submission to the Asian Women's Fund*, was carried out by two Japan-based researchers, Mayumi Yamamoto and William Horton, both of whom had conducted research on the Japanese occupation of the Netherlands East Indies.[65]

During this period, SOMJII members continued their outreach efforts in Indonesia, engaging in discussions with LBH and visits to surviving women such as Mardiyem, Suhanah, and Sukarlin, all of whom lived in Yogyakarta. SOMJII supporters such as Kimura's Korean wife, Kimura Otcho, reported back on these women's circumstances to supporters in their newsletter, noting in particular Sukarlin's dire poverty and her mistreatment by relatives.[66] In August 1998, Suhanah was invited to Japan by a solidarity group based in Chiba, just west of Tokyo. She was accompanied by Kimura Kōichi and Indonesian activist Vidiana, and she gave testimony on her experiences of forcible recruitment and maltreatment at a gathering of the Chiba Group for Considering War Time Responsibility. Suhanah testified that, at the age of sixteen, she was taken by Japanese soldiers from in front of her house and dragged away by her hair. She was a virgin and was raped first by a Japanese man and then a Japanese doctor, then repeatedly raped by five to ten men a day in the same room as other women, until she became ill. She explained to the Japanese audience her mixed feelings of being glad to meet them, but also sad to remember her painful past.[67]

Throughout August, LBH continued to act. They sent a letter to Japan's Foreign Minister Obuchi Keizō to inform him that in LBH's view, the AWF money had been misused by Indonesia's Ministry of Social Affairs. Drawing on renewed public attention to corruption in this period, he stated that the fact the minister of Social Affairs processed the money indicated potential corruption given that there was already money in the ministry's budget for these nursing homes. Hartono made an appeal stating, "even if our government is afraid and does not care about the fate of the former jugun ianfu we hope for the understanding of the Japanese PM for the sake of the self-worth of the former comfort women."[68]

This appeal reflected a deep sense of frustration at the lack of traction from the Indonesian government on this issue. Privately, in December 1999, Budi Hartono shared with SOMJII supporters that the survivors were disappointed with LBH because they had not been able to do anything for the women other than let them make their experiences known publicly.[69] The lack of support from Indonesian society further amplified the women's sense of disappointment and was adversely affecting their health. The women were elderly and in need of medical care and money, and the funds from the Civil Fund for Redress had ended. In response, SOMJII started what they called a Suara fund, named after their newsletter, to try and raise money for Indonesian survivors.

LBH continued to push for other forms of official government recognition of the women. After Suharto's fall, there was an almost immediate push to open up or "straighten out" Indonesian history.[70] There were calls for major revisions to the history curriculum. The first Education minister in the Habibie government, Juwono Sudarsono, immediately set to work on this new curriculum. He even suggested cases of human rights abuses, such as those in East Timor and Aceh, be included.[71] These calls from within the government to revise the history curriculum echoed those of the LBH and Mardiyem from a year earlier, and they continued to advocate for inclusion of the history of the "comfort women." In November 1998, LBH urged Minister Sudarsono to do so, saying, "history can't be avoided. We, especially the women of Indonesia who were made into jugun ianfu, indeed experienced a dark history. Yet don't consider this a stain. Our grandchildren need to know this. If not, their grandchildren will consider the women prostitutes."[72] He framed this request in terms of healing the wounds of the women who continued to be seen as "prostitutes." The general push to open up history, which importantly also came from community pressure, did lead to new initiatives. One of these was the formation in 1998 of a group called Women's Circle (Tutur Perempuan), whose members began to meet and hold discussions with women who had been victimized throughout Indonesian history.[73]

Interest in human rights was increasing more broadly in Indonesia, due not only to recent events, but to a great extent due to the lifting of restrictions on press freedom. In 1999, Internews, a source of radio news and other content for use by a syndicate of radio stations across Indonesia, began to explore the theme of human rights in their programming.[74] The women's program of Internews, coordinated by members of the progressive feminist *Jurnal Perempuan*, took up the theme of women's rights and violence against women. This led one young journalist, Eka Hindra, to the topic of the "comfort women" and an interview with Mardiyem.[75] A shortened version of her interview with Mardiyem was aired across fifty radio stations. Hindra had been drawn to this topic after an earlier meeting with Mardiyem and longtime activist Kimura Kōichi. From Kimura in particular, Hindra had learned a great deal about developments on this topic in Japan, which were not so widely known or understood in Indonesia.[76] From that point on, Hindra became a key activist for Indonesian women often accompanying and representing them at regional meetings.

Further significant changes in Indonesia happened in 1999, with the first democratic elections since 1955 held in June and the East Timor referendum on independence held in August. The vote for independence in East Timor was followed by widespread Indonesian military and militia-backed violence against the East Timorese. The combined effects of electing a new government and a new president and intense international scrutiny of Indonesia's human rights record escalated democratization, including the full withdrawal of the army from politics.

Indonesia's domestic crises and emerging democratization meant that Japanese activists paid increased attention to Indonesia. In 1999, the JFBA finally responded to the 1996 appeal filed by survivors and LBH in protest at the planned AWF deal with the Indonesian government. When it finally came, there was some puzzlement about why, given their significant interest in the case in the early 1990s, it had taken the JFBA three years to respond to these pleas.[77]

In December 1999, the JFBA sent a delegation of four lawyers to Indonesia to follow up on the plea. The delegation, their first since their high-profile visit in 1993, included Tokio Shigeru, Yamashita Kiyoshi, Yokoyama Knock, and Katō Yutaka.[78] During their visit the delegation met with representatives of the National Commission of Human Rights (Komnas HAM) to ascertain what they knew about the issue. The commissioners admitted that they did not really know how to deal with the issue, but they were willing to cooperate with the JFBA.[79] Although the commissioners expressed compassion for the women and agreed they had been hardly done right by in the AWF deal, in a recorded interaction with a group of survivors at the Komnas HAM office in Jakarta before the 2000 tribunal one commissioner suggested to the women, "*jugun ianfu* is a shameful term, it's better to say you were war victims. You are victims and that data can be used for a recommendation to lobby the Japanese embassy."[80]

This comment reflects the fact that even in human rights organizations, gendered violence was still seen as shameful. It appears that the JFBA did not consult the National Commission on Violence Against Women on this issue despite its more specific focus.

The JFBA team collected further testimonies from Indonesian survivors, including Mardiyem and Sukarlin, during this visit. In the course of an interview with Jainem, who had also been held in Telawang Boarding House with Mardiyem, she froze and stated that she had never been an "ianfu." Jainem had previously told Kawada and Kimura that she was raped at Telawang by the head of the boarding house and many other men, including two men from the Borneo newspaper. Kimura, who was acting as an interpreter at the time, noted that Jainem later explained her actions by stating, "I lied because talking about what Japanese men did to me was very shameful. I will speak the truth if [you] can really protect me."[81] The fact that she froze shocked Mardiyem and caused her to panic, thinking that perhaps the lawyers would think she was lying. This incident reminds us that the capacity of survivors to give testimony is shaped by circumstances. In contexts where public support was very low, women were more hesitant to share their experiences.

By 1999, after many years of advocacy, Mardiyem was feeling increasingly disheartened, especially because some of the friends and fellow survivors for whom she had striven to achieve compensation had passed away in poor conditions. She told a reporter that every time she met these friends, they would ask her how the struggle was going.[82] By then the women were feeling embarrassed because they felt like they had "stripped themselves naked."[83] Mardiyem explained, "They are already naked and ashamed because they have openly admitted they were jugun ianfu. Yet until now this struggle has not yet produced results that are sufficiently satisfying."[84]

There was a sense of hopelessness in Mardiyem's reflections and a hint that her activism had come to very little. She, like other women, was feeling exposed rather than supported.

The Road to the Women's International War Crimes Tribunal

The issue of the "comfort women" reached a climax internationally the following year, when activists held the Women's International War Crimes Tribunal on Japan's Military Sexual Slavery in Tokyo to try the Japanese government for crimes committed against women. Activists from the Japan-based Violence Against Women in War network (VAWW-Net) first proposed the tribunal in April 1998 at the Fifth Asian Women's Solidarity Conference in Seoul, where they gained support from conference delegates. They chose to use a people's tribunal to hear this case because of the perceived "failure of states to discharge their responsibility to ensure justice."[85] This included the failures immediately after World War II of states to prosecute most cases, and more recent setbacks including the multiple failed court cases brought by victims against the Japanese government. The AWF was seen as another effort to close down legal avenues for justice.

People's tribunals seek to use international laws to draw attention to ongoing injustices that have not been handled by other courts or relevant states. Organizers intended this tribunal to acknowledge this past, assign responsibility for the crimes committed in relation to this case, and advocate for individual reparations.[86] It was set up in the context of recent prosecutions of sexual violence in the international criminal courts for the former Yugoslavia and Rwanda. The organizers hoped that the tribunal would constitute a further step toward ending impunity for sexual violence.

Planning involved multiple preparatory meetings in the countries from which there was activist support for the tribunal, especially Japan and South Korea, but also North Korea, the Philippines, Taiwan, the United States, and the Netherlands. The key organizers were women from VAWW-Net, the Korean Council, and Lila Pilipina, but they eventually managed to gain support from ten prosecution teams representing Japan and women from North and South Korea, Taiwan, China, the Philippines, Malaysia, the Netherlands, East Timor, and Indonesia. In the long lead-up to the tribunal, it seems that Indonesians were only minimally engaged.[87] Kalyanamitra activist Ita Nadia, who had been prominent in activism related to justice for the victims of the May 1998 rapes, attended the first meeting where the tribunal was proposed. She strongly supported Indonesian participation and eventually joined the delegation to Japan. In December 1998, Apong Herlina represented LBH's Jakarta office at the conference "How to Hold the Women's International War Crimes Tribunal, Judging Japan's Military Sexual Slavery," sponsored by VAWW-Net at Waseda University, Japan. She reported to the conference on the situation of the Indonesian former "comfort women" who were shunned by society and suffered financial difficulties. She observed that due to social prejudices and the mental burdens on survivors and even family members, some women had given up on disclosing their pasts.[88] There was not, however, good coordination or information sharing about the plan for the tribunal across activist groups.

In preparing for the tribunal, the team of international organizers found it difficult to appoint a lead prosecutor to represent the Indonesian team. Among Korean and Japanese activists, there was doubt about Indonesia's ongoing support for this issue. This was perhaps because different Indonesian representatives were sent to planning meetings each time.[89] The tribunal organizers first invited prominent Indonesian lawyer Adnan Buyung Nasution, the chair of LBH, to join the initiative, but received no response. Indonesian support for the tribunal only escalated after Nursyahbani Katjasungkana, a founding member of LBH APIK, was brought onto the case in December 1999. She was approached by Matsui Yayori from VAWW-Net to lead the Indonesian prosecution team, no doubt due to her impressive credentials as a feminist lawyer who had long worked in the field of women's legal rights.

At that point, Katjasungkana recruited three other people to work with her on the Indonesian team. These were lawyers Asnifrianty Damanik from APIK, Paulus Mahulette from LBH, and Antarini Arna from the Women's Coalition (Koalisi Perempuan).[90] By this time, the prosecution team had to move quickly to gather data for their case. They were assisted by Kimura Kōichi, who introduced Katjasungkana to Japanese activist Mina Watanabe of VAWW-Net, who helped them find relevant Japanese documents. One key document this process uncovered was the autobiography of former Japanese Prime Minister Nasakone, in which he openly wrote about setting up "comfort stations" on the island of Borneo (see chapter 3).[91] Other documents included Japanese military archive material on the transportation of women.[92] The team also drew on the documents reproduced in Kawada Fumiko's book on Indonesian "comfort women" (see chapter 8). By the July 1999, prosecutors' meeting in Manila, the Indonesian team had prepared the first draft of their indictment.

The team worked closely with four survivors who were chosen to represent Indonesian women. These were Mardiyem, who was an obvious choice, Suhanah, Suharti, and Ema Kastimah, all of whom had been interviewed by Kawada Fumiko in 1996 (see chapter 8). Suharti and Mardiyem had remained friends since their experiences in South Borneo. All four were willing to speak in public about this issue, and Suhanah and Mardiyem had previously done so in forums in Japan and Korea.[93] In the lead-up to the tribunal, Mina Watanabe traveled to Indonesia to record video testimony with young Japanese filmmaker Tachikawa Tomoko and Indonesian filmmaker Lexy Rambadeta. The footage focused on the women's current lives and circumstances, the locations in which they were held by the Japanese during the occupation, and their narrations of their experiences.[94] In the case of Mardiyem, this included footage of her home and a trip she took in July 2000 with Watanabe, Kimura, Tachikawa, and an Indonesian activist, Vidiana, recreating her journey from fifty years earlier, from Yogyakarta via Surabaya to Borneo.[95] They were able to document the former location of the Telawang boarding house and the hospital where she was subjected to a forced abortion. Parts of this footage were used in the tribunal. The full footage was later included in the English-language film directed by Tachikawa Tomoko (then Kana Tomoko), titled *Mardiyem: Sex Slave of the Japanese Army*.[96]

The women's expectations of the tribunal varied. Reflecting on conversations with Suhanah in November 1999, Tachikawa suggested that Suhanah was not that clear on what the outcomes of the tribunal would be. She had asked Tachikawa "if I go to Tokyo for the tribunal in December, I will get money this time, right?"[97] Perhaps due to the complexity of the idea of a people's tribunal, Suhanah expected a more immediate result like compensation, which was highly unlikely given that the tribunal could really only act as a mechanism to pressure the Japanese government or the AWF for further action. Tachikawa's response was to call for more support from Japanese activists to collect money for the women, since many had already died in circumstances of poverty.[98]

On August 25, a meeting was held in Yogyakarta with two hundred participants in support of the tribunal. Key speakers at the meeting were Katjasungkana and Kimura Kōichi, as well as Suhanah and Mardiyem.[99] Katjasungskana explained that the premise of the Women's Tribunal was to address crimes against these women, to uncover the truth, and to make the Japanese government admit their offenses and apologize. On September 14, approximately fifty surviving women marched together to Yogyakarta's local assembly. The women presented their demands, including for the issue of the "comfort women" to be included in textbooks, for the assembly to hold the minister for Social Affairs,

Inten Soeweno, responsible for her actions, and that the Indonesian government should work with the Japanese government to dismiss the AWF and lobby the Japanese government to apologize to victimized Indonesian women.

The Indonesian delegation to the tribunal in Tokyo included the four survivors, the prosecution team, and other supporters, including Kimura Kōichi and Ita Nadia. In Japan, the Indonesian team was also supported by activists Kawada Fumiko and Tachikawa Tomoko and other SOMJII members.

The tribunal was held in a symbolic location: Kudan Kaikan Hall, used during the war as a military officers' club built in the Japanese imperial style. The hall is also close to the palace of the emperor, an accused party in the tribunal. The tribunal had a clear commemorative dimension to remember the women who had already passed away. Paintings by the victimized women and appeals and messages for peace were displayed, as well as photographs of survivors demonstrating in front of Japanese embassies or "showing the scars that still remain on their bodies."[100] On the evening before the tribunal began, survivors performed a procession, holding candles and walking across a stage featuring large portraits of survivors who had already passed away, such as Kim Hak-Sun. Participants were invited to jointly sing the protest song "We Shall Overcome." The words to this powerful song include the following: "We are not afraid, truth will set us free. Deep in our hearts we must believe, we are not alone today."[101] In the video footage taken of the tribunal by Lexy Rambadeta, it is noticeable that the Indonesian survivors did not sing along, perhaps because they did not understand the words, while the Indonesian lawyers, who were fluent in English, were singing.[102] The official language of the tribunal was English, with interpreters translating questions from country prosecutors in English. William Horton worked as an interpreter for the Indonesian women, using his skills in English, Japanese, and Indonesian. Even though survivors had access to some parts of the tribunal through translation, it is unclear how testimonies from women speaking other languages were communicated to audience members who did not speak either the original language or English.

The tribunal opened on December 8, 2000, with remarks from key organizers Matsui Yayori of VAWW-Net, India Lourdes Sajor of Lila Pilipina, and Yun Chung-Ok of the Korean Council. They thanked all survivors for attending and for making the tribunal possible, stressing that the court "did not belong to any government or power" and that "it was not just for survivors, but also for those who died and for generations to come."[103] The indictments against the Japanese government were read out, before each country presented its case. There was an audience of around one thousand people, with survivors seated in the front rows.[104] There were twenty-nine survivors from North and South Korea, twelve from Taiwan, nineteen from the Philippines, seven from

China, four from Indonesia, two from East Timor, two from the Netherlands, and one from Malaysia. The number of representative women from each country reflected the extent of support these women had. Indonesian women were relatively poorly supported.

Judge Gabrielle McDonald, the former president of the International Criminal Tribunal for the Former Yugoslavia, and three other high-profile human rights judges presided over the tribunal. The prosecutors argued that the rights of individuals could not be waived in postconflict treaties where there were "crimes against humanity" and harms committed against individuals where the state might be a perpetrator.[105] The tribunal organizers also presented this tribunal as a continuation of the Tokyo Charter (see chapter 4).[106]

During the three days of proceedings, sixty-four survivors gave testimony, repeating harrowing accounts of rape and captivity. Because of the flexible format, organizers tried to give survivors center stage, but at the same time "make the bodies of the perpetrators visible" through testimony that described the harmful acts these soldiers committed.[107] Two former soldiers, Kaneko Yasuji and Suzuki Yoshio, agreed to testify at the tribunal, providing firsthand accounts of how they had raped and abused women. Some senior military men were also named as accused. The entire proceedings were filmed, and a video was released afterward for public distribution. This was particularly significant in light of the fact that the Japanese broadcasting agency censored several aspects of their coverage, including the testimonies of many women and of the soldiers as well as the verdict of guilt, all of which was replaced by an interview with the conservative Japanese historian Hata Ikuhiko.[108] This censorship formed only part of a backlash in Japan against the tribunal. There were also demonstrations outside Kudan Kaikan Hall, in which survivors were accused of being voluntary sex workers.

The night before they gave their testimony, the Indonesian women went over their notes with the lawyers, getting instructions on which parts to highlight.[109] When the Indonesian delegation was called to the stage, the four survivors sat together wearing matching Javanese-style dress of red *kebaya* (lace tops) with purple *selendang* (shoulder scarves) and their hair styled in a *condet* or large bun (figure 4). The prosecutors sat behind them, and Katjasungkana stood at the podium to introduce the evidence for the Indonesian team, including some slides showing examples of documentary evidence.

The women provided an affidavit that they would only tell the truth in their testimonies. Video footage of Mardiyem's oral testimony was played to the audience. This included coverage of her talking about her experiences and her voyage to Borneo and back to Telawang. She emphasized having been treated "inhumanely like an animal."[110] The footage of her trip included a focus on

Figure 4. Photograph of Indonesian survivors at the 2000 tribunal, Tokyo. Photograph by Kimura Kōichi, reproduced with permission.

the location where she had been held, which was now a market, and the testimony of a local man who remembered women being held there. Their lawyer, Damanik, asked Mardiyem if she could have refused to serve the men, to which she responded no, she could not refuse or she would have faced punishment. Focusing on her most horrific experience, she was asked how she came to have a forced abortion. Mardiyem was invited to present her message to the court. She focused on three demands: (1) for Japan to admit its wrongs and ask for forgiveness, (2) for the younger generation to understand this history so it is not repeated, and (3) for the government to pay compensation to the women.

Suhanah also gave live testimony and testimony in video form. Her video testimony showed footage of Gedung Delapan, the house where she was detained, as she narrated her experiences of being forced into this work. She was briefly questioned by lawyer Antarini Arna about her experiences after the war and asked about her hopes for the tribunal. She replied, "My hope is that the government will ask for forgiveness and I am already old like this so I ask the Japanese government to give me compensation. I would also like the court to find Japan guilty."[111]

The Indonesian prosecution team concluded by noting that there was insufficient time to hear from Suharti and Emah, but their written testimonies would be submitted to the judges. In her closing remarks, Indonesia's lead prosecutor, Katjasungkana stated, "the facilities of military sexual slavery were systematic and a war crime and crimes against humanity. The perpetrators must be punished."[112] Although the tribunal had no legal weight, it sought to provide further evidence of the organized nature of the system and to demand accountability for this violence.

In the following press conference, Mardiyem thanked the lawyers and judges. She said, "I am proud and I have a hope that all the burdens from the past will be better. It's still dark and there is still a struggle ahead, but there is a little ray of hope. I thank you for your support for me and my friends in finding justice."[113] It seemed that the tribunal at least provided an unprecedented form of public recognition of the suffering of Mardiyem and her friends.

At the conclusion of the tribunal on December 12, the judges announced their preliminary results. They described the crimes against the women as a crime against humanity and found the emperor of Japan and the Japanese military and government criminally responsible. Video footage shows survivors flooding the stage, cheering and crying at the same time.[114] Katjasungkana described the tribunal as providing a "gorgeous feeling" because of the public recognition the tribunal provided for the women's suffering.[115]

There is some evidence that the tribunal enhanced the leverage of Indonesian women in their negotiations with the AWF. During its course, Katjasungkana was contacted by the head of the AWF to ask for a meeting together with the four Indonesian survivors.[116] The AWF wanted to offer the women compensation and for them to establish their own nursing homes since there was still money to fund five more homes. It was possible that the remaining ¥2 million could be given to representative organizations or to the women directly. Budi Hartono, Mardiyem, and Suharti refused the offer, but Suhanah and one other woman from Blitar agreed. This resulted in two more nursing homes being built in Bogor and Blitar. In Katjasungkana's view, the women were so poor and close to death that this was the only way to get money to assist them. Her previous requests to the Indonesian government to provide free health care for the women had received no response.[117]

Conclusion

In many ways, in the immediate post–New Order period, the attention demanded by the May 1998 riots and other contemporary and ongoing cases of sexual violence by the Indonesian military overshadowed the historical case of the "comfort women" of the Japanese occupation some fifty years earlier. It was only natural that the more recent cases involving crimes committed by the outgoing regime were seen as the most in need of advocacy. Nonetheless, activism for survivors persisted. The press continued to report on ongoing developments in this case internationally, such as Dutch women's receipt of money from the AWF. Indonesian survivor Mardiyem and other activists maintained connections with international partners, leading to new efforts to achieve justice. The Women's International Tribunal in Tokyo in 2000 provided an important opportunity for a select number of Indonesian survivors to join with those from other countries and finally receive a form of international recognition of their suffering and a form of symbolic justice.

Conclusion

Lessons from Indonesian Activism

The story of activism by and on behalf of Indonesian survivors of enforced military prostitution by the Japanese army holds many lessons for our understanding of transnational activism more broadly. Most critically, this case demonstrates the importance of visibility, resources, access to activist networks, and a conducive environment in terms of securing support. In the early years of evolving activism on this issue, Korean survivors (especially Kim Hak-Sun) achieved traction because of the support of both Korean and Japanese activists, who were motivated to pursue this case because of a deep engagement with the issue of wartime redress and critical reckonings with the legacies of Japanese colonialism and sexual violence against women, including military sexual violence. In Indonesia, despite the courageous act of Tuminah, who chose to testify as to her experiences in 1992 after hearing Kim Hak-Sun's story, there was not an immediately supportive reaction to her testimony. In fact, she was largely ignored. This was due to the combined effects of a lack of critical engagement with the legacies of the Japanese occupation, ongoing Indonesian economic dependence on Japan, the Indonesian military's disregard for human rights, the violent depoliticization of the once highly active women's movement, the missing tradition of history from below, and ongoing ambiguity about the occupation in Indonesian memory.

As a result of the visibility of Korean activism, Korean women were the first focus of both the 1995 AWF deals and more recently the only focus of the December 2015 agreement, which was supposed to "finally and irreversibly" settle the issue of the "comfort women," presumably for all survivors. Despite the fact that the deal ignored the wishes of Korean survivors, it was negotiated between the governments of the Republic of Korea and Japan, thereby ignoring survivors from many other countries.[1] Although geopolitics and a concern to reconcile Japan and Korea in particular in the context of the rise of China also underpinned the 2015 deal, at many points in the transnational activism for this issue, Indonesian women have been excluded or ignored by activists and representatives of the government of Japan. This dates back to the 1992 International Public Hearing organized by activists in Tokyo and extends through the 1995 AWF negotiations which at first did not recognize Indonesian survivors. Further reasons for the relative neglect of Indonesian women include the fact that no organization was devoted exclusively for advocacy of survivors. Instead, the most significant activism was carried out by larger organizations with more diverse agendas, such as Indonesian Legal Aid and the Communication Forum for Ex-Heiho.

Despite these obstacles, as the global movement progressed Indonesian survivors were repeatedly supported by a handful of Japanese activists and Japanese organizations. Largely due to the encouragement of the JFBA and then the interventions of the International Committee of Asia-Pacific War Victims Organizations Claiming Compensation, Indonesian activists first began to document survivors. Japanese activists Kawada Fumiko and Kimura Kōichi played central roles in publicizing the testimonies of Indonesian survivors in Japan and supporting key activist survivors (such as Mardiyem) on visits to Japan.

The observations Mardiyem shared about how she was first thrust in the limelight in 1993 by Indonesian Legal Aid and through to her experiences of engaging in activism, provide important insights into the dynamics between survivors and other activists and with the public more broadly. Her insights, which she shared in media interviews, in the 1997 book *The Sufferings of Forced Women*, and in her more extensive 2007 memoir, reveal confronting questions about the expectations placed on survivors and the toll activism has on them. Her story and those of other Indonesian survivors offer glimpses into the expectations journalists have sometimes placed on these women. This was the case when Indonesian reporters went in search of survivors and expected them to bear witness despite their clear reservations about doing so. Across different national contexts, some particularly resilient women, such as Henson in the Philippines, O'Herne in the Australia (representing the Netherlands), and Mardiyem in Indonesia, went on to become icons of the movement, especially if they were able to manage repeatedly sharing their stories and constantly being subjected to scrutiny.

Survivors chose to narrate their experiences for achieving rehabilitation in society for themselves and other survivors, as well as seeking forms of redress such as an apology and compensation from the Japanese government. One of the most important transformations that some survivors were able to achieve was to recalibrate the feelings of shame they had long attached to their experiences and instead direct blame at those who had perpetrated harms against them. This was particularly crucial in the context of Indonesia where notions of shame were collectively applied to a woman's family. This process of reconceptualizing experiences of sexual violence was not an easy or complete process, and some women seem to have continued to feel shame despite engaging in activism.

Activism for and on behalf of Indonesian survivors continued in the first two decades of the 2000s. This included new attention to this historical case from Komnas HAM. Between 2002 and 2007, Komnas HAM tried to advocate for survivors, but with little success. In 2010 they decided to focus on reducing the stigma experienced by survivors by sponsoring a position paper on this issue with the intention to better educate the public about these women.[2] The paper was compiled with the assistance of the advocacy group Jaringan Advokasi Jugun Ianfu Indonesia (Network for Indonesian Jugun Ianfu), which was founded in 2003 and led by activist Eka Hindra.

Eighty years after the beginning of the Japanese occupation of Indonesia, the number of people living who directly experienced this period has dwindled greatly. There are only a small number of survivors who remain active, yet their experiences are still carried forward in cultural memory and activism. Of all the demands laid out by Indonesian survivor activists, only one has been fulfilled, and that is inclusion in the Indonesian history curriculum. In 2008, Mardiyem's story was included in a guidebook for history education along with stories of *rōmusha*.[3] Her story was further memorialized in the release of a 2021 edition of her memoir.[4]

In addition to Mardiyem's story, Tuminah's story has been memorialized through a grave renovation project and a 2013 film project called *TUM* examining her life and legacy.[5] Perhaps most significantly, this film considers her life circumstances in the late colonial period, when she felt pressure to take up sex work. The film critically explores the structural nature of sexual violence and a continuum of violence, which Indonesian women like Tuminah experienced throughout their lives. Outside Indonesia, Tuminah's and Mardiyem's stories are included alongside that of Dutch survivor O'Herne in the Women's Active Museum in Tokyo, a museum dedicated to survivors and ongoing activism on this issue. In 2016 the museum hosted an exhibition on the experiences of Indonesian and Dutch survivors, which was one of the first efforts to link these cases of activism for women who were abused in the same colony yet remained divided by a crucial postcolonial fracture.[6]

Despite the personal costs to survivors, activism on the "comfort women" has contributed to a broader project of challenging sexual violence. In many ways this movement, combined with the effects of new global discourses on sexual violence, helped introduce critical framings of sexual violence to Indonesia. In this sense, this activism has made crucial contributions to advancing a human rights agenda. The struggle for recognition of historical cases of sexual violence in Indonesia and ongoing cases of sexual violence is far from complete. The other key contribution this activism has made is to draw attention to the experiences of women who were long marginalized historical subjects. In doing so, it has contributed to the project of democratizing Indonesian history and promoting a new questioning of what counts as history.

Glossary

aib: shame

bapak: father, also used to refer to President Suharto

bersiap: getting ready, refers to campaigns of violence against the Dutch and their assumed sympathizers by pro-independence supporters in late 1945 to 1946

bunkajin: person(s) of culture

cah nakal: lit. "immoral person"

"comfort women": women subjected to enforced military prostitution by members of the Japanese military; is a contested term for its euphemistic connotation that the women willingly provided "comfort" to Japanese men

"coolies": indentured, low-paid workers, including many from China, sometimes via British colonies, and a smaller number of Indians from British India. Dutch companies also recruited indentured laborers from Java to work on other islands

gunzoku: civilian auxiliaries

hakch'ul: one who has left school, a term coined for the wave of Korean students who in the 1970s and 1980s gave up their places at university to join factories

halmŏni: the Korean term for grandmothers. When used for survivors, it implies respect and affection.

hanbok: Korean female traditional dress

heiho: auxiliary soldiers

hibakusha: a victim of atomic bombing/nuclear radiation

ianfu: term used to describe women who were subjected to enforced military prostitution by Japanese military; see "comfort women"

ianjo: "comfort station," a term used to describe a variety of places where women were detained as part of the "comfort women" system

ibu: older woman and mother

ie: household

Indisch: those who had been born in the Netherlands and those who had lived for generations in the colony of the Netherlands East Indies, including many Eurasians

jūgun ianfu: military comfort women; see "comfort women"

kampung: urban village

karayukisan: Japanese girls and women in the late nineteenth and early twentieth centuries who were trafficked from poor agricultural prefectures in Japan to destinations in East Asia, Southeast Asia, Siberia, Manchuria, British India, and Australia, to serve as sex workers

keibitai: garrison

kekasihnya: her loved one

kekerasan: violence

kekersaan seksual: sexual violence

kenpeitai: military police force

keterbukaan: openness, a period of the New Order from 1989 to 1994

kisaeng: a hereditary status group of the Chosŏn dynasty who were trained from childhood as courtesans, often for high-ranking men

kodrat: lit. "god's will"; a concept that refers to predestined roles, especially in relation to gender

kokka mutōseki: Japanese legal principle of the irresponsibility of the state; a prewar doctrine holding that the government is not responsible to its citizens for the damages caused by the acts that it performs in exercising official authority

lola: grandmother (Tagalog)

mahakeret: term in the local language in Manado meaning "to scream," used to refer to the boarding house or "comfort station"

melayani: lit. "to serve men"; a term used to describe the role women carried out in relation to the soldiers; a deliberate softening of the experiences of sexual violence that conveys discomfort about calling out sexual violence

meluruskan sejarah: lit. "to straighten out history"

minshūshi: a trend in Japan for writing "people's history"

moffenhoeren: derogatory term used for a Dutch woman who had a romantic relationship with a German soldier during World War II, who were subject to vigilantism, in particular forced head shaving, after the war

moffenmeiden: a derogatory label meaning German maidens which refers to a Dutch woman who had a romantic relationship with a German soldier during World War II

nyai: a form of concubinage; live-in housekeepers who were sexually exploited by local and Dutch men by force or coerced negotiation; has links to colonial and feudal practices

Pancasila: five principles of Indonesian state ideology

pelacur: prostitute

perjuangan: lit. "struggle"; used to refer to the Indonesian Revolution/struggle for independence against the Dutch in 1945–49

perkosaan: rape

pingitan: traditional practice of seclusion in the home; an elite traditional Javanese custom for girls between the onset of menstruation and marriage

pribumi: lit. "native"

priyayi: members of the elite Javanese classes

rōmusha: lit. "laborer"; refers specifically to laborers recruited during the Japanese occupation, some voluntarily and others involuntarily

ronggeng: a term frequently used in the Indies to denote a sex worker; traditionally used to refer to Javanese female dancers who performed enticing dances and invited men to sensually dance with them in public for a fee

rusak: broken, damaged, or ruined

ryōriten shakufu: restaurant serving woman system

sakit hati: culturally specific term combining the two words *sakit* meaning ill or sick, and *hati*, which refers to the center of the body but also "the seat of emotions"

saski sejarah: historical witnesses

selendang: shoulder scarf

selir: concubine

taisō: a form of Japanese calisthenics

ternoda: stained

tuna susila: someone of loose morals

wanita penghibur: woman entertainer, sometimes used a referent for Indonesian "comfort women"

wanita-wanita tersesat: lit. "lost women"; refers to women who are deemed to have lost their way, which could mean sex workers and "comfort women"; also has religious connotations (both Muslim and Christian) of having veered from the path of a righteous life

zainichi kankojin/chōsenjin: Korean residents in Japan

Notes

Introduction

1. Elizabeth W. Son, *Embodied Reckonings: "Comfort Women," Performance, and Transpacific Redress* (Ann Arbor: University of Michigan Press, 2018), 147.

2. There are now monuments in the Philippines (2003), Japan (2006), the United States (2010, 2013, 2014, 2018), Canada (2015), Australia (2016, 2019), and China (2016, 2019).

3. Son, *Embodied Reckonings*, 149.

4. Eka Hindra, "The Bill of Ianfu: Breaking the Political Silence in Japan," in *Japanese Militarism and its War Crimes in Asia Pacific Region*, ed. Hendrajit (Jakarta: Global Future Institute, 2011), 119–20.

5. Elizabeth Son, "Statue Dedicated to 'Comfort Women' Removed in the Philippines," *UPI*, January 3, 2019.

6. On the economic relationships between the Philippines and Indonesia and Japan, see Galia Press-Baranathan, *The Political Economy of Transitions to Peace: A Comparative Perspective* (Pittsburgh: University of Pittsburgh Press, 2009), 82–106.

7. For discussion of the limited public and government recognition that survivors of the 1965 anticommunist violence have received, see Katharine McGregor and Ken Setiawan, "Shifting from International to 'Indonesian' Justice Measures: Two Decades of Addressing Past Human Rights Violations," *Journal of Contemporary Asia* 49, no. 5 (2019): 837–86; Katharine McGregor, "Historical Justice and the Case of the 1965 Killings," in *Routledge Handbook of Contemporary Indonesia*, ed. Robert Hefner (London: Routledge, 2018), 129–39; Katharine McGregor, "Exposing Impunity: Memory and Human Rights Activism in Indonesia and Argentina," *Journal of Genocide Research* 19, no. 4 (2017): 551–73.

8. Some exceptions are the monument to victims of the 1998 riots in Jakarta, a monument to the victims of the 2002 Bali bombings (an attack by Indonesian terrorists on a major nightclub called Paddy's Bar in the tourist area of Kuta), and a very small monument to select victims of the 1965 violence. See Andri Setiawan, "Makan Plumbon Jadi Situs Memori CIPDHUNESCO," *Historia*, January 16, 2020, https://

historia.id/politik/articles/makam-plumbon-jadi-situs-memori-cipdh-unesco-Pzd2O/ page/1. In addition to these monuments, there is a private museum dedicated to Munir, a high-profile human rights activist who was fatally poisoned. Vannessa Hearman, "Remembering Munir," *Inside Indonesia*, 115 (January–March 2014), https://www.in sideindonesia.org/remembering-munir.

9. Key studies of the empirical dimensions of the system are Bradley William Horton, "Comfort Women," in *Encyclopedia of Indonesia in the Pacific War*, ed. Peter Post, William H. Frederick, Iris Heidebrink, and Shigeru Satō (Leiden: Brill, 2010), 184–96; Yuki Tanaka, "'Comfort Women in the Dutch East Indies," in *Legacies of the Comfort Women of World War II*, ed Margaret D. Stetz and Bonnie Oh (New York: M. E. Sharpe, 2000), 42–68; Mayumi Yamamoto and William Bradley Horton, *Comfort Women in Indonesia: A Report on Dutch Archival Material* (Asian Women's Fund, revised version, December 1998); Naoko Yamada, "From War to Independence, 1942–1949: Ianfu in Indonesia" (MA thesis, Ohio University, 2000); Anna Mariana, *Perbudakan Seksual: Perbandingan Antara Masa Fasisme Jepang dan Neofasisme Orde Baru* (Tangerang Selatan: Marjin Kiri, 2015). A key study of postwar representations and justice-related dimensions of this topic is Yuki Tanaka, *Japan's Comfort Women: Sexual Slavery and Prostitution During World War II and the US Occupation* (New York: Routledge, 2002).

10. Vera Mackie, "In Search of Innocence: Feminist Historians Debate the Legacy of Wartime Japan," *Australian Feminist Studies* 20, no. 47 (2005): 208.

11. Some key studies focusing of Korean activism include C. Sarah Soh, *The Comfort Women: Sexual Violence and Postcolonial Memory in Korea and Japan* (Chicago: University of Chicago Press, 2008); Son, *Embodied Reckonings*; and Min Pyong Gap, *Korean "Comfort Women": Military Brothels, Brutality, and the Redress Movement* (New Brunswick, NJ: Rutgers University Press, 2021). The most comprehensive study of Chinese women's experiences, with some coverage of activism, is Qiu Peipei with Su Zhilang and Chen Lifei, *Chinese Comfort Women: Testimonies from Imperial Japan's Sex Slaves* (New York: Oxford University Press, 2013). Key studies of Japanese activism include Tai Eika, *Comfort Women Activism: Critical Voices from the Perpetrator State* (Hong Kong: Hong Kong University Press, 2020); and Kamila Szczepanska, *The Politics of War Memory in Japan: Progressive Civil Society Groups and Contestation of Memory of the Asia-Pacific War* (Abdingdon: Sheffield Centre for Japanese Studies, Routledge, 2014). A key study of Filipino women's activism is Katharina Mendoza, "'Freeing the Slaves of Destiny': The Lolas and the Filipino Comfort Women Movement," *Cultural Dynamics* 15, no. 3 (2003): 247–66. One of the most recent reflections on transnational activism on this topic is the edited volume Min Pyong Gap et al., eds., *The Transnational Redress Movement for the Victims of Japanese Military Sexual Slavery* (Berlin: De Gruyter Oldenbourg, 2020). One of the most insightful scholars on the dynamics of transnational activism is Vera Mackie. See Mackie, "In Search of Innocence"; Vera Mackie, "The Language of Globalization, Transnationality and Feminism," *International Feminist Journal of Politics*, 3 no. 2 (August 2002): 180–206; and Vera Mackie, "One Thousand Wednesdays: Transnational Activism from Seoul to Glendale," in *Women's Activism*

and Second Wave Feminism: Transnational Histories, ed. Barbara Molony and Jennifer Nelson (London: Bloomsbury Academic, 2017), 249–71.

12. See Sheila Miyoshi Jager and Rana Mitter, eds., *Ruptured Histories: War, Memory, and the Post-Cold War in Asia* (Cambridge, MA: Harvard University Press, 2007); Tessa Morris Suzuki, *East Asia Beyond the History Wars: Confronting the Ghosts of Violence* (Milton Park: Routledge, 2013); Kim Miyoung, ed., *Routledge Handbook of Memory and Reconciliation in East Asia* (London: Routledge, 2016). A recent exception to this pattern is Kevin Blackburn, *The Comfort Women of Singapore in History and Memory* (Singapore: National University of Singapore Press and University of Chicago Press, 2022).

13. Joan Tumbelty, "Introduction: Working with Memory as a Source and a Subject," in *Memory and History: Understanding Memory as a Subject and Source*, ed. Joan Tumbelty (London: Routledge, 2013), 2.

14. Astrid Erll, "Travelling Memory," *Parallax* 17, no. 4 (2011): 11.

15. Carol Gluck, "Operations of Memory: 'Comfort Women' and the World," in *Ruptured Histories*, ed. Sheila Miyoshi Jager and Rana Mitter (Cambridge, MA: Harvard University Press, 2007), 57.

16. Yifat Gutman, *Memory Activism: Reimagining the Past for the Future in Israel Palestine* (Nashville, TN: Vanderbilt University Press, 2017), 1–2.

17. Gutman, *Memory Activism*, 19.

18. Erll, "Travelling," 12.

19. You-me Park, "Compensation to Fit the Crime: Conceptualizing a Just Paradigm of Reparation for Korean 'Comfort Women,'" *Comparative Studies of South Asia, Africa and the Middle East* 30, no. 2 (2010): 204–13; Cheah Wui Ling, "Walking the Long Road in Solidarity and Hope: A Case Study of the 'Comfort Women' Movement's Deployment of Human Rights Discourse," *Harvard Human Rights Journal* 22, no. 1 (2009): 63–108.

20. Chakrabarty made these comments in reference to the very slow white Australian recognition of violence perpetrated against Aboriginal and Torres Strait Islander persons. Dipesh Chakrabarty, "History and the Politics of Recognition," in *History, Manifestos for History*, ed. K. Jenkins, S. Morgan, and A. Munslow (London: Routledge, 2007), 78.

21. Alon Confino, "Collective Memory and Cultural History: Problems of Method," *American Historical Review* 102, no. 5 (1997): 1390.

22. Yuki Tanaka, "'Comfort Women Bashing' and Japan's Social Formation of Hegemonic Masculinity," in *History Wars and Reconciliation in Japan and Korea: The Role of Historians, Artists and Activists*, ed. Michael Lewis (Sydney: Palgrave Macmillan, 2017), 163–82; and Nishino Rumiko, Kim Puja, and Onozawa Akane, eds., *Denying the Comfort Women: The Japanese State's Assault on Historical Truth* (London: Routledge, 2018).

23. Min, for example, points to the views of conservative historian Fujioka Nobukatsu, who believed that after the Kōno statement, Japanese history textbooks became too focused on "shameful modern history," arguing that there was no evidence the

Japanese military had forcibly mobilized the women. Min, *Korean "Comfort Women,"* 227. These claims that the women were not forcibly mobilized or forced to have sex are made not just by conservative Japanese academics but also more recently by a Harvard law professor and Japanese legal studies scholar, J. Mark Ramseyer, who claimed the forced sexual servitude of the women was "pure fiction." J. Mark Ramseyer, "Contracting for Sex in the Pacific War," *International Review of Law and Economics* 65 (2021): 1–8. For coverage of this, see Jeannie Suk Gersen, "Seeking the True Story of the Comfort Women," *New Yorker*, February 25, 2021.

24. For a fuller discuss of emotions and activism, see chapter 4 and Katharine McGregor, "Emotions and Activism for Former So-Called 'Comfort Women' of the Japanese Occupation of the Netherlands East Indies," *Women's Studies International Forum* 54 (2016): 67–78.

25. Shigeru Satō, "Various Terms for a Comfort Woman," in *The Encyclopedia of Indonesia in the Pacific War*, ed. Peter Post, William H. Frederick, Iris Heidebrink, and Shigeru Satō (Leiden: Brill, 2010), 196. He further explains that the term *jūgun ianfu*, which was not used during the war, began to be used more broadly after the 1973 book by Senda Kakō was published. Senda Kakō, *Jūgun Ianfu: "Koe Naki Onna: Hachiman-nin no Kokuhatsu"* (Tokyo: Futubasha, 1973).

26. Jan Ruff O'Herne, *Fifty Years of Silence: The Extraordinary Memory of a War Rape Survivor* (Sydney: Editions Tom Thompson, 1995), 137.

27. For example, on the website of the leading Korean advocacy organization, the Korean Council, which records survivor's testimony, this term is used. Furthermore, the museum in Taiwan is called the "Ama" Museum or "Grandmothers" Museum. Sharon Crozier-De Rosa and Vera Mackie, *Remembering Women's Activism* (Abingdon: Routledge, 2019), 185–87.

28. Dai Sil Kim-Gibson, "They Are Our Grandmas," *positions* 5, no. 1 (1997): 274.

29. The theme of the "comfort women" was taken up in the acclaimed novel *Cantik itu Luka* (later published in English as *Beauty is a Wound*), by Eka Kurniawan, which traces the life of a woman through several eras of Indonesian history. Eka Kurniawan, *Cantik itu Luka* (Jakarta: Gramedia Pustaka, 2002).

30. Budi Hartono and Dadang Juliantoro, *Derita Paksa Perempuan: Kisah Jugun Ianfu pada Masa Pendudukan Jepang, 1942–1945* (Jakarta: Pustaka Sinar Harapan, 1997).

31. This approach became far more common in the late 1990s after the fall of the Suharto regime, after which there was new attention in particular to the human rights violations committed in the 1965–68 genocide and an opportunity for survivors of that violence and activists to publish extensive life testimonies about such experiences. For an analysis of these narrations of human rights abuse, see Katharine E. McGregor and Vannessa Hearman, "The Challenges of Political Rehabilitation in Post New Order Indonesia: The Case of Gerwani (the Indonesian Women's Movement)," *Southeast Asia Research* 15, no. 3 (2007): 355–84.

32. For a similar point, see Vera Mackie, "Gender, Geopolitics and Gaps in Records: Women Glimpsed in the Military Archives," in *Sources and Methods in Histories of Colonialism: Approaching the Imperial Archive*, ed. Kirsty Reid and Fiona Paisley (London:

Routledge, 2017), 135–59; Tessa Morris Suzuki, "You Don't Want to Know about the Girls? The Comfort Women, the Japanese Military and the Allied Forces in the Asia-Pacific," *Asia Pacific Journal: Japan Focus* (August 3, 2015), https://apjjf.org/2015/13/31/Tessa-Morris-Suzuki/4352.html.

33. For a discussion of this push, see Michelle King, "Working with/in the Archives," in *Research Methods for History*, ed. Simon Gunn and Lucy Faire (Edinburgh: Edinburgh University Press, 2016), 20.

34. Michel-Rolph Trouillot, *Silencing the Past: Power and the Production of History* (Boston, MA: Beacon Press, 1995), 53.

35. Jacques Derrida, "Archive Fever: A Freudian Impression," *Diacritics* 25, no. 2 (1995): 12.

36. Laurie Sears, *Situated Testimonies: Dread and Enchantment in an Indonesian Literary Archive* (Honolulu: University of Hawai'i Press, 2013).

37. For example, Toer considers the historical position of *nyai* through the central character of Nyai Ontosoroh in his famous tetralogy *Bumi Manusia* (Jakarta: Hasta Mitra, 1980). He also published a book based on encounters on Buru Island between himself and other prisoners and survivors of the "comfort women" system; *Perawan Remaja Dalam Cengkeraman Militer* (Jakarta: Kepustakaan Populer Gramedia, 2001).

38. Pauline Stoltz, Gender, *Resistance and Transnational Memories of Violent Conflicts* (Cham: Palgrave Macmillan, 2020), 7–12.

39. Kirsty Reid and Fiona Paisley, "Introduction," in *Sources and Methods in Histories of Colonialism*, ed. Kirsty Reid and Fiona Paisley (Abingdon: Routledge, 2017), 3.

40. Antoinette Burton, "Archive Fever, Archive Stories," in *Archive Stories: Facts, Fiction and the Writing of History*, ed. Antoinette Burton (Durham, NC: Duke University Press, 2006), 6.

41. Patricia Viseur Sellers, "The Cultural Value of Sexual Violence," *Proceedings of the Annual Meeting (American Society for International Law)*, March 24–27, 1999, 319.

42. Kumagai Naoko, *The Comfort Women: Historical, Political, Legal and Moral Perspectives*, trans. David Noble (Tokyo: International House of Japan, 2016), 85.

43. Sellers, "Cultural Value," 318–19.

44. Taiwan Army Telegram 602, March 12, 1942, cited in Yoshimi Yoshiaki, *Comfort Women: Sexual Slavery in the Japanese Military during World War II* (New York: Columbia University Press, 2000), 81.

45. Morris Suzuki, "You Don't Want to Know about the Girls?," 1.

46. Yoshimi, *Comfort Women*, 34.

47. Ministry of Foreign Affaris Japan, Details of Exchanges between Japan and the Republic of Korea (ROK) Regarding the Comfort Women Issue—From the Drafting of the Statement to the Asian Women's Fund, June 20, 2014 (provisional translation), https://www.mofa.go.jp/files/000042171.pdf.

48. Hata Ikuhiko, *Comfort Women and Sex in the Battle Zone*, trans. Jason Michael Morgan (Lanham, MD: Hamilton Books, 2018).

49. Bart van Poelgeest, "Oosters Stille Dwang. Tewerkgesteld in de Japanse Bordelen van Nederlands-Indië," *ICODO Info* 10, no. 3 (1993): 13–21.

50. Tanaka, *Japan's Comfort Women*.

51. Yamamoto and Horton, *Comfort Women in Indonesia*, 1–22.

52. Katharine McGregor, "Living in a Conflict Zone: Gendered Violence during the Japanese Occupation of the Netherlands East Indies," in *Gendered Violence across Time and Space in Indonesia and East Timor*, ed. Katharine McGregor, Ana Dragojlovic, and Hannah Loney (London: Routledge, 2020), 39–58.

53. O'Herne, *Fifty Years of Silence*; and Maria Rosa Henson, *Comfort Woman: A Filipina's Story of Prostitution and Slavery under the Japanese Military* (London: Rowman and Littlefield, 1999).

54. Her story was first included in Hartono and Juliantoro, *Derita Paksa* (see chapter 8) then later published as a more complete memoir by Eka Hindra and Kimura Koichi, *Momoye Mereka Memanggilku* (Jakarta: Erlangga, 2007).

55. Marguerite Hamer de Froideville, *Geknakte Bloem: Acht Vrouwen Vertellen Hun Verhaal over Japanse Militaire Dwangprostitutie* (Delft: Elmar BV, 2013).

56. Kawada Fumiko, *Indoneshia no "Ianfu"* (Tokyo: Akashi Shoten, 1997).

57. Hilde Janssen, *Schaamte en Onschuld: Het Verdrongen Oorlogsverleden van Troostmeisjes in Indonesië* (Amsterdam: Nieuw Amsterdam, 2010).

58. Lampiran III: Hasil Wawancara Yugun Ianfu di Bandung, Bogor dan Sukabumi, in Forum Komunikasi Ex-Heiho, *Kompensasi Jugun Ianfu* (n.p., Forum Komunikasi Ex-Heiho, 1996), 23–56. For examples of accounts from survivors reported in *Suara*, see chapter 4.

59. Yoshiko Nozaki, "The Comfort Women Controversy: History and Testimony," *Japan Focus: The Asia Pacific Journal* 3, no. 7 (2005): 7.

60. Nozaki, "The Comfort Women Controversy," 10.

61. Hata, *Comfort Women and Sex*.

62. Hata, *Comfort Women and Sex*, 147.

63. Hata, *Comfort Women and Sex*, 148.

64. Kay Schaffer and Sidonie Smith, *Human Rights and Narrated Lives: The Ethics of Recognition* (New York: Palgrave Macmillan, 2004), 28–33.

65. For a useful discussion of alternative archives such as newsletters, human rights reports, poems, posters, flyers, and subversion trial defenses related to Indonesian student activism, see Doreen Lee, *Activist Archives: Youth Culture and the Political Past in Indonesia* (Durham, NC: Duke University Press, 2016), 25–32.

Chapter 1. Women, Sexual Exploitation, and Prostitution in the Netherlands East Indies

1. Barbara Andaya Watson, *The Flaming Womb: Repositioning Women in Early Modern Southeast Asia* (Honolulu: University of Hawai'i Press, 2006), 175.

2. Terence Hull, Endang Sulistyaningsih, and Gavin W. Jones, *Prostitution in Indonesia: Its History and Evolution* (Jakarta: Pustaka Sinar Harapan, 1999), 2.

3. Helen Creese, *Bali in the Early Nineteenth Century* (Leiden: Brill, 2016), 208–9.

4. Creese, *Bali*, 222.

5. Creese, *Bali*, 219–23.

6. Watson, *Flaming Womb*, 126.

7. Ann Laura Stoler, *Carnal Knowledge and Imperial Power: Race and the Intimate in Colonial Rule* (Berkeley: University of California Press, 2002), 48.

8. Jean Taylor, *The Social World of Batavia: Europeans and Eurasians in Colonial Indonesia* (Madison: University of Wisconsin Press, 2009), 14.

9. Watson, *Flaming Womb*, 145–46.

10. Eric Jones, *Wives, Slaves and Concubines: A History of the Female Underclass in Dutch Asia* (DeKalb: Northern Illinois University Press, 2010), 30–36.

11. Susan Abeyasekere, "Women as Cultural Intermediaries in Nineteenth-Century Batavia," in *Women's Work and Women's Roles: Economics and Everyday Life in Indonesia, Malaysia and Singapore*, ed. Lenore Manderson (Canberra: Australian National University Press, 1983), 21.

12. Nicole Lucas, "Trouwverbod, Inlandse Huishoudsters en Eropese Vrouwen: het Concubinaat in de Planterswereld aan Sumatra's Oostkust 1960–1940," in *Vrouwen in de Nederlandse Kolonien*, ed. Jeske Reijs et al. (Nijmegen: SUN, 1986), 82.

13. Susie Protschky, "Home at the Front: Violence against Indonesian Women and Children in Dutch Military Barracks during the Indonesian National Revolution," in *Gendered Violence Across Time and Space in Indonesia and East Timor*, ed. Katharine McGregor, Ana Dragojlovic, and Hannah Loney (London: Routledge, 2020), 60.

14. Hanneke Ming, "Barracks-Concubinage in the Indies, 1887–1920," *Indonesia* 35 (1983): 70–71.

15. Abeyasekere, "Women as Cultural Intermediaries," 23.

16. Liesbeth Hesselink, "Prostitution: A Necessary Evil," in *Indonesian Women in Focus: Past and Present Notions*, ed. Elsbeth Locher-Scholten and Anke Niehof (Leiden: KITLV Press, 1987), 209.

17. Ming, "Barracks-Concubinage," 71.

18. Sally White, "The Case of Nyi Anah: Concubinage, Marriage and Reformist Islam in the Late Colonial Dutch East Indies," *Review of Indonesian and Malaysian Affairs* 38, no. 1 (2004): 88.

19. Ann Laura Stoler and Karen Strassler, "Castings for the Colonial: Memory Work in 'New Order' Java," *Comparative Studies in Society and History* 42, no. 1 (2000): 16.

20. Tineke Hellwig, "Asian Women in the Lives of Dutch Tea Planters: Two Narratives from West Java," *Indonesia and the Malay World* 29, no. 85 (2001): 164.

21. Hellwig, "Asian Women," 168.

22. Abeyasekere, "Women as Cultural Intermediaries," 23.

23. Taylor, *Social World of Batavia*, 148.

24. Ming, "Barracks-Concubinage," 72–73.

25. Trude Jacobsen, *Sex Trafficking in Southeast Asia: A History of Desire, Duty and Debt* (London: Routledge, 2017), 65.

26. Stoler, *Carnal Knowledge*.

27. Ulbe Bosma and Remco Raben, *Being Dutch in the Indies: A History of Creolisation and Empire, 1500–1920*, trans. Wendie Shaffer (Athens: Ohio University Press; Singapore: NUS Press, 2008).

28. R. A. Soedirman, "Pergerakan Perempuan Perkawinan dan Perceraian," in *Kongres Perempuan Tinjauan Ulang*, ed. Susan Blackburn (Jakarta: Yayasan Obor Indonesia, KITLV Jakarta, 2007), 161.

29. Tien Sastrowirjo, "Bagaimana Pergerakan Kaum Perempuan Sekarang dan Nanti," in *Kongres Perempuan Pertama: Tinjauan Ulang*, ed. Susan Blackburn (Jakarta: Yayasan Obor Indonesia, KITLV Jakarta, 2007), 206.

30. Nieuwenhuys notes that sex ratios went from 471.6 to 884.5 women per 1,000 men. See R. Nieuwenhuys, *The Mirror of the Indies: A History of Dutch Colonial Literature* (Amherst: University of Massachusetts Press, 1982), 201, 327n6.

31. Stoler, *Carnal Knowledge*.

32. Ming, "Barracks-Concubinage," 71.

33. Hesselink, "Prostitution," 206.

34. Hesselink, "Prostitution," 207.

35. Hesselink, "Prostitution," 209.

36. For an overview, see Thio Termorshuizen, "Indentured Labour in the Dutch Colonial Empire 1800–1940," in *Dutch Colonialism, Migration and Cultural Heritage*, ed. Geert Oostinde (Leiden: KITLV Press, 2008), 261–314.

37. Termorshuizen, "Indentured Labour," 284–94.

38. Ann Laura Stoler, *Capitalism and Confrontation in Sumatra's Plantation Belt, 1870–1979* (Ann Arbor: University of Michigan Press, 1995), 32–33.

39. John Ingleson, "Prostitution in Colonial Java," in *Nineteenth and Twentieth Century Indonesia: Essays in Honour of J. D. Legge*, ed. David Chandler and Merle Ricklefs (Clayton: Centre of Southeast Asian Studies, Monash University, 1986), 124.

40. Ingelson, "Prostitution in Colonial Java," 130.

41. Hiroshi Shimizu, "Rise and Fall of the Karayukisan in the Netherlands Indies from the Late Nineteenth Century to the 1930s," *Review of Indonesian and Malaysian Affairs* 26, no. 2 (Summer 1992): 17–43.

42. Shimizu, "Rise and Fall of the Karayukisan," 26–27.

43. Lucas, "Trouwverbod," 86.

44. Shimizu, "Rise and Fall of the Karayukisan," 29–31.

45. Hesselink, "Prostitution," 207.

46. Shimizu, "Rise and Fall of the Karayukisan," 33.

47. Hayashi Hirofumi, "Japanese Comfort Women in Southeast Asia," *Japan Forum* 10, no. 2 (1998): 212–13.

48. R. D. G. P. Simons, "Indrukken over de Prostitutie en de Homosexueele Prostitutie en over het Voorkomen van Gelaschts-Zieken in Ned Oost-Indie en West-Indie," *Nederlands Tjidschrift voor Geneeskundig* 83, pt. 47 (1939): 5574–79. Translation provided by Paula Hendrix.

49. Simons, "Indrukken over de Prostitutie," 5574.

50. Christianity was one factor that enhanced petitions for the granting of European legal status in the Netherlands East Indies. Bart Luttikhuis, "Beyond Race Constructions of Europeaness in Late Colonial Legal Practice in the Dutch East Indies," *European Review of History: Revue Europeenne d'Historie* 20, no. 4 (2013): 542, 549.

51. Simons, "Indrukken over de Prostitutie," 5574–75.

52. Simons, "Indrukken over de Prostitutie," 5577.

53. Simons, "Indrukken over de Prostitutie," 5574.

54. Hesselink, "Prostitution," 216.

55. On this investigation, see Jessica P. Riley, "Claims to Protection: The Rise and Fall of Feminist Abolitionism in the League of Nations' Committee on the Traffic in Women and Children, 1919–1936?," *Journal of Women's History* 22, no. 4 (Winter 2010): 90–113; and Paul Knepper, "The Investigation into the Traffic in Women by the League of Nations: Sociological Jurisprudence as an International Social Project," *Law and History Review* 34, no. 1 (2016): 45–73.

56. Société des Nations, *Commission D'Enquête sur La Traite des Femmes et Des Enfants en Orient, Rapport au Conseil* (Geneva: Publications de la Société de Nations, 1933).

57. Société des Nations, *Commission D'Enquête*, 254.

58. Société des Nations, *Commission D'Enquête*, 263.

59. Creese, *Bali*, 222–3.

60. Société de Nations, *Traite des Femme et des Enfants: Travaux de le Conference de Bandoeng* (Geneva: Société de Nations, 1938), 27.

61. Société de Nations, *Traite des Femme et des Enfants*, 25–26.

62. Société de Nations, *Traite des Femme et des Enfants*, 41.

63. Société de Nations, *Traite des Femme et des Enfants*, 48.

64. Iris Borowy, *Coming to Terms with World Health: The League of Nations Health Organisation 1921–1946* (Frankfurt: Peter Lang, 2009).

65. Hesselink, "Prostitution," 210.

66. Hesselink, "Prostitution," 211.

67. Jean Gelman Taylor, "Nyai Dasima Portrait of a Mistress in Literature and Film," in *Fantasizing the Feminine in Indonesia*, ed. Laurie Sears (Durham, NC: Duke University Press, 1996), 225–58.

68. H. Kommer, *Tjerita Nyai Paina*, republished in Pramoedya Anata Toer, *Tempo Dulu Antologi Sastra Pra-Indonesia* (Jakarta: Lentera, Dipentara Jakarta, 2003). For further analysis of this anticolonial novel, see Diah Meutia Harum, "Representasi Kolonialisme dalam 'Tjerita Nji Paina' Karya H. Kommer," *Aksara* 29, no. 2 (December 2017): 155–69.

69. Joost Coté, "Tirto Adhi Soerjo and the Narration of Indonesian Modernity, 1909–1921: An Introduction to Two Stories," *Review of Indonesian and Malaysian Affairs* 32, no. 2 (1998): 17.

70. White, "The Case of Nyi Anah," 93.

71. For a detailed articulation of this view, see Sukarno's treatise *Sarinah* which was first published in 1947 as Indonesians were engaged in an independence struggle

with the Dutch. Soekarno, *Sarinah: Kewajiban Wanita dalam Perjuangan Republik Indonesia* (1947; Jakarta: Toko Gunung Agung, 2001).

72. Haji Agus Salim, "The Veiling and Isolation of Women" (1926), in *Regents, Reformers, and Revolutionaries: Indonesian Voices of Colonial Days: Selected Historical Readings, 1899–1949*, trans. Greta O. Wilson (Honolulu: University of Hawai'i Press, 1978), 69–70.

73. Kongres Wanita Indonesia, *Sejarah Setengah Abad Pergerakan Wanita Indonesia* (Jakarta: Balai Pustaka, 1978), 37.

74. Rasoena Said, *Panji Islam* 4, 23 (August 15, 1937): 494, quoted in Elsbeth Locher-Scholten, "Morals, Harmony, and National Identity: 'Companionate Feminism' in Colonial Indonesia in the 1930s," *Journal of Women's History* 14, no. 4 (2003): 48.

75. See A. K. Pringgodigdo, *Sedjarah Pergerakan Rakjat Indonesia* (Djakarta: Penerbit Dian Rajkat, 1967), 166; Susan Blackburn, *Women and the State in Modern Indonesia* (Cambridge: Cambridge University Press, 2004), 174–75.

76. P. de Kat Angelino, "Batikrapport," Inspecteur bij het Kantoor van Arbeid, Deel II, Midden-Java, Batavia, 1931.

77. Pringgodigdo, *Sedjarah Pergerakan Rakjat Indonesia*, 166.

78. Bill Mihalopoulos, *Sex in Japan's Globalization, 1870–1930: Prostitutes, Emigration and Nation-Building* (London: Pickering and Chatto, 2011), 7.

79. Mihalopoulos, *Sex in Japan's Globalization*, 35.

80. Mihalopoulos, *Sex in Japan's Globalization*, 35.

81. Amy Stanley, *Selling Women: Prostitution, Markets, and the Household in Early Modern Japan* (Berkeley: University of California Press, 2012), 3.

82. Stanley, *Selling Women*, 4–6.

83. Mark Driscoll, *Absolute Erotic, Absolute Grotesque: The Living, Dead, and Undead in Japan's Imperialism, 1895–1945* (Durham, NC: Duke University Press, 2010), 69.

84. See Jessica Flanigan and Lori Watson, *Debating Sex Work* (New York: Oxford University Press, 2019).

85. Michele Ford and Lenore Lyons, "Making the Best of What You've Got: Sex Work and Class Mobility in the Riau Islands," in *Women and Work in Indonesia*, ed. Michele Ford and Lyn Parker (London: Routledge, 2008), 174; Rebecca Surtees, "Traditional and Emergent Sex Work in Urban Indonesia," *Intersections: Gender, History and Culture in Asian Context* 10 (August 2004): 50.

86. See, for example, Stoler, *Carnal Knowledge*.

87. Gail Hershshatter, *Dangerous Pleasures: Prostitution and Modernity in Twentieth-Century Shanghai* (Berkeley: University of California Press, 1999).

88. Kimura Kōichi, "The Story of Tuminah the First Victim to Come Forward and Tell her Story about her Ordeal," *Asia Tsushin*, English edition, 4 (December 1996): 15–20.

89. Ardus M. Sawega, "Pengakuan Seorang 'Wanita Penghibur,'" *Kompas*, July 17, 1992, 16.

90. Jacobsen, *Sex Trafficking in Southeast Asia*, 2.

Chapter 2. The Japanese Occupation

1. See Mark R. Peattie, "Nanshin: The 'Southward Advance,' 1931–1941, as a Prelude to the Japanese Occupation of Southeast Asia," in *The Japanese Wartime Empire: Problems and Issues*, ed. Peter Duus et al. (Princeton, NJ: Princeton University Press, 1996), 200–220.

2. Ethan Mark, *Japan's Occupation of Java in the Second World War: A Transnational History* (London: Bloomsbury Academic, 2018), 48.

3. Mark, *Japan's Occupation of Java*, 3.

4. Mark, *Japan's Occupation of Java*, 41–42.

5. Jemma Purdey, Antje Missbach, and Dave McRae, *Indonesia: State and Society in Transition* (Boulder, CO: Lynne Rienner, 2020).

6. Peter Duus, "Introduction: Japan's Wartime Empire Problems and Issues," in *The Japanese Wartime Empire*, ed. Peter Duus, Ramon H. Myers, and Mark R. Peattie (Princeton, NJ: Princeton University Press, 1996), xxxiv.

7. Anthony Reid and Oki Akira, "Introduction," in *The Japanese Experience in Indonesia: Selected Memoirs 1942–1945*, ed. Anthony Reid and Oki Akira (Athens: Ohio Center for International Studies, 1986), 2.

8. Ooi Keat Gin, *The Japanese Occupation of Borneo, 1941–1945* (Abingdon: Routledge, 2011), 73–74.

9. Reid and Oki, "Introduction," 3.

10. Duus, "Introduction," xxii.

11. Duus, "Introduction," xxiii–xxv.

12. S. M. Gandasubrata, *An Account of the Japanese Occupation of Banjumas Residency, Java, March 1942 to August 1945*, trans. Leslie H. Palmer (Ithaca, NY: Cornell University, August 1953), 9.

13. Gandasubrata, *An Account*, 5.

14. Mark, *Japan's Occupation of Java*, 6–7.

15. Duus, "Introduction," xxxv.

16. Harry A. Poeze, "The Road to Hell: Construction of a Railway Line in West Java during the Japanese Occupation," in *Asian Labor in the Wartime Japanese Empire: Unknown Histories*, ed. Paul Kratoska (Armonk, NY: M. E. Sharp, 2005), 168–71. The 1926–27 rebellions took place in Java and Sumatra and were a response to increased Dutch government repression of the PKI and its promotion of Indonesian nationalism.

17. George M. Kahin, *Nationalism and Revolution in Indonesia* (Ithaca, NY: Cornell University Press, 1952), 112–13.

18. Okada Fumihide, "Okada's Report on his Administration, February 1944 (Extracts)," in *The Japanese Experience in Indonesia: Selected Memoirs of 1942–1945*, ed. Anthony Reid and Oki Akira (Athens: Ohio Center for International Studies, 1986), 154–55.

19. Elly Touwen-Bouwsma, "Japanese Minority Policy: The Eurasians on Java and the Dilemma of Ethnic Loyalty," in *Japan, Indonesia and the War: Myths and Realities*, ed. Peter Post and Elly Touwen-Bouwsma (Leiden: KITLV Press, 1997), 32–33.

20. "Announcement to Eurasians, January 12, 1943," in *Japanese Military Administration in Indonesia: Selected Documents*, ed. Harry J. Benda, James K. Irikura, and Kishi Kōichi (New Haven, CT: Yale University Press, 1965), 72.

21. Iris Heidebrink, "Introduction to Internment of Civilians: Introduction," in *Encyclopedia of Indonesia in the Pacific War*, ed. Peter Post, William H. Frederick, Iris Heidebrink, and Shigeru Satō (Leiden: Brill, 2010), 163–65.

22. Touwen-Bouwsma, "Japanese Minority Policy," 46–47.

23. Shigeru Satō, "'Economic Soldiers' in Java: Indonesian Laborers Mobilized for Agricultural Projects," in *Asian Labor in the Wartime Japanese Empire: Unknown Histories*, ed. Paul Kratoska (Armonk, NY: M. E. Sharp, 2005), 129.

24. Shigeru Satō, *War, Nationalism and Peasants: Java under the Japanese Occupation* (Sydney: Asian Studies Association of Australia in association with Allen and Unwin, 1994), 158.

25. Remco Raben, "Indonesian Romusha and Coolies under Naval Administration: The Eastern Archipelago, 1942–45," in *Asian Labor in the Wartime Japanese Empire: Unknown Histories*, ed. Paul Kratoska (Armonk, NY: M. E. Sharp, 2005), 197.

26. K. A. de Weerd, "The Japanese Occupation of the Netherlands Indies," statement prepared for International Prosecution Section of the International Military Tribunal for the Far East, 1946, 73.

27. Satō, "'Economic Soldiers,'" 148.

28. Japanese Military Administration in Indonesia, "Principles Governing the Administration of Occupied Southern Areas," Adopted at the Liaison Conference between Imperial Headquarters and the Government, November 20, 1941, in *Japanese Military Administration in Indonesia: Selected Documents*, ed. Harry J. Benda, James K. Irikura, and Kishi Kōichi (New Haven, CT: Yale University Press, 1965), 2.

29. Aiko Kurasawa-Inomata, "Rice Shortage and Transportation," in *Japan, Indonesia and the War*, ed. Peter Post and Elly Touwen-Bouwsma (Leiden: KITLV Press, 1997), 112–15.

30. Satō, *War, Nationalism and Peasants*, 165–75.

31. Tan Malaka, *Dari Penjara ke Penjara* (Yogyakarta: Teplok Press, 2000), 147–48, as quoted in Poeze, "The Road to Hell," 165.

32. E. Bruce Reynolds, "History, Memory, Compensation and Reconciliation: The Abuse of Labor along the Thailand-Burma Railway," in *Asian Labor in the Wartime Japanese Empire: Unknown Histories*, ed. Paul Kratoska (Armonk, NY: M. E. Sharp, 2005), 329.

33. de Weerd, "Japanese Occupation," 74.

34. Cindy Adams, *Sukarno: An Autobiography as Told to Cindy Adams* (Hong Kong: Gunung Agung, 1965), 160–61.

35. Adams, *Sukarno*, 177–79, 192.

36. Kaori Maekawa, "The Heiho during the Japanese Occupation of Indonesia," in *Asian Labor in the Wartime Japanese Empire: Unknown Histories*, ed. Paul Kratoska (Armonk, NY: M. E. Sharpe, 2005), 185–89.

37. de Weerd, "Japanese Occupation," 70.

38. Maekawa, "Heiho," 188.

39. Maekawa, "Heiho," 192.

40. Maekawa, "Heiho," 191. The locations included Surabaya, Jakarta, Malang, Semarang, Jatigede, Bandung, and Sukabumi in Java; Tanjung Melawang, Medan, and Belawan in Sumatra; Makassar and Manado in Sulawesi; Singaraja in the Lesser Sundas; and Banjarmasin and Tarakan in Borneo.

41. de Weerd, "Japanese Occupation," 70.

42. Maekawa, "Heiho," 195.

43. Mark, *Japan's Occupation of Java*, 250.

44. Java Service Association, "Bylaws of the Constitution of the Java Service Association (Jawa Hōkōkai Kiyaku Saisoku), Section 4 Women's Associations, 1944," in *Japanese Military Administration in Indonesia: Selected Documents*, ed. Harry J. Benda, James K. Irikura, and Kishi Kōichi (New Haven, CT: Yale University Press, 1965), 158.

45. Siti Fatimah, "Fujinkai (Women's Association)," trans. Shigeru Satō, in *The Encyclopedia of Indonesia in the Pacific War*, ed. Peter Post, William H. Frederick, Iris Heidebrink, and Shigeru Satō (Leiden: Brill, 2010), 292.

46. Siti Fatimah, "Fujinkai," 292.

47. Sandra Wilson, "Family or State? Nation, War and Gender in Japan, 1937–45," *Critical Asian Studies* 38, no. 2 (2006): 215.

48. Wilson, "Family or State?," 215.

49. Wilson, "Family or State?," 215.

50. Chin Sung Chung, "The Origin and Development of the Military Sexual Slavery Problem in Imperial Japan," *positions*, 5 no. 1 (1997): 230.

51. Java Service Association, "Bylaws of the Constitution," 158.

52. Gandasubrata, *An Account of the Japanese Occupation*, 3.

53. Sarah Kovner, *Occupying Powers: Sex Workers and Servicemen in Postwar Japan* (Stanford, CA: Stanford University Press, 2019), 10–11.

54. Caroline Norma, *The Japanese Comfort Women and Sexual Slavery during the China and Pacific Wars* (London: Bloomsbury Academic, 2016), 80.

55. For one of the most detailed studies of their experiences, see Sachiyo Tsukamoto, *The Politics of Trauma and Integrity: Stories of Japanese "Comfort Women"* (London: Routledge, 2022).

56. Song Youn-Uk, "Japanese Colonial Rule and State-Managed Prostitution: Korea's Licensed Prostitutes," *positions* 5, no. 1 (1997): 175–76.

57. Song, "Japanese Colonial Rule," 181.

58. Song, "Japanese Colonial Rule," 144.

59. Kovner, *Occupying Powers*, 13.

60. Kovner, *Occupying Powers*, 13

61. Song, "Japanese Colonial Rule," 186.

62. Yoshimi, *Comfort Women*, 43.

63. Yoshimi, *Comfort Women*, 44.

64. Yoshimi, *Comfort Women*, 45.

65. Bonnie B. C. Oh, "The Japanese Imperial System and the Korean 'Comfort Women' of World War II," in *Legacies of the Comfort Women of World War II*, ed. Margaret D. Stetz and Bonnie B. C. Oh (Armonk, NY: M. E. Sharpe, 2001), 9.

66. Qiu with Su and Chen, *Chinese Comfort Women*, 6.

67. Kumagai, *The Comfort Women*, 17–18.

68. Kumagai, *The Comfort Women*, 17–18

69. Yoshimi, *Comfort Women*, 92–93.

70. Yoshimi, *Comfort Women*, 46.

71. Cynthia Enloe, *Does Khaki Become You: The Militarisation of Women's Lives* (London: Pluto, 1983), 19–20.

72. Chunghee Sarah Soh, "Prostitutes versus Sex Slaves: The Politics of Representing the 'Comfort Women,'" in *Legacies of the Comfort Women of World War II*, ed. Margaret D. Stetz and Bonnie B. C. Oh (Armonk, NY: M. E. Sharpe, 2001), 73–75.

73. Soh, "Prostitutes versus Sex Slaves," 77.

74. Tanaka, *Japan's Comfort Women*, 30.

75. Sensō Sekinin Shiryō Sentā, "Shiryō Chōsa Dai'ichiji Happhō," *Kikan Sensō Sekinin Kenkyū* (July 1993): 21, quoted (in translation) in Yamada, "From War to Independence," 20.

76. Sensō Sekinin Shiryō Sentā, "Shiryō Chōsa Dai'ichiji Happhō," 21.

77. For a broader perspective on the Japanese strategy toward Muslims in occupied China and the Netherlands East Indies and how this drew on German and Italian models, see Kelly A. Hammond, "Managing Muslims: Imperial Japan, Islamic Policy and Axis Connections during the Second World War," *Journal of Global History* 12 (2017): 251–73.

78. Tanaka, *Comfort Women*, 21.

79. Tanaka, *Comfort Women*, 64–65.

80. "Lists of Names of War Criminals. List of charges against Japanese war criminals, Pontianak with reports," Algemene Secretarie va de Nederlands-Indische Regering en Daarbij Gedeponeerde Archiven (1942) 1944–1950, inv. no. 5307.

81. Nakasone Yasuhiro, "Nijūsansai de Sanzen nin no Sōshikikan," in *Owarinaki Kaigun: Wakai Sedai e Tsutaetai Nokoshitai*, ed. Matsuura Takanori (Tokyo: Bunka Hōsō Kaihatsu Sentā Shuppanbu, 1978). Translations from Kimura Kōichi.

82. Horton, "Comfort Women," 187.

83. Elly Touwen-Bouwsma, "Japanse Legerprostitutie in Nederlands Indië 1942–1945," in *Oorlogsdocumentatie 40–45* (Amsterdam: Vijfde Jaarboek van het Rijksinstituut voor Oorlogsdocumentatie, 1994), 33.

84. Touwen-Bouwsma, "Japanse Legerprostitutie," 33.

85. Touwen-Bouwsma, "Japanse Legerprostitutie," 33.

86. Yamada, "From War to Independence," 21–23.

87. Tanaka, *Japan's Comfort Women*, 28.

88. Bart van Poelgeest, "Report of a Study of Dutch Government Documents on the Forced Prostitution of Dutch Women in the Dutch East Indies during the Japanese

Occupation," unofficial translation, NIOD Library, 1994, 5; Yamamoto and Horton, *Comfort Women in Indonesia*, 28.

89. Kimura Kōichi, "Brutal Abuse of Young Girls as Military Sex Slaves," *Asia Tsushin*, English edition no. 4 (December 1996): 3.

90. Budi Setiyono, "Ianfu di Indonesia," *Historia* 3 (2021): 53. (Data from Forum Komunikasi Ex-Heiho; see map 2.)

91. Raben, "Indonesian Romusha," 203.

Chapter 3. Patterns across the "Comfort Women" System in the Netherlands East Indies

1. Ema Kastinah, testimony. See also Ema, interview with Kawada Fumiko, March 29, 1996, trans. Kimura Kōichi, in Forum Komunikasi Ex-Heiho, *Kompensasi Jugun Ianfu* (n.p., 1996), 27–28.

2. King, "Working with/in the Archives," 13–29.

3. For a similar discussion of the labels and judgments that layer these records and further reflections on how accounts in them can be understood, see McGregor, "Living in a Conflict Zone," 44–45.

4. Eveline Buchheim, "Victim, Accomplice or Culprit? Marie-Therese Brandenburg van Olstende's Relations with the Japanese Occupier," in *Under Fire: Women and World War II* (Amsterdam/Hilversum: Verloren, 2014), 127–40.

5. National Archives of the Netherlands, The Hague (Nl-HaNA), Netherlands East Indies Forces Intelligence Service (NEFIS), 2.10.37.02, inv. no. 3, 6, 8, 13.

6. Monika Diederichs, "Stigma and Silence: Dutch Women, German Soldiers and Their Children," in *Children of War: The Hidden Enemy Legacy*, ed. Kjesti Ericsson and Eva Simonsen (London: Bloomsbury, 2005), 151.

7. On the search for traitors and collaborators, see Robert Cribb, "Avoiding Clemency: The Trial and Transfer of Japanese War Criminals in Indonesia, 1946–1949," *Japanese Studies* 31, no. 2 (2011): 151–70.

8. Consistent with the requirements of both the Nl-HaNA and the NIOD, the names of those involved in either setting up or running such facilities, and the names of individuals held in them, are not reproduced here.

9. Morris Suzuki, "You Don't Want to Know about the Girls?," 1–3.

10. Norma, *The Japanese Comfort Women*, 4, 94, 134.

11. Account from a Japanese veteran stationed in West Sumatra in 1942, published in 1978, Ryūji Takashi, *100-satsu ga kataru "ianjo," otoko no hone: Ajia zen'iki ni "ianjo" go atta* (Tokyo: Nashinokisha, 1994), as cited in Norma, *The Japanese Comfort Women*, 101.

12. Yamamoto and Horton, *Comfort Women in Indonesia*, 26; Nl-HaNA, Algemene Secretarie van de Nederlands-Indische Regering en de daarbij gedeponeerde Archieven (Alg. Secretarie Ned.-Ind. Regering; General Office of the Netherlands Indies Government and thereby deposited Archives), 2.10.14, inv. no. 5307, "Extracts from Interrogation Reports from Japanese War Criminals at Pontianak," and inv. no. 5309, "Report

on Enforced Prostitution in Western Borneo during Japanese Naval Occupation, Batavia, July 5, 1946."

13. Kimura Kōichi, "The Story of Tuminah," 15.

14. Note the word *selir* means concubine.

15. Adams, *Sukarno*, 163.

16. Adams, *Sukarno*, 163–64, emphasis added.

17. Adams, *Sukarno*, 164.

18. According to Kikumaru's biographer, she signed up to be a "comfort woman" to escape indentured prostitution and based in part on the false perception that her spirit would, like that of Japanese soldiers, be enshrined in Yasukuni shrine because of her patriotic duty. Sachiyo Tsukamoto, "A More Miserable Life than Living in the Jungle: A Japanese 'Comfort Woman' Story," *Gender and History* (November 2021): 7.

19. Tanaka, *Japan's Comfort Women*, 67.

20. Tanaka, *Japan's Comfort Women*, 22.

21. Min, *Korean "Comfort Women,"* 88.

22. Sutarbini, testimony in Hilde Janssen, *Schaamte en Onschuld: Het Verdrongen Oorlogsverleden van Troostmeisjes in Indonesië* (Amsterdam: Nieuw Amsterdam, 2010), 99–100.

23. "Wanita Penghibur Tentara Jepang Melapor ke LBH: Siang Melayani Tentara, Malam Sipil," *Bernas*, April 27, 1993.

24. Hartono and Juliantoro, *Derita*, 61.

25. Hartono and Juliantoro, *Derita*, 90.

26. Lasiyem's testimony, quoted in Hartono and Juliantoro, *Derita*, 89.

27. Mardiyah, account provided in Janssen, *Schaamte en Onschuld*, 26–29.

28. Mardiyah, account provided in Janssen, *Schaamte en Onschuld*, 34, 37–38.

29. Sharon Bessell, "The Politics of Child Labour in Indonesia: Global Trends and Domestic Policy," *Pacific Affairs* 72, no. 3 (1999): 354.

30. Bessell, "Child Labour," 357–58.

31. Encik Siti Marjam, "Pidato Encik Siti Marjam," in *Kongres Perempuan Pertama: Tinjauan Ulang*, ed. Susan Blackburn (Jakarta: Yayasan Obor Indonesia, KITLV Jakarta), 206.

32. Perhaps due to the early date of these records the term *troostmeisje* or *troostvrouwen*, "comfort girl" or "comfort woman," is only used twice. Nl-HaNA, NEFIS en Centrale Militaire Inlichtingendienst (CMI) in Nederlands-Indië, 1944 (2.10.62 inv. no. 44) and 1946 (2.10.62 inv. no. 2245).

33. Ide Anak Agung Gde Agung, *Kenangan Masa Lampau: Zaman Kolonial Hindia Belanda dan Zaman Pendudukan Jepang di Bali* (Jakarta: Yayasan Obor Indonesia, 1993), 91–194.

34. Tanaka, *Japan's Comfort Women*, 23.

35. Norma, *Comfort Women*, 80.

36. Jan Banning and Hilde Janssen, *Comfort Women, TroostMeisjes* (Utrecht: Ipso Facto, 2010), 87. See also Kasinem account in Janssen, *Schaamte en Onschuld*, 71–73.

37. Nl-HaNA, NEFIS/CMI, 2.10.62, inv. no. 2003, "NEFIS Interrogation Report No 311," n.d.

38. Nl-HaNA, NEFIS/CMI, 2.10.62, inv. no. 47, "Compilation of NEFIS Interrogation Reports Nos 200, 204–14, 229–45 (Not Issued), 8 September 1944."

39. Rosa, testimony in Hilde Janssen, *Schaamte en Onschuld: Het Verdrongen Oorlogsverleden van Troostmeisjes in Indonesië* (Amsterdam: Nieuw Amsterdam, 2010), 113–16.

40. Janssen, *Schaamte en Onschuld*, 111.

41. Sintha Melati, "In the Service of the Underground: The Struggle against the Japanese," trans. David Bourchier, in *Local Opposition and Underground Resistance to the Japanese in Java, 1942–1945*, ed. Anton Lucas (Clayton, Victoria: Monash Papers on Southeast Asia, 1986), 128. The piece was originally written under a pseudonym due to Umi Sardjono's detention by the Suharto regime and concerns about making political statements.

42. Toer, *Perawan Remaja*, 10–12.

43. Qiu with Su and Chen, *Chinese Comfort Women*, 43–45.

44. Melati, "In the Service of the Underground," 128–29.

45. Hartono and Juliantoro, *Derita*, 91.

46. Hartono and Juliantoro, *Derita*, 61.

47. Hartono and Juliantoro, *Derita*, 69.

48. Hartono and Juliantoro, *Derita*, 61.

49. Nl-HaNA, NEFIS/CMI, 2.10.62, inv. no. 47, "Compilation of NEFIS Interrogation Reports Nos 252–60 (Not Issued), September 2, 1944," and inv. no. 49, "Compilation of NEFIS Interrogation Reports Nos 366–78, 404–7 and 410–17 (Not Issued), October 29, 1944."

50. Nl-HaNA, NEFIS/CMI, 2.10.62, inv. no. 53, "NEFIS Interrogation Report No 1244, March 9, 1945."

51. Nl-HaNA, NEFIS/CMI, 2.10.62, inv. no. 2110, "Registers of Charges against Japanese War Criminals, Pontianak, 1946."

52. Nl-HaNA, NEFIS/CMI, 2.10.62, inv. no. 48, "Compilation of NEFIS Interrogation Reports Nos 296–327 (Not Issued separately), 10 October 1944."

53. Nl-HaNA, NEFIS/CMI, 2.10.62, inv. no. 2387, "Interrogation Report no 111, Batavia, January 14, 1946."

54. Nl-HaNA, NEFIS/CMI, 2.10.62, inv. no. 47, "Compilation of NEFIS Interrogation Reports Nos 200, 204–14, 229–45 (Not Issued), September 8, 1944."

55. Touwen-Bouwsma, "Japanse Legerprostitutie," 33.

56. Nl-HaNA, Alg. Secretarie Ned.-Ind. Regering (1942), 1944–50, 2.10.14, inv. no. 5307, "Lists of Names of War Criminals. List of Charges against Japanese War Criminals, Pontianak with Reports."

57. Nl-HaNA, Alg. Secretarie Ned.-Ind. Regering, 2.10.14, inv. no. 5307.

58. Tanaka, *Japan's Comfort Women*, 65.

59. Nl-HaNA, NEFIS/CMI, 2.10.62, inv. no. 1016, "Dagrapport, Batavia, November 26, 1945"; inv. no. 1020, "Dagrapport, Batavia, January 15, 1946"; inv. no. 1024,

"Dagrapport Batavia, Juni 24, 1946"; inv. no. 2245, "Interrogation Report, Semarang, April 26, 1946"; and inv. no. 2388, "Interrogation Report, Semarang, April 3, 1946." Nl-HaNA, NEFIS, 2.10.37.02, inv. nos. 1, 3, 4, 6, 8, 14, 21.

60. Nl-HaNA, NEFIS, 2.10.37.02, inv. nos. 4, 8, 14, 21.

61. Nl-HaNA, NEFIS, 2.10.37.02, inv. nos. 4, 8, 13; and 2.10.62, inv. no. 2245, "Interrogation Report, Semarang, April 26, 1946"; inv. no. 2387, "Interrogation Report, Padang, January 14, 1946."

62. Nl-HaNA, NEFIS/CMI, 2.10.62, inv. no. 2387, "Interrogation Report, Padang, January 14, 1946."

63. Toer, *Perawan Remaja*, 9–10.

64. Toer, *Perawan Remaja*, 10. See also Melati, "In the Service of the Underground," 128.

65. Suharti's story was recorded by Kawada Fumiko in 1997 and later by Hilde Janssen. She also testified at the 2000 Tokyo Tribunal. Kawada, *Indoneshia no "Ianfu,"* 31; Suharti, account provided in Janssen, *Schaamte en Onschuld*, 87–90.

66. See Blackburn, *The Comfort Women of Singapore*, 83–108.

67. Nl-HaNA, NEFIS/CMI, 2.10.62, inv. no. 44, "Interrogation of Two Native Sailors, Escapees from Timika (South New Guinea), February 21, 1944."

68. Nl-HaNA, NEFIS/CMI, 2.10.62, inv. no. 44, "Interrogation Report of Petrus Katuuk, Fireman 1st Cl. R.N.N. July 1, 1944."

69. Nl-HaNA, NEFIS/CMI, 2.10.62, inv. no. 49, "Compilation of NEFIS Interrogation Reports Nos 438–41, 448–9, 451–4 (Not Issued Separately), November 4, 1944."

70. Nl-HaNA, NEFIS, 2.10.37.02, inv. no. 1966, "Declaration in Preparation for Temporary Court-Martial Makassar, May 18, 1946."

71. Nl-HaNA, NEFIS, 2.10.37.02. inv. no. 1967, "Declaration in Preparation for Temporary Court-Martial Makassar, June 11, 1946."

72. Gandasubrata, *An Account of the Japanese Occupation*, 10.

73. Ken'ichi Gotō, "'Bright Legacy' or 'Abortive Flower': Indonesian Students in Japan during World War 2," in *Japanese Cultural Policies in Southeast Asia during World War 2*, ed. Grant K. Goodman (New York: St. Martin's Press, 1991), 7–20.

74. Mardiyem, Testimony, in Kana, *Mardiyem: Sex Slave of the Japanese Army*.

75. Hartono and Juliantoro, *Derita*, 65–66.

76. Toer, *Perawan Remaja*, 10.

77. C. Sarah Soh, "Aspiring to Craft Modern Gendered Selves: 'Comfort Women' and Chŏngsindae in Late Colonial Korea," *Critical Asian Studies* 36, no. 2 (2004): 176.

78. Morris Suzuki, "You Don't Want to Know About the Girls?," 5–6.

79. Qiu with Su and Chen, *Chinese Comfort Women*, 36–39.

80. Emi, Interview with Kawada Fumiko, March 28, 1996, translated by Kimura Kōichi, in Forum Komunikasi Ex-Heiho, *Kompensasi Jugun Ianfu*, 26. In his account of the occupation, Gandasubrata explains that the Japanese encouraged people to strengthen their bodies by performing *taisō* to the radio together outside their houses or in public spaces. Gandasubrata, *An Account of the Japanese Occupation*, 9.

81. Suhanah, Interview with Kawada Fumiko, March 28, 1996, trans. Kimura Kōichi, in Forum Komunikasi Ex-Heiho, *Kompensasi Jugun Ianfu*, 33.

82. Omoh, Interview with Kawada Fumiko, March 29, 1996, trans. Kimura Kōichi, in Forum Komunikasi Ex-Heiho, *Kompensasi Jugun Ianfu*, 29.

83. Emi, Suhanah, and Omoh interviews.

84. Janssen, *Schaamte en Onschuld*, 78.

85. Sri Sukanti, Testimony, in Eka Hindra, "Nona Djawa," *National Geographic* (Indonesia), August 2020, 36. The words she used were "saat itu rasanya saya ingin mati. Bukan manusia lagi."

86. Janssen, *Schaamte en Onschuld*, 100.

87. Gandasubrata, *An Account of the Japanese Occupation*, 3.

88. Hasniah Saleh Kaharuddin Yunus, Interview, quoted in Rasyaad Aminuddin, "Rahmah El Yunusiyyah: Kartini Perguruan Islam," in *Manusia dalam Kemelut Sejarah*, ed. Taufik Abdullah, Aswab Mahasin, and Daniel Dhakidae (Jakarta: LP3ES, 1978), 235.

89. Nl-HaNA, NEFIS/CMI, 2.10.62, inv. no. 44, "Report on the Interrogation of 55 Javanese, May 25, 1944."

90. Nl-HaNA, NEFIS/CMI, 2.10.62, inv. no. 49, "Compilation of NEFIS Interrogation Reports Nos 455 to 469 (Not Issued Separately), November 4, 1944."

91. Nl-HaNA, NEFIS/CMI, 2.10.62, inv. no. 44, "Report on the Interrogation of 55 Javanese, May 25, 1944."

92. Nl-HaNA, Alg. Secretarie Ned.-Ind. Regering, 2.10.14, inv. no. 5284.

93. Nl-HaNA, NEFIS/CMI, 2.10.62, inv. no. 45, "Compilation of NEFIS Interrogation Reports Nos 185–92, 10 August 1944."

94. Nl-HaNA, NEFIS/CMI, 2.10.62, inv. nos. 2000 and 2001.

95. Nl-HaNA, NEFIS/CMI, 2.10.62, inv. nos. 2000 and 2001.

96. van Poelgeest, "Oosters Stille Dwang," 13–21.

97. See advertisement reproduced in Hindra, "Nona Djawa," *National Geographic* (Indonesia), August 2020.

98. van Poelgeest, "Oosters Stille Dwang," 14.

99. Jeroen Kemperman, "Internment of Civilians," in *The Encyclopedia of Indonesia in the Pacific War*, ed. Peter Post, William H. Frederick, Iris Heidebrink, and Shigeru Satō (Leiden: Brill, 2010), 167.

100. International Military Tribunal for the Far East, Tokyo, 1946, 13, 487–13, 488 as given in Tanaka, *Japan's Comfort Women*, 67.

101. Helen Colijn, *Song of Survival: Women Interned* (Alexandria, NSW: Millennium Books, 1996), 148.

102. Tanaka, *Japan's Comfort Women*, 68–69.

103. Heidebrink, "Internment of Civilians," 163–65.

104. Nl-HaNA, NEFIS/CMI, 2.10.62, inv. no. 2388, "Interrogation Report dated March 19, 1946, Kandy."

105. Nl-HaNA, NEFIS/CMI, 2.10.62, inv. no. 2245, "Interrogation Report dated April 26, 1946, Semarang."

106. Nl-HaNA, NEFIS/CMI, 2.10.62, inv. no. 1971.

107. Nl-HaNA, NEFIS/CMI, 2.10.62, inv. no. 1971, "Summary of Examination dated January 24, 1946, Padang."

108. Nl-HaNA, NEFIS/CMI, 2.10.62, inv. no. 1971. On military police protection, see also inv. no. 1977, "Translation of the official report of the latest camp command of the women interned in Sumatra West Coast."

109. For some detailed examples, see van Poelgeest, *Oosters Stille Dwang*, 14–19.

110. Tanaka, *Japan's Comfort Women*, 72–74.

111. Horton, "Comfort Women," 187.

112. van Poelgeest, *Oosters Stille Dwang*, 14.

113. This paragraph draws on the narrated memoir of Ellen van der Ploeg in Jos Goos, *Gevoelloos op Bevel: Ervarringen in Jappenkampen* (Utrecht: Het Spectrum H.V., 1995), 11–12.

114. Nl-HaNA, NEFIS, 2.10.37.02, inv. no. 21.

115. O'Herne, *Fifty Years of Silence*, 66–68.

116. Tanaka, *Japan's Comfort Women*, 72.

117. Norma, *The Japanese Comfort Women*, 96.

118. NL-HaNA, Alg. Secretarie Ned.-Ind. Regering, 2.10.14, inv. no. 5282, 5309; Nl-HaNA, NEFIS, 2.10.37.02, inv. no. 4; Nl-HaNA, NEFIS/CMI, 2.10.62, inv. nos. 44, 46, 48–50, 2442, 3612. NIOD, Indische Collectie, entry no. 400, inv. no. 5647, "Documentation of the Temporary Court-Martial in Balikpapan." For a detailed account of the so-called Semarang case, see Yamamoto and Horton, *Comfort Women in Indonesia*, 16–20; and Tanaka, *Japan's Comfort Women*, 72–77.

119. Nl-HaNA, NEFIS/CMI, 2.10.62, inv. no. 50.

120. Hindra and Kimura, *Momoye*, 92.

121. Hindra and Kimura, *Momoye*, 119.

122. Janssen, *Schaamte en Onschuld*, 89.

123. Hindra and Kimura, *Momoye*, 108.

124. Kimura, "The Story of Tuminah," 15–16.

125. Lucia Juningsih, *Dampak Kekerasan Seksual pada Jugun Ianfu* (Yogyakarta: Kerjasama Ford Foundation dengan Pusat Penelitian Kependudukan Universitas Gadjah Mada, 1999), 28.

126. Nl-HaNA, NEFIS/CMI, 2.10.62, inv. no. 1969.

127. Nl-HaNA, NEFIS/CMI, 2.10.62, inv. no. 1952.

128. Hindra and Kimura, *Momoye*, 112.

129. Ahn Yonson, "Yearning for Affection: Traumatic Bonding between Korean 'Comfort Women' and Japanese Soldiers during World War II," *European Journal of Women's Studies* 26, no. 4 (2019): 365.

130. Nl-HaNA, Alg. Secretarie Ned.-Ind. Regering, 2.10.14, "Lists of Names of War Criminals. List of Charges against Japanese War Criminals, Pontianak with Reports," inv. no. 5307.

131. Nl-HaNA, NEFIS/CMI, 2.10.62, inv. nos. 1961 and 1967.

132. Norma, *The Japanese Comfort Women*, 108.

133. Nl-HaNA, NEFIS/CMI, 2.10.62, inv. no. 46, "Interrogation Report No 246."

134. Nl-HaNA, NEFIS/CMI, 2.10.62, inv. no. 48, "Interrogation Report No 442, October 23, 1944." See also Nl-HaNA, NEFIS/CMI, 2.10.62, inv. no. 2003.

135. Nl-HaNA, NEFIS/CMI, 2.10.62, inv. no. 53, "March 8, 1945."

136. Dai Sil Kim-Gibson, "They Defiled My Body, Not My Spirit: The Story of Korean Comfort Woman, Chung Seo Woon (Interview)," in *Making Waves: New Writing by Asian American Women*, ed. Elaine H. Kim and Lilia V. Villanueva (Boston: Beacon Press, 1997), 177–83.

137. Kim-Gibson, "They Defiled My Body," 182–83.

138. See Horton, "Comfort Women," 186.

139. Nl-HaNA, NEFIS/CMI, 2.10.62, inv. no. 2442.

140. Hindra and Kimura, *Momoye*, 93–94.

141. Suharti's Japanese name and the Japanese names of other survivors who have identified themselves are provided in Mariana, *Perbudakan Seksual*, 81, 89.

142. Kasinem, Testimony, in Hilde Janssen, *Schaamte en Onschuld: Het Verdrongen Oorlogsverleden van Troostmeisjes in Indonesië* (Amsterdam: Nieuw Amsterdam, 2010), 67.

143. O'Herne, *Fifty Years of Silence*, 79.

144. Mariana, *Perbudakan Seksual*, 81.

145. Janssen, *Schaamte en Onschuld*, 78–79.

146. van Poelgeest, "Report of a Study of Dutch Government," 4.

147. Ni-HaNA, Alg. Secretarie Ned-Ind. Regering (1942), 1944–1950, 2.10.14, inv. no. 5284.

148. Qiu with Su and Chen, *Chinese Comfort Women*, 67.

149. Nl-HaNA, NEFIS/CMI, 2.10.62, inv. no. 44, "Interrogation Report of Two Natives from Waigeo Captured R. N. N. Submarine on April 24, 1944, May 8, 1944."

150. Nl-HaNA, NEFIS/CMI, 2.10.62, inv. no. 44, "Report on the Interrogation of 55 Javanese, May 25, 1944."

151. Nl-HaNA, NEFIS/CMI, 2.10.62, inv. no. 44, "Report on the Interrogation of 55 Javanese, May 25, 1944" and "Detailed Report to Interrogation Report of 32 Javanese captured at Korako and Aitape, July 3, 1944."

152. Kawada, *Indonesia no "Ianfu,"* 51–90.

153. Nur, Testimony, in Hilde Janssen, *Schaamte en Onschuld: Het Verdrongen Oorlogsverleden van Troostmeisjes in Indonesië* (Amsterdam: Nieuw Amsterdam, 2010, 58–59.

154. Mardiyah, Testimony, in Hilde Janssen, *Schaamte en Onschuld: Het Verdrongen Oorlogsverleden van Troostmeisjes in Indonesië* (Amsterdam: Nieuw Amsterdam, 2010), 29.

155. Paini, Testimony, in Hilde Janssen, *Schaamte en Onschuld: Het Verdrongen Oorlogsverleden van Troostmeisjes in Indonesië* (Amsterdam: Nieuw Amsterdam, 2010), 49–52.

156. Siyem, Testimony, in Hilde Janssen, *Schaamte en Onschuld: Het Verdrongen Oorlogsverleden van Troostmeisjes in Indonesië* (Amsterdam: Nieuw Amsterdam, 2010), 65.

157. Kemperman, "Internment of Civilians," 169.

158. Kimura Kōichi, interview with author, Fukuoka, February 17, 2015.

159. Nl-HaNA, NEFIS/CMI, 2.10.62, inv. no. 1950, "Interrogation Report dated December 7, 1945."

160. Nl-HaNA, NEFIS/CMI, 2.10.62, inv. no. 1951, "Summary of Examination dated March 19, 1946."

161. Nl-HaNA, NEFIS/CMI, 2.10.62, inv. no. 2389, "Interrogation Report dated March 12, 1946, Semarang."

162. Nl-HaNA, NEFIS/CMI, 2.10.62, inv. no. 1971.

163. I also discuss this practice in McGregor, "Living in a Conflict Zone," 48–50.

164. This kind of domestic servitude and forced "marriage" was recognized in 1998 by the UN Special Rapporteur as another form of sexual slavery. Gay J. McDougall, "Contemporary Forms of Slavery: Systematic Rape, Sexual Slavery and Slavery-like Practices during Armed Conflict," *Final Report Special UN Special Rapporteur, United Nations Economic and Social Council,* June 22, 1998, 9–10.

165. Nl-HaNA, NEFIS/CMI, 2.10.62, inv. no. 44, "Interrogation Report of 13 Seroeanese Evacuees, evacuated on 26 March 1944, April 12, 1944."

166. Nl-HaNA, NEFIS/CMI, 2.10.62, inv. no. 48, "Interrogation Reports No 184 (Part III), October 18, 1944."

167. Nl-HaNA, NEFIS, 2.10.37.02, inv. nos. 4 and 6; Nl-HaNA, NEFIS/CMI, 2.10.62, inv. no. 2433.

168. Nl-HaNA, NEFIS, 2.10.37.02, inv. no. 8.

169. Nl-HaNA, NEFIS/CMI, 2.10.62, inv. no. 1966.

170. Nl-HaNA, NEFIS, 2.10.37.02, inv. no. 6.

171. Nl-HaNA, NEFIS/CMI, 2.10.62, inv. no. 1961.

172. Nl-HaNA, NEFIS, 2.10.37.02, inv. no. 1.

173. Nl-HaNA, NEFIS, 2.10.37.02, inv. nos. 1 and 14.

Chapter 4. Life after the War

1. Niyem's account is provided in Banning and Janssen, *Comfort Women, Troost-Meisjes,* 90.

2. Sandra Wilson, Robert Cribb, Beatrice Trefault, and Dean Aszkielowicz, *Japanese War Criminals: The Politics of Justice after the Second World War* (New York: Columbia University Press, 2017), 1.

3. "Rescue of Javanese Girls Planned," *Morning Bulletin,* September 17, 1945, 4.

4. Morris Suzuki, "You Don't Want to Know about the Girls?," 1–3.

5. Mackie, "Gender, Geopolitics and Gaps," 135–59.

6. As quoted in Mackie, "Gender, Geopolitics and Gaps," 143.

7. Emi, interview, 27.

8. Emi, interview, 27.

9. Ema, interview, 29.

10. Suhanah, interview, 34.

11. Iteng, Testimony, in Hilde Janssen, "Breaking the Silence," in *Japanese Militarism and Its War Crimes in Asia Pacific Region*, ed. Hendrajit (Jakarta: Global Future Institute, 2011), 141.

12. Veena Das, *Life and Words: Violence and the Descent into the Ordinary* (Berkeley: University of California Press, 2006), 48–49. The term "social death" was originally coined by Orlando Patterson, *Slavery and Social Death: A Comparative Study* (Cambridge, MA: Harvard University Press, 1982).

13. Hindra and Kimura, *Momoye*, 156.

14. Hindra and Kimura, *Momoye*, 158.

15. Hindra and Kimura, *Momoye*, 169.

16. Hindra and Kimura, *Momoye*, 163–80.

17. Hindra and Kimura, *Momoye*, 187.

18. Mutsuyo Ōki, "52 Nichi-kan no 'Shi no Kōshin': Suharuthi-san no Kunan to Kōfuku," *Suara*, no. 11 (March 26, 2001): 6.

19. Mutsuyo, "52 Nichi-kan," 6.

20. Mutsuyo, "52 Nichi-kan," 6.

21. Hindra and Kimura, *Momoye*, 172.

22. Hindra and Kimura, *Momoye*, 171–72.

23. Toer, *Perawan Remaja*.

24. Toer, *Perawan Remaja*. These interviews were conducted by Harun Rosidi and Sutikno W. S. The details of who these interviewers are, and indeed of the interviews Pramoedya conducted, are not clearly referenced throughout the text, which is a significant limitation, but the source remains valuable for the rare accounts that it provides into women left on this island. For more detailed analysis of this work, see Bradley William Horton, "Pramoedya and the Comfort Women of Buru: A Textual Analysis of *Perawan Remaja dalam Cengkeraman Militer*" [Teenage virgins in the grasp of the military], *Journal of Asia Pacific Studies* 14 (2010): 71–88.

25. Toer, *Perawan Remaja*, 37.

26. Toer, *Perawan Remaja*, 38.

27. Toer, *Perawan Remaja*, 39. For a more detailed discussion of the concept of being stained, see chapter 7.

28. Toer, *Perawan Remaja*, 50.

29. Mutsuyo, "52 nichi-kan," 6.

30. Das, *Life and Words*, refers to the care provided by parents and husbands for women stigmatized by others for being victims of sexual violence.

31. Juningsih, *Dampak Kekerasan Seksual*, 37.

32. Cited from Fusayama Takao, *Sumatora no Yoake* (Kodansha, Tokyo, 1981), 95–96, in Shigeru Satō, "The Japanese Army and Comfort Women in World War II," in *Sex, Power and Slavery*, ed. Gwyn Campbell and Elizabeth Elbourne (Athens: Ohio University Press, 2014), 397.

33. Diederichs, "Stigma and Silence," 151.

34. Juningsih, *Dampak Kekerasan*, 28–31.

35. Juningsih, *Dampak Kekerasan*, 32.

36. Juningsih, *Dampak Kekerasan*, 32.

37. Phillip Shaver, Upekkha Murdaya, and R. Chris Fraley, "Structure of the Indonesian Emotion Lexicon," *Asian Journal of Social Psychology* 4, no. 3 (2001): 206.

38. Susan Rees and Derrick Silove, "Sakit Hati: A State of Chronic Mental Distress Related to Resentment and Anger amongst West Papuan Refugees Exposed to Persecution," *Social Science and Medicine* 73, no. 1 (2011): 107.

39. Shibata Yaichiro, "Surabaya after the Surrender," in *The Japanese Experience in Indonesia*, ed. Anthony Reid and Oki Akira (Athens: Ohio University Press, 1986), 347–48.

40. See also Katharine McGregor and Vera Mackie, "Transcultural Memory and the Troostmeisjes/Comfort Women Photographic Project," *History and Memory* 30, no. 1 (Spring/Summer 2018): 116–50.

41. Juningsih, *Dampak Kekerasan*.

42. Mayumi Yamamoto, "Whispers and Gazes: A Postscript to the Semarang Comfort Women Incident," *Journal of Asia Pacific Studies* 18 (2012): 197–98.

43. NEFIS 2.10.62, inv. no. 2388.

44. O'Herne, *Fifty Years of Silence*, 115.

45. O'Herne, *Fifty Years of Silence*, 120.

46. William Frederick, "The Killing of Dutch and Eurasians in Indonesia's National Revolution (1945–1949): A Brief Genocide Reconsidered," *Journal of Genocide Research* 14, nos. 3–4 (2012): 359–80; Esther Captain and Onno Sinke, "Hatred of Foreign Elements and Their 'Accomplices': Extreme Violence in the First Phase of the Indonesian Revolution (17 August 1945 to 31 March 1946)," in *Beyond the Pale: Dutch Extreme Violence in the Indonesian War of Independence, 1945–1949*, ed. Gert Oostindie et al. (Amsterdam: Amsterdam University Press, 2022), 141–76.

47. O'Herne, *Fifty Years of Silence*, 128.

48. Katharine McGregor, "Transnational and Japanese Activism on Behalf of Indonesian and Dutch Victims of Enforced Military Prostitution During World War II," *Asia Pacific Journal* 14, no. 7 (2016), https://apjjf.org/2016/16/McGregor.html.

49. Andrew Goss, "From Tong-Tong to Tempo Doeloe: Eurasian Memory Work and the Bracketing of Dutch Colonial History, 1957–1961," *Indonesia* 70 (2000): 14.

50. O'Herne, *Fifty Years of Silence*, 131–32.

51. Goos, *Gevoelloes Op Bevel*, 105–6.

52. O'Herne, *Fifty Years of Silence*, 110–11.

53. This paragraph draws on Hamer de Froideville, *Geknakte Bloem*, 137.

54. T. van Boetzelaar, "Between Nation and Gender: The Representation of Former Military Comfort Women in the Netherlands and South Korea" (MA thesis, Leiden University, 2016), 25.

55. Hamer de Froideville, *Geknakte Bloem*, 139. See also Eveline Buchheim, "'Hide and Seek': Children of Japanese-Indisch Parents," in *Forgotten Captives in Japanese Occupied Asia*, ed. Karl Hack and Kevin Blackburn (London: Routledge, 2008), 260–77.

56. Ana Dragojlovic, "Did You Know My Father? The Zone of Unspeakability as Postcolonial Legacy," *Australian Feminist Studies* 26, no. 69 (2011): 319–34.

57. Frederick, "The Killing of Dutch and Eurasians," 365; Captain and Sinke, "Hatred of Foreign Elements," 150n507.

58. See the new series of books released in 2022 by the researchers behind a major project on this topic with Amsterdam University Press, including Gert Oostindie et al., eds., *Beyond the Pale: Dutch Extreme Violence in the Indonesian War of Independence, 1945–1949* (Amsterdam: Amsterdam University Press, 2022).

59. Katharine McGregor, "From National Sacrifice to Compensation Claims: Changing Indonesian Representations of the Captain Westerling Massacres in South Sulawesi (1946–1947)," in *Colonial Counterinsurgency and Mass Violence: The Dutch Empire in Indonesia*, ed. Bart Luttikhius and Dirk Moses (London: Taylor and Francis, 2014), 282–307.

60. "Court Says Dutch State Must Compensate Women for Rape 67 Years Ago," *Dutch News NL*, January 27, 2016, https://www.dutchnews.nl/news/2016/01/84093-2/; Liesbeth Zegveld, "Netherlands Liable for Rape of Woman in Dutch East Indies: State Must Allow Investigation in Dutch National Archives," December 18, 2016, http://www.liesbethzegveld.com/en/whats-going-on/netherlands-liable-for-rape-of-woman-in-dutch-east-indies-state-must-allow-investigation-in-dutch-national-archives/. For some preliminary scholarly analysis of this trend, see Stef Scagliola and Natalya Vince (in collaboration with Khedidja Adel and Galuh Ambar), "The Places, Traces, and Politics of Rape in the Indonesian and the Algerian Wars of Independence," in *Empire's Violent End*, ed. Brocades Zaalberg and Bart Luttikhuis (Ithaca, NY: Cornell University Press, 2022), 96–119.

61. Protschky, "Home at the Front," 60.

62. Tanaka, *Japan's Comfort Women*, 110–40. To date no research has been conducted on whether the Allied forces perpetrated sexual violence in Indonesia despite hints of this possibility in the work of Morris Suzuki. Suzuki, "You Don't Want to Know about the Girls?," 16. Similarly, the work of Indonesian scholar Anna Mariana (*Perbudakan Seksual*) draws broader links between Japanese practices of sexual violence and those of Indonesian military from the onset of the New Order in the 1965 anticommunist genocide.

63. Aleksandra Babovic, *The Tokyo Trial: Justice and the Postwar International Order* (Singapore: Springer Singapore, 2019), 4.

64. Nicola Henry, "Memory of an Injustice: The Comfort Women and the Legacy of the Tokyo Trial," *Asian Studies Review* 37, no. 3 (2013): 366–67.

65. Henry, "Comfort Women," 368–69.

66. Frederic Borch, *Military Trials of War Criminals in the Netherlands East Indies, 1946–1949* (Oxford: Oxford University Press, 2017), 35.

67. Borch, *Military Trials*, 128.

68. Borch, *Military Trials*, 36–37.

69. Iris Heidebrink, "Military Tribunals in the Netherlands East Indies," in *The Encyclopedia of Indonesia in the Pacific War*, ed. Peter Post, William H. Frederick, Iris Heidebrink, and Shigeru Satō (Leiden: Brill, 2010), 414.

70. Heidebrink, "Military Tribunals," 412.

71. Heidebrink, "Military Tribunals," 414.

72. Yamada, "From War to Independence," 77.

73. Yamamoto, "Whispers and Gazes," 194.

74. For close analysis of these trials, see Borch, *Military Trials*, 134–47.

75. Tanaka, *Japan's Comfort Women*, 52.

76. Yamada, "From War to Independence," 78.

77. Yamada, "From War to Independence," 78.

78. Yamada, "From War to Independence," 79–80.

79. Babovic, *Tokyo Trial*, 123–28.

80. Babovic, *Tokyo Trial*, 146–50.

81. Suehiro Akira, "The Road to Economic Reentry: Japan's Policy Toward Southeast Asian Development in the 1950s and 1960s," *Social Science Japan Journal* 2, no. 1 (1999): 85.

82. Sutan Sjahrir, *Our Struggle* (Ithaca, NY: Modern Indonesia Project, Southeast Asia Program, Dept. of Asian Studies, Cornell University, 1968).

83. Kurasawa Aiko, *Peristiwa 1965: Persepsi dan Sikap Jepang* (Jakarta: Penerbit Buku Kompas, 2015), 55.

84. Treaty of Peace between Japan and the Republic of Indonesia (1958) and Reparations Agreement between Japan and the Republic of Indonesia (1958), accessed September 26, 2021, https://www.mofa.go.jp/region/asia-paci/indonesia/epa0708/agreement.pdf.

85. Suehiro, "Road to Economic Reentry," 85–105.

86. "4 Kontroversi Ratna Sari Dewi Soekarno yang Menggerakan," *Merdeka*, November 5, 2013.

87. Baskara Wardaya, *Indonesia Melawan Amerika: Konflik Perang Dingin, 1953–1963* (Yogyakarta: Galang Pers, 2008).

88. Katharine McGregor, Annie Pohlman, and Jess Melvin, "New Interpretations of the Causes, Dynamics and Legacies of the Indonesian Genocide," in *The Indonesian Genocide: Causes, Dynamics and Legacies*, ed. Katharine McGregor, Jess Melvin, and Annie Pohlman (London: Palgrave Macmillan, 2018), 1–26.

89. Kurasawa, *Peristiwa 1965*, 160–66.

90. Bradley R. Simpson, *Economists with Guns: Authoritarian Development and US-Indonesian Relations 1960–1968* (Stanford, CA: Stanford University Press, 2008), 183.

91. Simpson, *Economists with Guns*, 212.

92. Mossadeq Bahri, "International Aid for Development? An Overview of Japanese ODA to Indonesia," *Makara Seri Sosial Humaniora* 8, no. 1 (2004): 42–43.

93. Ken'ichi Gotō, "Multilayered Postcolonial Space: Indonesia, the Netherlands, Japan and East Timor," in *A New East Asia: Toward a Regional Community*, ed. Mori Kazuko and Hirano Ken'ichoro (Singapore: NUS Press, 2007), 34.

94. Gotō, "Multilayered Postcolonial Space," 34.

95. Elizabeth van Kampen, "Memories of the Dutch East Indies: From Plantation Society to Prisoner of Japan," *Asia Pacific Journal* 7, no. 1 (2009), https://apjjf.org/-Elizabeth-Van-Kampen/3002/article.html.

96. Marijke Schuurmans, "Indies Memories in Bronze and Stone," *Inside Indonesia* 103 (January–March 2011), http://www.insideindonesia.org/indies-memories-in-bronze-and-stone.

97. Rudy Kousbroek, *Het Oostindisch Kampsyndroom* (Amsterdam: Muelenhoff, 1992).

98. Gotō, "Multilayered Postcolonial Space," 34.

99. Schuurmans, "Indies Memories."

100. See, for example, Colijn, *Song of Survival.*

101. See, for example, Touwen-Bouwsma, "Japanse Legerprostitutie."

102. The term "honorary" in the title refers to the demands of the foundation that the Japanese government "pays its respect and honors its obligations to the Dutch from Netherlands East Indies." See "Introduction to the Foundation of Japanese Honorary Debts," Stichting Japanse Ereschulden, accessed August 23, 2022, https://www.japanse-ereschulden.nl/english/.

103. van Kampen, "Memories of the Dutch East Indies."

104. Borch, *Military Trials.*

105. Ethan Mark, "Suharto's New Order Remembers Japan's New Order," in *Representing the Japanese Occupation of Indonesia*, ed. Remco Raben (Zwolle: Waanders, 1999), 72–84.

106. Mark, "Suharto's New Order," 72–84.

107. Gotō, "Multilayered Postcolonial Space," 28.

108. "New Order" is the term used by the Suharto regime to refer to the beginning of a new era under Suharto as a break from the period of the old order under Sukarno. Pancasila is the national philosophy of Indonesia.

109. Gotō, "Multilayered Postcolonial Space," 28.

110. Pandir Kelana, *Kadarwati Wanita dengan Lima Nama* (Jakarta: Penerbit Sinar Harapan, 1982).

111. Sri Indrayati and Ōkawa Seiichi, "Kisah Kadarwati yang Sebenarnya," *Tempo*, July 25, 1992.

112. Indrayati and Ōkawa, "Kisah Kadarwati." Cheong Yong Mun, "Indonesia: Questions of Stability," *Southeast Asian Affairs* 5 (1978): 119; Salim Said, *Genesis of Power: General Sudirman and the Indonesian Military in Politics 1945–1949* (North Sydney: Allen and Unwin, 1992), 104.

113. Other novels included *Ibu Sinder* (Jakarta: Penerbit Sinar Harapan, 1983) and *Kereta Api Terakhir* (Jakarta: Gramedia Pustaka Utama, 1983).

114. Sophan Sophiaan, dir., *Kadarwati Wanita dengan Lima Nama*, Gramedia Film, 1983.

115. Kelana, *Kadarwati*, 17.

116. Kelana, *Kadarwati*, 22.

117. Kelana, *Kadarwati*, 27.

118. Kelana, *Kadarwati*, 64–65.

119. Kelana, *Kadarwati*, 66

120. Kelana, *Kadarwati*, 87.

121. Kelana, *Kadarwati*, 89.

122. Kelana, *Kadarwati*, 129.

123. Kelana, *Kadarwati*, 179.

124. Kelana, *Kadarwati*, 181.

125. Kelana, *Kadarwati*, 182.

126. Kelana, *Kadarwati*, 194.

127. Gotō, "Multilayered Postcolonial Space," 29.

Chapter 5. Pathways to Activism in Japan and Korea, 1980s–1990s

1. Park Jon-Seok and Shin Dong-Yun, *My Wish Is . . .* , Korea Centre for Investigative Journalism, January 6, 2016, https://newstapa.org/article/7LiYc?lang=eng.

2. This aspect of advocacy has received less scholarly attention than that of the women's activist movement. The major studies of Japanese and Korean feminist activism on this issue are quoted below. Key studies of Japanese legal activism tend to focus on activism for forced laborers. One example is Petra Schmidt, "Japan's Wartime Compensation: Forced Labour," *Asia Pacific Journal on Human Rights and Law* 2 (2000): 1–54.

3. JFBA, *Japan Federation of Bar Associations*, pamphlet provided to the author, Tokyo, n.d., 18.

4. JFBA pamphlet, 11, 37.

5. Agreement on the Settlement of Problems Concerning Property and Claims and on Economic Cooperation (1965), https://treaties.un.org/doc/Publication/UNTS /Volume% 20583/volume-583-I-8473-English.pdf.

6. Misook Lee, "The Japan-Korea Solidarity Movement in the 1970s and 1980s: From Solidarity to Reflexive Democracy," *Asia-Pacific Journal* 12, no. 1 (2014): 2.

7. Shin Hae Bong, "Compensation for Victims of Wartime Atrocities: Recent Developments in Japan's Case Law," *Journal of International Criminal Justice* 3, no. 1 (2005): 190.

8. Bong, "Compensation for Victims," 188.

9. Elazar Barkan, *The Guilt of Nations: Restitution and Negotiating Historical Injustices* (New York: Norton, 2000), xvii.

10. A key author here is Takagi Ken'ichi. He has published the following books considering compensation: Takagi Ken'ichi, *Saharin to Nihon no Sengo Sekinin* (Tokyo: Gaifū Sha, 1990); Takagi Ken'ichi, *Jūgun Ianfu to Sengo Hoshō—Nihon no Sengo Sekinin* (Tokyo: San'ichi Shobō, 1992); Takagi Ken'ichi, *Ima Naze Sengo Hoshō ka* (Tokyo: Kōdan Sha, 2001); and Takagi Ken'ichi, *Sengo Hoshō no Ronri: Higaisha no Koe o Dō kiku ka* (Tokyo: Renga Shobō Shinsha, 1994). Other lawyers who have written on this are Murayama Akira, *Bengoshi ga Mita Sengo Hoshō to Jinken* (Tokyo: Buraku Mondai Kenkyūjo, 1995); Uchida Masatoshi, *Sengo Hoshō o Kangaeru* (Tokyo: Kôdansha, 1994); and Totsuka Etsurō, *Nihon ga Shiranai Sensō Sekinin: Kokuren no Jinken Katsudō to Nihongun Jūgun Ianfu Mondai* (Tokyo: Gendai Jinbunsha, 1999).

11. Hirowatari Seigo, "Kenpō to Sengo Sekinin: Sengo 50 nen, Nihon to Doitsu," *Hōritsu Jihō* 67, no. 6 (1995): 11–17; Imamura Tsuguo, Takagi Yoshitaka, and Suzuki Isomi, *Sengo Hoshō Hō* (Tokyo: Akashi Shoten, 1999).

12. On the importance of family experiences of the war in shaping the views, see Philip Seaton, *Japan's Contested War Memories: The Memory Rifts in Historical Consciousness of World War II* (London: Routledge, Taylor and Francis, 2007).

13. Takagi Ken'ichi, interview, Tokyo, February 20, 2015.

14. Patricia G. Steinoff, "Japan: Student Activism in an Emerging Democracy," in *Student Activism in Asia: Between Protest and Powerlessness*, ed. Meredith Weiss and Edward Aspinall (Minneapolis: University of Minnesota Press, 2012), 63–66.

15. Lee, "Japan-Korea Solidarity Movement," 1.

16. Takagi, interview.

17. Schmidt, "Japan's Wartime Compensation," 20.

18. Association of Pacific War Victims and Bereaved Families, *The Issue of Korean Human Rights during and after the Pacific War*, March 1, 1993, 25.

19. Schmidt, "Japan's Wartime Compensation," 21–25.

20. Cathleen Kozen, "Redress as American-Style Justice: Congressional Narratives of Japanese American Redress at the End of the Cold War," *Time and Society* 21, no. 1 (2012): 104–20.

21. Takagi, interview.

22. Bong, "Compensation for Victims."

23. Schmidt, "Japan's Wartime Compensation," 28–29.

24. Nozaki, "The Comfort Women Controversy."

25. Japan Federation of Bar Associations, "Recommendations on the Issue of the 'Comfort Women,'" JFBA, January 1995, 11.

26. For a discussion of cases brought in the 1990s, see Totsuka Etsurô, "Commentary on a Victory for 'Comfort Women': Japan's Judicial Recognition of Military Sexual Slavery," *Pacific Rim Law and Policy Journal* 8, no. 1 (1999): 47–61.

27. Ayako Kano, *Japanese Feminist Debates: A Century of Contention on Sex, Love, and Labor* (Honolulu: University of Hawai'i Press, 2016), 46–48.

28. Kano, *Japanese Feminist Debates*, 18.

29. This title is a translation of the original Japanese text by Yamazaki Tomoko, *Sandakan Hachiban Shōkan-Teihen Joseishi Joshō* (Tokyo: Chukumo Shobō, 1972).

30. On this field of history, see Carol Gluck, "The People in History: Recent Trends in Japanese Historiography," *Journal of Asian Studies* 38, no. 1 (1978): 25–50.

31. Gluck, "People in History," 47.

32. For an overview of criticisms of people's history, see Ethan Mark, "Translator's Introduction: The People in the War," in Yoshimi Yoshiaki, *Grassroots Fascism: The War Experience of the Japanese People* (New York: Columbia University Press), 24.

33. Yamazaki Tomoko, *Sandakan Brothel No. 8: An Episode in the History of Lower-Class Japanese Women*, trans. Karen Colligan-Taylor (Armonk, NY: M. E. Sharpe, 1999). All citations below come from this English-language text.

34. James Warren, "Review Essay: New Lands, Old Ties and Prostitution: A Voiceless Voice," *Intersections: Gender, History and Culture in the Asian Context* 4 (2000): 2.

35. Yamazaki, *Sandakan Brothel No. 8*, 52, 62.

36. Warren, "Review Essay," 7.

37. Yamazaki, *Sandakan Brothel No. 8*, 52.

38. Yamazaki, *Sandakan Brothel No. 8*, 63.

39. Yamazaki, *Sandakan Brothel No. 8*, 57.

40. Yamazaki, *Sandakan Brothel No. 8*, 192.

41. Warren, "Review Essay," 1.

42. Warren, "Review Essay," 1.

43. Warren, "Review Essay"; James Warren, *Ah Ku and Karayukisan: Prostitution in Singapore, 1870–1940* (Singapore: Oxford University Press, 1993).

44. Erik Ropers, *Voices of the Korean Minority in Postwar Japan: Histories against the Grain* (New York: Routledge, 2019), 115.

45. Senda, *Jūgun Ianfu*.

46. Ropers, *Voices of the Korean Minority*, 119.

47. Ropers, *Voices of the Korean Minority*, 128.

48. Soh, *The Comfort Women*, 148.

49. Michael Weiner and David Chapman, "Zainichi Koreans in History and Memory," in *Japan's Minorities: The Illusion of Homogeneity*, ed. Michael Weiner (London: Routledge, 2009), 172.

50. Vera Mackie, *Feminism in Modern Japan: Citizenship, Embodiment and Sexuality* (Cambridge: Cambridge University Press, 2003), 218. For some analysis of these oral histories of laborers, see Ropers, *Voices of the Korean Minority*.

51. Weiner and Chapman, "Zainichi Koreans."

52. Mackie, *Feminism in Modern Japan*, 148.

53. Matthew Allen, "Okinawa, Ambivalence, Identity and Japan," in *Japan's Minorities: The Illusion of Homogeneity*, ed. Michael Weiner (Abingdon: Routledge, 2009), 188–89.

54. Mackie, *Feminism in Modern Japan*, 218.

55. Hayashi Hirofumi, "Government, the Military and Business in Japan's Wartime Comfort Women System." *Asia-Pacific Journal* 5, no. 1 (2007): 4, https://apjjf.org/-Hayashi-Hirofumi/2332/article.html; Tanaka, *Japan's Comfort Women*, 85.

56. Tanaka, *Japan's Comfort Women*, 111–12. Tanaka also documents US sexual violence against these women in the postwar era.

57. Lee Jeong-gyu, "Remembering Bae Bong-gi, the First Comfort Woman to Testify about Her Experiences," *Hankyoreh*, March 18, 2019, http://english.hani.co.kr/arti/english_edition/e_international/886367.html.

58. "Senjichū Okinawa ni Renkō no Kankoku Josei 30 nen buri 'Jiyū' o Teni: Fukō na Kako Hōmushō Tokubetsu Zairyū o Kyoka," *Kōchi Shimbun*, October 22, 1975.

59. Tai, *Comfort Women Activism*, 14.

60. The 1979 film was called *Okinawa no Harumoni: Shōgen: Jugun Ianfu.* The book was called *Okinawa no Harumoni: Dainippon Baishunshi* (Tokyo: Bansheisha, 1979). Soh, *The Comfort Women,* 156.

61. Kawada Fumiko, interview with author, Tokyo, September 20, 2017.

62. "Senjichū Okinawa."

63. Kawada, interview.

64. Fujino Yutaka, *Sengo Nihon no Jinshin Baibai* (Tokyo: Ōtsuki Shoten, 2012); Kawada, interview.

65. Kawada, interview.

66. Kawada Fumiko, *Akagawara no Ie: Chōsen kara Kita Jūgun Ianfu* (Tokyo: Chikuma Shobō, 1987). She also published a book about Okinawan women, including women working in fisheries, agriculture, and red-light districts. Kawada Fumiko, *Ryūkyūko no Onnatachi* (Tokyo: Tō jusha, 1983).

67. Min, *Korean "Comfort Women,"* 53–54.

68. Matsui Yayori, "Why I Oppose Kisaeng Tours," originally published in Japanese in 1974, extract in *International Feminism: Networking against Female Sexual Slavery, Report of the Global Feminist Workshop to Organize against Traffic in Women, Rotterdam, the Netherlands, April 6–15, 1983,* ed. Kathleen Barry, Charlotte Bunch, and Shirley Castley (New York: International Women's Tribune Center, 1984), 69.

69. "History from AWA to AJWRC," Asia-Japan Women's Resource Center, accessed August 23, 2022, http://www.ajwrc.org/eng/modules/pico1/index.php? content _id=2.

70. Yamane Kazuyo, "Yayori Matsui and the Women's Active Museum on War and Peace," *Social Alternatives* 29, no. 1 (2010): 25.

71. Matsui Yayori, *Women's Asia* (London: Zed Books, 1989).

72. Mackie, *Feminism in Modern Japan,* 203.

73. Lee, "Japan-Korea Solidarity," 2–3, 6–7.

74. Lee, "Japan-Korea Solidarity," 4–6.

75. Mackie, *Feminism in Modern Japan,* 204.

76. Yamane, "Yayori Matsui," 27.

77. Yayori Matsui, "Kankoku-fujin no Ikita Michi," *Asahi Shinbun,* November 2, 1984, 5, cited in Nozaki, "The Comfort Women Controversy."

78. Nozaki, "The Comfort Women Controversy."

79. Mackie, *Feminism in Modern Japan,* 205.

80. Mackie, *Feminism in Modern Japan,* 205.

81. "The Women Who Came to Rotterdam," in *International Feminism: Networking against Female Sexual Slavery, Report of the Global Feminist Workshop to Organize against Traffic in Women, Rotterdam, the Netherlands, April 6–15, 1983,* ed. Kathleen Barry, Charlotte Bunch, and Shirley Castley (New York: International Women's Tribune Center, 1984), 15–20.

82. Charlotte Bunch and Shirley Castley, "Introduction," in *International Feminism: Networking against Female Sexual Slavery, Report of the Global Feminist Workshop to Organize against Traffic in Women, Rotterdam, the Netherlands, April 6–15, 1983,* ed.

Kathleen Barry, Charlotte Bunch, and Shirley Castley (New York: International Women's Tribune Center, 1984), 10–11.

83. Ruth Barraclough, *Factory Girl Literature: Sexuality, Violence, and Representation in Industrializing Korea* (Los Angeles: University of California Press, 2012), 59, 76.

84. Barraclough, *Factory Girl Literature*, 73.

85. Barraclough, *Factory Girl Literature*, 140.

86. Barraclough, *Factory Girl Literature*, 111.

87. Barraclough, *Factory Girl Literature*, 80.

88. Miriam Ching Yoon Louie, "Minjung Feminism: Korean Women's Movement for Gender and Class Liberation," *Women's Studies International Forum* 18, no. 4 (1995): 418. The term *minjung* specifically refers to a mass movement and the exploitation of the working classes in particular.

89. Kyungja Jung, *Practicing Feminism in South Korea* (London: Routledge, 2014), 9.

90. Louie, "Minjung Feminism," 418.

91. Barraclough, *Factory Girl Literature*, 101. The term *hakch'ul* means those who have departed school and was coined in the 1970s for those who left school to work in factories.

92. Jung, *Practicing Feminism*, 23–25.

93. Louie, "Minjung Feminism," 420.

94. Jung, *Practicing Feminism*, 12–13.

95. Jung, *Practicing Feminism*, 13–14.

96. Jung, *Practicing Feminism*, 19–23.

97. Louie, "Minjung Feminism," 423.

98. Louie, "Minjung Feminism," 423.

99. Material in this paragraph is based on the Association of Pacific War Victims and Bereaved Families, *The Issue of Korean Human Rights during and after the Pacific War*, 2–4 (March 1, 1993): 22–25.

100. Hee Soon Kwon, "The Military Sexual Slavery Issue and Asian Peace," paper presented at the First East Asian Women's Forum, Japan, October 20–22, 1994, 6.

101. Kwon, "Military Sexual Slavery Issue," 2.

102. Kwon, "Military Sexual Slavery Issue," 2.

103. Alice Yun Chai, "Asian-Pacific Feminist Coalition Politics," *Korean Studies* 17 (1993): 67–91.

104. Oh, "The Japanese Imperial System," 15.

105. Oh, "The Japanese Imperial System," 15–16.

106. Kwon, "Military Sexual Slavery Issue," 5.

107. Kwon, "Military Sexual Slavery Issue," 5.

108. Kwon, "Military Sexual Slavery Issue," 5.

109. Kwon, "Military Sexual Slavery Issue," 5.

110. Jung, *Practicing Feminism*, 82.

111. Chunghee Sarah Soh, "The Korean 'Comfort Women' Movement for Redress," *Asian Survey* 36, no. 12 (1996): 1235.

112. Association of Pacific War Victims and Bereaved Families, *Korean Human Rights*, 2–3.

113. Association of Pacific War Victims and Bereaved Families, *Korean Human Rights*, 4.

114. Soh, *Comfort Women*, 43.

115. Soh, *Comfort Women*, 43.

116. Different sources provide different numbers of claimants.

117. Min, *Korean "Comfort Women,"* 67.

118. Soh, *Comfort Women*, 43.

119. Takagi, interview.

120. Photograph of the demonstration on December 7, 1991, Association of Pacific War Victims and Bereaved Families, *Korean Human Rights*, 33.

121. Takagi, interview.

122. Takagi, interview.

123. This account is adapted from the translated account of Kim Hak-Sun's experiences provided by Soh, *Comfort Women*, 130–31.

124. JFBA, "Recommendations," 13.

125. Hata, *Comfort Women and Sex*, 17.

126. Yoshimi, *Comfort Women*, 33–35.

127. Yoshimi, *Comfort Women*, 35.

128. Yoshimi Yoshiaki, *Grassroots Fascism: The War Experience of the Japanese People*, trans. Ethan Mark (New York: Columbia University Press, 2015).

129. *Asahi Shimbun*, January 11, 1992, 1, cited in Yoshimi, *Comfort Women*, 35.

130. Yoshimi, *Comfort Women*, 35.

131. Kwon, "Military Sexual Slavery Issue," 8–9.

132. Kwon, "Military Sexual Slavery Issue," 8–9.

133. Kwon, "Military Sexual Slavery Issue," 1.

134. Soh, "Korean Comfort Women," 1235.

135. Hayashi Hirofumi, "The Japanese Movement to Protest Wartime Sexual Violence: A Survey of Japanese and International Literature," *Critical Asian Studies* 33, no. 4 (2001): 574.

136. Democratic People's Republic of Korea, Minister for Foreign Affairs, Letter to the Secretary-General, August 2, 1993, United Nations, file A/48/302.

137. Letter, United Nations, file A/48/302.

138. This organization expanded to become the Asia-Japan Women's Resource Center in 1994.

139. *War Victimization and Japan: International Public Hearing Report*, The Executive Committee International Public Hearing (Osaka-shi: Tōhō Shuppan, 1993).

140. Murayama Akira, "Realities of War Victims and Japan's Measures for War Responsibility," in *War Victimization and Japan, International Public Hearing Report*, The Executive Committee International Public Hearing (Osaka-shi: Tōhō Shuppan, 1993), 135.

141. Murayama Akira, interview, Tokyo, February 23, 2015.

142. Murayama, interview.

143. Murayama, interview. Murayama explained that the reasons for sending missions to Indonesia and other countries was based on an understanding that the victims themselves would be unable to attend hearings or provide testimony in Japan.

144. Szczepanska, *The Politics of War Memory in Japan*, 32.

145. Hayashi, "Japanese Movement," 574.

146. Soh, *Comfort Women*, 65.

147. Kwon, "Military Sexual Slavery Issue," 8–9.

148. Mackie, "In Search of Innocence," 209.

149. Gluck, "Operations of Memory," 59–65.

150. *War Victimization and Japan*, 2–3.

Chapter 6. The Early 1990s

1. Bunga Surawijaya and Ōkawa Seiichi, "Jeritan dari Rumah Bamboo," *Tempo*, August 8, 1992, 56.

2. Katharine McGregor, *History in Uniform: Military Ideology and the Construction of the Indonesian Past* (Singapore: NUS Press, 2007).

3. John Taylor, *East Timor: The Price of Freedom* (New York: Zed Books, 1999).

4. Annie Pohlman, *Women, Sexual Violence and the Indonesian Killings of 1965–66* (New York: Routledge, 2015); Hannah Loney, *In Women's Words: Violence and Everyday Life during the Indonesian Occupation of East Timor, 1975–1999* (Brighton: Sussex Academic Press, 2018).

5. Ruth India Rahayu, "Politik Gender Orde Baru: Tinjauan Organisasi Perempuan Sejak 1980an," *Prisma* 5, no. 25 (1996): 29–42.

6. Saskia Wieringa, *Sexual Politics in Indonesia* (New York: Palgrave Macmillan, 2002), 140.

7. Sulami, "The Birth and Growth of the Indonesian Women's Movement," *Women of the Whole World* (Part 2), 1 (1959): 30. A section of this report was titled "Indonesian women suffer Japanese occupation."

8. Katharine McGregor, "Indonesian Women, the Women's International Democratic Federation and the Struggle for 'Women's Rights,' 1946–1965," *Indonesia and the Malay World* 40, no. 117 (2012): 193–208.

9. McGregor, "Indonesian Women."

10. Donald Hindley, *The Communist Party of Indonesia 1951–1963* (Berkeley: University of California Press, 1964), 201–8.

11. Wieringa, *Sexual Politics in Indonesia*.

12. Pohlman, *Women, Sexual Violence*.

13. Nori Andriyani, "Hak Asasi Perempuan Dalam Orde Baru," in *Demokrasi Antara Represi dan Resistensi: Catatan Keadaan Hak Asasi Manusia*, ed. Mulyana W. Kusuma (Jakarta: Yayasan Lembaga Bantuan Hukum, 1993), 108–9.

14. Andriyani, "Hak Asasi," 106.

15. Andriyani, "Hak Asasi," 106.

16. Julia Suryakasuma, "The State and Sexuality in New Order Indonesia," in *Fantasizing the Feminine in Indonesia*, ed. Laurie Sears (Durham, NC: Duke University Press, 1996), 99–119.

17. Krishna Sen, "Indonesian Women at Work: Reframing the Subject," in *Gender and Power in Affluent Asia*, ed. Krishna Sen and Maila Stivens (London: Routledge, 1998), 35–62.

18. Andriyani, "Hak Asasi," 104.

19. Soedjatmoko, "The Indonesian Historian and His [*sic*] Time," in *An Introduction to Indonesian Historiography*, ed. Soedjatmoko, Mohammd Ali, G. J. Resink, and G. M. Kahin (Ithaca, NY: Cornell University Press, 1965), 404–15.

20. Ruth McVey, "The Enchantment of the Indonesian Revolution: History and Action in an Indonesian Communist Text," in *Perceptions of the Past in Southeast Asia*, ed. Anthony Reid and David Marr (Kuala Lumpur: Asian Studies Association of Australia, Heineman Education Books, 1979), 340–58.

21. Blackburn, *Women and the State*, 199–200.

22. Ruth Indiah Rahayu, "Konstruksi Historiografi Feminisme dari Tutur Perempuan," in *Historiografi Indonesia: Di Antara Historiografi Nasional dan Alternatif*, Pusat Studi Sosial Asia Tenggara and ARC, Hotel Yogya Plaza, July 2–4, 2007. The term *pribumi* refers to so-called indigenous Indonesians, but here it is used to accentuate the fact that ethnic minorities are frequently excluded from Indonesian historiography.

23. Sartono Kartodirdjo, *The Peasants' Revolt of Banten in 1918: Its Conditions, Course and Sequel: A Case Study of Social Movements in Indonesia* (s'Gravenhage: Martinus Nijhoff, 1966).

24. Erwiza Erman, "Penggunan Sejarah Lisan dalam Historiografi Indonesia," *Jurnal Masyarakat dan Budaya* 13, no. 1 (2011): 4.

25. Erman, "Penggunan Sejarah," 11.

26. John Roosa, Ayu Ratih, and Hilmar Farid, eds., *Tahun Yang Tak Pernah Berakhir: Memahami Pengalaman Korban 65 Esai-esai Sejarah Lisan* (Jakarta: ELSAM, 2004).

27. Saparinah Sadli, "Feminism and Indonesia in an International Context," in *Women in Indonesia: Gender, Equity and Development*, ed. Kathy Robinson and Sharon Bessell (Singapore: Institute of Southeast Asian Studies, 2002), 81.

28. Sadli, "Feminism and Indonesia," 83.

29. A. Nunuk P. Murniati, *Gerakan Anti-Kekerasan terhadap Perempuan* (Yogyakarta: Penerbit Kanisius, 1998), 22.

30. Ruth Indiah Rahayu, former member of Kalyanamitra, personal correspondence, May 2019.

31. Rahayu, personal correspondence.

32. Saraswati Sunindyo, "She Who Earns: The Politics of Prostitution in Java" (MA thesis, University of Wisconsin–Madison, 1993), 33.

33. Rachel Rinaldo, *Mobilizing Piety: Islam and Feminism in Indonesia* (New York: Oxford University Press, 2013).

34. Dina Afrianty, "Agents for Change, Local Women's Organizations and Domestic Violence in Indonesia," *Bijdragen tot de taal-, land-en volkenkunde* 174, no. 1 (2018): 35–36. For more on LBH APIK, see chapter 7.

35. Blackburn, *Women and the State*, 203.

36. Murniati, *Gerakan Anti-Kekerasan*, 22.

37. Murniati, *Gerakan Anti-Kekerasan*, 53.

38. Jafar Suryomenggolo, "Factory Employment, Female Workers Activism, and Authoritarianism in Indonesia: Reading Ira Irianti's Pembelaan," *Critical Asian Studies* 44, no. 4 (2012): 602–5.

39. Murniati, *Gerakan Anti-Kekerasan*, 23–25.

40. Leena Avonius, "From Marsinah to Munir: Grounding Human Rights in Indonesia," in *Human Rights in Asia: A Reassessment of the Asian Values Debate*, ed. Damien Kingsbury and Leena Avonius (Basingstoke: Palgrave Macmillan, 2008), 99–119.

41. Yayasan Lembaga Bantuan Hukum, "Kasus Marsinah," in *Demokrasi Antara Represi dan Resistensi: Catatan Keadaan Hak Asasi Manusia* (Jakarta: Yayasan Lembaga Bantuan Hukum, 1994), 231–32.

42. On the significance of language to activism, see Mackie, "The Language of Globalization," 197.

43. On Filipino women's positions in these debates, see Mina Roces, "Prostitution, Women's Movement and the Victim Narrative in the Philippines," *Women's Studies International Forum* 32 (2009): 271, 274.

44. Sunindyo, "She Who Earns," 2.

45. Sunindyo, "She Who Earns," 212.

46. Flower Aceh, "Profil," accessed August 23, 2022, http://floweraceh.or.id/pro fil/.

47. Blackburn, *Women and the State*, 195.

48. Edward Aspinall, *Opposing Suharto: Compromise, Resistance, and Regime Change in Indonesia* (Stanford, CA: Stanford University Press, 2005), 35.

49. Aspinall, *Opposing Suharto*, 43.

50. Anja Jetschke, "Linking the Unlinkable? International Norms and Nationalism in Indonesia and the Philippines," in *The Power of Human Rights: International Norms and Domestic Change*, ed. Thomas Risse, Stephen Ropp, and Kathryn Sikkink (Cambridge: Cambridge University Press, 1999), 134–71.

51. Ken Setiawan, *Promoting Human Rights, National Human Rights Commissions in Indonesia and Malaysia* (Leiden: Leiden University Press, 2013), 35.

52. Ken Setiawan, "From Hope to Disillusion: The Paradox of Komnas HAM, the Indonesian Human Rights Commission," *Bijdragen tot de taal-, land- en volkenkunde* 172, no. 1 (2016): 8.

53. Gluck, "Operations of Memory," 69.

54. Ueno Chizuko, "The Politics of Memory: Nation, Individual and Self," trans. Jordan Sand, *History and Memory* 11, no. 2 (1999): 137.

55. See Seichi Ōkawa and ADN, "Maaf, Kata Miyazawa," *Tempo*, January 25, 1992, 82.

56. Janet Steele, *Wars Within: The Story of* Tempo *an Independent Magazine in Soeharto's Indonesia* (Jakarta: Equinox Pub. and Institute of Southeast Asian Studies, 2005), xi.

57. Krishna Sen and David Hill, *Media Culture and Politics in Indonesia* (Melbourne: Oxford University Press, 2000), 11–12.

58. Steele, *Wars Within*, 155–58.

59. George Hicks, *The Comfort Women: Japan's Brutal Regime of Enforced Prostitution in the Second World War* (New York: Norton, 1995), 142–48. For some highly critical reviews of Hicks's work, see Katharine H. S. Moon, "Review: 'The Comfort Women: Japan's Brutal Regime of Enforced Prostitution in the Second World War,'" *Contemporary Sociology* 25, no. 5 (1996): 630–31; Chunghee Sarah Soh, "Uncovering the Truth about the 'Comfort Women,'" *Women's Studies International Forum* 21, no. 4 (1998): 452. One *Tempo* article translated into English and republished is Amsakasasi et al., trans. Alison Garrod, Heidi Lindgren, and Kat Napthali, "Screams from the Bamboo Hut," *RIMA* 26, no. 2 (Summer 1992): 77–90.

60. Steele, *Wars Within*, 190.

61. Kepustakaan Populer Gramedia, *Cerita di Balik Dapur Tempo* (Jakarta: Tempo, 2011), 145.

62. Ōkawa and ADN, "Maaf," 82.

63. Ōkawa and ADN, "Maaf," 82.

64. Ōkawa and ADN, "Maaf," 82.

65. Ueno Chizuko, *Nationalism and Gender*, trans. Beverley Yamamoto (Melbourne: Trans Pacific Press, 2004), 74.

66. "Indonesia Wants More Data on 'Comfort Women,'" *Kyodo News International*, July 13, 1992.

67. "Indonesia Urges Japan to Act on 'Comfort Women,'" *Reuters*, July 13, 1992.

68. "Pengakuan Seorang 'Wanita Penghibur,'" *Kompas*, July 17, 1992, 16.

69. Kimura, "The Story of Tuminah," 17.

70. I thank Rhiannon Paget and Vera Mackie for assisting me in identifying this image. It is titled "Nakano-chō in the Yoshiwara." For more details, see the catalog entry by the Museum of Fine Arts in Boston, accessed August 23, 2022, https://collections.mfa.org/objects/237766.

71. Giacomo Puccini, *Madama Butterfly: Opera in Three Acts*, 1920; Arthur Golden, *Memoirs of a Geisha* (New York: Knopf, 1997). For a more complicated interpretation of Madame Butterfly, see Mari Yoshihara, "The Flight of the Japanese Butterfly: Orientalism, Nationalism and Performances of Japanese Womanhood," *American Quarterly* 56, no. 4 (2004): 975–1001.

72. Bambang Bujono, "Jugun Ianfu" (Laporan Utama), *Tempo*, July 25, 1992, 13. Ford and Lyons explain that the word *pelacur* has strong negative moral overtones. Ford and Lyons, "Making the Best of What You've Got," 181.

73. Didi Prambada and Ōkawa Seiichi, "Setelah Jepang tak Bisa Mengelak Lagi," *Tempo*, July 25, 1992, 14. For reports in Japanese, see "'Ianfu' Seifu Kan'yo Mitomeru: Kyōseirenkō wa Hitei," *Asahi Shimbun*, July 7, 1992, 1; Yamamoto Kentarō, "Jūgun Ianfu

Mondai no Keii: Kōno Danwa o Meguru Ugoki o Chūshin ni," *Refarensu*, September 2013, 68–69.

74. Bujono, "Jugun Ianfu," 13.

75. Prambada and Ōkawa, "Setelah," 14.

76. Prambada and Ōkawa, "Setelah," 15.

77. Prambada and Ōkawa, "Setelah."

78. Prambada and Ōkawa, "Setelah," 15

79. Indrayati and Ōkawa, "Kisah Kardarwati," 17–18.

80. Indrayati and Ōkawa, "Kisah Kardarwati," 18.

81. Indrayati and Ōkawa, "Kisah Kardarwati," 18.

82. Prambadi and Krishna, "Pengakuan dari Semarang," *Tempo*, July 25, 1992, 21.

83. Surawijaya and Ōkawa, "Jeritan," 51–60; Priyono B. Sumbogo, Kastyo Ramelan, Andi Reza Rohadin, Waspada Santing, and Mochtar Touwe, "Mereka Pun Tak Punya Pilihan," *Tempo*, August 8, 1992, 61–64.

84. Surawijaya and Ōkawa, "Jeritan," 51.

85. See McGregor, "Living in a Conflict Zone," 39–58.

86. Surawijaya and Ōkawa, "Jeritan," 52.

87. Surawijaya and Ōkawa, "Jeritan," 52.

88. Surawijaya and Ōkawa, "Jeritan," 52.

89. Surawijaya and Ōkawa, "Jeritan," 53.

90. Surawijaya and Ōkawa, "Jeritan," 53.

91. On this point, see McGregor and Mackie, "Transcultural Memory," 116–41.

92. Nogi Harumichi, *Kaigun Tokubetsu Keisatsutai: Ambontō BC kyū Senpan no Shuki* (Tokyo: Taihei Shuppansha, 1975).

93. Surawijaya and Ōkawa, "Jeritan," 56.

94. Surawijaya and Ōkawa, "Jeritan," 59.

95. Kanō Mikiyo, "The Problem with the 'Comfort Women' Problem," *AMPO Japan Asia Quarterly Review* 24, no. 2 (1993): 41–42. See also McGregor, "Transnational and Japanese Activism."

96. Surawijaya and Ōkawa, "Jeritan," 59.

97. Surawijaya and Ōkawa, "Jeritan," 59–60.

98. Surawijaya and Ōkawa, "Jeritan," 60.

99. Surawijaya and Ōkawa, "Jeritan," 60.

100. Sumbogo et al., "Mereka," 63.

101. Sumbogo et al., "Mereka," 61.

102. Sumbogo et al., "Mereka," 64.

103. Cheah, "Walking the Long Road," 73

104. Janssen, *Schaamte en Onschuld.*

105. Annie Pohlman, "Testimonio and Telling Women's Narratives of Genocide, Torture and Political Imprisonment in Post-Suharto Indonesia," *Life Writing* 5, no. 1 (2008): 47–60.

106. For more on this topic, see chapter 7 and Schaffer and Smith, *Human Rights and Narrated Lives.*

Chapter 7. The Japan Federation of Bar Associations and Escalating Indonesian Activism

1. Cheah, "Walking the Long Road," 79.
2. Murayama Akira, interview by author, Tokyo, February 23, 2015.
3. Murayama, interview.
4. Murayama, interview.
5. PERADIN was established in 1963 as a means to unify the law profession and engage in law reform, professional independence, and constitutionalism. See Daniel Lev, *Legal Evolution and Political Authority in Indonesia: Selected Essays* (The Hague: Kluwer Law, 2000), 315–20.
6. Jetschke, "Linking the Unlinkable?," 140.
7. Murayama, interview.
8. Murayama, interview.
9. Agus Basri and Nunik Iswardhani, "Korban-Korban Serdadu Jepang," *Tempo*, April 24, 1993, 33.
10. "Watanabe Apologizes for R. P Comfort Women," *Jiji Press English News Service*, February 3, 1993.
11. Jetschke, "Linking the Unlinkable?," 141.
12. Knut D. Asplund, "Resistance to Human Rights in Indonesia: Asian Values and Beyond," *Asia-Pacific Journal on Human Rights and the Law* 10, no. 1 (2009): 27–47.
13. Nico Schuldt Nordholt, "Aid and Conditionality: the case of Dutch-Indonesian Relationships," in *Aid and Political Conditionality*, ed. Olav Stokke (London: Frank Cass, 1995), 152–54.
14. Jetschke, "Linking the Unlinkable?," 141.
15. See Hartono and Juliantoro, *Derita Paksa*, 183.
16. Murayama, interview.
17. JFBA, *Sensōhigai Kaigaichōsa Hōkokusho* (Tokyo: Japanese Federation of Bar Associations, 1993), 178–79.
18. JFBA, *Sensōhigai*, 180–82.
19. JFBA, *Sensōhigai*, 182.
20. Murayama, interview.
21. Basri and Iswardhani, "Korban-Korban," 33.
22. Basri and Iswardhani, "Korban-Korban," 33.
23. Basri and Iswardhani, "Korban-Korban," 33.
24. Adnan Buyung Nasution, "Defending Human Rights in Indonesia," *Journal of Democracy in Indonesia* (July 1994): 117.
25. Budi Hartono, "Foreword," in Eka Hindra and Kimura Kōichi, *Momoye Mereka Memanggilku* (Jakarta: Erlangga, 2007), viii–ix.
26. Nasution, "Defending Human Rights," 119.
27. Nasution, "Defending Human Rights," 119.
28. Nursyahbani Katjasungkana, interview with author, Skype, September 11, 2014.

29. Nursyahbani Katjasungkana, "Gender and Transformative Legal Aid," in *Women's Participation in Social Development: Experiences from Asia, Latin America and the Caribbean*, ed. Karen Mokate (Washington, DC: Inter American Bank, 2004), 150–51.

30. Katjasungkana, "Gender and Transformative," 150.

31. Blackburn, *Women and the State in Indonesia*, 196. Challenges to this law commenced in 2012. The bill on sexual violence was finally passed in April 2022. The law is victim-centered and provides a means to prosecute perpetrators for nine forms of sexual violence, including nonphysical sexual harassment, physical sexual harassment, forced contraception, forced sterilization, forced marriage, electronic-based sexual violence, sexual torture, sexual exploitation, and sexual slavery. "RUU TPKS Disahkan setelah Berbagai Penolakan Selama Enam Tahun, Apa Saja Poin Penting," *BBC Indonesia*, April 12, 2022, https://www.bbc.com/indonesia/indonesia-61077691.

32. Katjasungkana, "Gender and Transformative Legal Aid," 142–62.

33. Lubis, "Defending Human Rights," 117.

34. Daniel Levy and Natan Sznaider, *Human Rights and Memory* (University Park: Pennsylvania State University Press, 2010), 6–12.

35. Aspinall, *Opposing Suharto*, 103.

36. Hartono and Juliantoro, *Derita*.

37. Hartono and Juliantoro, *Derita*, vii.

38. Winarta Hadiwiyono, interview with Hani Yulindrasari, Yogyakarta, November 3, 2014.

39. Hadiwiyono, interview.

40. Hartono and Juliantoro, *Derita*, Lampiran 1.

41. Hadiwiyono, interview.

42. Hadiwiyono, interview.

43. Hadiwiyono, interview.

44. Korean Council for Women Drafted for Military Sexual Slavery by Japan, *True Stories of the Comfort Women: Testimonies*, trans. Yong Joo Lee (London: Cassell, 1995).

45. Hadiwiyono, interview.

46. Aspinall, *Opposing Suharto*, 105.

47. "Pengakuan Para Ianfu Kandungnya Digugurkan," *Kedaulatan Rakyat*, April 27, 1993.

48. "Eks Ianfu Yogya and Semarang Tuntut Jepang Minta Maaf," *Wawasan*, April 27, 1993.

49. "Pengakuan Bekas Ianfu," *Jawa Pos*, April 29, 1993.

50. Hindra and Kimura, *Momoye*, 198–99.

51. Hindra and Kimura, *Momoye*, 199.

52. Hartono and Juliantoro, *Derita*, Lampiran 1. Note that 249 women registered or were registered by others, including 29 women who had died during or since the occupation and 46 women who were missing since the war, meaning they presumably never returned home.

53. Barkan, *The Guilt of Nations*, 47.

54. "South Koreans Protest at Japanese Embassy over WWII 'Sex Slaves,'" *Associated Press*, January 15, 1992; Rangsook Yoon, "Erecting the Comfort Women Memorials from Seoul to San Francisco," *De Arte* 53, no. 2 (2018): 70–85.

55. "Filipina Comfort Woman Seeks Apology from Japan," *Reuters*, September 18, 1992; Yuki Tanaka, "Introduction," in Maria Rosa Henson, *Comfort Woman: A Filipina Woman's Story of Prostitution and Slavery under the Japanese Military* (Lanham, MD: Rowman and Littlefield, 1999), xviii.

56. "Philippine Ex-Sex Slave Seeks Tokyo Compensation," *Reuters*, October 15, 1993.

57. Henson, *Comfort Women*, 33–38.

58. Mari Yamaguchi, "Asian, Dutch Former Sex Slaves Testify on Abuses," *Associated Press*, December 9, 1992.

59. O'Herne, *Fifty Years of Silence*, 64–106.

60. O'Herne, *Fifty Years of Silence*, 138.

61. For similar analysis of this choice, see McGregor, "Emotions and Activism."

62. "Wanita Penghibur Tentara Jepang Melapor ke LBH," *Bernas*, April 27, 1993; "Eks Ianfu," *Wawasan*; "Pengakuan Para Ianfu," *Kedaulatan Rakyat*; "Pengakuan Bekas Ianfu," *Jawa Pos*.

63. Shim Sung-won, "South Korea Protests Nagano's Remarks on 'Comfort Women,'" *Reuters*, May 7, 1994.

64. Sawega, "Pengakuan Seorang," 16.

65. Kimura, "'The Story of Tuminah," 16.

66. Sawega, "Pengakuan," 16.

67. Hilary Gorman, "Marginalisation of 'Immoral Women': Experiences of Young Women Street Sex Workers in Surabaya, Indonesia," *Intersections: Gender and Sexuality in Asia and the Pacific* 26 (2011): 1.

68. Sawega, "Pengakuan," 16.

69. Soh, *Comfort Women*, 46–56.

70. Ueno, *Nationalism and Gender*, 89.

71. Ueno, *Nationalism and Gender*, 82.

72. Yamashita Yeong-ae, "Revisiting the 'Comfort Women': Moving beyond Nationalism," trans. Malaya Ileto, in *Transforming Japan: How Feminism and Diversity Are Making a Difference*, ed. Kumiko Fujimura-Fanselow (New York: Feminist Press and CUNY, 2011), 273–74.

73. Yamashita, "Revisiting the 'Comfort Women,'" 275.

74. For full proceedings, see *War Victimization and Japan*.

75. These women included Kang Soon-Ae (Republic of Korea), Kim Yong-Sil (Democratic Republic of Korea), Wan Ai Hua (China), and an anonymous Taiwanese woman who was held on Timor Island.

76. Soh, *Comfort Women*, 64.

77. *War Victimization and Japan*, viii.

78. Hindra and Kimura, *Momoye*, 201.

79. Hindra and Kimura, *Momoye*, 102.

80. For a more detailed discussion of Mardiyem's emotions, see McGregor, "Emotions and Activism," 67–78.

81. She lists all her friends with the dates of their passing: Mangun 1979, Ribu 1996, Atemo 1994, Sarmini 1993, Sukarlin 2000, Partiyem 2001, Jainem 2002, Ginem 1995, Lagiyem 1995, and Suharti and Lasiyem (these last two were still alive at the time of publication of the memoir). Hindra and Kimura, *Momoye*, 201.

82. Hindra and Kimura, *Momoye*, 197–98.

83. Hindra and Kimura, *Momoye*, 199.

84. Hindra and Kimura, *Momoye*, 199.

85. Hindra and Kimura, *Momoye*, 211. Mardiyem reported the same experience to journalists in 1997. See "Comfort Women Continue to Suffer," *Jakarta Post*, March 30, 1997.

86. Hindra and Kimura, *Momoye*, 211.

87. "Sudah 13 Romusha Lapor ke LBH," *Bernas*, May 8, 1993.

88. Hartono and Juliantoro, *Derita*, vii–viii.

89. Hartono and Juliantoro, *Derita*, 201–2.

90. Hartono, "Foreword," viii.

91. Hadiwiyono, interview.

92. Hadiwiyono, interview.

93. Hadiwiyono, interview.

94. Hadiwiyono, interview.

95. "Eks Ianfu," *Wawasan*.

96. "Seorang Ianfu dan Romusha Mengadu ke LBH Yogyakarta," *Kompas*, April 29, 1993.

97. "LBHI Perjuangkan Nasib Ianfu dan Romusha," *Kedaulatan Rakyat*, May 9, 1993.

98. Hadiwiyono, interview.

99. Hadiwiyono, interview.

100. Hadiwiyono, interview.

101. "Pengakuan Bekas Ianfu," *Jawa Pos*.

102. Murayama, interview.

103. For a brief summary of the results of the 1993 study, see "On the Issue of Wartime Comfort Women," Asian Women's Fund, accessed August 23, 2022, https://awf.or.jp/e6/statement-03.htm. For a five-volume report in Japanese on documents analyzed for this report, see "Historical Materials Regarding Comfort Women Issue," Asian Women's Fund, accessed August 23, 2022, https://awf.or.jp/e6/document.html.

104. Kōno Yōhei, Statement by the Chief Cabinet Secretary (Kōno Yōhei) on the results of the Japanese government study on the issue of "comfort women," August 4, 1993, https://www.mofa.go.jp/a_o/rp/page25e_000343.html.

105. "Setelah Minta Maaf, Apa?," *Jawa Pos*, August 7, 1993.

106. "Setelah," *Jawa Pos*.

107. "North Korea Forms Committee for Comfort Women Compensation," *Kyodo News International*, August 10, 1992; "South Korean President to Visit Japan

Next Month," *Reuters*, October 22, 1992; Abby Tan, "Japan's Record in War Blights Tour of Asia," *The Times*, August 24, 1994.

108. JFBA, *Sensōhigai*.

109. "Lawyers' Federation Urges Compensation for War Victims," *Kyodo News International*, September 13, 1993.

110. Murayama, interview.

111. JFBA lawyers, interview with author, February 23, 2015.

112. Murayama, interview.

113. Murayama, interview.

114. Yoshiko Nozaki, *War Memory, Nationalism and Education in Postwar Japan, 1945–2007: The Japanese History Textbook Controversy and Ienaga Saburo's Court Challenges* (New York: Routledge, 2008), 141.

115. Hadiwiyono, interview. Two letters addressed to Prime Minister Tomeichi Murayama (dated August 2, 1995) and Prime Minister Ryutaro Hashimoto (dated February 7, 1996) are included as appendices in the Hartono and Juliantoro, *Derita*, 217–20.

116. Hadiwiyono, interview.

117. Tim Lindsey and Melissa Crouch, "Cause Lawyers in Indonesia: A House Divided," *Wisconsin International Journal of Law* 3 (2013): 622.

118. Lindsey and Crouch, "Cause Lawyers," 624.

119. Hartono and Juliantoro, *Derita*, 175.

120. Cheah, "Walking the Long Road," 79.

121. Eka Hindra, interview with author, Jakarta, June 23, 2014.

122. Hadiwiyono, interview.

123. See Leslie Dwyer and Degung Santikarma, "Speaking from the Shadows: Memory and Mass Violence in Bali," in *After Mass Crime: Rebuilding States and Communities*, ed. Béatrice Pouligny, Simon Chesterman, and Albrecht Schnabel (Tokyo: United Nations University Press, 2007), 190–214.

Chapter 8. The Asian Women's Fund and Increasing International Outreach, 1995–1997

1. International Commission of Jurists, *Comfort Women: An Unfinished Ordeal* (Geneva: International Commission of Jurists, 1994). For commentary on the report, see Soh, *Comfort Women*, 47.

2. Soh, *Comfort Women*, 44.

3. Soh, *Comfort Women*, 44.

4. Kumagai Naoko, "Asian Women's Fund Revisited," *Asia Pacific Review* 21, no. 2 (2014): 119.

5. Murayama remained closely associated with the AWF and served as its president for many years. Hugo Dobson and Caroline Rose, "The Afterlives of Postwar Japanese Prime Ministers," *Journal of Contemporary Asia* 49, no. 1 (2019): 140–41.

6. These included the following people named in the Public Appeal for Funds: Akamatsu Ryōko, Ashida Jinnosuke, Etō Shinkichi, Okita Toshiko, Ōtaka Yoshiko,

Ōnuma Yasuaki, Okamato Yukio, Katō Taki, Shimomura Mitsuko, Suzuki Kenji, Sunobe Ryōzō, Takahashi Yoshikatsu, Tsurumi Shunsuke, Noda Aiko, Nonaka Kuniko, Hagiwara Nobutoshi, Miki Mutsuko, Miyazaki Isamu, Yamamoto Tadashi, and Wada Haruki. "An Appeal for Donations for the Asian Women's Fund," Digital Museum: The Comfort Women and the Asian Women's Fund, accessed May 30, 2022, http://awf.or.jp/e2/foundation-01.html.

7. See Soh, *Comfort Women*, 96, 239; Kumagai, "Asian Women's Fund Revisited," 117–48.

8. Office of the United Nations High Commissioner for Human Rights (OHCHR), *15 Years of the United Nations Special Rapporteur on Violence Against Women, Its Causes and Consequences (1994–2009): A Critical Review*, OHCHR, 2009, https://www.unwomen.org/en/docs/2009/1/15-years-of-the-un-special-rapporteur-on-violence-against-women.

9. Radhika Coomaraswamy, *Report of the Mission to the Democratic People's Republic of Korea, the Republic of Korea and Japan on the Issue of Military Sexual Slavery in Wartime, Economic and Social Council*, E/CN.4/1996/53/Add.1, 24–25.

10. Aspinall, *Opposing Suharto*, 191.

11. Takagi, interview.

12. Takagi Ken'ichi, "Keynote Speech to International Committee of Asia-Pacific War Victims Organizations Claiming Compensation," in Forum Komunikasi Ex-Heiho, *Laporan Pertemuan: The International Committee of Asia-Pacific War Victims Organizations Claiming Compensation*, Forum Komunikasi Ex-Heiho Indonesia, Kota Chiba, Japan, August 9–10, 1996, 26.

13. Takagi, "Keynote," 28

14. Mira Pojskic, "Consequence of Rape, Report from Bosnia," in Forum Komunikasi Ex-Heiho, *Laporan Pertemuan: The International Committee of Asia-Pacific War Victims Organisations Claiming Compensation*, Forum Komunikasi Ex-Heiho Indonesia, Kota Chiba, Japan, August 9–10, 1996, 63–77.

15. Persatuan Heiho Indonesia-Jepang, *Indonesia Petisi dari Para Heiho* (Tokyo: Persatuan Heiho Indonesia-Jepang, Nashinoki-sha, 1993), 10. On Morotai, see Steve Bullard, "Australia's War in New Guinea and Australia in the Liberation of the Netherlands East Indies," in *The Encyclopedia of Indonesia in the Pacific War*, ed. Peter Post, William H. Frederick, Iris Heidebrink, and Shigeru Satō (Leiden: Brill, 2010), 29.

16. Such as Mizuno Kōsuke of Kyoto University, Matsuno Akihisa of Osaka Foreign Language University, and Utsumi Aiko of Keisen University. These scholars have published respectively on Indonesian culture and the independence of East Timor (Matsuno) and wartime compensation and Japan's wartime responsibility in the 1990s (Utsumi). Matsuno has also been involved with researching the "comfort women" in East Timor and South Sulawesi.

17. Takagi, interview.

18. Takagi, interview. See Kokusai Fōramu Jikkō Iinkai (hen.), eds., *Sengo Hoshō o Kangaeru* (Osaka: Tōhō Shuppan, 1992), 63–68.

19. Prambadi and Ōkawa, "Setelah Jepang," 15.

20. Ute Frevert, *Emotions in History Lost and Found* (New York: Central European University Press, 2011), 67–68.

21. Persatuan Heiho Indonesia-Jepang, *Indonesia Petisi dari Para Heiho*, 20–21.

22. See letters reproduced in Forum Komunikasi Ex-Heiho Indonesia, *Laporan*, 2–3.

23. Tanaka, "Introduction," xviii.

24. Takagi, interview.

25. Takagi, interview.

26. Takagi Keni'chi, personal communication, April 3, 2015.

27. Takagi, personal communication.

28. Takagi, interview.

29. Proceedings of the International Forum on War Compensation for the Asian-Pacific Region, Seiryō Kaikan, Nagata chō, 7, August 13–14, 1995. Please note elsewhere this organization is referred to as the International Committee for Asia-Pacific War Victims Organizations Claiming Compensation.

30. "Moto Jūgun Ianfu ga Senjichū no Taiken o Shōgen: Kyō Yokohama de Tsudoi/Kanagawa," *Asahi Shimbun*, December 7, 1995.

31. Hindra and Kōichi, *Momoye*, 13.

32. Takagi, interview.

33. Brief data from these interviews in Bogor appears in Forum Komunikasi Ex-Heiho, *Kompensasi Jugun Ianfu* (Jakarta, Forum Komunikasi Ex-Heiho, 1996), 52–56.

34. Takagi, interview.

35. Letter to Prime Minister Murayama Tomiichi, August 2, 1995, reproduced in Hartono and Juliantoro, *Derita*, 217–20.

36. For some analysis of how the forum used emotions in their advocacy, see McGregor, "Emotions and Activism," 67–78.

37. Forum Komunikasi Ex-Heiho, *Kompensasi Jugun Ianfu*, 6–7, 10.

38. "28.500 Dollar untuk Setiap Ianfu," *Koran Rakyat*, May 13, 1996. This is based on a report from *Antara* as quoted in Hilde Janssen, "Breaking the Silence," in *Japanese Militarism and Its War Crimes in Asia Pacific Region*, ed. Hendrajit (Jakarta: Global Future Institute, 2011),145, n10.

39. Kimura, interview. The results and a sample questionnaire are presented in Forum Komunikasi Ex-Heiho, *Kompensasi Jugun Ianfu*, 58–62. A collation of results to these questions was published in Kimura Kōichi, "The Result of Investigation into the Condition of Indonesian Former Jugun Ianfu," *Asia Tsushin*, English Edition no. 4 (December 1996): 11–14.

40. Forum Komunikasi Ex-Heiho, *Kompensasi Jugun Ianfu*, 59–63.

41. Forum Komunikasi Ex-Heiho, *Kompensasi Jugun Ianfu*, 61.

42. Takagi, interview.

43. Forum Komunikasi Ex-Heiho, *Kompensasi Jugun Ianfu*, 8.

44. Takagi, interview.

45. Kimura, "Brutal Abuse," 2–3.

46. Forum Komunikasi Ex-Heiho, *Kompensasi Jugun Ianfu*, 7.

47. Forum Komunikasi Ex-Heiho, *Kompensasi Jugun Ianfu*, 11.

48. Forum Komunikasi Ex-Heiho, *Kompensasi Jugun Ianfu*, 2.

49. Forum Komunikasi Ex-Heiho, *Kompensasi Jugun Ianfu*, 2.

50. Shigeru Satō, "Heiho Entry (Lexicon)," in *The Encyclopedia of Indonesia in the Pacific War*, ed. Peter Post, William H. Frederick, Iris Heidebrink, and Shigeru Satō (Leiden: Brill, 2010), 506.

51. Takagi, "Keynote," 27.

52. Takagi, "Keynote," 28.

53. Cheah, "Walking the Long Road," 71, n31.

54. For details of their efforts to lobby the UN, see Eun Hee Chi, "South Korea Why the Private Fund Cannot Be the Solution to the Comfort Women Issue," *Proceedings Fourth Asian Women's Solidarity Conference*, March 27–30, 1996, Manila, Philippines, 7.

55. List of Participants, in *Proceedings Fourth Asian Women's Solidarity Conference*, March 27–30, 1996, Manila, Philippines.

56. "Adoption of Resolution and Closing Ceremony," in *Proceedings Fourth Asian Women's Solidarity Conference*, 29.

57. Chunghee Sarah Soh, "Human Rights and the 'Comfort Women,'" *Peace Review* 12, no. 1 (2000): 125.

58. Soh, "Human Rights," 125.

59. Soh, *Comfort Women*, 96.

60. Soh, "Human Rights," 126.

61. Soh, "Human Rights," 128.

62. Hideko Mitsui, "The Politics of National Atonement and Narratives of War," *Inter-Asia Cultural Studies* 9, no. 1 (2008): 48.

63. Mitsui, "The Politics of National Atonement," 58.

64. Yamashita, "Revisiting the 'Comfort Women,'" 221.

65. Public address by the Coalition of Citizens for Resolving the Issue of Sexual Slavery under the Japanese Military, March 1, 1997, quoted in Yamashita, "Revisiting the 'Comfort Women,'" 221.

66. Soh, "Human Rights," 125.

67. Maria Rosa Luna Henson, "My Views on the Asian Women's Fund," in Forum Komunikasi Ex-Heiho, *Laporan Pertemuan: The International Committee of Asia-Pacific War Victims Organisations Claiming Compensation* (Jakarta: Forum Komunikasi Ex-Heiho, 1996), 92.

68. Henson, "My Views," 92.

69. Tanaka, "Introduction," xix.

70. "Projects by Country or Region - Philippines," Asian Women's Fund Digital Museum, accessed August 23, 2022, http://www.awf.or.jp/e3/philippine-01.html.

71. Soh, "Human Rights," 126.

72. Arimitsu Ken, interview with author, Tokyo, September 23, 2017.

73. Arimitsu, interview.

74. Hartono and Juliantoro, *Derita*, 185.

75. The Ministry of Foreign Affairs 1995, quoted in Mitsui, "The Politics of National Atonement," 52. This quote is replicated on the Asian Women's Fund website under "An Appeal for Donations for the Asian Women's Fund."

76. C. Sarah Soh, "Japan's National Asian Women's Fund for 'Comfort Women,'" *Pacific Affairs* 76, no. 2 (2003): 217.

77. Kawada, *Indoneshia no "Ianfu,"* 3–4.

78. Kawada, *Indoneshia no "Ianfu,"* 3–4.

79. Kawada, *Indoneshia no "Ianfu,"* 47.

80. Kawada, *Indoneshia no "Ianfu,"* 43–46.

81. Kawada, *Indoneshia no "Ianfu,"* 120–46.

82. Kawada, *Indoneshia no "Ianfu,"* 53.

83. Thanks to Mayuko Itoh for making this observation.

84. Kawada, *Indoneshia no "Ianfu,"* 24–26.

85. Kawada, *Indoneshia no "Ianfu,"* 35–36.

86. Kawada, *Indoneshia no "Ianfu,"* 15–20.

87. Kawada, *Indoneshia no "Ianfu,"* 150–55.

88. The film was directed by Owaki Michiyo. Kimura, interview.

89. "Indoneshia Moto Ianfu, Jinken Kyūsai o Uttae Nichibenren ni Mōshitatesho," *Asahi Shimbun*, July 25, 1996, 30.

90. Hartono and Juliantoro, *Derita*, 184–85.

91. Hartono and Juliantoro, *Derita*, 185.

92. Komnas HAM, *Menggugat Negara Indonesia atas Pengabaian Hak-hak Asasi (Pembiaran) Jugun Ianfu Sebagai Budak Seks Militer dan Sipil Jepang 1942–1945* (Jakarta: Komnas HAM, 2010), 23.

93. Hindra and Kimura, *Momoye*, 16.

94. Yoong Mee-Hyang, interview with author, Seoul, February 26, 2015.

95. Yoong, interview.

96. Aspinall, *Opposing Suharto*, 191–93.

97. For example, "(Shohyō) Watashi wa Ianfu dewa Nai: Sensō Giseisha o Kokoro ni Kizamu Kai hen," *Asahi Shimbun*, September 21, 1997, 16.

98. Hartono and Juliantoro, *Derita*, 181.

99. In February 1998, AWF Director Hara Bunbe reported that ¥38,000,000 had already been paid out per year for 1996 and 1997 (*Suara*, no. 1 [April 20, 1998]: 6). It was clarified later by the Ministry of Foreign Affairs that the money was first paid in 1997 (*Suara*, nos. 5 and 6 [August 5, 1999]: 1).

100. See Asian Women's Fund Digital Museum, Projects by region of Country, Indonesia, accessed August 23, 2022, http://www.awf.or.jp/e3/indonesia-00.html.

101. Aspinall, *Opposing Suharto*, 23.

102. Phillip Eldridge, "Human Rights and Democracy in Indonesia and Malaysia: Emerging Contexts and Discourse," *Contemporary Southeast Asia* 18, no. 3 (1996): 300.

103. Some examples are Republic of Indonesia, Ministry of Social Affairs, *Petunjuk Teknis Penanganan Masalah Sosial Tuna Susila* (Jakarta: Directorate General Bina

Rehabilitasi Sosial, 1991); Republic of Indonesia, Ministry of Social Affairs, *Buku Putih Rehabilitasi Sosial* (Jakarta: Directorate General Bina Rehabilitasi Sosial, 1994).

104. Hull, Sulistyaningsih, and Jones, *Prostitution in Indonesia*, 64–66.

105. See Asian Women's Fund Digital Museum, Projects by region of Country, Indonesia, accessed August 23, 2022, http://www.awf.or.jp/e3/indonesia-00.html.

106. Aspinall, *Opposing Suharto*, 180–81.

107. Aspinall, *Opposing Suharto*, 189.

108. Memorandum of Understanding between the Department of Social Affairs Republic of Indonesia and the Asian Women's Fund, Asian Women's Fund Digital Museum, accessed August 23, 2022, https://www.awf.or.jp/pdf/0206.pdf.

109. Memorandum of Understanding.

110. Memorandum of Understanding. For press coverage, see "Comfort Women Continue to Suffer," *Jakarta Post*; and "Comfort Women Fight for Rights at Home, Abroad," *Jakarta Post*, March 30, 1997.

111. Ōmura Tetsuo, "SOMJII Gaimushō e, Motto NGO tono Renkei o," *Suara*, nos. 5 and 6 (August 5, 1999): 2.

112. "Hidup Saya Sudah Kosong, Saya Hanya Ingin Jadi Saksi Sejarah," *Bernas*, February 23, 1997.

113. "Bukan Pampasan Perang," *Republika*, April 13, 1997.

114. "Comfort Women Threaten Suit against Minister," *Jakarta Post*, April 19, 1997.

115. "Comfort Women Threaten."

116. This organization was headed by Nunik Murniati and formed in November 1996 in Jakarta with a home base in the city of Yogyakarta. "Women and Violence, Indonesia Anti Violence Against Women," *WIN News* 24, no. 3 (Summer 1998): 37

117. "Batalkan Pengalihan Dana Mantan 'Jugun Ianfu,'" *Kompas*, May 30, 1997.

118. Kawada, *Indoneshia No "Ianfu,"* 150–57.

119. Kawada, *Indoneshia No "Ianfu,"* 157–78.

120. Kimura, interview.

121. Kimura, interview.

122. "Film 'Jugun Ianfu' Banyak Tanggapan dari Rakyat Jepang," *Yogya Pos*, June 24, 1997. The documentary "NNN Dokyumento 96 Ianfu: Indonesia no baai niwa" was broadcast on September 30, 1996.

123. "Televisi Jepang Akan Membuat Film Dokumen tentang Ianfu," *Suara Merdeka*, June 24, 1997. This documentary was broadcast as "NNN Dokyumento 97 Koe Tozasarete, Soshite: Indoneshia no 'Ianfu' tachi, Tokushū Sensō no Jidai ni," December 8, 1997.

124. *Suara*, no. 1 (April 20, 1998): 10. The named members of SOMJII printed in the first bulletin of the organization were Aijek Kushajatie, Ikeda Eriko, Ishida Kimie, Utsumi Aiko, Osono Hiroshi, Ogasawara Toshifumi, Okamoto Yukie, Ōmura Tetsuo, Katō Kazunari, Katō Hisako, Katō Jirō, Kawakami Sonoko, Kawada Fumiko, Kinomura Terumi, Kim Puja, Suzuki Takashi, Takagi Makoto, Tsuji Yusaku, Tokunaga Risa, Naoi Hiroko, Nakamura Akemi, Pak Eiko, Matsuno Akihisa, Yajima Mitsuharu, Yamakawa Yuriko, Yoshida Takashi, and Yoshimi Yoshiaki.

125. On their appeal to the AWF, see their newsletters, *Suara*, no. 1 (April 20, 1998): 4–5; *Suara*, no. 2 (August 1, 1998): 5; *Suara*, nos. 5 and 6 (August 5, 1999): 1–5; *Suara*, no. 7 (December 1, 1998): 4–5; *Suara*, no. 8 (May 12, 2000): 10–11.

126. "Bila Dana Cair, Kami Gugat," *Media Indonesia*, July 13, 1997.

127. "Bila Dana," *Media Indonesia*.

128. "Jugun Ianfu dan Santuan Ganti Rugi," *Media Indonesia*, July 13, 1997.

129. "25 Mantan Jugun Ianfu Gelar Poster di LBH Yogya," *Kedaulatan Rakyat*, July 24, 1997; "LBH Yogya Kembali Masalahkan Jugun Ianfu," *Yogya Post*, September 3, 1997.

130. "Tuntut Pembayaran Ganti Rugi," *Kedaulatan Rakyat*, August 12, 1997.

131. "Kakek-Kakek Mendemo ke Dubes Jepang," *Jawa Pos*, August 21, 1997.

132. "Comfort Women Fight for Rights at Home, Abroad."

133. "Gambaran Murni Perempuan Bila Dianggap Ibu," *Kedaulatan Rakyat*, August 3, 1997.

134. "Jepang tidak Bisa Serahkan Ganti Rugi pada Jugun Ianfu," *Kedaulatan Rakyat*, October 18, 1997.

135. "Jepang," Kedaulatan Rakyat.

136. *Suara*, no. 1 (April 20, 1998): 4.

137. *Suara*, no. 1 (April 20, 1998): 5.

138. As quoted in Newsletter of the Asian Women's Fund, no. 6.

139. *Suara*, no. 1 (April 20, 1998): 5.

140. *Suara*, no. 1 (April 20, 1998): 5.

141. *Suara*, no. 2 (August 1, 1998): 1–2.

142. Ōmura, "SOMJII Gaimushō," 1–2.

Chapter 9. The End of Suharto

1. Hartono and Juliantoro, *Derita*.

2. "Lima Jugun Ianfu Gugat Mensos," *Jawa Pos*, November 13, 1997.

3. "Bentuk Protes Mantan Jugun Ianfu terhadap Kepasifan Pemerintah RI," *Wawasan*, November 13, 1997.

4. "LBH Yogya akan Luncurkan Buku tentang Jugun Ianfu," *Bernas*, November 13, 1997.

5. "Five Former Comfort Women to Sue Inten," *Jakarta Post*, November 17, 1997.

6. Hartono and Juliantoro, *Derita*, 105–53.

7. Yayasan Lembaga Bantuan Hukum, "Kasus Marsinah."

8. On Marsinah as a symbol for labor, see Michele Ford, "Beyond the Femina Fantasy: Female Industrial and Overseas Domestic Labour in Indonesian Discourses of Women's Work," *Review of Indonesian and Malaysian Affairs* 37, no. 2 (2003): 93–94.

9. Hartono and Juliantoro, *Derita*, 91.

10. "Ny Mardiyem: Mereka Antre Seperti Mau Nonton Bioskop," *Wawasan*, November 15, 1997.

11. Shalendra D Sharma, *The Asian Financial Crisis: Crisis, Reform and Recovery* (Manchester: Manchester University Press, 2003), 143.

12. Hartono and Juliantoro, *Derita*, 4.

13. Ueno, *Nationalism and Gender*, 73.

14. Ueno, *Nationalism and Gender*, 73.

15. Hartono and Juliantoro, *Derita*.

16. "Peluncuran Buku Derita Paksa Perempuan: Fakta Sejarah Jangan Ditutupi," *Kedaulatan Rakyat*, November 15, 1997.

17. "Dukunglah Kami, 'Selak' Pada Mati," *Bernas*, November 15, 1997. The word "ration" here implies being shared around.

18. "Ratapan dan Gelegak Emosi," *Pikiran Rakyat*, November 15, 1997.

19. "Jugun Ianfu Agar Masuk Kurikulum Pendidikan Sejarah," *Republika*, November 15, 1997.

20. "Peluncuran Buku," *Kedaulatan Rakyat*.

21. "Peluncuran Buku," *Kedaulatan Rakyat*.

22. Avonius, "From Marsinah to Munir," 108–9.

23. Ōmura Tetsuo, "'Tōkai Shusai 'Indoneshia no Moto 'Ianfu' wa Ima . . . ,' Shūkai deno Kimura Kōichi-san no Kōen kara," *Suara*, no. 2 (August 1998): 4.

24. Jemma Purdey, *Anti-Chinese Violence in Indonesia, 1996–1999* (Singapore: NUS Press, 2006), 124.

25. Purdey, *Anti-Chinese Violence*, 169.

26. Rita Serena Kolibonso, "The Gender Perspective: A Key to Democracy in Indonesia," in *Reformasi Crisis and Change in Indonesia*, ed. Arief Budiman, Barbara Hatley, and Damien Kingsbury (Clayton, Victoria: Monash Asia Institute, 1999), 336.

27. Kolibonso, "Gender Perspectives," 336.

28. "Sekarang Pacar Saya pun Merasa Jijik," *Nyata*, June 4, 1998, 6–7, quoted in James T. Siegel, "Early Thoughts on the Violence of May 13 and 14, 1998, in Jakarta," *Indonesia* 66 (October 1998): 96–98.

29. Ariel Heryanto, "Rape, Race and Reporting," in *Reformasi Crisis and Change in Indonesia*, ed. Arief Budiman, Barbara Hatley, and Damien Kingsbury (Clayton, Victoria: Monash Asia Institute, 1999), 302.

30. Purdey, *Anti-Chinese Violence*, 159.

31. Purdey, *Anti-Chinese Violence*, 147. See also Jemma Purdey, "Problematizing the Place of Victims in Reformasi Indonesia: A Contested Truth about the May 1998 Violence," *Asian Survey* 42, no. 4 (2002): 605–22.

32. The argument was made by some members of the Tim Gabungan Pencari Fakta that medical examination of victims was necessary proof of rape or sexual assault. Purdey, *Anti-Chinese Violence*, 146. See also Karen Strassler, "Gendered Visibilities and the Dream of Transparency: The Chinese Indonesian Rape Debate in Post-Suharto Indonesia," *Gender and History* 16, no. 3 (November 2004): 695; Galuh Wandita, "The Tears Have Not Stopped, the Violence Has Not Ended: Political Upheaval, Ethnicity and Violence against Women in Indonesia," *Gender and Development* 6, no. 3 (November 1998): 35–36.

33. Heryanto, "Rape, Race and Reporting," 308–9.

34. Gadis Arivia, "Logika Kekerasan Negara terhadap Perempuan," in *Negara dan Kekerasan terhadap Perempuan* (Jakarta: Yayasan Jurnal Perempuan and Asia Foundation, 2000), 4–10.

35. Melani Budianta, "The Blessed Tragedy: The Making of Women's Activism during the Reformasi Years," in *Challenging Authoritarianism in Southeast Asia*, ed. Ariel Heryanto and Sumit Mandal (London: Routledge and Curzon, 2003), 165.

36. Budianta, "Blessed Tragedy," 165.

37. "Sengketa di Timor Timur Memang Kejam," *Gatra* 40, no. 47 (October 10, 1998): 29.

38. *Suara Pembaruan*, September 7, 1998, 3.

39. Ōmura Tetsuo, "'Suharto go' no Indoneshia no Media ni Miru 'Ianfu' Mondai," *Suara*, no. 3 (August 1, 1998): 1–2.

40. Strassler, "Gendered Visibilities," 705.

41. Budianta, "Blessed Tragedy," 165–66; Dewi Anggraeni, *Tragedi Mei 1998 dan Lahirnya Komnas Perempuan* (Jakarta: Penerbit Buku Kompas, 2014).

42. Harikristuti Harikrisnowo, "Perempuan dan Hak Asasi Manusia dalam Perspektif Yuridis," in *Negara dan Kekerasan terhadap Perempuan*, ed. Yayasan Jurnal Perempuan (Jakarta: Yayasan Jurnal Perempuan and Asia Foundation, 2000), 211–12.

43. Radhika Coomaraswamy, *Report of the Special Rapporteur on Violence against Women, its Causes and Consequences, Addendum Mission to Indonesia and East Timor on the issue of Violence against Women (20 November–4 December 1998)*, Economic and Social Council, E/CN.4/1999/68/Add.3, 10.

44. Kolibonso, "Gender Perspective," 340.

45. Budianta, "Blessed Tragedy," 175n10.

46. Blackburn, *Women and the State*, 201.

47. Blackburn, *Women and the State*, 209.

48. Coomaraswamy, *Report of the Special Rapporteur*, 10.

49. Coomaraswamy, *Report of the Special Rapporteur*, 14.

50. Blackburn, *Women and the State*, 209.

51. Blackburn, *Women and the State*, 211.

52. For example, the entry on Indonesia for 2000 on violence against women covers the May riots, the cases of violence against refugee East Timorese women in West Timor, and women in East Timor and Aceh, but no mention of historical cases. Due to the alphabetical listing, following directly after this report was one on Japan, focused exclusively on the "comfort women" issue with brief updates on the AWF (no country specific details) and on all court cases relating to this case held in Japan and the United States. Report from the Special Rapporteur on Violence against Women, *Integration of the Human Rights of Women and Gender Perspective, Violence against Women, Violence against Women Perpetrated and/or Condoned by the State during Times of Armed Conflict (1997–2000)*, A/CN.4/2001/73.

53. Report from the Special Rapporteur on Violence against Women, *Integration of the Human Rights of Women and Gender Perspective*.

54. Marguerite Hamer-Monod de Froideville, interview, The Hague, September 7, 2015.

55. Hamer de Froideville, *Geknakte Bloem*, 46.

56. Hamer de Froideville, *Geknakte Bloem*, 47–48.

57. Hamer de Froideville, *Geknakte Bloem*, 48.

58. Hamer de Froideville, *Geknakte Bloem*, 110–11.

59. PICN, Evaluation Report of the Project Implementation Committee in the Netherlands, January 2001, 7, http://www.awf.or.jp/pdf/0208.pdf.

60. Hamer-Monod de Froideville, interview; Rumi Sakamoto, "The Women's International War Crimes Tribunal on Japan's Military Sexual Slavery: A Legal Feminist Approach to the 'Comfort Women' Issue," *New Zealand Journal of Asian Studies* 3, no. 1 (June 2001): 55.

61. "Jugun Ianfu Belanda Dapat Ganti Rugi," *Solo Post*, July 21, 1998.

62. "LBH Yogya Tolak Dana AWF," *Kedaulatan Rakyat*, July 22,1998.

63. "LBH Yogya Tolak Dana AWF," *Kedaulatan Rakyat*.

64. "Indoneshia 'Ianfu' Mondai no Nagare," *Suara*, nos. 5 and 6 (August 5, 1999): 12.

65. Yamamoto and Horton, "Comfort Women in Indonesia."

66. Kimura Otcho, "Mardiyemu-san no Tatakai: Indonesia Shakai no 'Nihon ni Taisuru Zōo' to 'Ibu tachi eno Keibetsu' wa Koin no Ryōmen," *Suara*, no. 5 (August 5, 1998): 8–10.

67. Ōsono Hiroshi, "Indoneshia kara Moto 'Ianfu' ga Rainichi' Hiroshi Osono," *Suara*, no. 7 (December 1, 1998): 2.

68. "Tarik Dana AWF dari Depsos," *Solo Post*, August 4, 1998. The term *wanita penghibur* is used in the second reference to "comfort women" in this quote.

69. Kimura Kōichi, "Jaiemu-san wa Naze 'Gishō' Shitanoka: Nihongun Seidoreisei Higaisha (Ianfu) no Jinkenkyūsai Mōshitate de Nichibenren ga Hōmon Chōsa," *Suara*, no. 8 (May 12, 2000): 3.

70. Adrian Vickers and Katharine McGregor, "Public Debates about History: Comparative Notes from Indonesia," *History Australia* 2, no. 2 (June 2005): 44.1–13.

71. "Menghapus Kisah Heroik Soeharto," *Gatra* 40, no. 48 (October 17, 1998): 92–93.

72. "Desak Jugun Ianfu Masuk Sejarah," *Jawa Pos*, November 23, 1998.

73. Rahayu, "Kontrusksi Historiografi."

74. Eka Hindra, interview with author, Jakarta, June 23, 2014.

75. Hindra, interview.

76. Hindra, interview.

77. Kimura, "Jaiemu-san wa Naze," 1.

78. "Pengacara Jepang Natalan dengan Ianfu," *Jateng Post*, December 13, 1999.

79. Kimura, "Jaiemu-san wa Naze," 3.

80. Tomoko, *Mardiyem*.

81. Kimura, "Jaiemu-san wa Naze," 1.

82. "Trauma dengan Wajah Brewokan," *Jateng Post*, December 13, 1999.

83. "Trauma," *Jateng Post.*

84. "Trauma," *Jateng Post.*

85. Women's International War Crimes Tribunal Judgement, The Hague, Netherlands, December 4, 2001, 1.

86. Tribunal Judgement, 2.

87. Katjasungkana, interview.

88. "Tōjisha ni Yorisou Tachiba kara Nihonjin no Kyōryoku o Motomeru: LBH Bengoshi Apong Herlina-shi ni Kiku," *Suara*, no. 4 (February 1, 1999): 1.

89. Katjasungkana, interview.

90. Katjasungkana, interview.

91. Quoted in Tribunal Judgement, 65.

92. Quoted in Tribunal Judgement, 64–66.

93. Katjasungkana, interview.

94. Footage focusing on Indonesian women and the tribunal appears in Lexy Rambadeta, *The Indonesian Comfort Women*, Lexy Rambadeta Films, 2000; and in Kana Tomoko, *Mardiyem.*

95. Hindra and Kimura, *Momoye*, 18–19.

96. Tomoko, *Mardiyem.*

97. Tachikawa Tomoko, "Mardiyemu-san no 'Tabi': Imawashii Kako o Tazunete," *Suara*, no. 11 (March 26, 2001): 3.

98. Tachikawa, "Mardiyemu-san no 'Tabi,'" 3.

99. Ōmura Tetsuo, "Indoneshia de 'Ianfu' Mondai ga Futatabi Kurōzuappu," *Suara*, no. 10 (November 10, 2000): 3.

100. Sakamoto, "The Women's International War Crimes Tribunal," 50.

101. Video Juku, *Breaking the History of Silence: Women's International War Crimes Tribunal on Japan's Military Sexual Slavery*, VAWW-Net, 2001.

102. Rambadeta, *The Indonesian Comfort Women.*

103. Video Juku, *Breaking the History of Silence.*

104. Sakamoto, "Women's International War Crimes Tribunal."

105. Cheah, "Walking the Long Road," 97–98.

106. Tribunal Judgement, 19–20.

107. Mitsui, "The Politics of National Atonement," 56.

108. Video Juku, *Breaking the History of Silence.* On the broadcast censoring and resulting court case, see Norma Field, "The Courts, Japan's Military Comfort Women and the Conscience of Humanity: The Ruling in VAWW-Net Japan v NHK," *The Asia Pacific Journal* 5, no. 2 (February 2, 2007), https://apjjf.org/-Norma-Field/2352/article.html.

109. Rambadeta, *The Indonesian Comfort Women.*

110. Rambadeta, *The Indonesian Comfort Women.*

111. Rambadeta, *The Indonesian Comfort Women.*

112. Rambadeta, *The Indonesian Comfort Women.*

113. Rambadeta, *The Indonesian Comfort Women.*

114. Video Juku, *Breaking the History of Silence.*

115. Katjasungkana, interview.

116. Katjasungkana, interview.

117. Katjasungkana, interview.

Conclusion

1. Ministry of Foreign Affairs Japan, *Japan-Republic of Korea Relations*, 2015 https://www.mofa.go.jp/a_o/na/kr/page4e_000365.html.

2. Ifhdal Kasim, "Kata Pengantar," in Komnas HAM, *Menggugat Negara Indonesia Atas Pengabaian Hak-Hak Asasi Manusia (Pembiaran) Jugun Ianfu Sebagai Budak Seks Militer & Sipil Jepang, 1942–1945* (Jakarta: Komnas HAM, 2010), v–vi.

3. Hindra, interview.

4. Hindra and Kōichi, *Momoye.*

5. Fanny Chotimah, *TUM*, 2013. For a brief discussion of the film, see Ajeng Nindias, "Fanny Chotimah: Film, Sejarah, Diri dan Upaya Merawat Ingatan," *Infoscreening*, November 30, 2020.

6. For some analysis of a 2015 exhibition covering Dutch and Indonesian women, see McGregor, "Transnational and Japanese Activism."

Bibliography

Archival Sources

National Archives of the Netherlands, The Hague:
Nl-HaNA, NEFIS
Folder: 2.10.37.02
Inventory nos.: 1, 3, 4, 6, 8, 13, 14, 21, 1996, 1967.

Nl-HaNA, Algemene Secretarie van de Nederlands-Indische Regering en de daarbij gedeponeerde Archieven [Alg. Secretarie Ned.-Ind. Regering, Nl-HaNA, NEFIS en Centrale Militaire Inlichtingendienst (CMI) in Nederlands-Indië, 1944] [General Office of the Netherlands Indies Government and thereby deposited archives]
Folder: 2.10.14
Inventory nos.: 5284, 5307, 5282, 5284, 5307, 5309

Nl-HaNA, NEFIS en Centrale Militaire Inlichtingendienst (CMI) in Nederlands-Indië, 1944
Folder: 2.10.62
Inventory nos.: 46, 47, 48, 49, 50, 1950, 1951, 1952, 1961, 1966, 1969, 1971, 1977, 2000, 2001, 2003, 2110, 2245, 2387, 2388, 2389, 2442, 3612

Films

Chotimah, Fanny, dir. *TUM*, 2013.
Kana, Tomoko, dir. *Mardiyem: Sex Slave of the Japanese Army*. Kana Tomoko, 2001.
NNN Dokyumento 96 Ianfu: Indoneshia no baai niwa [NNN documentary 96 ianfu: Cases in Indonesia]. Broadcast on September 30, 1996.
NNN Dokyumento 97 Koe Tozasarete, Soshite: Indoneshia no "Ianfu" tachi, Tokushū Sensō no Jidai ni [NNN Documentary 97 voices were robbed, and: "Ianfu" in Indonesia—special feature in the age of war]. December 8, 1997.
Park Jon-Seok and Shin Dong-Yun, dirs. *My Wish Is . . .* Korea Centre for Investigative Journalism, January 6, 2016. https://newstapa.org/article/7LiYc?lang=eng.

Rambadeta, Lexy, dir. *The Indonesian Comfort Women.* Lexy Rambadeta Films, 2000.

Sophiaan, Sophan, dir. *Kadarwati Wanita dengan Lima Nama* [Kadarwati the woman with five names]. Gramedia Film, 1983.

Video Juku, dir. *Breaking the History of Silence: Women's International War Crimes Tribunal on Japan's Military Sexual Slavery.* Produced by VAWW-Net and Video Juku, 2001.

Treaties, Agreements, Statements, and Declarations

Agreement on the Settlement of Problems Concerning Property and Claims and on Economic Cooperation, 1965. https://treaties.un.org/doc/Publication/UNTS/Volume%20583/volume-583-I-8473-English.pdf.

Announcement to Eurasians, January 12, 1943. In *Japanese Military Administration in Indonesia: Selected Documents*, edited by Harry J. Benda, James K. Irikura, and Kishi Kōichi, 72. New Haven, CT: Yale University Press, 1965.

Declaration on the Elimination of Violence against Women. United Nations Human Rights Office of the High Commissioner. Accessed October 4, 2021. https://www.ohchr.org/en/professionalinterest/pages/violenceagainstwomen.aspx.

de Weerd, K. A. "The Japanese Occupation of the Netherlands Indies." Statement prepared for International Prosecution Section of the International Military Tribunal for the Far East, 1946.

Kōno Yōhei. Statement by the Chief Cabinet Secretary on the Results of the Study on the Issue of "Comfort Women." August 4, 1993. https://www.mofa.go.jp/policy/women/fund/state9308.html.

Memorandum of Understanding between the Department of Social Affairs Republic of Indonesia and the Asian Women's Fund. Accessed October 4, 2021. https://www.awf.or.jp/pdf/0206.pdf.

Ministry of Foreign Affairs Japan. *Details of Exchanges between Japan and the Republic of Korea (ROK) Regarding the Comfort Women Issue—From the Drafting of the Statement to the Asian Women's Fund.* June 20, 2014 (provisional translation). https://www.mofa.go.jp/files/000042171.pdf.

Ministry of Foreign Affairs Japan, *Japan-Republic of Korea Relations*, 2015 https://www.mofa.go.jp/a_o/na/kr/page4e_000365.html.

Treaty of Peace between Japan and the Republic of Indonesia and Reparations Agreement between Japan and the Republic of Indonesia. 1958. https://www.mofa.go.jp/region/asia-paci/indonesia/epa0708/agreement.pdf.

Women's International War Crimes Tribunal Judgement. The Hague, December 4, 2001.

Memoirs, Testimony Collections, and Testimonials Related to Survivors

Ema. Interview by Kawada Fumiko, March 29, 1996. In Forum Komunikasi Ex-Heiho, *Kompensasi Jugun Ianfu* [Compensation for the comfort women], translated by Kimura Kōichi, 27–28. n.p.: Forum Komunikasi Ex-Heiho, 1996.

Ema Kastinah. Testimony. In Kana Tomoko (dir.), *Mardiyem: Sex Slave of Japanese Army*. Kana Tomoko, 2001.

Emi. Interview by Kawada Fumiko, March 28, 1996. In Forum Komunikasi Ex-Heiho, *Kompensasi Jugun Ianfu*, translated by Kimura Kōichi, 26–27, n.p.: Forum Komunikasi Ex-Heiho, 1996.

Goos, Jos. *Gevoelloos Op Bevel: Ervaringen in Jappenkampen* [Emotionless on command: The experiences of Ellen van der Ploeg in Japanese camps]. Utrecht: Het Spectrum, 1995.

Hamer de Froideville, Marguerite. *Geknakte Bloem: Acht Vrouwen vertellen hun Verhaal over Japanse Militaire Dwangprostitutie* [Broken flower: Eight women tell their stories about the Japanese military forced prostitution]. Delft: Elmar, Uitgeverij, 2013.

Hartono, Budi, and Dadang Juliantoro. *Derita Paksa Perempuan: Kisah Jugun Ianfu pada Masa Pendudukan Jepang, 1942–1945* [The sufferings of forced women: Stories of "comfort women" during the Japanese occupation, 1942–1945]. Jakarta: Pustaka Sinar Harapan, LBH Yogyakarta, Yayasan Lapera Indonesia, and Ford Foundation, 1997.

Henson, Maria Rosa. *Comfort Woman: A Filipina's Story of Prostitution and Slavery under the Japanese Military*. London: Rowman and Littlefield, 1999.

Hindra, Eka. "Nona Djawa" [Young Javanese women]. *National Geographic* (Indonesia) (August 2020): 32–47.

Hindra, Eka, and Kimura Kōichi. *Momoye Mereka Memanggilku* [They called me Momoye]. Jakarta: Erlangga, 2007.

Iteng. Testimony. In Hilde Janssen, "Breaking the Silence," in *Japanese Militarism and Its War Crimes in Asia Pacific Region*, edited by Hendrajit, 141. Jakarta: Global Future Institute, 2011.

Janssen, Hilde. *Schaamte en Onschuld: Het Verdrongen Oorlogsverleden van Troostmeisjes in Indonesië* [Shame and innocence: The repressed history of comfort women in Indonesia]. Amsterdam: Nieuw Amsterdam, 2010.

Kasinem. Testimony. In Hilde Janssen, *Schaamte en Onschuld: Het Verdrongen Oorlogsverleden van Troostmeisjes in Indonesië*, 71–73. Amsterdam: Nieuw Amsterdam, 2010.

Kimura, Kōichi. "The Story of Tuminah the First Victim to Come Forward and Tell her Story about Her Ordeal." *Asia Tsushin*, English edition, December 1996, 15–20.

Mardiyah. Testimony. In Hilde Janssen, *Schaamte en Onschuld: Het Verdrongen Oorlogsverleden van Troostmeisjes in Indonesië*, 26–41. Amsterdam: Nieuw Amsterdam, 2010.

Mardiyem. Testimony. In Kana Tomoko (dir.), *Mardiyem: Sex Slave of the Japanese Army*. Kana Tomoko, 2001.

Nur. Testimony. In Hilde Janssen, *Schaamte en Onschuld: Het Verdrongen Oorlogsverleden van Troostmeisjes in Indonesië*, 57–61. Amsterdam: Nieuw Amsterdam, 2010.

O'Herne, Jan Ruff. *Fifty Years of Silence: The Extraordinary Memory of a War Rape Survivor*. Sydney: Editions Tom Thompson, 1994.

Omoh. Interview by Kawada Fumiko, March 29, 1996. In Forum Komunikasi Ex-Heiho, *Kompensasi Jugun Ianfu*, translated by Kimura Kōichi, 29–31. n.p.: Forum Komunikasi Ex-Heiho, 1996.

Paini. Testimony. In Hilde Janssen, *Schaamte en Onschuld: Het Verdrongen Oorlogsverleden van Troostmeisjes in Indonesië*, 43–63. Amsterdam: Nieuw Amsterdam, 2010.

Rosa. Testimony. In Hilde Janssen, *Schaamte en Onschuld: Het Verdrongen Oorlogsverleden van Troostmeisjes in Indonesië*, 113–18. Amsterdam: Nieuw Amsterdam, 2010.

Siyem. Testimony. In Hilde Janssen, *Schaamte en Onschuld: Het Verdrongen Oorlogsverleden van Troostmeisjes in Indonesië*, 65–66. Amsterdam: Nieuw Amsterdam, 2010.

Sri Sukanti. Testimony. In Eka Hindra, "Nona Djawa," *National Geographic* (Indonesia) (August 2020), 32–37.

Suhanah. Interview by Kawada Fumiko, March 28, 1996. In Forum Komunikasi Ex-Heiho, *Kompensasi Jugun Ianfu*, translated by Kimura Kōichi, 33–34. n.p.: Forum Komunikasi Ex-Heiho, 1996.

Sutarbini. Testimony. In Hilde Janssen, *Schaamte en Onschuld: Het Verdrongen Oorlogsverleden van Troostmeisjes in Indonesië*, 99–103. Amsterdam: Nieuw Amsterdam, 2010.

Reports and Conference Proceedings

Association of Pacific War Victims and Bereaved Families. *The Issue of Korean Human Rights during and after the Pacific War*. March 1, 1993.

Barry, Kathleen, Charlotte Bunch, and Shirley Castley, eds. *International Feminism: Networking Against Female Sexual Slavery, Report of the Global Feminist Workshop to Organize against Traffic in Women, Rotterdam, the Netherlands, April 6–15, 1983*. New York: International Women's Tribune Center, 1984.

Bunch, Charlotte, and Shirley Castley, "Introduction," in *International Feminism: Networking against Female Sexual Slavery, Report of the Global Feminist Workshop to Organize against Traffic in Women, Rotterdam, the Netherlands, April 6–15, 1983*, eds. Kathleen Barry, Charlotte Bunch, and Shirley Castley, 8–14, New York: International Women's Tribune Center, 1984.

Chi, Eun-Hee. "South Korea Why the Private Fund Cannot Be the Solution to the Comfort Women Issue." In *Proceedings Fourth Asian Women's Solidarity Conference*, Manila, Philippines, March 27–30, 1996.

Coomaraswamy, Radhika. *Report of the Mission to the Democratic People's Republic of Korea, the Republic of Korea and Japan on the Issue of Military Sexual Slavery in Wartime, Economic and Social Council*. E/CN.4/1996/53/Add.1. January 4, 1996.

Coomaraswamy, Radhika. *Report of the Special Rapporteur on Violence against Women, its Causes and Consequences, Addendum Mission to Indonesia and East Timor on the Issue of Violence against Women (20 November–4 December 1998)*. Economic and Social Council, E/CN.4/1999/68/Add.3. January 21, 1999.

de Kat Angelino, P. "Batikrapport." Inspecteur bij het Kantoor van Arbeid. Deel II. Midden-Java [Batik report by P. de Kat Angelino, inspector of the Labour Office, part 2, Central-Java]. Batavia, 1931.

Democratic People's Republic of Korea, Minister for Foreign Affairs. Letter to the UN Secretary General, August 2, 1993. United Nations, file A/48/302.

Forum Komunikasi Ex-Heiho, *Laporan Pertemuan [Report of the meeting of]: The International Committee of Asia-Pacific War Victims Organisations Claiming Compensation*, 92. Jakarta: Forum Komunikasi Ex-Heiho, 1996.

Forum Komunikasi Ex-Heiho. *Kompensasi Jugun Ianfu* [Compensation for the comfort women]. n.p.: Forum Komunikasi Ex-Heiho, 1996.

Henson, Maria Rosa Luna. "My Views on the Asian Women's Fund." In Forum Komunikasi Ex- Heiho, *Laporan Pertemuan: The International Committee of Asia-Pacific War Victims Organisations Claiming Compensation*, 92. Jakarta: Forum Komunikasi Ex-Heiho, 1996.

International Commission of Jurists. *Comfort Women: An Unfinished Ordeal*. Geneva: International Commission of Jurists, 1994.

Japan Federation of Bar Associations. *Recommendations on the Issue of the "Comfort Women."* Tokyo: JFBA, January 1995.

Japan Federation of Bar Associations. *Sensōhigai Kaigaichōsa Hōkokusho* [Report of the overseas investigation into war-time victimizations]. Tokyo: JFBA, 1993.

Japanese Military Administration in Indonesia. "Principles Governing the Administration of Occupied Southern Areas, Adopted at the Liaison Conference between Imperial Headquarters and the Government, November 20, 1941." In *Japanese Military Administration in Indonesia: Selected Documents*, edited by Harry J. Benda, James K. Irikura, and Kishi Kōichi, 1–3. New Haven, CT: Yale University Press, 1965.

Java Service Association. "Bylaws of the Constitution of the Java Service Association (Jawa Hōkōkai Kiyaku Saisoku), Section 4 Women's Associations, 1944." In *Japanese Military Administration in Indonesia: Selected Documents*, edited by Harry J. Benda, James K. Irikura, and Kishi Kōichi, 158–60. New Haven, CT: Yale University Press, 1965.

Kimura Kōichi. "The Result of Investigation into the Condition of Indonesian Former Jugun Ianfu." *Asia Tsushin*, English edition, no. 4 (December 1996): 11–14.

Komnas HAM. *Menggugat Negara Indonesia atas Pengabaian Hak-hak Asasi (Pembiaran) Jugun Ianfu Sebagai Budak Seks Militer dan Sipil Jepang 1942–1945* [Accusing the Indonesian state of abandoning the human rights of comfort women and military sex slaves of the Japanese military and civilians 1942–1945]. Jakarta: Komnas HAM, 2010.

Kwon, Hee Soon. "The Military Sexual Slavery Issue and Asian Peace." Paper presented at the First East Asian Women's Forum, Japan, October 20–22, 1994.

Murayama, Akira. "Realities of War Victims and Japan's Measures for War Responsibility." In *War Victimization and Japan: International Public Hearing*, 135–47. Executive Committee International Public Hearing, Osaka-shi, Japan, 1993.

McDougall, Gay J. "Contemporary Forms of Slavery: Systematic Rape, Sexual Slavery and Slavery-like Practices during Armed Conflict." Final Report Special UN Special Rapporteur, United Nations Economic and Social Council. June 22, 1998.

Office of the United Nations High Commissioner for Human Rights (OHCHR). *15 Years of the United Nations Special Rapporteur on Violence Against Women, Its Causes and Consequences (1994–2009): A Critical Review*. 2009. https://www.unwomen.org/en/docs/2009/1/15-years-of-the-un-special-rapporteur-on-violence-against-women.

PICN. *Evaluation Report of the "Project Implementation Committee in the Netherlands".* January 2001. http://www.awf.or.jp/pdf/0208.pdf.

Pojskic, Mira. "Consequence of Rape, Report from Bosnia." In Forum Komunikasi Ex-Heiho, *Laporan Pertemuan [Report of the meeting of]: The International Committee of Asia-Pacific War Victims Organisations Claiming Compensation,* 63–77. Forum Komunikasi Ex-Heiho Indonesia, Kota Chiba, Japan, August 9–10, 1996.

Proceedings Fourth Asian Women's Solidarity Conference. Manila, Philippines. March 27–30, 1996.

Proceedings of the International Forum on War Compensation for the Asian-Pacific Region. Seiryō Kaikan, Nagata chō. August 13–14, 1995.

Report from the Special Rapporteur on Violence against Women. *Integration of the Human Rights of Women and Gender Perspective, Violence against Women: Violence against Women Perpetrated and/or Condoned by the State during Times of Armed Conflict (1997–2000).* E/CN.4/2001/73. January 23, 2001.

Republic of Indonesia, Ministry of Social Affairs. *Buku Putih Rehabilitasi Sosial* [White book for social rehabilitation]. Jakarta: Directorate General Bina Rehabilitasi Sosial, 1994.

Republic of Indonesia, Ministry of Social Affairs. *Petunjuk Teknis Penanganan Masalah Sosial Tuna Susila* [Technical instructions for handling the social problems of persons of loose morals]. Jakarta: Directorate General Bina Rehabilitasi Sosial, 1991.

Simons, R. D. G. P. "Indrukken over de Prostitutie en de Homosexueele Prostititite en over het Voorkomen van Gelaschts-Zieken in Ned Oost-Indie en West-Indie" [Impressions about prostitution and homosexual prostitution and the prevention of sexual diseases in the Dutch East Indies and the West Indies]. *Nederlands Tjidschrift voor Geneeskundig* 83, pt. 47 (1939): 5574–79.

Société des Nations. *Commission D'Enquête sur La Traite des Femmes et Des Enfants en Orient, Rapport au Conseil* [Commission of inquiry into the trafficking of women and children in the east, report to the board]. Geneva: Publications de la Société de Nations, 1933.

Société de Nations. *Traite des Femme et des Enfants: Travaux de le Conference de Bandoeng* [The trafficking of women and children: Proceedings of the Bandoeng Conference]. Geneva: Société de Nations, 1938.

Takagi, Ken'ichi. Keynote Speech, International Committee of Asia-Pacific War Victims Organizations Claiming Compensation. In Forum Komunikasi Ex-Heiho, *Laporan Pertemuan: The International Committee of Asia-Pacific War Victims Organisations Claiming Compensation,* 26–28. Ketiga Utusan dari Forum Komunikasi Ex-Heiho Indonesia di Kota Chiba, Jepang, August 9–10, 1996.

van Poelgeest, Bart. "Oosters Stille Dwang. Tewerkgesteld in de Japanse bordelen van Nederlands-Indië" [Eastern silent compulsion: Employed in the Japanese brothels of the Dutch East Indies]. *ICODO Info* 10, no. 3 (1993): 13–21.

van Poelgeest, Bart. *Report of a Study of Dutch Government Documents on the Forced Prostitution of Dutch Women in in the Dutch East Indies during the Japanese Occupation,*

1993 report. Unofficial translation. January 24, 1994. https://www.awf.or.jp/pdf/0205.pdf.

War Victimization and Japan: International Public Hearing Report. Executive Committee International Public Hearing. Osaka-shi: Tōhō Shuppan, 1993.

Yamamoto, Mayumi, and William Bradley Horton. *Comfort Women in Indonesia. A Report on Dutch Archival Material*. Asian Women's Fund, revised version. December 1998.

Yayasan Lembaga Bantuan Hukum. "Kasus Marsinah" [The case of Marsinah]. In *Demokrasi Antara Represi dan Resistensi: Catatan Keadaan Hak Asasi Manusia* [Democracy between repression and resistance: Notes on the state of human rights]. Jakarta: Yayasan Lembaga Bantuan Hukum, 1994.

Unattributed Newspaper Articles

"4 Kontroversi Ratna Sari Dewi Soekarno yang Menggerakan" [4 controversies Ratna Sari Dewi Soekarno started]. *Merdeka*, November 5, 2013.

"25 Mantan Jugun Ianfu Gelar Poster di LBH Yogya" [25 former comfort women make posters at LBH Yogya]. *Kedaulatan Rakyat*, July 24, 1997.

"28.500 Dollar untuk Setiap Ianfu" [28,500 dollars for each comfort woman]. *Koran Rakyat*, May 13, 1996.

"Batalkan Pengalihan Dana Mantan 'Jugun Ianfu'" [Stop the distribution of former "comfort women" funds]. *Kompas*, May 30, 1997.

"Bentuk Protes Mantan Jugun Ianfu terhadap Kepasifan Pemerintah RI" [A form of protest by former comfort women on the passivity of the government of the Republic of Indonesia]. *Wawasan*, November 13, 1997.

"Bila Dana Cair, Kami Gugat" [When the money flows, we will accuse]. *Media Indonesia*, July 13, 1997.

"Bukan Pampasan Perang" [Not spoils of war]. *Republika*, April 13, 1997.

"Comfort Women Continue to Suffer." *Jakarta Post*, March 30, 1997.

"Comfort Women Fight for Rights at Home, Abroad." *Jakarta Post*, March 30, 1997.

"Comfort Women Threaten Suit against Minister." *Jakarta Post*, April 19, 1997.

"Court Says Dutch State Must Compensate Women for Rape 67 Years Ago." *Dutch News*, January 27, 2016. https://www.dutchnews.nl/news/2016/01/84093-2/.

"Desak Jugun Ianfu Masuk Sejarah" [Push for the comfort women to be included in history]. *Jawa Pos*, November 23, 1998.

"Dukunglah Kami, 'Selak' Pada Mati" [Support us, "close" to death]. *Bernas*, November 15, 1997.

"Eks Ianfu Yogya dan Semarang Tuntut Jepang Minta Maaf" [Ex comfort women of Yogyakarta and Semarang sue Japan to apologize]. *Wawasan*, April 27, 1993.

"Filipina Comfort Woman Seeks Apology from Japan." *Reuters*, September 18, 1992.

"Film 'Jugun Ianfu' Banyak Tanggapan dari Rakyat Jepang" [Film about the comfort women gets a large response from the Japanese people]. *Yogya Pos*, June 24, 1997.

"Five Former Comfort Women to Sue Inten." *Jakarta Post*, November 17, 1997.

"Gambaran Murni Perempuan Bila Dianggap Ibu." [There will be a pure picture of the women if they are considered ibu]. *Kedaulatan Rakyat*, August 3, 1997.

"Hidup Saya Sudah Kosong, Saya Hanya Ingin Jadi Saksi Sejarah" [My life is already empty, I only want to become a historical witness]. *Bernas*, February 23, 1997.

"'Ianfu' Seifu Kan'yo Mitomeru: Kyōsei Renkō wa Hitei" ["Ianfu" the government admitted its involvement: Forced recruitment was denied]. *Asahi Shimbun*, July 7, 1992.

"Indoneshia 'Ianfu' Mondai no Nagare" [The timeline of the issue of "ianfu" in Indonesia]. *Suara* 5–6 (August 5, 1999): 12.

"Indoneshia Moto Ianfu, Jinken Kyūsai o Uttae Nichibenren ni Mōshitatesho" [Indonesian ex-ianfu submit a plea to the Japan Federation of Bar Associations for human rights protection]. *Asahi Shimbun*, July 25, 1996, 30.

"Indonesia Urges Japan to Act on Comfort Women." *Reuters*, July 13, 1992.

"Indonesia Wants More Data on 'Comfort Women.'" *Kyodo News International*, July 13, 1992.

"Jepang tidak Bisa Serahkan Ganti Rugi pada Jugun Ianfu" [Japan cannot hand over compensation to the jugun ianfu]. *Kedaulatan Rakyat*, October 18, 1997.

"Jugun Ianfu Agar Masuk Kurikulum Pendidikan Sejarah" [Calls for the comfort women to be included in the history education curriculum]. *Republika*, November 15, 1997.

"Jugun Ianfu Belanda Dapat Ganti Rugi" [Dutch comfort women get compensation]. *Solo Pos*, July 21, 1998.

"Jugun Ianfu dan Santuan Ganti Rugi" [Comfort women and compensation aid]. *Media Indonesia*, July 13, 1997.

"Kakek-Kakek Mendemo ke Dubes Jepang" [Older men demonstrate at the Japanese embassy]. *Jawa Pos*, August 21, 1997.

"Lawyers' Federation Urges Compensation for War Victims." *Kyodo News International*, September 13, 1993.

"LBHI Perjuangkan Nasib Ianfu dan Romusha" [LBHI fights for the fate of comfort women and forced laborers]. *Kedaulatan Rakyat*, May 9, 1993.

"LBH Yogya akan Luncurkan Buku tentang Jugun Ianfu" [LBH Yogya will launch a book about comfort women]. *Bernas*, November 13, 1997.

"LBH Yogya Kembali Masalahkan Jugun Ianfu" [LBH Yogya revisits the comfort women issue]. *Yogya Post*, September 3, 1997.

"LBH Yogya Siap Menggugat Mensos" [LBH Yogya is ready to sue the minister for Social Affairs]. *Kedaulatan Rakyat*, September 1, 1997.

"LBH Yogya Tolak Dana AWF" [LBH Yogya rejects the AWF funds]. *Kedaulatan Rakyat*, July 22, 1998.

"Lima Jugun Ianfu Gugat Mensos" [Five comfort women sue the minister of Social Affairs]. *Jawa Pos*, November 13, 1997.

"Menghapus Kisah Heroik Soeharto" [Erasing the heroic image of Soeharto]. *Gatra* 40, no. 48 (October 17, 1998): 92–93.

"Moto Jūgun Ianfu ga Senjichū no Taiken o Shōgen: Kyō Yokohama de Tsudoi/ Kanagawa" [An ex-jūgun ianfu testifies about her war-time experience: Gathering will be held in Yokohama/ Kanagawa today]. *Asahi Shimbun*, December 7, 1995.

"North Korea Forms Committee for Comfort Women Compensation." *Kyodo News International*, August 10, 1992.

"Ny Mardiyem: Mereka Antre Seperti Mau Nonton Bioskop" [Mrs Mardiyem: They queued as if they wanted to watch a movie at the cinema]. *Wawasan*, November 15, 1997.

"Peluncuran Buku Derita Paksa Perempuan: Fakta Sejarah Jangan Ditutupi" [Launch of the book the sufferings of forced women: Don't cover up the facts of history]. *Kedaulatan Rakyat*, November 15, 1997.

"Pengacara Jepang Natalan dengan Ianfu" [Japanese lawyers have Christmas with the comfort women]. *Jateng Post*, December 13, 1999.

"Pengakuan Bekas Ianfu dari Yogya: 'Sehari Saya Harus Melayani 20 Orang'" [Confession of a former comfort woman from Yogya: "In one day I had to serve 20 people"]. *Jawa Pos*, April 29, 1993.

"Pengakuan Para Ianfu Kandungnya Dipaksa Digugurkan" [Confession of a comfort woman that she was forced to abort the fetus in her womb]. *Kedaulatan Rakyat*, April 27, 1993.

"Pengakuan Seorang 'Wanita Penghibur'" [Confession of a "comfort woman"]. *Kompas*, July 17, 1992, 16.

"Philippine Ex-Sex Slave Seeks Tokyo Compensation." *Reuters*, October 15, 1993.

"Ratapan dan Gelegak Emosi" [Emotions of despair and rage]. *Pikiran Rakyat*, November 15, 1997.

"Rescue of Javanese Girls Planned." *Morning Bulletin*, September 17, 1945, 4.

"RUU TPKS Disahkan setelah Berbagai Penolakan Selama Enam Tahun, Apa Saja Poin Penting" [The TPKS law is ratified after several setbacks across six years, what are the most important points]. *BBC Indonesia*, April 12, 2022. https://www.bbc.com/indonesia/indonesia-61077691.

"Sengketa di Timor Timur Memang Kejam" [The dispute in East Timor was indeed cruel]. *Gatra* 40, no. 47 (October 10, 1998), 29.

"Senjichū Okinawa ni Renkō no Kankoku Josei 30 nen buri 'Jiyū' o Teni: Fukō na Kako Hōmushō Tokubetsu Zairyū o Kyoka" [A Korean woman taken to Okinawa in the wartime obtained "freedom" for the first time in 30 years: For her unfortunate past, the Ministry of Justice granted her a special residence permit]. *Kōchi Shimbun*, October 22, 1975.

"Seorang Ianfu dan Romusha Mengadu ke LBH Yogyakarta" [A comfort woman and a former forced laborer complain to LBH Yogyakarta]. *Kompas*, April 29, 1993.

"Setelah Minta Maaf, Apa?" [After asking for an apology, what next?]. *Jawa Pos*, August 7, 1993.

"(Shohyō) Watashi wa Ianfu dewa Nai: Senso Giseisha o Kokoro ni Kizamu Kai hen" [(Book review) I am not an ianfu: Group for remembering war-time victims (ed.)]. *Asahi Shimbun*, September 21, 1997, 16.

"South Korean President to Visit Japan next Month." *Reuters*, October 22, 1992.

"South Koreans Protest at Japanese Embassy over WWII 'Sex Slaves.'" *Associated Press*, January 15, 1992.

"Sudah 13 Romusha Lapor ke LBH" [13 former forced laborers have already reported to LBH]. *Bernas*, May 8, 1993.

"Tarik Dana AWF dari Depsos" [Pull the funds from the AWF from the Department of Social Affairs]. *Solo Pos*, August 4, 1998.

"Televisi Jepang akan Membuat Film Dokumen tentang Ianfu" [Japanese television will make a documentary film about comfort women]. *Suara Merdeka*, June 24, 1997.

"Tōjisha ni Yorisou Tachiba kara Nihonjin no Kyōryoku o Motomeru: LBH Bengoshi Apon Herunina-shi ni Kiku" [We seek the cooperation of Japanese people from the standpoint of being close to the victims: Interview with Apong Herlina, lawyer at LBH]. *Suara* 4 (February 1, 1999), 1.

"Trauma dengan Wajah Brewokan" [Trauma from face with a moustache]. *Jateng Post*, December 13, 1999.

"Tuntut Pembayaran Ganti Rugi" [Demanding the payment of compensation]. *Kedaulatan Rakyat*, August 12, 1997.

"Wanita Penghibur Tentara Jepang Melapor ke LBH: Siang Melayani Tentara, Malam Sipil" [Comfort women of the Japanese army report to LBH: In the day they served the soldiers, in the night civilians]. *Bernas*, April 27, 1993.

"Watanabe Apologizes for R. P. Comfort Women." *Jiji Press English News Service*, February 3, 1993.

"Women and Violence, Indonesia Anti Violence Against Women." *WIN News* 24, no. 3 (Summer 1998): 37.

Secondary Sources

Abeyasekere, Susan. "Women as Cultural Intermediaries in Nineteenth-Century Batavia." In *Women's Work and Women's Roles: Economics and Everyday life in Indonesia, Malaysia and Singapore*, edited by Lenore Manderson, 15–30. Canberra: Australian National University Press, 1983.

Adams, Cindy. *Sukarno: An Autobiography as Told to Cindy Adams*. Hong Kong: Gunung Agung, 1965.

Afrianty, Dina. "Agents for Change: Local Women's Organizations and Domestic Violence in Indonesia." *Bijdragen tot de taal-, land-en volkenkunde* 174, no. 1 (2018): 24–46.

Agung, Ide Anak Agung Gde. *Kenangan Masa Lampau: Zaman Kolonial Hindia Belanda dan Zaman Pendudukan Jepang di Bali* [Reminiscences from the past: The colonial East Indies and the Japanese occupation in Bali]. Jakarta: Yayasan Obor Indonesia, 1993.

Allen, Matthew. "Okinawa, Ambivalence, Identity and Japan." In *Japan's Minorities: The Illusion of Homogeneity*, edited by Michael Weiner, 188–205. 2nd ed. Abingdon and New York: Routledge, 2009.

Aminuddin, Rasyaad "Rahmah El Yunusiyyah: Kartini Perguruan Islam" [Rahmah El Yunusiyyah: Kartini Islamic College]. In *Manusia dalam Kemelut Sejarah* [People in historical conflict], edited by Taufik Abdullah, Aswab Mahasin, and Daniel Dhakidae, 219–43. Jakarta: LP3ES, 1978.

Amsakasasi et al. "Screams from the Bamboo Hut." Translated by Alison Garrod, Heidi Lindgren, and Kate Napthali. *RIMA: Review of Indonesian and Malaysian Affairs* 26, no. 2 (Summer 1992): 77–90.

Andriyani, Nori. "Hak Asasi Perempuan Dalam Orde Baru" [The rights of women in the New Order]. In *Demokrasi Antara Represi dan Resistensi: Catatan Keadaan Hak Asasi Manusia 1993* [Democracy between repression and resistance: Notes on the state of human rights 1993], edited by Mulyana W. Kusuma, 102–9. Jakarta: Yayasan Lembaga Bantuan Hukum, 1994.

Anggraeni, Dewi. *Tragedi Mei 1998 dan Lahirnya Komnas Perempuan* [The May Tragedy and the creation of the National Commission on Violence against Women]. Jakarta: Penerbit Buku Kompas, 2014.

Arivia, Gadis. "Logika Kekerasan Negara terhadap Perempuan" [The logic of state violence against women]. In *Negara dan Kekerasan terhadap Perempuan* [The State and violence against women], edited by Yayasan Jurnal Perempuan, 4–10. Jakarta: Yayasan Jurnal Perempuan and Asia Foundation, 2000.

Aspinall, Edward. *Opposing Suharto: Compromise, Resistance, and Regime Change in Indonesia.* Stanford, CA: Stanford University Press, 2005.

Asplund, Knut D. "Resistance to Human Rights in Indonesia: Asian Values and Beyond." *Asia-Pacific Journal on Human Rights and the Law* 10, no. 1 (2009): 27–47.

Avonius, Leena. "From Marsinah to Munir: Grounding Human Rights in Indonesia." In *Human Rights in Asia: A Reassessment of the Asian Values Debate*, edited by Damien Kingsbury and Leena Avonius, 99–119. Basingstoke: Palgrave Macmillan, 2008.

Babovic, Aleksandra. *The Tokyo Trial, Justice and the Postwar International Order.* Singapore: Springer Singapore, 2019.

Bahri, Mossadeq. "International Aid for Development? An Overview of Japanese ODA to Indonesia." *Makara Seri Sosial Humaniora* 8, no. 1 (2004): 39–44.

Banning, Jan, and Hilde Janssen. *Comfort Women, TroostMeisjes.* Utrecht: Ipso Facto, 2010.

Barkan, Elazar. *The Guilt of Nations: Restitution and Negotiating Historical Injustices.* New York: Norton, 2000.

Barraclough, Ruth. *Factory Girl Literature: Sexuality, Violence and Representation in Industrializing Korea.* Los Angeles: University of California Press, 2012.

Basri, Agus, and Nunik Iswardhani. "Korban-Korban Serdadu Jepang" [Victims of the Japanese soldiers]. *Tempo*, April 24, 1993, 32–33.

Bessell, Sharon. "The Politics of Child Labour in Indonesia: Global Trends and Domestic Policy." *Pacific Affairs* 72, no. 3 (1999): 353–71.

Blackburn, Kevin. *The Comfort Women of Singapore in History and Memory.* Singapore: National University of Singapore Press and University of Chicago Press, 2022.

Blackburn, Susan. *Women and the State in Modern Indonesia.* Cambridge: Cambridge University Press, 2004.

Bong, Shin Hae. "Compensation for Victims of Wartime Atrocities: Recent Developments in Japan's Case Law." *Journal of International Criminal Justice* 3, no. 1 (2005): 187–206.

Borch, Frederic. *Military Trials of War Criminals in the Netherlands East Indies, 1946–1949*. Oxford: Oxford University Press, 2017.

Borowy, Iris. *Coming to Terms with World Health: The League of Nations Health Organisation 1921–1946*. Frankfurt: Peter Lang, 2009.

Bosma, Ulbe, and Remco Raben. *Being Dutch in the Indies: A History of Creolisaiton and Empire, 1500–1920*. Translated by Wendie Shaffer. Athens: Ohio University Press; Singapore: NUS Press, 2008.

Buchheim, Eveline. "'Hide and Seek': Children of Japanese-Indisch Parents." In *Forgotten Captives in Japanese Occupied Asia*, edited by Karl Hack and Kevin Blackburn, 260–77. London: Routledge, 2008.

Buchheim, Eveline. "Victim, Accomplice or Culprit? Marie-Therese Brandenburg van Olstende's Relations with the Japanese Occupier." In *Under Fire: Women and World War II*, edited by Eveline Buchheim and Ralf Futselaar, 127–40. Amsterdam: Verloren, 2014.

Budianta, Melani. "The Blessed Tragedy: The Making of Women's Activism during the Reformasi Years." In *Challenging Authoritarianism in Southeast Asia*, edited by Ariel Heryanto and Sumit Mandal, 145–76. London: Routledge Curzon, 2003.

Bujono, Bambang. "Jugun Ianfu" [The "comfort women"]. *Tempo*, July 25, 1992, 13.

Bullard, Steve. "Australia's War in New Guinea and Australia in the Liberation of the Netherlands East Indies." In *Encyclopedia of Indonesia in the Pacific War*, edited by Peter Post, William H. Frederick, Iris Heidebrink, and Shigeru Satō, 24–29. Leiden: Brill, 2010.

Burton, Antoinette. "Archive Fever, Archive Stories." In *Archive Stories: Facts, Fiction and the Writing of History*, edited by Antoinette Burton, 1–24. Durham, NC: Duke University Press, 2006.

Captain, Esther, and Onno Sinke. "Hatred of Foreign Elements and Their 'Accomplices': Extreme Violence in the First Phase of the Indonesian Revolution (17 August 1945 to 31 March 1946)." In *Beyond the Pale: Dutch Extreme Violence in the Indonesian War of Independence, 1945–1949*, edited by Gert Oostindie, Ben Schoenmaker, and Frank Van Vree, 141–76. Amsterdam: Amsterdam University Press, 2022.

Chai, Alice Yun. "Asian-Pacific Feminist Coalition Politics: The 'Chŏngshindae/Jūgunianfu' ('Comfort Women') Movement." *Korean Studies* 17 (1993): 67–91.

Chakrabarty, Dipesh. "History and the Politics of Recognition." In *Manifestos for History*, edited by K. Jenkins, S. Morgan, and A. Munslow, 77–87. London: Routledge, 2007.

Cheah Wui Ling. "Walking the Long Road in Solidarity and Hope: A Case Study of the 'Comfort Women' Movement's Deployment of Human Rights Discourse." *Harvard Human Rights Journal* 22, no. 1 (2009): 63–107.

Cheong Yong Mun. "Indonesia: Questions of Stability." *Southeast Asian Affairs* 5 (1978): 107–21.

Chung, Chin Sung. "The Origin and Development of the Military Sexual Slavery Problem in Imperial Japan." *positions* 5, no. 1 (1997): 219–53.

Colijn, Helen. *Song of Survival: Women Interned*. Alexandria, NSW: Millennium Books, 1996.

Confino, Alon. "Collective Memory and Cultural History: Problems of Method." *American Historical Review* 102, no. 5 (1997): 1386–403.

Coté, Joost J. P. "Tirto Adhi Soerjo and the Narration of Indonesian Modernity, 1909–1921: An Introduction to Two Stories." *RIMA: Review of Indonesian and Malaysian Affairs* 32, no. 2 (1998): 1–43.

Creese, Helen. *Bali in the Early Nineteenth Century*. Leiden: Brill, 2016.

Cribb, Robert. "Avoiding Clemency: The Trial and Transfer of Japanese War Criminals in Indonesia, 1946–1949." *Japanese Studies* 31, no. 2 (2011): 151–70.

Cribb, Robert. *Digital Atlas of Indonesian History*. Copenhagen: NIAS Press, 2010.

Crozier-De Rosa, Sharon, and Vera Mackie. *Remembering Women's Activism*. Abingdon, UK: Routledge, 2019.

Das, Veena. *Life and Words: Violence and the Descent into the Ordinary*. Berkeley: University of California Press, 2006.

Derrida, Jacques. "Archive Fever: A Freudian Impression." *Diacritics* 25, no. 2 (1995): 9–63.

Diederichs, Monika. "Stigma and Silence: Dutch Women, German Soldiers and Their Children." In *Children of War: The Hidden Enemy Legacy*, edited by Kjersti Ericsson and Eva Simonsen, 151–64. London: Bloomsbury, 2005.

Dobson, Hugo, and Caroline Rose. "The Afterlives of Postwar Japanese Prime Ministers." *Journal of Contemporary Asia* 49, no. 1 (2019): 127–50.

Dragojlovic, Ana. "Did You Know My Father? The Zone of Unspeakability as Postcolonial Legacy." *Australian Feminist Studies* 26, no. 69 (2011): 319–34.

Driscoll, Mark. *Absolute Erotic, Absolute Grotesque: The Living, Dead, and Undead in Japan's Imperialism, 1895–1945*. Durham, NC: Duke University Press, 2010.

Duus, Peter. "Introduction: Japan's Wartime Empire Problems and Issues." In *The Japanese Wartime Empire, 1931–1945*, edited by Peter Duus, Ramon H. Myers, and Mark R. Peattie, xi–xlvii. Princeton, NJ: Princeton University Press, 1996.

Dwyer, Leslie, and Degung Santikarma. "Speaking from the Shadows: Memory and Mass Violence in Bali." In *After Mass Crime: Rebuilding States and Communities*, edited by Béatrice Pouligny, Simon Chesterman, and Albrecht Schnabel, 190–214. Tokyo: United Nations University Press, 2007.

Eldridge, Phillip. "Human Rights and Democracy in Indonesia and Malaysia: Emerging Contexts and Discourse." *Contemporary Southeast Asia* 18, no. 3 (1996): 298–319.

Enloe, Cynthia. *Does Khaki Become You: The Militarisation of Women's Lives*. London: Pluto, 1983.

Erll, Astrid. "Travelling Memory." *Parallax* 17, no. 4 (2011): 4–18.

Erman, Erwiza. "Penggunan Sejarah Lisan dalam Historiografi Indonesia" [The use of oral history in Indonesian historiography]. *Jurnal Masyarakat dan Budaya* 13, no. 1 (2011): 1–22.

Fatimah, Siti. "Fujinkai (Women's Association)," translated by Shigeru Satō. In *Encyclopedia of Indonesia in the Pacific War*, edited by Peter Post, William H. Frederick, Iris Heidebrink, and Shigeru Satō, 290–300. Leiden: Brill, 2010.

Field, Norma. "The Courts, Japan's Military Comfort Women and the Conscience of Humanity: The Ruling in VAWW-Net Japan v NHK." *Asia Pacific Journal* 5, no. 2 (2007). https://apjjf.org/-Norma-Field/2352/article.html.

Flanigan, Jessica, and Lori Watson. *Debating Sex Work*. New York: Oxford University Press, 2019.

Ford, Michele. "Beyond the Femina Fantasy: Female Industrial and Overseas Domestic Labour in Indonesian Discourses of Women's Work." *RIMA: Review of Indonesian and Malaysian Affairs* 37, no. 2 (2003): 83–113.

Ford, Michele, and Lenore Lyons. "Making the Best of What You've Got: Sex Work and Class Mobility in the Riau Islands." In *Women and Work in Indonesia*, edited by Michele Ford and Lyn Parker, 173–94. London: Routledge, 2008.

Frederick, William. "The Killing of Dutch and Eurasians in Indonesia's National Revolution (1945–49): A Brief Genocide Reconsidered." *Journal of Genocide Research* 14, nos. 3–4 (2012): 359–80.

Frevert, Ute. *Emotions in History Lost and Found*. Natalie Zemon Davis Annual Lecture Series. New York: Central European University Press, 2011.

Fujino, Yutaka. *Sengo Nihon no Jinshin Baibai* [Human trafficking in the postwar Japan]. Tokyo: Ōtsuki Shoten, 2012.

Gandasubrata, S. M. *An Account of the Japanese Occupation of Banjumas Residency, Java, March 1942 to August 1945*. Translated by Leslie H Palmer. Ithaca, NY: Cornell University Press, 1955.

Gluck, Carol. "Operations of Memory 'Comfort Women' and the World." In *Ruptured Histories: War, Memory, and the Post-Cold War in Asia*, edited by Sheila Miyoshi Jager and Rana Mitter, 47–77. Cambridge, MA: Harvard University Press, 2007.

Gluck, Carol. "The People in History: Recent Trends in Japanese Historiography." *Journal of Asian Studies* 38, no. 1 (1978): 25–50.

Golden, Arthur. *Memoirs of a Geisha*. New York: Knopf, 1997.

Gorman, Hilary. "Marginalisation of 'Immoral Women': Experiences of Young Women Street Sex Workers in Surabaya, Indonesia." *Intersections: Gender and Sexuality in Asia and the Pacific* 26 (August 2011). http://intersections.anu.edu.au/issue 26/gorman.htm.

Goss, Andrew. "From Tong-Tong to Tempo Doeloe: Eurasian Memory Work and the Bracketing of Dutch Colonial History, 1957–1961." *Indonesia* 70 (2000): 9–36.

Gotō, Ken'ichi. "Bright Legacy or Abortive Flower: Indonesian Students in Japan during World War 2." In *Japanese Cultural Policies in Southeast Asia during World War 2*, edited by Grant K. Goodman, 7–20. New York: St. Martin's Press, 1991.

Gotō, Ken'ichi. "Multilayered Postcolonial Space: Indonesia, the Netherlands, Japan and East Timor." In *A New East Asia: Toward a Regional Community*, edited by Mori Kazuko and Hirano Ken'ichirō, 20–43. Singapore: NUS Press, 2007.

Gutman, Yifat. *Memory Activism: Re-imagining the Past for the Future in Israel Palestine*. Nashville, TN: Vanderbilt University Press, 2017.

Hammond, Kelly A. "Managing Muslims: Imperial Japan, Islamic Policy and Axis Connections during the Second World War." *Journal of Global History* 12 (2017): 251–73.

Harikrisnowo, Harikristuti. "Perempuan dan Hak Asasi Manusia dalam Perspectif Yuridis" [Women and human rights from a judicial perspective]. In *Negara dan Kekerasan terhadap Perempuan*, edited by Yayasan Jurnal Perempuan, 205–18. Jakarta: Yayasan Jurnal Perempuan and Asia Foundation, 2000.

Hartono, Budi. "Foreword." In Eka Hindra and Kimura Kōichi, *Momoye Mereka Memanggilku*, vi–x. Jakarta: Erlangga, 2007.

Harum, Diah Meutia. "Representasi Kolonialisme dalam 'Tjerita Nji Paina' Karya H. Kommer" [Representations of colonialism in "Tjerita Nji Paina" by H. Kommer]. *Aksara* 29, no. 2 (December 2017): 155–69.

Hata, Ikuhiko. *Comfort Women and Sex in the Battle Zone*. Translated by Jason Michael Morgan. Lanham, MD: Hamilton Books, 2018.

Hayashi Hirofumi. "Government, the Military and Business in Japan's Wartime Comfort Women System." *Asia-Pacific Journal* 5, no. 1 (2007). https://apjjf.org/-Hayashi -Hirofumi/2332/article.html.

Hayashi Hirofumi. "Japanese Comfort Women in Southeast Asia." *Japan Forum* 10, no. 2 (1998): 211–19.

Hayashi Hirofumi. "The Japanese Movement to Protest Wartime Sexual Violence: A Survey of Japanese and International Literature." *Critical Asian Studies* 33, no. 4 (2001): 572–80.

Hearman, Vannessa. "Remembering Munir." *Inside Indonesia* 115 (January–March 2014). https://www.insideindonesia.org/remembering-munir.

Heidebrink, Iris. "Internment of Civilians: Introduction." In *Encyclopedia of Indonesia in the Pacific War*, edited by Peter Post, William H. Frederick, Iris Heidebrink, and Shigeru Satō, 163–65. Leiden: Brill, 2010.

Heidebrik, Iris. "Military Tribunals in the Netherlands East Indies." In *Encyclopedia of Indonesia in the Pacific War*, edited by Peter Post, William H. Frederick, Iris Heidebrink, and Shigeru Satō, 411–21. Leiden: Brill, 2010.

Hellwig, Tineke. "Asian Women in the Lives of Dutch Tea Planters: Two Narratives from West Java." *Indonesia and the Malay World* 29, no. 85 (2001): 161–79.

Henry, Nicola. "Memory of an Injustice: The 'Comfort Women' and the Legacy of the Tokyo Trial." *Asian Studies Review* 37, no. 3 (2013): 362–80.

Hersshatter, Gail. *Dangerous Pleasures: Prostitution and Modernity in Twentieth-Century Shanghai*. Berkeley: University of California Press, 1999.

Heryanto, Ariel. "Rape, Race and Reporting." In *Reformasi Crisis and Change in Indonesia*, edited by Arief Budiman, Barbara Hatley, and Damien Kingsbury, 299–334. Clayton, Vic.: Monash Asia Institute, 1999.

Hesselink, Liesbeth. "Prostitution: A Necessary Evil." In *Indonesian Women in Focus: Past and Present Notions*, edited by Elsbeth Locher-Scholten and Anke Niehof, 205–24. Dordrecht: Foris, 1987.

Hicks, George. *The Comfort Women: Japan's Brutal Regime of Enforced Prostitution in the Second World War*. New York: Norton, 1995.

Hindley, Donald. *The Communist Party of Indonesia 1951–1963*. Berkeley: University of California Press, 1964.

Hindra, Eka. "The Bill of Ianfu: Breaking the Political Silence in Japan." In *Japanese Militarism and Its War Crimes in Asia Pacific Region*, edited by Hendrajit, 109–36. Jakarta: Global Future Institute, 2011.

Hirowatari Seigo. "Kenpō to Sengo Sekinin: Sengo 50 nen, Nihon to Doitsu" [Constitutions and wartime responsibility: 50 years since the end of the war, Japan and Germany]. *Hōritsu Jihō* 67, no. 6 (1995): 11–17.

Horton, Bradley William. "Comfort Women." In *Encyclopedia of Indonesia in the Pacific War*, edited by Peter Post, William H. Frederick, Iris Heidebrink, and Shigeru Satō, 184–96. Leiden: Brill, 2010.

Horton, Bradley William. "Pramoedya and the Comfort Women of Buru: A Textual Analysis of 'Perawan Remaja dalam Cengkeraman Militer'" [Teenage virgins in the grasp of the military]. *Journal of Asia Pacific Studies* 14 (2010): 71–88.

Hull, Terence, Endang Sulistyaningsih, and Gavin W Jones. *Prostitution in Indonesia: Its History and Evolution*. Jakarta: Pustaka Sinar Harapan, 1999.

Imamura Tsuguo, Takagi Yoshitaka, and Suzuki Isomi. *Sengo Hoshō Hō* [Postwar compensation law]. Tokyo: Akashi Shoten, 1999.

Indrayati, Sri, and Ōkawa Seiichi. "Kisah Kadarwati yang Sebenarnya." [The story of the true Kadarwati]. *Tempo*, July 25, 1992, 17–18.

Ingleson, John. "Prostitution in Colonial Java." In *Nineteenth and Twentieth Century Indonesia: Essays in Honour of J. D. Legge*, edited by David Chandler and Merle Ricklefs, 123–40. Clayton, Vic.: Monash University, 1986.

Jacobsen, Trude. *Sex Trafficking in Southeast Asia: A History of Desire, Duty and Debt*. London: Routledge, 2017.

Jager, Sheila Miyoshi, and Rana Mitter, eds. *Ruptured Histories: War, Memory, and the Post-Cold War in Asia*. Cambridge, MA: Harvard University Press, 2007.

Janssen, Hilde. "Breaking the Silence." In *Japanese Militarism and Its War Crimes in Asia Pacific Region*, edited by Hendrajit, 137–52. Jakarta: Global Future Institute, 2011.

Jetschke, Anja. "Linking the Unlinkable? International Norms and Nationalism in Indonesia and the Philippines." In *The Power of Human Rights: International Norms and Domestic Change*, edited by Thomas Risse, Stephen C. Ropp, and Kathryn Sikkink, 134–71. Cambridge: Cambridge University Press, 1999.

Jones, Eric. *Wives, Slaves and Concubines: A History of the Female Underclass in Dutch Asia*. DeKalb: Northern Illinois University Press, 2010.

Jung, Kyungja. *Practicing Feminism in South Korea*. London: Routledge, 2014.

Juningsih, Lucia. *Dampak Kekerasan Seksual pada Jugun Ianfu* [The effects of sexual violence on the comfort women]. Yogyakarta: Kerjasama Ford Foundation dengan Pusat Penelitian Kependudukan Universitas Gadjah Mada, 1999.

Kahin, George M. T. *Nationalism and Revolution in Indonesia*. Ithaca, NY: Cornell University Press, 1952.

Kano, Ayako. *Japanese Feminist Debates: A Century of Contention on Sex, Love, and Labor*. Honolulu: University of Hawai'i Press, 2016.

Kanō Mikiyo. "The Problem with the 'Comfort Women' Problem." *AMPO Japan Asia Quarterly Review* 24, no. 2 (1993): 42–63.

Kartodirdjo, Sartono. *The Peasants' Revolt of Banten in 1918: Its Conditions, Course and Sequel: A Case Study of Social Movements in Indonesia.* s'Gravenhage: Martinus Nijhoff, 1966.

Kasim, Ifhdal. "Kata Pengantar" [Foreword]. In Komnas HAM, *Menggugat Negara Indonesia Atas Pengabaian Hak-Hak Asasi Manusia (Pembiaran) Jugun Ianfu Sebagai Budak Seks Militer & Sipil Jepang, 1942–1945* [Accusing the Indonesian state of abandoning the human rights of jugun iangu as the sex slaves of the Japanese military and civilians, 1942–1945], v–vi. Jakarta: Komnas HAM, 2010.

Katjasungkana, Nursyahbani. "Gender and Transformative Legal Aid." In *Women's Participation in Social Development: Experiences from Asia, Latin America and the Caribbean,* edited by Karen Mokate, 147–62. Washington, DC: Inter American Bank, 2004.

Kawada Fumiko. *Akagawara no Ie: Chōsen kara Kita Jūgun Ianfu* [A house with a red tile roof: A military comfort woman from Korea]. Tokyo: Chikuma Shobō, 1987.

Kawada Fumiko. *Indoneshia no "Ianfu"* ["Comfort women" in Indonesia]. Tokyo: Akashi Shoten, 1997.

Kawada Fumiko. *Ryūkyūko no Onnatachi* [Women in Ryūkyū Islands]. Tokyo: Tō jusha, 1983.

Kelana, Pandir. *Ibu Sinder* [Mrs. Cinder]. Jakarta: Sinar Harapan, 1983.

Kelana, Pandir. *Kadarwati Wanita dengan Lima Nama* [Kadarwati the woman with five names] Jakarta: Sinar Harapan, 1982.

Kelana, Pandir. *Kereta Api Terakhir* [The last train]. Jakarta: Gramedia Pustaka Utama, 1991.

Kemperman, Jeroen. "Internment of Civilians." In *Encyclopedia of Indonesia in the Pacific War,* edited by Peter Post, William H. Frederick, Iris Heidebrink, and Shigeru Satō, 163–73. Leiden: Brill, 2010.

Kepustakaan Populer Gramedia. *Cerita di Balik Dapur Tempo* [The story behind Tempo]. Jakarta: Kepustakaan Populer Gramedia bekerja sama dengan Majalah Tempo, 2011.

Kim Miyoung, ed. *Routledge Handbook of Memory and Reconciliation in East Asia.* London: Routledge, 2016.

Kim-Gibson, Dai Sil. "They Are Our Grandmas." *Positions* 5, no. 1 (1997): 255–74.

Kim-Gibson, Dai Sil. "They Defiled My Body, Not My Spirit: The Story of Korean Comfort Woman, Chung Seo Woon (Interview)." In *Making Waves: New Writing by Asian American Women,* edited by Elaine H. Kim and Lilia V. Villanueva, 177–83. Boston: Beacon Press, 1997.

Kimura Kōichi. "Brutal Abuse of Young Girls as Military Sex Slaves." *Asia Tsushin,* English edition 4, December 1996, 11–14.

Kimura Kōichi. "Jaiemu-san wa Naze 'Gishō' Shita noka: Nihongun Seidoreisei Higaisha (Ianfu) no Jinken Kyūsai Mōshitate de Nichibenren ga Hōmon Chōsa" [Why Jainem made "false testimony": The Japan Federation of Bar Associations visited the victims of Japan's military sexual slavery (ianfu) to investigate their human rights protection claims]. *Suara* 8 (May 12, 2000): 1–4.

Kimura Otcho. "Mardiemu-san no Tatakai: Indoneshia Shakai no 'Nihon ni Taisuru Zōo' to 'Ibu tachi eno Keibetsu' wa Koin no Ryōmen" [The fight of Mardiyem: Indonesian society's "hatred of Japan" and "contempt for women" are two sides of the same coin]. *Suara* 5–6 (August 5, 1998): 8–10.

King, Michelle T. "Working with/in the Archives." In *Research Methods for History*, edited by Simon Gunn and Lucy Faire, 13–29. Edinburgh: Edinburgh University Press, 2016.

Knepper, Paul. "The Investigation into the Traffic in Women by the League of Nations: Sociological Jurisprudence as an International Social Project." *Law and History Review* 34, no. 1 (2016): 45–73.

Kokusai Fōramu Jikkō Iinkai, ed. *Sengo Hoshō o Kangaeru* [Considering wartime compensation]. Osaka: Tōhō Shuppan, 1992.

Kolibonso, Rita Serena. "The Gender Perspective: A Key to Democracy in Indonesia." In *Reformasi Crisis and Change in Indonesia*, edited by Arief Budiman, Barbara Hatley, and Damien Kingsbury, 335–41. Clayton, Vic.: Monash Asia Institute, 1999.

Kongres Wanita Indonesia. *Sejarah Setengah Abad Pergerakan Wanita Indonesia* [The history of a half century of the Indonesian women's movement]. Jakarta: Balai Pustaka, 1978.

Korean Council for Women Drafted for Military Sexual Slavery by Japan, eds. *True Stories of the Comfort Women: Testimonies*. Translated by Yong Joo Lee. London: Cassell, 1995.

Kousbroek, Rudy. *Het Oostindisch Kampsyndroom* [The East Indies camp syndrome]. Amsterdam: Muelenhoff, 1992.

Kovner, Sarah. *Occupying Powers: Sex Workers and Servicemen in Postwar Japan*. Stanford, CA: Stanford University Press, 2019.

Kozen, Cathleen. "Redress as American-Style Justice: Congressional Narratives of Japanese American Redress at the End of the Cold War." *Time and Society* 21, no. 1 (2012): 104–20.

Kumagai Naoko. "Asian Women's Fund Revisited." *Asia Pacific Review* 21, no. 2 (2014): 117–48.

Kumagai Naoko. *The Comfort Women: Historical, Political, Legal and Moral Perspectives*. Translated by David Noble. Tokyo: International House of Japan, 2016.

Kurasawa, Aiko. *Peristiwa 1965: Persepsi dan Sikap Jepang* [The 1965 incident: The perceptions and attitude of Japan]. Jakarta: Penerbit Buku Kompas, 2015.

Kurasawa-Inomata, Aiko. "Rice Shortage and Transportation." In *Japan, Indonesia and the War: Myths and Realities*, edited by Peter Post and Elly Touwen-Bouwsma, 111–33. Leiden: KITLV Press, 1997.

Kurniawan, Eka. *Cantik itu Luka* [Beauty is a wound]. Jakarta: Gramedia Pustaka, 2002.

Lee, Doreen. *Activist Archives: Youth Culture and the Political Past in Indonesia*. Durham, NC: Duke University Press, 2016.

Lee, Jeong-gyu. "Remembering Bae Bong-gi, the First Comfort Woman to Testify about her Experiences." *Hankyoreh*, March 18, 2019. http://english.hani.co.kr/arti/_edition/e_international/886367.html.

Lee, Misook. "The Japan-Korea Solidarity Movement in the 1970s and 1980s: From Solidarity to Reflexive Democracy." *Asia-Pacific Journal* 12, issue 38, no. 1 (September 22, 2014). https://apjjf.org/2014/12/38/Misook-Lee/4187.html.

Lev, Daniel. *Legal Evolution and Political Authority in Indonesia: Selected Essays.* The Hague: Kluwer Law International, 2000.

Levy, Daniel, and Natan Sznaider. *Human Rights and Memory.* University Park: Pennsylvania State University Press, 2010.

Lindsey, Tim, and Melissa Crouch. "Cause Lawyers in Indonesia: A House Divided." *Wisconsin International Journal of Law* 31, no. 3 (2013): 620–45.

Locher-Scholten, Elsbeth. "Morals, Harmony, and National Identity: 'Companionate Feminism' in Colonial Indonesia in the 1930s." *Journal of Women's History* 14, no. 4 (2003): 38–58.

Loney, Hannah. *In Women's Words: Violence and Everyday Life during the Indonesian Occupation of East Timor, 1975–1999.* Brighton, UK: Sussex Academic Press, 2018.

Louie, Miriam Ching Yoon. "Minjung Feminism: Korean Women's Movement for Gender and Class Liberation." *Women's Studies International Forum* 18, no. 4 (1995): 417–30.

Lucas, Nicole. "Trouwverbod, Inlandse Huishoudsters en Eropese Vrouwen: het Concubinaat in de Planterswereld aan Sumatra's Oostkust 1960–1940" [The marriage ban, local housekeepers and European women: Concubinage in the world of plantations on Sumatra's east coast 1860–1940]. In *Vrouwen in de Nederlandse Kolonien* [Women in the Dutch colonies], edited by Jeske Reij, Els Kloek, Ulla Jansz, Annemarie de Wildt, Suzanne van Norden, Mirjam de Baar, 78–97. Nijmegen: SUN, 1986.

Luttikhuis, Bart. "Beyond Race Constructions of Europeanness in Late Colonial Legal Practice in the Dutch East Indies." *European Review of History: Revue Europeenne d'Historie* 20, no. 4 (2013): 539–58.

Mackie, Vera. *Feminism in Modern Japan: Citizenship, Embodiment and Sexuality.* New York: Cambridge University Press, 2003.

Mackie, Vera. "Gender, Geopolitics and Gaps in Records: Women Glimpsed in the Military Archives." In *Sources and Methods in Histories of Colonialism: Approaching the Imperial Archive,* edited by Kirsty Reid and Fiona Paisley, 135–59. London: Routledge, 2017.

Mackie, Vera. "The Language of Globalization, Trasnationality and Feminism." *International Feminist Journal of Politics* 3, no. 2 (2001): 180–206.

Mackie, Vera. "In Search of Innocence: Feminist Historians Debate the Legacy of Wartime Japan." *Australian Feminist Studies* 20, no. 47 (2005): 207–17.

Mackie, Vera. "One Thousand Wednesdays: Transnational Activism from Seoul to Glendale." In *Women's Activism and Second Wave Feminism: Transnational Histories,* edited by Barbara Molony and Jennifer Nelson, 249–71. London: Bloomsbury Academic, 2017.

Maekawa, Kaori. "The Heiho during the Japanese Occupation of Indonesia." In *Asian Labor in the Wartime Japanese Empire: Unknown Histories,* edited by Paul Kratoska, 179–96. Armonk, NY: M. E. Sharpe, 2005.

Malaka, Tan. *Dari Penjara ke Penjara* [From jail to jail]. Yogyakarta: Teplok Press, 2000.

Mariana, Anna. *Perbudakan Seksual: Perbandingan Antara Masa Fasisme Jepang dan Neofasisme Orde Baru* [Sexual slavery: A comparison between the fascism of the Japanese and the neo-fascism of the New Order]. Tangerang Selatan: Marjin Kiri, 2015.

Marjam, Encik Siti. "Pidato Encik Siti Marjam" [Speech of Siti Marjam]. In *Kongres Perempuan Pertama: Tinjauan Ulang* [The first women's congress: Revisited], edited by Susan Blackburn, 106–13. Jakarta: Yayasan Obor Indonesia, KITLV Jakarta, 2007.

Mark, Ethan. *Japan's Occupation of Java in the Second World War: A Transnational History*. London: Bloomsbury Academic, 2018.

Mark, Ethan. "Suharto's New Order Remembers Japan's New Order." In *Representing the Japanese Occupation of Indonesia: Personal Testimonies and Public Images in Indonesia, Japan, and the Netherlands*, edited by Remco Raben, 72–84. Zwolle: Waanders, 1999.

Mark, Ethan. "Translator's Introduction: The People in the War." In Yoshimi Yoshiaki, *Grassroots Fascism: The War Experience of the Japanese People*, 1–40. New York: Columbia University Press, 2015.

Matsui, Yayori. "Why I Oppose Kisaeng Tours." Extract in *International Feminism: Networking against Female Sexual Slavery Report of the Global Feminist Workshop to Organize against Traffic in Women, Rotterdam, the Netherlands, April 6–15, 1983*, edited by Kathleen Barry, Charlotte Bunch, and Shirley Castley, 64–73. New York: International Women's Tribune Center, 1984.

Matsui, Yayori. *Women's Asia*. London: Zed Books, 1989.

McGregor, Katharine. "Emotions and Activism for Former So Called 'Comfort Women' of the Japanese Occupation of the Netherlands East Indies." *Women's Studies International Forum* 54 (January–February 2016): 67–78.

McGregor, Katharine. "Exposing Impunity: Memory and Human Rights Activism in Indonesia and Argentina." *Journal of Genocide Research* 19, no. 4 (2017): 551–73.

McGregor, Katharine. "From National Sacrifice to Compensation Claims: Changing Indonesian Representations of the Captain Westerling Massacres in South Sulawesi (1946–1947)." In *Colonial Counterinsurgency and Mass Violence: The Dutch Empire in Indonesia*, edited by Bart Luttikhius and Dirk Moses, 282–307. London: Taylor and Francis, 2014.

McGregor, Katharine. "Historical Justice and the Case of the 1965 Killings." In *Routledge Handbook of Contemporary Indonesia*, edited by Robert Hefner, 129–39. London: Routledge, 2018.

McGregor, Katharine. *History in Uniform: Military Ideology and the Construction of the Indonesian Past*. Singapore: NUS Press, 2007.

McGregor, Katharine. "Indonesian Women, the Women's International Democratic Federation and the Struggle for 'Women's Rights,' 1946–1965." *Indonesia and the Malay World* 40, no. 117 (2012): 193–208.

McGregor, Katharine. "Living in a Conflict Zone: Gendered Violence during the Japanese Occupation of the Netherlands East Indies." In *Gendered Violence across*

Time and Space in Indonesia and East Timor, edited by Katharine McGregor, Ana Dragojlovic, and Hannah Loney, 39–58. London: Routledge, 2020.

McGregor, Katharine. "Transnational and Japanese Activism on Behalf of Indonesian and Dutch Victims of Enforced Military Prostitution during World War II." *Asia-Pacific Journal* 14, issue 16, no. 7 (2016). https://apjjf.org/2016/16/McGregor.html.

McGregor, Katharine E., and Vannessa Hearman. "The Challenges of Political Rehabilitation in Post New Order Indonesia: The Case of Gerwani (the Indonesian Women's Movement)." *Southeast Asia Research* 15, no. 3 (2007): 355–84.

McGregor, Katharine, and Vera Mackie. "Transcultural Memory and the Troostmeisjes/Comfort Women Photographic Project." *History and Memory* 30, no. 1 (Spring/Summer 2018): 116–50.

McGregor, Katharine, Annie Pohlman, and Jess Melvin. "New Interpretations of the Causes, Dynamics and Legacies of the Indonesian Genocide." In *The Indonesian Genocide: Causes, Dynamics and Legacies*, edited by Katharine McGregor, Jess Melvin, and Annie Pohlman, 1–26. London: Palgrave Macmillan, 2018.

McGregor, Katharine, and Ken Setiawan. "Shifting from International to 'Indonesian' Justice Measures: Two Decades of Addressing Past Human Rights Violations." *Journal of Contemporary Asia* 49, no. 5 (2019): 837–86.

McVey, Ruth. "The Enchantment of the Indonesian Revolution: History and Action in an Indonesian Communist Text." In *Perceptions of the Past in Southeast Asia*, edited by Anthony Reid and David Marr, 340–58. Kuala Lumpur: Heineman Education Books, 1979.

Melati, Sintha. "In the Service of the Underground: The Struggle against the Japanese." In *Local Opposition and Underground Resistance to the Japanese in Java, 1942–1945*, edited by Anton Lucas, 123–264. Translated and annotated by David Bourchier. Clayton, Vic.: Centre of Southeast Asian Studies, 1986.

Mendoza, Katharina. "'Freeing the Slaves of Destiny': The Lolas and the Filipino Comfort Women Movement." *Cultural Dynamics* 15, no. 3 (2003): 247–66.

Mihalopoulos, Bill. *Sex in Japan's Globalization, 1870–1930: Prostitutes, Emigration and Nation-Building*. London: Pickering and Chatto, 2011.

Min Pyong Gap. *Korean "Comfort Women": Military Brothels, Brutality and the Redress Movement*. New Brunswick, NJ: Rutgers University Press, 2021.

Min Pyong Gap, Thomas R. Chung, and Sejung Sage Yim, eds. *The Transnational Redress Movement for the Victims of Japanese Military Sexual Slavery*. Berlin: De Gruyter Oldenbourg, 2020.

Ming, Hanneke. "Barracks-Concubinage in the Indies, 1887–1920." *Indonesia* 35 (1983): 65–94.

Mitsui Hideko. "The Politics of National Atonement and Narratives of War." *Inter-Asia Cultural Studies* 9, no. 1 (2008): 47–61.

Moon, Katharine H. S. "Review: The Comfort Women: Japan's Brutal Regime of Enforced Prostitution in the Second World War." *Contemporary Sociology* 25, no. 5 (1996): 630–31.

Morris Suzuki, Tessa. *East Asia beyond the History Wars: Confronting the Ghosts of Violence*. Milton Park: Routledge, 2013.

Morris Suzuki, Tessa. "You Don't Want to Know about the Girls? The 'Comfort Women', the Japanese Military and the Allied Forces in the Asia-Pacific." *Asia Pacific Journal* 13, issue 31, no. 1 (August 3, 2015), https://apjjf.org/2015/13/31/Tessa-Morris-Suzuki/4352.html.

Murayama, Akira. *Bengoshi ga Mita Sengo Hoshō to Jinken* [Wartime compensation and human rights viewed by a lawyer]. Tokyo: Buraku Mondai Kenkyūjo, 1995.

Murniati, A. Nunuk P. *Gerakan Anti-Kekerasan terhadap Perempuan* [Movement to oppose violence against women]. Yogyakarta: Penerbit Kanisius, 1998.

Mutsuyo, Ōki. "52 nichi-kan no 'Shi no Kōshin': Suharuthi-san no Kunan to Kōfuku" [52 days of a "death march": Suharti's suffering and happiness]. *Suara* 11 (March 26, 2001): 4–7.

Nasution, Adnan Buyung. "Defending Human Rights in Indonesia." *Journal of Democracy* 5, no. 3 (1994): 114–23.

Nieuwenhuys, R. *The Mirror of the Indies: A History of Dutch Colonial Literature*. Amherst: University of Massachusetts Press, 1982.

Nindias, Ajeng. "Fanny Chotimah: Film, Sejarah, Diri dan Upaya Merawat Ingatan." [Fanny Chotimah: Film, history, self and efforts to craft memories]. *Infoscreening*, November 30, 2020.

Nishino, Rumiko, Kim Puja, and Onozawa Akane, eds. *Denying the Comfort Women: The Japanese State's Assault on Historical Truth*. London: Routledge, 2018.

Nogi Harumichi. *Kaigun Tokubetsu Keisatsutai: Ambontō BC kyū Senpan no Shuki* [The Navy's special police squad: The memoir of BC class war-criminal stationed in Ambon Island]. Tokyo: Taihei Shuppansha, 1975.

Norma, Caroline. *The Japanese Comfort Women and Sexual Slavery during the China and Pacific Wars*. London: Bloomsbury, 2016.

Nozaki, Yoshiko. "The 'Comfort Women' Controversy: History and Testimony." *Asia-Pacific Journal* 3, no. 7 (July 2005). https://apjjf.org/-Yoshiko-Nozaki/2063/article.html.

Nozaki, Yoshiko. *War Memory, Nationalism and Education in Postwar Japan, 1945–2007: The Japanese History Textbook Controversy and Ienaga Saburo's Court Challenges*. New York: Routledge, 2008.

Oh, Bonnie B. C. "The Japanese Imperial System and Korean 'Comfort Women' of World War II." In *Legacies of the Comfort Women of World War II*, by Margaret D. Stetz and Bonnie B. C. Oh, 3–25. Armonk, NY: M. E. Sharpe, 2001.

Okada, Fumihide. "Okada's Report on His Administration, February 1944 (Extracts)." In *The Japanese Experience in Indonesia: Selected Memoirs of 1942–1945*, edited by Anthony Reid and Oki Akira, 127–58. Athens: Ohio Center for International Studies, 1986.

Ōkawa, Seiichi, and ADN. "Maaf, Kata Miyazawa" [Sorry, says Miyazawa]. *Tempo*, January 25, 1992, 82.

Ōmura Tetsuo. "Indoneshia de 'Ianfu' Mondai ga Futatabi Kurōzuappu" [The issue of ianfu is re-focused in Indonesia]. *Suara* 10 (November 10, 2000): 3–5.

Ōmura Tetsuo. "SOMJII Gaimushō e: Motto NGO tono Renkei o" [SOMJII's visit to the Ministry of Foreign Affairs: More cooperation with NGOs required]. *Suara* 5–6 (August 5, 1999): 1–3.

Ōmura Tetsuo. "'Suharto go' no Indoneshia no Media ni Miru 'Ianfu' Mondai" [The issue of "comfort women" in the Indonesian media in the "post-Suharto" period]. *Suara* 2 (August 1, 1998): 1–2.

Ōmura Tetsuo. "Tōkai Shusai 'Indoneshia no Moto 'Ianfu' wa Ima . . . ' Shūkai deno Kimura Kōichi-san no Kōen kara" [Extracts from Kimura Kōichi's speech made at the gathering entitled "Ex-Ianfu in Indonesia Now" organized by SOMJII]. *Suara* 2 (August 1, 1998): 3–5.

Ooi, Keat Gin. *The Japanese Occupation of Borneo, 1941–1945.* Abingdon, UK: Routledge, 2011.

Oostindie, Gert, Ben Schoenmaker, and Frank Van Vree, eds. *Beyond the Pale: Dutch Extreme Violence in the Indonesian War of Independence, 1945–1949.* Amsterdam: Amsterdam University Press, 2022.

Ōsono, Hiroshi. "Indoneshia kara Moto 'Ianfu' ga Rainichi" [The ex "ianfu" visited Japan from Indonesia]. *Suara* 7 (December 1, 1998): 1–2.

Park, You-me. "Compensation to Fit the Crime: Conceptualizing a Just Paradigm of Reparation for Korean 'Comfort Women.'" *Comparative Studies of South Asia, Africa and the Middle East* 30, no. 2 (2010): 204–13.

Patterson, Orlando. *Slavery and Social Death: A Comparative Study.* Cambridge, MA: Harvard University Press, 1982.

Peattie, Mark R. "Nanshin: The 'Southward Advance,' 1931–1941, as a Prelude to the Japanese Occupation of Southeast Asia." In *The Japanese Wartime Empire: Problems and Issues,* edited by Peter Duus, Ramon H. Myers, and Mark R. Peattie, 200–220. Princeton, NJ: Princeton University Press, 1996.

Persatuan Heiho Indonesia-Jepang. *Indonesia Petisi dari Para Heiho* [Indonesia petition from the heiho]. Tokyo: Persatuan Heiho Indonesia-Jepang, Nashinoki-sha, 1993.

Poeze, Harry A. "The Road to Hell: Construction of a Railway Line in West Java during the Japanese Occupation." In *Asian Labour in the War Time Japanese Empire: Unknown Histories,* edited by Paul Kratoska, 152–78. Armonk, NY: M. E. Sharp, 2005.

Pohlman, Annie. "Testimonio and Telling Women's Narratives of Genocide, Torture and Political Imprisonment in Post-Suharto Indonesia." *Life Writing* 5, no. 1 (2008): 47–60.

Pohlman, Annie. *Women, Sexual Violence and the Indonesian Killings of 1965–66.* New York: Routledge, 2015.

Prambadi, Didi, and Krishna. "Pengakuan dari Semarang" [Confession from Semarang]. *Tempo,* July 25, 1992, 19–21.

Prambadi, Didi, and Ōkawa Seiichi. "Setelah Jepang tak Bisa Mengelak Lagi" [Now Japan can no longer dodge it]. *Tempo,* July 25, 1992, 14–16.

Press-Baranathan, Galia. *The Political Economy of Transitions to Peace: A Comparative Perspective.* Pittsburgh: University of Pittsburgh Press, 2009.

Pringgodigdo, A. K. *Sedjarah Pergerakan Rakjat Indonesia* [History of the movement of the Indonesian people]. Djakarta: Penerbit Dian Rajkat, 1967.

Protschky, Susie. "Home at the Front: Violence against Indonesian Women and Children in Dutch Military Barracks during the Indonesian National Revolution." In *Gendered Violence across Time and Space in Indonesia and East Timor*, edited by Katharine McGregor, Ana Dragojlovic, and Hannah Loney, 59–83. Abingdon, UK: Routledge, 2020.

Puccini, Giacomo. *Madame Butterfly: Opera in Three Acts*. 1920.

Purdey, Jemma. *Anti-Chinese Violence in Indonesia, 1996–1999*. Singapore: NUS Publishing, 2006.

Purdey, Jemma. "Problematizing the Place of Victims in Reformasi Indonesia: A Contested Truth about the May 1998 Violence." *Asian Survey* 42, no. 4 (2002): 605–22.

Purdey, Jemma, Antje Missbach, and Dave McRae. *Indonesia: State and Society in Transition*. Boulder CO: Lynne Rienner, 2020.

Qiu Peipei, Su Zhilang, and Chen Lifei. *Chinese Comfort Women: Testimonies from Imperial Japan's Sex Slaves*. Oxford: Oxford University Press, 2013.

Raben, Remco. "Indonesian Romusha and Coolies Under Naval Administration: The Eastern Archipelago, 1942–45." In *Asian Labor in the Wartime Japanese Empire*, edited by Paul H. Kratoska, 197–212. Armonk, NY: M. E. Sharpe, 2005.

Rahayu, Ruth Indiah. "Kontruksi Historiografi Feminisme dari Tutur Perempuan" [The Women's Circle's constructions of feminist history]. *Historiografi Indonesia: di Antara Historiografi Nasional dan Alternatif* [Indonesian historiography: Between national and alternative historiography]. Pusat Studi Sosial Asia Tenggara and ARC, Hotel Yogya Plaza, July 2–4, 2007.

Rahayu, Ruth Indiah. "Politik Gender Orde Baru: Tinjauan Organisasi Perempuan Sejak 1980an" [The politics of gender in the New Order: A review of women's organizations since the 1980s]. *Prisma* 5, Tahun 25 (1996): 29–42.

Ramseyer, J. Mark. "Contracting for Sex in the Pacific War." *International Review of Law and Economics* 65 (2021): 105971.

Rees, Susan, and Derrick Silove, "Sakit Hati: A State of Chronic Mental Distress Related to Resentment and Anger amongst West Papuan Refugees Exposed to Persecution." *Social Science and Medicine* 73, no. 1 (2011): 103–10.

Reid, Anthony, and Oki Akira. "Introduction." In *The Japanese Experience in Indonesia: Selected Memoirs of 1942–1945*, edited by Anthony Reid and Oki Akira, 1–5. Athens: Ohio Center for International Studies, 1986.

Reid, Kirsty, and Fiona Paisley. "Introduction." In *Sources and Methods in Histories of Colonialism: Approaching the Imperial Archive*, edited by Kirsty Reid and Fiona Paisley, 1–12. Abingdon, UK: Routledge, 2017.

Reynolds, E. Bruce. "History, Memory, Compensation and Reconciliation: The Abuse of Labour along the Thailand-Burma Railway." In *Asian Labor in the Wartime Japanese Empire: Unknown Histories*, edited by Paul Kratoska, 326–48. Armonk, NY: M. E. Sharpe, 2005.

Riley, Jessica P. "Claims to Protection: The Rise and Fall of Feminist Abolitionism in the League of Nations' Committee on the Traffic in Women and Children, 1919–1936." *Journal of Women's History* 22, no. 4 (Winter 2010): 90–113.

Rinaldo, Rachel. *Mobilizing Piety: Islam and Feminism in Indonesia*. New York: Oxford University Press, 2013.

Roces, Mina. "Prostitution, Women's Movement and the Victim Narrative in the Philippines." *Women's Studies International Forum* 32 (2009): 270–80.

Roosa, John, Ayu Ratih, and Hilmar Farid. *Tahun Yang Tak Pernah Berakhir: Memahami Pengalaman Korban 65 Esai-esai Sejarah Lisan* [The year that never ended: Understanding the experiences of victims of 1965 essays from oral history]. Jakarta: ELSAM, 2004.

Ropers, Erik. *Voices of the Korean Minority in Postwar Japan: Histories against the Grain*. New York: Routledge, 2019.

Sadli, Saparinah. "Feminism and Indonesia in an International Context." In *Women in Indonesia: Gender, Equity and Development*, edited by Kathy Robinson and Sharon Bessell, 80–91. Singapore: Institute of Southeast Asian Studies, 2002.

Said, Salim. *Genesis of Power: General Sudirman and the Indonesian Military in Politics 1945–1949*. North Sydney: Allen and Unwin, 1992.

Sakamoto, Rumi. "The Women's International War Crimes Tribunal on Japan's Military Sexual Slavery: A Legal Feminist Approach to the 'Comfort Women' Issue." *New Zealand Journal of Asian Studies* 3, no. 1 (June 2001): 49–58.

Salim, Haji Agus. "The Veiling and Isolation of Women" (1926). In *Regents, Reformers, and Revolutionaries: Indonesian Voices of Colonial Days: Selected Historical Readings, 1899–1949*, edited by Greta O. Wilson, 69–70. Honolulu: University of Hawai'i Press, 1978.

Sastrowirjo, Tien. "Bagaimana Pergerakan Kaum Perempuan Sekarang dan Nanti" [What about the women's movement now and then]. In *Kongres Perempuan Pertama: Tinjauan Ulang*, edited by Susan Blackburn, 193–206. Jakarta: Yayasan Obor Indonesia, KITLV Jakarta, 2007.

Satō, Shigeru. "'Economic Soldiers' in Java: Indonesian Laborers Mobilized for Agricultural Projects." In *Asian Labor in the Wartime Japanese Empire*, edited by Paul Kratoska, 129–51. Armonk, NY: M. E. Sharpe, 2006.

Satō, Shigeru. "Heiho Entry (Lexicon)." In *Encyclopedia of Indonesia in the Pacific War*, edited by Peter Post, William H. Frederick, Iris Heidebrink, and Shigeru Sato, 506. Leiden: Brill, 2010.

Satō, Shigeru. "The Japanese Army and Comfort Women in World War II." In *Sex, Power and Slavery*, edited by Gwyn Campbell and Elizabeth Elbourne, 389–406. Athens: Ohio University Press, 2014.

Satō, Shigeru. "Various Terms for a Comfort Woman." In *Encyclopedia of Indonesia in the Pacific War*, edited by Peter Post, William H. Frederick, Iris Heidebrink, and Shigeru Sato, 196. Leiden: Brill, 2010.

Satō, Shigeru. *War, Nationalism and Peasants: Java under the Japanese Occupation*. Sydney: Asian Studies Association of Australia in association with Allen and Unwin, 1994.

Sawega, Ardus M. "Pengakuan Seorang 'Wanita Penghibur'" [Confession of a comfort woman]. *Kompas*, July 17, 1992, 16.

Scagliola, Stef, and Natalya Vince (in collaboration with Khedidja Adel and Galuh Ambar). "The Places, Traces, and Politics of Rape in the Indonesian and the Algerian Wars of Independence." In *Empire's Violent End*, edited by Brocades Zaalberg and Bart Luttikhuis, 96–119. Ithaca, NY: Cornell University Press, 2022.

Schaffer, Kay, and Sidonie Smith. *Human Rights and Narrated Lives: The Ethics of Recognition*. Hampshire: Palgrave Macmillan, 2004.

Schmidt, Petra. "Japan's Wartime Compensation: Forced Labour." *Asia Pacific Journal on Human Rights and Law* 1, no. 2 (2000): 1–54.

Schulte Nordholt, Nico. "Aid and Conditionality: The Case of Dutch-Indonesian Relationships." In *Aid and Political Conditionality*, edited by Olav Stokke, 129–61. London: Frank Cass, 1995.

Schuurmans, Marijke. "Indies Memories in Bronze and Stone." *Inside Indonesia* 103 (January–March 2011). http://www.insideindonesia.org/indies-memories-in-bronze -and-stone.

Sears, Laurie. *Situated Testimonies: Dread and Enchantment in an Indonesian Literary Archive*. Honolulu: University of Hawai'i Press, 2013.

Seaton, Philip. *Japan's Contested War Memories: The Memory Rifts in Historical Consciousness of World War II*. London: Routledge and Taylor and Francis, 2007.

Sen, Krishna. "Indonesian Women at Work: Reframing the Subject." In *Gender and Power in Affluent Asia*, edited by Krishna Sen and Maila Stivens, 35–62. London: Routledge, 1998.

Sen, Krishna, and David Hill. *Media Culture and Politics in Indonesia*. Melbourne: Oxford University Press, 2000.

Senda Kakō. *Jūgun Ianfu: "Koe Naki Onna: Hachimannin no Kokuhatsu"* [Military comfort women: The grievances of 80,000 voiceless women]. Tokyo: Futubasha, 1973.

Setiawan, Andri. "Makan Plumbon Jadi Situs Memori CIPDH-UNESCO [The Plumbon grave becomes a CIPDH-UNESCO memorial site]." *Historia*, January 16, 2020. https://historia.id/politik/articles/makam-plumbon-jadi-situs-memori-cipdh -unesco-Pzd2O/page/1.

Setiawan, Ken. "From Hope to Disillusion: The Paradox of Komnas HAM, the Indonesian Human Rights Commission." *Bijdragen tot de taal-, land- en volkenkunde* 172, no. 1 (2016): 1–32.

Setiawan, Ken. *Promoting Human Rights, National Human Rights Commissions in Indonesia and Malaysia*. Leiden: Leiden University Press, 2013.

Setiyono, Budi. "Ianfu di Indonesia." *Historia* 3 (2012): 52–53.

Sharma, Shalendra D. *The Asian Financial Crisis: Crisis, Reform, and Recovery*. Manchester: Manchester University Press, 2003.

Shaver, Phillip, Upekkha Murdaya, and Chris Fraley. "Structure of the Indonesian Emotion Lexicon." *Asian Journal of Social Psychology* 4, no. 3 (2001): 201–24.

Shibata Yaichirō. "Surabaya after the Surrender." In *The Japanese Experience in Indonesia: Selected Memoirs of 1942–1945*, edited by Anthony Reid and Oki Akira, 341–74. Athens: Ohio University Press, 1986.

Shim, Sung-won. "South Korea Protests Nagano's Remarks on 'Comfort Women.'" *Reuters*, May 7, 1994.

Shimizu, Hiroshi. "Rise and Fall of the Karayukisan in the Netherlands Indies from the Late Nineteenth Century to the 1930s." *RIMA: Review of Indonesian and Malaysian Affairs* 26 no. 2 (Summer 1992): 17–43.

Siegel, James T. "Early Thoughts on the Violence of May 13 and 14, 1998 in Jakarta." *Indonesia* 66 (October 1998): 74–108.

Simpson, Bradley R. *Economists with Guns: Authoritarian Development and US-Indonesian Relations 1960–1968*. Stanford, CA: Stanford University Press, 2008.

Soedirman, R. A. "Pergerakan Perempuan Perkawinan dan Perceraian" [The women's movement marriage and divorce]. In *Kongres Perempuan Pertama: Tinjauan Ulang*, edited by Susan Blackburn, 158–63. Jakarta: Yayasan Obor Indonesia, KITLV Jakarta, 2007.

Soedjatmoko. "The Indonesian Historian and His [*sic*] Time." In *An Introduction to Indonesian Historiography*, edited by Soedjatmoko, 404–15. Ithaca, NY: Cornell University Press, 1965.

Soekarno. *Sarinah: Kewajiban Wanita dalam Perjuangan Republik Indonesia* [Sarinah: The duties of women in the struggle of the Republic of Indonesia]. 1947; Jakarta: Toko Gunung Agung, 2001.

Soh, C. Sarah. "Aspiring to Craft Modern Gendered Selves: 'Comfort Women' and Chŏngsindae in Late Colonial Korea." *Critical Asian Studies* 36, no. 2 (2004): 175–98.

Soh, C. Sarah. *The Comfort Women: Sexual Violence and Post-colonial Memory in Korea and Japan*. Chicago: University of Chicago Press, 2008.

Soh, Chunghee Sarah. "Human Rights and the 'Comfort Women.'" *Peace Review* 12, no. 1 (2000): 123–29.

Soh, C. Sarah. "Japan's National Asian Women's Fund for 'Comfort Women.'" *Pacific Affairs* 76, no. 2 (2003): 209–33.

Soh, Chunghee Sarah. "The Korean 'Comfort Women': Movement for Redress." *Asian Survey* 36, no. 12 (1996): 1226–40.

Soh, Chunghee Sarah. "'Prostitutes versus Sex Slaves': The Politics of Representing the 'Comfort Women.'" In *Legacies of the Comfort Women of World War II*, edited by Margaret D. Stetz and Bonnie B. C. Oh, 69–90. Armonk, NY: M. E. Sharpe, 2001.

Soh, Chunghee Sarah. "Uncovering the Truth about the 'Comfort Women.'" *Women's Studies International Forum* 21, no. 4 (1998): 451–54.

Son, Elizabeth W. *Embodied Reckonings: "Comfort Women," Performance, and Transpacific Redress*. Ann Arbor: University of Michigan Press, 2018.

Son, Elizabeth. "Statue Dedicated to 'Comfort Women' Removed in the Philippines." *UPI*, January 3, 2019. https://www.upi.com/Top_News/World-News/2019/01/03/Statue-dedicated-to-comfort-women-removed-in-the-Philippines/4461546541049/.

Song, Youn-ok. "Japanese Colonial Rule and State-Managed Prostitution: Korea's Licensed Prostitutes." *positions* 5, no. 1 (1997): 171–219.

Stanley, Amy. *Selling Women: Prostitution, Markets, and the Household in Early Modern Japan*. Berkeley, CA: University of California Press, 2012.

Steele, Janet E. *Wars Within: The Story of Tempo, an Independent Magazine in Soeharto's Indonesia*. Jakarta: Equinox Publishers, Institute of Southeast Asian Studies, 2005.

Steinoff, Patricia G. "Japan: Student Activism in an Emerging Democracy." In *Student Activism in Asia: Between Protest and Powerlessness*, edited by Meredith Weiss and Edward Aspinall, 57–78. Minneapolis: University of Minnesota Press, 2012.

Stoler, Ann Laura. *Capitalism and Confrontation in Sumatra's Plantation Belt, 1870–1979*. 2nd ed. Ann Arbor: University of Michigan Press, 1995.

Stoler, Ann Laura. *Carnal Knowledge and Imperial Power: Race and the Intimate in Colonial Rule*. Berkeley: University of California Press, 2002.

Stoler, Anne Laura, and Karen Strassler. "Castings for the Colonial: Memory Work in 'New Order' Java." *Comparative Studies in Society and History* 42, no. 1 (2000): 4–48.

Stoltz, Pauline. *Gender, Resistance and Transnational Memories of Violent Conflicts*. Cham: Palgrave Macmillan, 2020.

Strassler, Karen. "Gendered Visibilities and the Dream of Transparency: The Chinese Indonesian Rape Debate in Post-Suharto Indonesia." *Gender and History* 16, no. 3 (November 2004): 689–725.

Suehiro, Akira. "The Road to Economic Reentry: Japan's Policy toward Southeast Asian Development in the 1950s and 1960s." *Social Science Japan Journal* 2, no. 1 (1999): 85–105.

Suk Gersen, Jeannie. "Seeking the True Story of the Comfort Women." *New Yorker*, February 25, 2021. https://www.newyorker.com/culture/annals-of-inquiry/seeking -the-true-story-of-the-comfort-women-j-mark-ramseyer.

Sulami. "The Birth and Growth of the Indonesian Women's Movement." *Women of the Whole World*, pt. 2, no. 1 (1959): 30–31.

Sumbogo, Priyono B., Kastyo Ramelan, Andi Reza Rohadin, Waspada Santing, dan Mochtar Touwe. "Mereka Pun Tak Punya Pilihan" [They had no choice]. *Tempo*, August 8, 1992, 61–64.

Sunindyo, Saraswati. "She Who Earns: The Politics of Prostitution in Java." MA thesis, University of Wisconsin–Madison, 1993.

Surawijaya, Bunga, and Ōkawa Seiichi. "Jeritan dari Rumah Bamboo" [Screams from the bamboo hut]. *Tempo*, August 8, 1992, 51–60.

Surtees, Rebecca. "Traditional and Emergent Sex Work in Urban Indonesia." *Intersections, Gender, History and Culture in Asian Context* 10 (August 2004). http://inter sections.anu.edu.au/issue10/surtees.html.

Suryakasuma, Julia. "The State and Sexuality in New Order Indonesia." In *Fantasizing the Feminine in Indonesia*, edited by Laurie Sears, 92–119. Durham, NC: Duke University Press, 1996.

Suryomenggolo, Jafar. "Factory Employment, Female Workers Activism and Authoritarianism in Indonesia: Reading Ira Irianti's Pembelaan." *Critical Asian Studies* 44, no. 4 (2012): 597–626.

Sjahrir, Sutan. *Our Struggle*. Ithaca, NY: Modern Indonesia Project, Southeast Asia Program, Dept. of Asian Studies, Cornell University, 1968.

Szczepanska, Kamila. *The Politics of War Memory in Japan: Progressive Civil Society Groups and Contestation of Memory of the Asia-Pacific War*. Abingdon: Sheffield Centre for Japanese Studies, Routledge, 2014.

Tachikawa Tomoko. "Marudiemu-san no 'Tabi': Imawashii Kako o Tazunete" [Mardiyem's journey: Visiting a disgusting past]. *Suara* 11 (March 26, 2001): 1–3.

Tai Eika. *Comfort Women Activism: Critical Voices from the Perpetrator State*. Hong Kong: Hong Kong University Press, 2020.

Takagi Ken'ichi. *Ima Naze Sengo Hoshō ka* [Why postwar compensation now]. Tokyo: Kōdan Sha, 2001.

Takagi Ken'ichi. *Jūgun Ianfu to Sengo Hoshō—Nihon no Sengo Sekinin* [The military comfort women and postwar compensation—Japan's postwar responsibility]. Tokyo: San'ichi Shobō, 1992.

Takagi Ken'ichi. *Saharin to Nihon no Sengo Sekinin* [Japan's postwar responsibility for Sakhalin]. Tokyo: Gaifū Sha, 1990.

Takagi Ken'ichi. *Sengo Hoshō no Ronri: Higaisha no Koe o Dō Kiku ka* [The logic of postwar compensation: How to listen to the victims' voices]. Tokyo: Renga Shobō Shinsha, 1994.

Tan, Abby. "Japan's Record in War Blights Tour of Asia." *The Times*, August 24, 1994.

Tanaka, Yuki. "'Comfort Women Bashing' and Japan's Social Formation of Hegemonic Masculinity." In *History Wars and Reconciliation in Japan and Korea: The Role of Historians, Artists and Activists*, edited by Michael Lewis, 163–82. Sydney: Palgrave Macmillan, 2017.

Tanaka, Yuki. "'Comfort Women' in the Dutch East Indies." In *Legacies of the Comfort Women of World War II*, edited by Margaret D. Stetz and Bonnie Oh, 42–68. Armonk, NY: M. E. Sharpe, 2000.

Tanaka, Yuki. "Introduction." In Maria Rosa Henson, *Comfort Women: A Filipina Woman's Story of Prostitution and Slavery under the Japanese Military*, ix–xxi. Lanham, MD: Rowman and Littlefield, 1999.

Tanaka, Yuki. *Japan's Comfort Women: Sexual Slavery and Prostitution during World War II and the US Occupation*. London: Routledge, 2002.

Taylor, Jean Gelman. "Nyai Dasima Portrait of a Mistress in Literature and Film." In *Fantasizing the Feminine in Indonesia*, edited by Laurie Sears, 225–58. Durham, NC: Duke University Press, 1996.

Taylor, Jean. *The Social World of Batavia: Europeans and Eurasians in Colonial Indonesia*. 2nd ed. Madison: University of Wisconsin Press, 2009.

Taylor, John J. *East Timor: The Price of Freedom*. New York: Zed Books, 1999.

Termorshuizen, Thio. "Indentured Labour in the Dutch Colonial Empire 1800–1940." In *Dutch Colonialism, Migration and Cultural Heritage*, edited by Gert Oostinde, 261–314. Leiden: KITLV Press, 2008.

Toer, Pramoedya Anata. *Bumi Manusia* [This earth of mankind]. Jakarta: Hasta Mitra, 1980.

Toer, Pramoedya Ananta. *Perawan Remaja dalam Cengkeraman Militer* [Teenage virgins in the grasp of the military]. Jakarta: Kepustakaan Populer Gramedia, 2001.

Toer, Pramoedya Anata. *Tempo Dulu Antologi Sastra Pra-Indonesia* [The past: An anthology of pre-Indonesian literature]. Jakarta: Lentera, Dipentara Jakarta, 2003.

Totsuka Etsurō. "Commentary on a Victory for 'Comfort Women': Japan's Judicial Recognition of Military Sexual Slavery." *Pacific Rim Law and Policy Journal* 8, no. 1 (1999): 47–61.

Totsuka Etsurō. *Nihon ga Shiranai Sensō Sekinin: Kokuren no Jinken Katsudō to Nihon-gun Jūgun Ianfu Mondai* [Wartime responsibility that Japan does not know: Human rights protections at the United Nations and the issue of the Japanese military comfort women]. Tokyo: Gendai Jimbunsha, 1999.

Touwen-Bouwsma, Elly. "Japanese Minority Policy: The Eurasians on Java and the Dilemma of Ethnic Loyalty." In *Japan, Indonesia and the War: Myths and Realities*, edited by Peter Post and Elly Touwen-Bouwsma, 31–50. Leiden: KITLV Press, 1997.

Touwen-Bouwsma, Elly. "Japanse Legerprostitutie in Nederlands Indië 1942–1945" [Japanese Army prostitution in the Netherlands Indies 1942–1945]. In *Oorlogsdocu-mentatie 40–45*, 31–45. Amsterdam: Vijfde Jaarboek van het Rijksinstituut voor Oorlogsdocumentatie, 1994.

Trouillot, Michel-Rolph. *Silencing the Past: Power and the Production of History.* Boston: Beacon Press, 1995.

Tsukamoto, Sachiyo. "A More Miserable Life than Living in the Jungle: A Japanese 'Comfort Woman' Story." *Gender and History* (November 2021): 1–18.

Tsukamoto, Sachiyo. *The Politics of Trauma and Integrity: Stories of Japanese "Comfort Women."* London: Routledge, 2022.

Tumbelty, Joan. "Introduction: Working with Memory as a Source and a Subject." In *Memory and History: Understanding Memory as a Subject and Source*, edited by Joan Tumbelty, 1–16. London: Routledge, 2013.

Uchida Masatoshi. *Sengo Hoshō o Kangaeru* [Considering postwar compensation]. Tokyo: Kōdansha, 1994.

Ueno Chizuko. *Nationalism and Gender.* Translated by Beverley Yamamoto. Melbourne: Trans Pacific Press, 2003.

Ueno Chizuko. "The Politics of Memory: Nation, Individual and Self." *History and Memory* 11, no. 2 (1999): 129–52.

van Boetzelaar, T. "Between Nation and Gender: The Representation of Former Military Comfort Women in the Netherlands and South Korea." MA thesis, Leiden University, 2016.

van Kampen, Elizabeth. "Memories of the Dutch East Indies: From Plantation Society to Prisoner of Japan." *Asia-Pacific Journal* 7, no. 1 (January) 2009. https://apjjf.org/-Elizabeth-Van-Kampen/3002/article.html.

Vickers, Adrian, and Katharine McGregor. "Public Debates about History: Comparative Notes from Indonesia." *History Australia* 2, no. 2 (June 2005): 44.1–13.

Viseur Sellers, Patricia. "The Cultural Value of Sexual Violence." *Proceedings of the Annual Meeting American Society for International Law* 93 (March 24–27, 1999).

Wandita, Galuh. "The Tears Have Not Stopped, the Violence Has Not Ended: Political Upheaval, Ethnicity and Violence against Women in Indonesia." *Gender and Development* 6, no. 3 (1998): 34–41.

Wardaya, Baskara. *Indonesia Melawan Amerika: Konflik Perang Dingin, 1953–1963* [Indonesia opposes America: Cold War conflict, 1953–1963]. Yogyakarta: Galang Pers, 2008.

Warren, James. *Ah Ku and Karayukisan: Prostitution in Singapore, 1870–1940*. Singapore: Oxford University Press, 1993.

Warren, James. "New Lands, Old Ties and Prostitution: A Voiceless Voice." *Intersections: Gender, History and Culture in the Asian Context* 4 (September 2000). http://intersections.anu.edu.au/issue5/sandakan.html.

Watson, Barbara Andaya. *The Flaming Womb: Repositioning Women in Early Modern Southeast Asia*. Honolulu: University of Hawai'i Press, 2006.

Weiner, Michael, and David Chapman. "Zainichi Koreans in History and Memory." In *Japan's Minorities: The Illusion of Homogeneity*, edited by Michael Weiner, 162–87. London: Routledge, 2009.

White, Sally. "The Case of Nyi Anah: Concubinage, Marriage and Reformist Islam in the late Colonial Dutch East Indies." *RIMA: Review of Indonesian and Malaysian Affairs* 38, no. 1 (2004): 87–97.

Wieringa, Saskia. *Sexual Politics in Indonesia*. New York: Palgrave Macmillan, 2002.

Wilson, Sandra. "Family or State? Nation, War, and Gender in Japan, 1937–45." *Critical Asian Studies* 38, no. 2 (2006): 209–38.

Wilson, Sandra, Robert Cribb, Beatrice Trefault, and Dean Aszkielowicz. *Japanese War Criminals: The Politics of Justice after the Second World War*. New York: Columbia University Press, 2017.

Yamada, Naoko. "From War to Independence, 1942–1949 Ianfu in Indonesia." MA thesis, Ohio University, 2000.

Yamaguchi, Mari. "Asian, Dutch Former Sex Slaves Testify on Abuses." *Associated Press*, December 9, 1992.

Yamamoto Kentarō. "Jūgun Ianfu Mondai no Keii: Kōno Danwa o Meguru Ugoki o Chūshin ni" [Circumstances of the issue of military comfort women: On discussions around the Kōno statement]. *Refarensu* (September 2013): 68–69.

Yamamoto, Mayumi. "Whispers and Gazes: A Postscript to the Semarang Comfort Women Incident." *Journal of Asia Pacific Studies* 18 (March 2012): 193–201.

Yamane Kazuyo. "Yayori Matsui and the Women's Active Museum on War and Peace." *Social Alternatives* 29, no. 1 (2010): 25–28.

Yamashita Yeong-ae. "Revisiting the 'Comfort Women': Moving beyond Nationalism." In *Transforming Japan: How Feminism and Diversity Are Making a Difference*, edited by Kumiko Fujimura-Fanselow, 267–83. Translated by Malaya Ileto. New York: Feminist Press and CUNY, 2011.

Yamatani Tetsuo. *Okinawa no Harumoni: Dai Nihon Baishun Shi* [An old woman in Okinawa: A history of prostitution in greater Japan]. Tokyo: Banseisha, 1979.

Yamazaki Tomoko. *Sandakan Brothel No 8: An Episode in the History of Lower-Class Japanese Women*. Translated by Karen Colligan-Taylor. Armonk, NY: M. E. Sharpe, 1999.

Yamazaki Tomoko. *Sandakan Hachiban Shōkan-Teihen Joseishi Joshō* [Sandakan brothel no 8: A prologue of the history of Japanese lower-class women]. Tokyo: Chukumo Shobō Tokyo, 1972.

Yasuhiro, Nakasone. "Nijūsansai de Sanzen-nin no Sōshikikan" [Commander of three thousand soldiers at the age of twenty-three]. In *Owarinaki Kaigun: Wakai Sedai e Tsutaetai Nokoshitai* [Never ending navy: Memories that we want to hand down to young generations], edited by Matsuura Takanori, 90–98. Tokyo: Bunka Hōsō Kaihatsu Sentā Shuppanbu, 1978.

Yonson, Ahn. "Yearning for Affection: Traumatic Bonding between Korean 'Comfort Women' and Japanese Soldiers during World War II." *European Journal of Women's Studies* 26, no. 4 (2019): 360–74.

Yoon, Rangsook. "Erecting the Comfort Women Memorials from Seoul to San Francisco." *De Arte* 53, nos. 2–3 (2018): 70–85.

Yoshihara, Mari. "The Flight of the Japanese Butterfly: Orientalism, Nationalism and Performances of Japanese Womanhood." *American Quarterly* 56, no. 4 (2004): 975–1001.

Yoshimi Yoshiaki. *Comfort Women: Sexual Slavery in the Japanese Military during World War II.* Translated by Suzanne O'Brien. New York: Columbia University Press, 2000.

Yoshimi Yoshiaki. *Grassroots Fascism: The War Experience of the Japanese People.* Translated by Ethan Mark. New York: Columbia University Press, 2015.

Zegveld, Liesbeth. "Netherlands Liable for Rape of Woman in Dutch East Indies: State Must Allow Investigation in Dutch National Archives." December 18, 2016.

Websites

Asia-Japan Women's Resource Center. Accessed August 23, 2022. http://www.ajwrc.org/eng/index.php.

Asian Women's Fund Digital Museum. "An Appeal for Donations for the Asian Women's Fund." Accessed August 23, 2022. http://awf.or.jp/e2/foundation-01.html.

Asian Women's Fund Digital Museum. "Historical Materials Regarding Comfort Women Issue." Accessed August 23, 2022. https://awf.or.jp/e6/document.html.

Asian Women's Fund Digital Museum. "On the Issue of War-time Comfort Women." Accessed August 23, 2022. https://awf.or.jp/e6/statement-03.html.

Asian Women's Fund Digital Museum. "Projects by Country or Region - Indonesia." Accessed August 23, 2022. http://www.awf.or.jp/e3/indonesia-00.html.

Asian Women's Fund Digital Museum. "Projects by Country or Region - Philippines." Accessed August 23, 2022. http://www.awf.or.jp/e3/philippine-01.html.

Flower Aceh. "Profil." Accessed August 23, 2022. http://floweraceh.or.id/profil/.

Index

Page numbers followed by "f" indicate illustrations.

compensation, 18, 120, 163; survivors' expectations of, 157–58, 201. *See also* wartime redress; AWF; International Public Hearing on Japan's Postwar Compensation; Women's International War Crimes Tribunal on Japan's Military Sexual Slavery

concubinage: in feudal court, 27–32; in Netherlands East Indies, 14, 27–43; under Japanese Occupation, 81–82, 137–40. *See also* "comfort women"; *nyai*

Confino, Alan, 12

Confucian values, 113

Coomaraswamy, Radhika: and "comfort women," 165, 172, 187; visit to Indonesia and report on militarized sexual violence, 192–93. *See also* May 1998 riots; Reform Era

Coté, Joost, 39

court-martials, 16, 63, 77–78, 85, 92–94; on sexual violence crimes, 93. *See also* Semarang Affair; war crimes prosecutions

Creese, Helen, 29, 37

Crouch, Melissa, 160

Damanik, Asnifrianty: women's tribunal, 200, 204

Danusudirdjo, Slamet, 99, 136

Das, Veena, 87

de Weerd, Klaas, 51

Declaration on the Elimination on Violence against Women, 165. *See also* Coomaraswamy, Radhika

democratization: in Indonesia, 184–97 (*see also* Reform Era); in Korea, 16, 112–15 (*see also* Minjung movement)

Derita Paksa Perempuan (Hartono and Juliantoro), 19, 68, 185–88, 208

Derrida, Jacques, 20

Diet, the, 116

Driscoll, Mark, 41

East Timor: Dili massacre, 131; independence referendum and violence, 197; Indonesia's annexation and occupation, 125; response from international community, 158. *See also* New Order

enforced military prostitution, 7, 45 archival records of, 63, 68–70, 118; background, 20–22, 55–57 brothels: Japanese navy, 58, 69; licenses, 58; locations, 58–60, 64, 67–68, 72; management of, 69; conditions, 76

health and disease, 56–57, 67; planning for Indonesia, 57–61

recruitment, 55–56, 61–62, 64–70 age of women, 67; coercion, 82; heiho, involvement in, 69, 138; local involvement in, 64–65; rationalization, 56–57

resistance and opposition to, 72–73; sexual violence and rape, 72, 79–82; former soldier's testimony of, 203. *See also* "comfort women"; Japanese Occupation; Japanese imperialism

Enloe, Cynthia, 56

Erll, Astrid, 10

Ethical Policy, 33. *See also* Netherlands East Indies

Ewha University: women's studies department, 114–15

Fatimah, 146. *See also* survivor testimony

film: on "comfort women," 99, 111, 245n60; by Japanese, 176, 180; about Tuminah, 209; women's tribunal, use at, 201

on *rōmusha*, 98–99

Flower Aceh, 131. *See also* women's organizations

forced labor, 15; recruitment, 50–52; redress and commemoration, 98–99, 150–51, 157, 187, 209. See also *heiho*; Japanese Occupation; *rōmusha*

Wiranto, Gen., 191. *See also* May 1998 riots

Women's Active Museum on War and Peace, 25, 209. *See also* survivor testimony; Women's International War Crimes Tribunal on Japan's Military Sexual Slavery

Women's Coalition for Justice and Democracy, 192. *See also* Katjasungkana, Nursyahbani

Women's Commission of the Ecumenical Association of Third World Theologians and the Asian Women and Culture Movement, 129

Women's International Democratic Federation, 125

Women's International War Crimes Tribunal on Japan's Military Sexual Slavery (2000), xi, 9, 18, 19, 25, 176, 199–206; censorship and opposition in Japan, 203; Indonesia's participation, 200–202, 204f. *See also* "comfort women"; enforced military prostitution; survivor testimony; Mardiyem

women's organizations, Indonesian, 45, 125; advocacy opposing violence against women, 129–31; under Japanese Occupation, 52–53

women's studies: in Indonesia, 128; in Korea, 114. *See also* Sadli, Saparinah

worker's rights: activism in Indonesia, 125, 186. *See also* Marsinah; Indonesian Congress for Women

World War II: Battle of Singapore, 46; bombings of Hiroshima and Nagasaki, 84; in Europe, 46; Japanese surrender, 84–85

Yamashita Kiyoshi, 198. *See also* JFBA

Yamashita Yeong-ae, 154, 173. *See also* Korean Council

Yamatani Tetsuo, 111

Yamazaki Tomoko, 108–9

Yayasan Anisa Swasti (YASANTI), 130. *See also* women's organizations

YLBHI. *See* Indonesian Legal Aid Foundation

Yokoyama Knock, 198. *See also* JFBA

Yonson, Ahn, 77

Yoong Mee-Hyang, 176. *See also* Korean Council

Yoshiko Nozaki, 23

Yoshimi Yoshiaki: archival documentation on "comfort women," 118, 120–21, 136, 175; estimated numbers of "comfort women," 56, 170

Young Virgins in the Grasp of the Military (Toer), 88–89

Yun Chung-Ok, 115, 202. *See also* Korean Council

Critical Human Rights

Printed in the USA
CPSIA information can be obtained
at www.ICGtesting.com
LVHW010040091223
765978LV00004B/11